A GUIDE TO
Learning Independently
5e

WITHDRAWN

A GUIDE TO
Learning Independently
5e

Lorraine Marshall and Frances Rowland

Pearson Australia
Unit 4, Level 3
14 Aquatic Drive
Frenchs Forest NSW 2086

www.pearson.com.au

Acquisitions Editor: Lucy Elliott
Project Editor: Liz de Rome
Production Coordinator: Caroline Stewart
Copy Editor: Jo Hoban
Proofreader: Nicole Le Grand
Copyright and Pictures Editors: Lisa Woodland and Jodie Streckeisen
Indexer: Barbara Bessant
Cover and internal design by Natalie Bowra
Cover photographs from © Shutterstock: Yuri Arcurs, Blend Images, Cozyta, Deklofenak, doglikehorse, Marie C Fields, Warren Goldswain, Dan Kosmayer, Christine Langer-Pueschel, Sergey Nivens, Mykhaylo Palinchak, Pressmaster, Laurin Rinder, Yuri Sheftsoff, Kuttelvaserova Stuchelova, Marko Tomicic and ZouZou.
Typeset by Midland Typesetters, Australia

Printed in Malaysia, CTP-PJB

1 2 3 4 5 18 17 16 15 14

National Library of Australia
Cataloguing-in-Publication Data

Author:	Marshall, Lorraine A., author.
Title:	A guide to learning independently / Lorraine Marshall and Frances Rowland.
Edition:	5 edition.
ISBN:	9781442559363 (paperback)
Notes:	Includes index.
Subjects:	Study skills—Handbooks, manuals, etc.
	College student orientation—Handbooks, manuals, etc.
Other Authors/ Contributors:	Rowland, Frances, author.
Dewey Number:	378.170281

ALWAYS LEARNING

PEARSON

Contents

List of tables

About the authors

Professor **Lorraine Marshall**, as a foundation staff member of Murdoch University, has provided national leadership in the development of student learning support, much of the philosophy of which was embedded in the first edition of this book, and continues to inform this fifth edition. Besides leading student academic learning support for many years, more recently Lorraine has facilitated Murdoch's involvement in Open Universities Australia (OUA), including coordinating her popular first year introductory OUA unit, which is also offered at Murdoch. In addition to developing two student support videos and online interactive learning materials, Lorraine is the author of *A Learning Companion*. Her current research in interdisciplinary learning and teaching coincides with her long-term leadership of Murdoch's first year interdisciplinary foundation units.

Frances Rowland is currently an Adjunct Senior Lecturer at Murdoch University. She enjoys working directly with students and has been teaching at Murdoch and elsewhere for more than 30 years. In particular, Frances has taught and learnt from first year and external students, and students in equity programs, in multidisciplinary courses and in social sciences and education.

Frances' dual career as a writer and a teacher has involved developing and teaching community courses, professional education seminars and staff development and mentoring programs.

Thanks

We would like to thank the many people who gave us encouragement and advice on each edition, especially those who helped and supported our writing, put time into reading the manuscripts and assisted us with individual chapters. For the fifth edition thanks to Margaret Jones and Jean Coleman. Thank you also to the hundreds of students who have told us (sometimes via their tutors) how important earlier editions of this book were in helping them through their studies. Their comments in the street, in emails and online have truly motivated us in the completion of this fifth edition.

A special thanks to Jim for his patience and support throughout, for his endless reading of the drafts and for simply being there. And thanks also to our daughter Suzannah who, although not involved in the first edition, helped with subsequent editions. Thanks to Murdoch University and academic staff from a range of disciplines for their contribution over the five editions of this book.
LORRAINE MARSHALL

My personal thanks to John Holt, who reminded me of what I believe about teaching; to Ann, who taught me about learning; and to Ann's babysitters, without whom I wouldn't have written the first edition of this book.
FRANCES ROWLAND

Preface to the fifth edition

As a comprehensive guide to tertiary study, we are confident that this latest edition of *A Guide to Learning Independently* will continue to be a useful reference throughout undergraduate study. Despite the plentiful learning skills advice online, it is invaluable to have a guidebook that you can use wherever you study and can just open and quickly find what you need. This book will save you having to trawl through many websites to find solid study skills suggestions, and the many cross-references in the *Guide* act like hyperlinks.

The book does not simply take an instrumental approach, where study is primarily a means to an end. It offers plenty of practical strategies and user-friendly activities from which you can select to build up your own learning skills repertoire. As well as 'how to' strategies, the *Guide* discusses why you might use the strategies, and how they reflect fundamental approaches to learning and teaching at university. The book also offers distinctive chapters such as those on 'Remembering what you learn', 'Asking your own questions' and 'Developing your writing'.

The learning skills tactics in the *Guide* are realistic so that, for example, we don't assume that all lectures are perfect, that all tutors are expert teachers, or that you have easy access to academic staff at all times. We offer tips to save you time in a busy life, but we also explain how you can fully develop particular skills if you want to become a really proficient student.

You

It is over 30 years since the first edition of *A Guide to Learning Independently* was published. Some of the ideas it contains were first formulated in the 1970s when access to higher education was expanding in Western societies. This was a time of structural and social change. There was increasing recognition of what it means to live in a culturally diverse society, and of the influence of class, ethnicity and gender on people's opportunities. It was also a time of focus on individual growth; and *A Guide to Learning Independently,* with its emphasis on 'you', originated in that time. By contrast, in the early twenty-first century higher education has instead become focused on national economic goals.

This edition of the *Guide* still offers techniques to help you do what is expected of you by teachers. But rather than providing only a workbook to help you jump successfully through the hoops held by other people, the book still argues that your study should be centred on you and on your reasons for learning. It still rests on the premise that it is possible for you to change your approach to learning; any advice is directed to you as an individual student because it is you who must write the essays and reports, pass the exams and manage your time in order to be successful in the tertiary education system.

To some academics (and possibly some students), this focus on you may seem out of touch with the reality of increasing pressures on universities, and this fifth edition of the *Guide* takes into account factors such as worsening staff–student ratios. The effect of ongoing changes and funding cuts in universities have been more profound than at the time of previous editions. We try to take a sensible approach to what can be expected of teachers and students, while at the same time reiterating the traditional role of universities in valuing learning for its own sake. We claim that it is even more important in such times for students to take charge of their own learning as much as possible; and any help that this book can give is worthwhile.

Key concepts

We have modified material in the light of teaching experience, curriculum planning practice, and work with Open Universities Australia. For example, 'Planning your study' has been revised as a result of extensive use by students and staff at Murdoch University; 'Participating in discussions' places more emphasis on collaborative and online groups; and 'Becoming a university student' considers various pathways which students follow to arrive at university. However, there are three educational principles which remain central to the *Guide*.

- The importance of *clear goals* in shaping learning is considered particularly in Chapter 1 and applied throughout the book. At a time when extrinsic vocational orientations are emphasised, the *Guide* values lifelong learning and studying at university because of an intrinsic love of learning.

- The book continues to frame the development of students' learning within a *critical thinking* context, and we reinforce the centrality of reflecting and questioning. The *Guide* takes as one of its starting points that a distinguishing feature of a university education is being able to analyse and to generate complex arguments. Such emphasis is increasingly necessary in fast-paced times and as students interact with instantaneous multiple technologies which discourage sustained attention.

- In the first edition of the book, students were urged to link *content with process*—to link what they are learning with how they learn it. Research into developing student learning skills has strengthened this basic premise and the need for such linking has been reinforced in this edition.

Key changes

Themes with increased relevance have been emphasised—themes such as learning independently, collaborative learning, and using clear research questions. In addition, the content takes into account some recent developments in educational theory and in the evolution of our own thinking. The changes in three broad areas—students, the nature of higher education, and technology—have informed most of the updates and reorganisation in the fifth edition; and rapid change in all three areas is an underlying theme of the book.

Students

We know from feedback that many students use the *Guide* throughout their degree, but this edition has more explicit consideration of the first year experience. A greater emphasis on increased participation in higher education has resulted in a new cohort of students, many of whom might not have previously seen university as an option. A consequence of this shift is that many new students are unfamiliar with university culture and with the expectations of university study. As with any student, people in this group can be highly motivated and often excel, but staff also report that such students often need greater support in their first year.

Another major change is students' everyday use of electronic technology, especially social media. While this has produced a generation accustomed to researching their interests on the Internet, it has also led to students with more fragmented attention, and with expectations of being entertained and constantly stimulated. Because of these characteristics, an ability to filter and evaluate Internet information is now an essential skill for academic learning.

We recognised in previous editions that the escalating complexity of students' lives can often result in more students feeling isolated and becoming disengaged from campus life and study. Such complexity increases the challenge of becoming an independent learner, and means that having clear goals is particularly important if personal and financial problems are not to result in withdrawal from study. It is paradoxical that spending time with other students has become more difficult when such support and contact is more necessary, and we encourage students to seek opportunities for face-to-face or online collaboration with other students. And the 'learning independently' of the book's title is still central—it is even more vital now for students to be self-directed and proactive, and to locate where they can go for help when needed. Such support, for example from a learning skills adviser or a counsellor, now may often be either face-to-face or online.

Higher education

Much of the new material in this edition springs from changes in higher education. While established universities in Australia and elsewhere still have a substantial presence, it is no longer accurate to speak only of 'the' university, or to assume that students will enrol in and connect with a single institution. Provision of tertiary education is now more global; there is a wider range of private providers; and 'open access' pathways into all or part of university education are more diverse.

In various chapters, the book integrates strategies that take into account the consequences of changing global markets for the learning environment. For example, international students from different cultural and educational backgrounds affect the way in which courses are planned and units taught. Being a university student is even more likely to involve learning with people who have come from cultures which differ from your own, and you may even find yourself in global courses where your fellow students live in other countries.

Technology

As in each of the four previous editions, the major current technological changes which affect learning have been taken into account. While we argue that technology should support rather than direct learning, electronic technologies are transforming the life of every student. For example, study is becoming increasingly flexible with many students learning online. And while in previous editions we have been keenly aware of distance education students as a distinct category, and while living in rural and remote areas has often meant limited access to current technology, now such students are likely to be one subset of online learners.

Another major change in the last decade is that universities now place more academic material online, and that administrative contact with students is via computer. This means that a computer is no longer an optional tool for tertiary study—at the least, regular access to one is essential.

Changes to how students engage with learning because of new technologies are dealt with in the appropriate chapters. For example, the chapter on libraries and information sources has been substantially revised yet again; and we again draw attention to the possibilities that electronic communications offer for student to student contact. The Internet allows curriculum planners to make use of blended learning where face-to-face and virtual interactions are combined. And the use of the web for research and communication means that new types of information literacy are necessary.

Since the rapid changes in technology will only continue, we have tried to think through possible developments in the next decade, such as the implications of students working with a variety of new software and hardware. We have also taken the precaution throughout the book of usually avoiding mention of specific currently popular technologies (such as Facebook or Twitter), as in the decades since the first edition of the *Guide* we have seen many such technologies come and go.

* * *

Our thanks again to the many people who have taken the time to tell us that they have found the earlier editions of the *Guide* helpful and to make suggestions for improvements. We hope that the fifth edition of the book will prove as useful.

Read this first!

If you are looking for a book that does more than describe techniques to help you succeed in your formal education, *A Guide to Learning Independently* is the book for you. It will help you with learning tasks such as writing assignments, reading textbooks, making notes and concentrating when you study, and it presents a range of techniques to help you meet the requirements of your teachers and courses.

However, *A Guide to Learning Independently* is also designed to help you discover your own learning goals and how you learn best. It will help you articulate your knowledge about your own learning, and encourage you to think about (or become 'metacognitive' about) your learning. It doesn't set out to prescribe how you should learn, but offers a repertoire of ideas and techniques from which you can choose. These alternatives are presented in the context of encouraging you to use tertiary institutions for your own purposes. To set the ideas and techniques in a broader framework, we also discuss learning in general and tertiary education in particular.

You

This book focuses on you—who you are and what you bring to your learning. Throughout the book you are encouraged to examine your purposes and what you want to learn. You are also encouraged to reflect on how you learn informally, and to build on this self-knowledge in your formal learning. Implicit in this approach are the beliefs that there is no single way of learning that suits everyone, and that it is your right and responsibility to shape your own learning.

You are encouraged to explore your past experience of learning, to clarify why you learn as you do. *Within each chapter* you will find questions and ideas about you as a learner. These are intended to centre the book on you and to help you discover your goals, aims and approaches to learning. Actually take time to focus on and answer the questions. Don't just gloss over them. Read them carefully, take time to reflect, and return to them again later. Because the questions are based on the premise that only you can answer them, we don't prescribe one 'best' way to learn. When we suggest study techniques, we give reasons for these so that you can decide how useful they are for your aims, and we encourage you to try them as you actually learn and study to find those which suit you. Often these techniques are presented in the framework of 'before', 'during' and 'after' stages of a learning activity, such as in the chapters on 'Researching a topic' and 'Reading'.

User-friendly

This is a reference book, rather than a text to be read from start to finish, so strategies are used to make it accessible and readable.

We have provided pathways to quickly locate specific sections.

- There is an overall *contents* table at the start of the book, and a detailed contents list at the start of each chapter.
- The *Index* is comprehensive.
- The book contains frequent *cross-references* to other sections of the book. These direct you to other relevant sections or chapters.

In addition, the *Ten Tips* at the end of each chapter are a source of quick practical advice and suggestions.

And *quotations* from a variety of sources are used to offer different perspectives, to reinforce what is in the text—and to entertain you.

Chapter contents

Each chapter in *A Guide to Learning Independently* has a particular focus. However, the ideas and techniques mentioned in any one chapter cannot be neatly separated from those in any other chapter, any more than your learning can be segmented.

- Use this introduction and the 'What to do now' section, below, to familiarise yourself with the whole book.
- Use the contents list to become familiar with the focus of each chapter.
- When working with a chapter, use the index and cross-references to move backwards and forwards through the book, to think about the ideas and techniques in different contexts.

The *first four chapters* of the book concentrate on you and on being a student at university. They focus on those aspects of your self and your lifestyle that affect your learning and planning your study. They discuss the nature of university and the decisions and adjustments you make when beginning tertiary studies.

The *next seven chapters* look at how you can find, take in and evaluate information and ideas when pursuing your own and other people's questions. The importance of asking your own questions in your learning is emphasised, as is learning in ways that suit you so that you remember what you learn. These chapters deal with analysing and researching a topic, finding and using information sources, and reading and listening to lectures.

The *last six chapters* look at communicating, using, critiquing and presenting what you learn. They deal with participating in discussions, with developing your writing, and with writing and presenting essays and reports. The book concludes with a chapter on evaluating your learning.

Who the book is for

This book is intended primarily as *a guide and reference* for people who have some opportunity for independent learning. It is mostly intended for students who are past the age of compulsory schooling, and for people who want to discover how to use the resources of formal tertiary education for their own goals in learning. However, the learning techniques presented in the book can be used in a range of structured classes, and sections of the book can be used by people who need help with activities such as journal writing, learning portfolios, producing business reports and running discussion groups.

- You will find the book invaluable if you are a student at university, especially in first or second year.

- Postgraduate and advanced students will also find sections of the book very helpful, such as the chapters on 'Asking your own questions' and 'Using information sources'.

- If you are a student who has little contact with teachers—perhaps because you belong to a large institution or because you are studying online, part-time and/or at a distance—the book offers information otherwise available from frequent face-to-face contact with teachers.

- If you are returning to study after an absence from it, you can use our suggestions to help you gain confidence in yourself as a learner.

- If you are a student entering university straight from a highly structured secondary school or a TAFE college, the book will help you adjust to taking primary responsibility for your studies and introduce you to essential university skills.

- If you have left school and are taking a technical or training course, the book will help you with basic learning skills.

- You will find the book useful if you are in the final years of high school, whether or not you are going on to tertiary study.

How to use the book

A Guide to Learning Independently can be used in several different ways, each of which involves actively trying the ideas and techniques in your learning and studying. Don't simply read the book. Acquaint yourself with its contents, then use it as a guide and reference when the need arises.

- You can use the book *on your own*. Refer to it, for example, when you need help with how to use a library or write an essay. Read chapters such as 'Becoming a university student', 'Engaging with university', and 'Learning from evaluation', if you are thinking about the nature of formal tertiary education. The *Guide* can be especially useful if you are studying mostly online because you are remote from campus or have a busy life outside study.

- The book can be used when studying and learning *collaboratively*. You might, for example, use the chapter on 'Developing your writing', to work on your writing with other students. The process of learning with other students can enrich your education and make it less solitary. Use the book when working on your learning skills with a teacher, so you both can relate our suggestions to your particular learning activity. For example, refer to 'Choosing and analysing a topic', 'Researching a topic', and 'Writing essays' when working on how to prepare and write an essay.

- *Teachers* can use this book too. A teacher within a unit can refer students to sections of the book that would be most helpful to a particular individual or group. Learning skills advisers and counsellors can also use the book in their classes or with individual students.

However, all the ideas, information, techniques and suggestions we offer are of little value to you as a student unless you are reading, writing, listening, talking, asking questions, experimenting, and stretching your mind—unless you are engaged in learning. Exploring and practising alternative approaches to learning and studying provide a basis from which you can choose the approaches that are most effective and satisfying for you. This experience with alternative ways of learning is also essential if you are to change habits that no longer suit you. Such changes take time and practice, and suggestions which are easy for us to make may take courage and persistence for you to apply. But defining your goals, reflecting on your learning, thinking critically, and building on your strengths and working on your weaknesses as a student are all crucial to learning independently. This book is intended to help you discover these challenges and pleasures.

* * *

'Students' minds are like containers to be filled.'
'Education is to sharpen that tool which is the mind.'
'Knowledge is to be built up, block by block.'

These are a few of the metaphors commonly used to describe formal education. But such metaphors describe learning as essentially confined and defined, rather than as a process of growing and changing.

Each of us is born with a great curiosity, and this curiosity is essential for us to survive and learn. We learn as we ask and think about what we need to know. We are learning all the time, whether or not we realise it. We learn from what we do, from what happens to us, from our jobs and our pastimes—the list is endless. And we learn more easily when actively involved and when using what we learn in doing or talking, thinking or dreaming.

Learning is often thought of largely as an approved activity that happens in certain places (schools, colleges and universities) at certain ages (usually between 5 and 21) and in certain ways (in classrooms, according to a curriculum taught by teachers). But this formal study is only one part of our learning, and is designed to achieve only particular outcomes. At the heart of all our significant learning, formal and informal, are the questions we ask because of who we are and what we want to know.

Formal educational institutions can help you ask and pursue your own questions and solve problems. There are teachers in these institutions who care about teaching and about you as a learner, who can convey to you the fierce and gentle pleasures of the mind. Having teachers who help you ask your own questions, who share their knowledge and experience and who are also questioning and learning for themselves is an invaluable part of formal education. There are also students with whom you can talk and argue, theorise and imagine.

However, formal education may channel learning in directions that can seem irrelevant to you. But without your own questions that arise from your curiosity, you are limited to learning what is presented to you rather than discovering how to learn, and to communicate and exchange ideas. Knowing how to learn makes it possible for you to continue learning long after you finish formal education. Otherwise, you are restricted to learning a particular body of knowledge that may soon become outdated.

Using the resources of an educational institution for your own goals entails thinking about what is expected of you, and why. Who decides what you should learn, and how and when this should be taught? Who decides how and when you should be required to prove what you have learned? These decisions, made partly by teachers, reflect what many others see as the roles of a university or college in our society. These 'others' include government bodies, academic committees, administrators, professional organisations, employers, and individuals who make key decisions in our society. If you want to use formal education as part of your goals for learning rather than simply following other people's objectives, try to identify and examine and question the assumptions and purposes of the people who shape tertiary education. Will you accept what these people expect, what they require? If not, think about your options.

Formal educational institutions expect a lot of you. As with most work, sometimes you will be involved and enthusiastic, and sometimes you will have other priorities in your life that detract from your study. Learning is a personal process, not simply a commodity or a meal ticket that you will acquire after a set program of study, so keep your questions and your goals in mind. Play with ideas—speculate, hypothesise, fantasise. Do the ideas offered excite you or make sense to you? If so, grab them with both halves of your brain. Read, write, draw, critique, experiment, for the sake of your own learning and for the pleasure and discovery of a craft. Learn how to communicate your own questions and ideas, and try hard to understand what others are communicating. Don't reject an idea or a topic or a unit out of hand because of your biases or laziness or fears. Be willing to take a risk, to reach a little further than you think you can. Don't expect to understand all you read or hear.

Real, active learning of your own isn't easy—it's hard work. But the hard work is not that of a dutiful conscience, it arises from the joy of intense involvement. One of the greatest challenges you can take on is attempting to be aware of your goals for learning, to reflect profoundly on what and how you learn, to communicate your ideas clearly, and to understand and critically evaluate the thoughts of others. This learning is a process of growing and changing, a process that is much more exciting than filling bins or sharpening tools or building with blocks.

What to do now

1 Read through the initial Contents list.

2 Flick through the book and use the Contents list for each chapter to select one which would be especially useful to you now. If you can't decide, start with Chapter 1, 'You', or Chapter 2, 'Becoming a university student'. Skim through the quotations, and then read the chapter thoroughly.

3 Choose a topic that interests you, look it up in the Index and read the relevant pages of the book.

4 Turn to Table 10.1, 'The anatomy of a book', and apply the questions in this table to *A Guide to Learning Independently*.

5 Look back over 'Read this first!'

6 Go to the final chapter and the last pages of the book. Read 'A learning portfolio' and consider how you might begin a portfolio now.

7 Any questions or ideas? Ask someone else—another student, a teacher, or a friend—for their thoughts on your questions and ideas.

You

1

We shall not cease from exploration
And the end of our exploring
Will be to arrive where we started
And to know the place for the first time.

T. S. ELIOT

Your physical and emotional self
    Body rhythms
    Sleep
    Food and drink
    Physical exercise
    Senses
    Health and wellbeing
    Tension and relaxation
    Emotions
    Reflections

Your cultural self
    Ways of thinking and learning
    Beliefs and values
    Your goals

Your social self
    The people in your life
    Social groupings
    Your virtual social self

This book begins with you. It begins with you because asking questions and thinking about yourself, your lifestyle and your background can give you insights into your individual learning style. You can then use these insights to make your learning and study more effective and satisfying.

Your body and your emotions, your cultural background and your beliefs, and the people in your life—all these affect your learning. Your physical state and your emotions influence your ability to learn, and too little sleep or exercise may affect your enthusiasm for and ability to study. A belief in the value of hard work may make you a conscientious student. An argument with the people in your household can create difficulties when you try to concentrate on study, and moving house or changing jobs can leave little time and energy for formal learning.

As people and students we are all different. If you are a meticulous and deliberate thinker, a study task might take you longer. This may leave you feeling inadequate, or you might enjoy the leisurely savouring of new ideas. At the other extreme, if you have a high energy level and live at a fast pace, you might wish you could occasionally slow down enough to integrate in more depth what you learn, or you might enjoy the speed with which new insights come to you. There is no single way to learn and study that suits everyone. And because you change daily, weekly and monthly, there is no one way of studying that always suits you. So you need to know more about these aspects of yourself, and examine how your culture and surroundings affect your learning.

- Read each set of questions in turn and write down your answers or ideas on them, perhaps in a special notebook or journal (see 'Learning journals or logs', Chapter 13). When you have read and thought about the whole chapter, look back over it and revise any notes.

- Read through the whole chapter and reflect on these questions and suggestions which are relevant to you at present. Later re-read the chapter and focus on other questions. Rethink your responses if you or your lifestyle has changed significantly.

- Discuss the questions with one or two friends or with a group of people (see 'Playing your part during discussions', Chapter 12).

Your physical and emotional self

As a first step to thinking about your self, centre your attention on your body. Stop for a few minutes. Centre your attention on your face—think about your forehead, eyes, nose, mouth and jaw. Are they relaxed/strong/tired/tense? Move your awareness down to your neck, shoulders and spine. Focus on each part of your body, from your head down to your toes. How does your whole body feel now?

What do you like most about your body?

What do you like least?

When does your body feel really good? What circumstances lead you to feel good about your body (such as when you do lots of exercise, after a good night's sleep or when you eat healthy food)?

How does your body feel now?

Now **stop**. Did you actually spend time thinking about and answering these questions, or did you just passively read them? If you didn't answer them, go back and think about them seriously. Get in touch with your body before you go on to the next set of questions. This chapter centres on you, but can only be effective if you become actively involved with the questions and ideas it contains.

Body rhythms

Certainly people show consistent, life-long predilections for morning or night activity. Physiological differences may be found in the circadian rhythms of the so-called lark people, who are most alive by morning, and the owls, who perform at their best late in the day, yet the owls are generally penalised by the usual scheduling of school hours.

GAY GAER LUCE

Your body has many rhythms and cycles. Each day, for example, your temperature and pulse rate fluctuate slightly, and you pass through the same pattern of dreaming several times each night. Perhaps you go through cycles where your desire for physical activity alternates with your desire for mental activity. The lives we lead often make it difficult to stay in tune with our natural body rhythms, and interruptions to our sleep patterns from part-time or shift work, young children, all night partying or long study hours all interfere with these natural rhythms.

Discovering your individual body rhythms can help you plan study times when you are more mentally active. One of the difficulties in studying for final exams in the spring or early summer can be that you often need to stay inside and be mentally active when you would prefer to be outside and physically active as the seasons change. If you are a night person you may be unwilling to leave your bed to attend an early lecture on a gloomy winter morning, or if you are a day person you may find it difficult to concentrate during an evening class. A cup of coffee may revive you for that evening class but, in the long run, regularly using stimulants to help you cope with study is self-defeating.

Are you a lark or an owl?

Are you aware of patterns in your body's need for sleep, exercise, food and sex?

How is your study related to these patterns?

- Determine the times during the day when you are usually most mentally alert and when you feel physically ready to study.
- Try to schedule your study during your alert times. If it is necessary to study when your energy level is low, plan to do work which demands less intense concentration.

Sleep

> I haven't been to sleep for over a year. That's why I go to bed early. One needs more rest if one doesn't sleep. EVELYN WAUGH

Sleep needs vary for different people and sleep deprivation can have an impact on you emotionally and physically. If you are frequently irritable and can't cope as well as usual with minor problems, you are possibly getting too little sleep. How well you concentrate on study is influenced by how much sleep you have.

○○○ *Do you often sleep so much that your mind feels drugged?*

What effect does a late night or an interrupted night's sleep have on your concentration the next day, for example, if you are short of sleep because of an active social life?

Can you think clearly after a nap? Does a brief nap or a couple of hours' sleep refresh you for long periods of study?

When do your sleep needs vary (for example, when you are emotionally upset or physically active)?

Do you often have to change your sleep times, for example, because of shift work or a restless baby? How do these changes affect your study?

- Determine your minimum sleep needs and the amount of sleep you think you need for a good night's rest. Think about a time when you have been very relaxed and were able to sleep as much as you needed.
- Consider your sleep patterns for the past two weeks and how they have helped or interfered with your learning.
- Try to plan your most demanding study periods for times when you are not short of sleep.
- On a night when you can't fall asleep, try deep breathing exercises and relaxing your body completely (see 'Tension and relaxation', later in this chapter). If this doesn't work, get up and do something rather than lying in bed and worrying about not sleeping.
- The 'blue light' from electronic devices can interfere with your body's readiness for sleep if you use them at bedtime.
- If you have an ongoing sleep problem and it is interfering with your study, seek professional help.

- If you often have difficulty getting enough sleep, allow time to wind down before going to bed, and don't drink or eat foods that contain caffeine during the evening. Give yourself two or three periods of deep relaxation during the day. Relaxing your body fully from head to toe can be almost as refreshing as sleeping.

Food and drink

One cannot think well, love well, sleep well, if one has not dined well.   VIRGINIA WOOLF

A breakfast that is more nourishing than tea and toast, or lunch that is more than a bag of chips, a doughnut or a bowl of rice, helps you concentrate during class or private study. A light evening meal instead of a large dinner makes it easier to focus on your study or an evening class. Studying is especially difficult if you feel tired and irritable because of poor eating or heavy drinking.

Do you prefer to eat one large meal a day or frequent small meals? Do you try to study after a large meal?

When settling to study, does preparing something to eat or drink help or hinder you?

Do you often drink so much alcohol that you cannot think clearly the next day?

Are there some foods, such as certain additives, that adversely affect your concentration?

- Make sure your diet is well balanced and includes protein, carbohydrates and plenty of fruit and vegetables. Essential protein is available from complex carbohydrates such as beans or rice as well as from meat and dairy products, but refined carbohydrates such as ice cream, alcohol and soft drinks add little to your diet except kilojoules. If you generally lack energy, check that your diet isn't deficient in minerals and vitamins, particularly iron and the vitamin B complex. If you don't have much money or have dietary restrictions, eating properly takes more planning and a knowledge of nutrition, but it can be done.
- Avoid planning study after a heavy meal.
- If you feel the need for food during a study session a piece of fruit can boost your serotonin levels, or have a small amount of protein food such as a piece of cheese, a glass of soy milk or a handful of peanuts.
- A judiciously chosen treat can help you when you settle to work or reward you when you finish.

Physical exercise

Not taking care of your body is like not paying the rent; you end up with no place to live.
                                                                GAYLE OLINEKOVA

Physical exercise can provide a welcome break from mental activity. Exercise helps you study because it reduces tension, increases the oxygen supply to your brain, improves your digestion and helps you sleep more soundly. Long periods without exercising your body can make it difficult to exercise your mind effectively. However, immediately after strenuous physical exercise some people find it difficult to settle down to study.

○○○ *What form of physical exercise do you enjoy, for example, a team sport, cycling, swimming, sailing, yoga, sex, dancing, table tennis, walking, or skating?*

If you are a physically active person, do you find it difficult to sit still for long periods to read, write or listen to a lecture?

Does exercise usually refresh or fatigue you for learning?

Do you renew your concentration during a study session by taking a short break to move about?

● Choose exercise that feels good to you and do it regularly. Include activity that exercises your whole body, including your heart and lungs, and activity that stretches your body and helps you loosen up.

● Plan to study and exercise when these two activities help rather than conflict with each other.

● If your work is physically tiring, allow yourself time to relax and eat something nourishing before you try to study.

● At times when you need to be especially mentally alert, such as during exams, regular physical exercise helps increase your alertness and concentration.

Senses

All creative activity, as well as much of your pleasure in life, depends on your sensory awareness. Even your ability to absorb and use second-hand information depends on your ability to relate it to your own first-hand observations. Yet, constantly exposed to second-hand information, you may forget to use your senses and may become, to some degree, cut off from the world immediately around you. FRED MORGAN

Your earliest learning is through your senses, but as you come to rely more on abstract reasoning it is easy to forget how vital your senses are to your learning.

○○○ *Stop for a moment. Shut your eyes. What can you smell? What can you hear? What tastes do you have in your mouth? What sensations do you feel on your skin? Now open your eyes. What can you see?*

What is your strongest sense? Do you learn best by hearing, seeing, touching, or a combination of these?

● At the end of each day ask yourself what you remember most vividly—which sight, sound, smell, taste or touch comes instantly to your mind? Conjure up these sense impressions as you drift off to sleep, or write a description of them in a daily journal.

- When you feel like relaxing, take a few minutes to become deeply aware of the smells, sounds, tastes, touch and sights you are experiencing.
- In your study utilise as many of your senses as you can. For example, when trying to learn something you find difficult don't just read it silently and use only your sense of sight. Speak it aloud so that you hear it, and make notes using patterns and colours so that you use your visual sense more fully (see 'Patterns and principles', Chapter 5). The act of writing by hand also uses the sense of touch.

Health and wellbeing

Health is a state of complete physical, mental and social well-being, and not merely the absence of disease or infirmity.   WORLD HEALTH ORGANIZATION

Many factors in your life and environment can have an impact on your physical and psychological health and wellbeing, and in turn your health can have a major impact on your study. For some people, a diagnosed condition can make everyday study more challenging than usual.

Do you consider yourself to be healthy?

Do you have any physical or psychological ailments that might affect your study?

How often do you see a doctor? Do you go for regular physical examinations?

Do you regularly see the dentist, the optometrist or other practitioners such as a physiotherapist or chiropractor?

Can you identify any factors, such as your eating or where you live, that might be having a positive or negative affect on your health?

- If you are basically healthy maintain this with good food and sufficient sleep and exercise.
- If you are unwell during semester and visit a doctor, ask for a medical certificate in case you need to request an extension for an assignment.
- If you become ill unexpectedly, even from a winter cold, let your teacher know if you think you might need to request an extension. You don't need to struggle on when, if you are genuinely ill and follow the correct procedures, you will be able to get an extension.
- If you often feel unwell, seek professional help. If you cannot identify a cause, speak to a counsellor or the university nurse or doctor for advice on the best professional to consult.
- If you have a diagnosed condition (physical or psychological) which makes everyday study more challenging than usual, seek advice well in advance of

semester about the challenges and adjustments you will face with your study. It is helpful if you can get to know both the campus and any counselling and equity support staff. In particular, contact the relevant support staff such as a student adviser or the health services and explain your condition.

- Depending on your problem, check out the relevant services and facilities. As well as providing practical support so that you are not placed at an unfair disadvantage, there may be options to help you to become part of the university community more easily. Find out about alternatives that might make study less challenging for you. For example:
  — check if there are alternative means of assessment which might be helpful, and if flexible modes of taking exams are an option
  — if necessary, find out about special parking arrangements
  — ask about technical equipment such as voice-activated word processors or text-enlarged computers
  — find out about services such as library assistance, perhaps with online searches and photocopying, and
  — if you have handwriting difficulties, request that you be assigned a lecture notetaker.

Tension and relaxation

How did I live to be a hundred years old? Well, when I moves I moves slow. When I sits, I sits loose. And when I worries, I goes to sleep.   LIZ CARPENTER

If you are reasonably relaxed you can learn more effectively. To relax and de-stress, you may need to put aside problems for a while, exercise more often, or learn how to relax your body consciously from head to toe.

○○○ *Where in your body do you usually feel anxiety or tension?*

Do you feel relaxed now? If so, why? If not, why not?

Can you study when you feel tense and stressed? If not, do you know how to relax?

While you are studying or listening to a lecture, do you occasionally check to see if any parts of your body are tense?

After a period of study or a session at the keyboard do you suffer from eye strain, headaches or tension in your shoulder muscles?

Do you habitually rely on drugs or herbal remedies to help you relax?

- Learn and practise relaxation techniques that help your whole body to relax fully, for example, deep breathing, yoga, gentle exercise, massage, a hot bath.
- If you think your tension is due to physical causes such as eye strain, seek appropriate help.

- When reading or writing or using a computer, stretch and change positions occasionally, rest your eyes by focusing on a distant object, and yawn and take several deep breaths to ease tension around your mouth and jaw. There are 'on the spot' exercises that are quick to do and designed specifically to relieve keyboard stress.

- Search for software that reminds you to take a break when working for long stretches. Some software fades out your computer screen at intervals for a length of time of your choice. Some programs remind you to stretch and re-focus your eyes, some provide exercises, and some play restful music.

- Get some whole body exercise following a long study session.

Emotions

Last night I was seized by a fit of despair that found utterance in moans, and that finally drove me to throw the dining room clock into the sea.   MARIE BASHKIRTSEFF

The ups and downs of your emotions influence your learning. If you are feeling cheerful you probably find it easy to study; if you are feeling depressed you may have difficulty concentrating or absorbing new ideas. Most students have emotional problems at one time or another, including anxiety or guilt about study.

What are the most positive aspects in your life at present? List them.

What are the most positive aspects of your studies?

What are you most worried about? List these worries.

Which aspects of your studies worry you the most?

How do you deal with stress and anxiety?

- Write down what is worrying you before you begin studying or if you continue to be distracted as you study. Ask yourself whether it is more urgent to go on studying or to tackle your worries. Plan another time to deal with whichever is less urgent.

- Allow yourself a set time during the day to think about your problems and try to put them aside for the rest of the day. Talk to a friend about them or write them out.

- Practise physical relaxation techniques or activities which help you deal with your emotions.

- Reading for pleasure can give you a respite from your worries and stress.

- Spend some time away from the place where you seem to worry most. Going for a walk or visiting friends can put your problems in perspective.

- If you have a persistent problem, discuss it with a close friend, a sympathetic 'outsider' or a trained counsellor.

- If your difficulties are connected with your learning or lack of it, do some work. A few hours of concentrated study often works wonders if you are feeling overwhelmed with study demands. If you are stuck on a problem, discuss it with your teacher or with other students—often other people have the same problem. Read the relevant sections in this guide for some useful suggestions.

- If you are anxious about a responsibility such as taking an exam or giving a seminar paper, find out as precisely as possible what you want to know about your subject, and study it as thoroughly as you can. Talk to someone with experience in the techniques of exams or seminars, or read the relevant sections in this book. A certain amount of anxiety and tension can help motivate you to learn.

Reflections

> Reflection must be reserved for solitary hours; whenever she was alone, she gave way to it as the greatest relief; and not a day went by without a solitary walk, in which she might indulge in all the delight of . . . reflections.　　　　　JANE AUSTEN

Reflection is one of the keys to understanding, to remembering, to learning and to thinking critically. It is central to integrating what you learn into your existing knowledge and belief system, and in deciding how to act. Thinking about your own thinking, or 'metacognition', will give you insights into how you go about your learning, and is important if you want to change or adapt study behaviours.

○○○ *Do you enjoy spending time alone?*

Are you able to spend enough time with your own thoughts?

Do you write down your reflections? Do you share them with someone else? Who with?

Do you live life at such a fast pace that you have no time to make sense of your experiences and learning?

How do your emotions influence your reflections?

Can you think of recent examples where your reflections have led you to act differently?

- If you can manage to have time alone without interruption, reflect on your life, your interests, your concerns and your learning. Try to set up both intellectual and physical space to reflect on what you are learning.

- When you have completed a study task, such as writing or reading a report, or giving a seminar, think back over the process you went through and write down how you went about it and what you would change next time.

- You may want to document your reflections in a personal or learning journal (see Chapter 13, 'Developing your writing').

Your cultural self

It is important to consider the impact of your cultural background on your thinking and learning, so begin by reflecting on your beliefs and values, and how these affect your study.

Stop for a moment and think about your cultural background in your wider society and then within your tertiary institution.

Which cultural groups have been influential in shaping who you are? Do you identify with a strong cultural or ethnic group in your country?

Were you born in this country or are you a migrant or an overseas student? If you were born here, for how many generations has your family been in this country?

To what socioeconomic class does your family belong?

Are you from a group whose numbers in this society are small, for example, a recent migrant or refugee group or a religious minority?

Are you from a country town, a remote area or the city?

Are you the first member of your family to attend university? Are you the first among your friends to attend university?

For many years, most tertiary education communities in countries such as Australia and Britain consisted primarily of school leavers from affluent families. This has changed, and university communities have become more varied. There has been an influx of students from overseas; and tertiary study now attracts students from diverse backgrounds, including mature-age people, Indigenous peoples, migrants, minority ethnic groups, refugees and people from lower socioeconomic groups.

Ways of thinking and learning

All of us are living and thinking subjects . . . Everybody both acts and thinks. The way people act or react is linked to a way of thinking, and of course thinking is related to tradition.   MICHEL FOUCAULT

It is valuable to spend some time thinking about how your cultural and social background might influence your thinking and how you go about your learning.

Do the cultural groups with which you identify value learning?

How has your background helped or hindered you in your desire for a tertiary education?

With which cultural groups in your university community do you identify?

How does your background affect your view of the world? How does this world view affect your study? For example, how is your interpretation of what you read and hear different from that of other students?

How does your background give you particular strengths in your learning? Do you ever feel that there are gaps in your learning because of your background?

- If you are studying because it is a cultural or social expectation and not because you want to, think about your alternatives. If you are to continue with a formal education, you need to be clear about your learning goals and objectives so that the time and effort you invest does not seem like a waste of time (see 'Making choices and decisions', Chapter 2). If one of your life goals is to complete a tertiary education but in pursuing this you are at odds with others in your cultural or social group, consider how you can handle this opposition and look for support from within your university or college (see 'Engaging with others', Chapter 3).

- Try to identify how your background might strengthen your learning at university, and how there might be areas on which you need to work. For example, if your family has experience with books and academic learning, you may understand how university students are expected to approach study, but you may also be subject to family pressure to achieve at a high level. If you come from a society where teachers are highly respected and where questioning the teacher is not acceptable, it may take you time to become accustomed to more informal teacher–student interactions, but your respect for teachers perhaps means that you are more ready to listen carefully to lectures. If you are a student from a developing country, your formal education may have suffered because of limited access to books and resources, but your learning can be enriched by the cross-cultural comparisons you can make. If your background includes experience with questioning and critiquing the world around you, you will find the critical culture of a university easier to adapt to.

- Once you become involved in your studies, you will find that your way of interpreting what you read and what is discussed in tutorials sometimes differs noticeably from that of other students. This difference reflects your background, experiences, world view, interests and previous schooling. You are entitled to your own interpretation, which should be supported by evidence, examples and explanations. If you are a lone voice presenting a particular point of view, you need to think through your interpretation as fully and critically as possible, and you may have to work harder to have your ideas considered or accepted. Remember, however, that diversity of opinions is important in academic debate in a university, and that everyone has a contribution to make.

Beliefs and values

> Ideally, our choices will be made on the basis of the values we hold; but frequently, we
> are not clear about our own values.   SIDNEY B. SIMON et al.

What you believe and value directly affects your learning. It can affect your choice of courses, your work within units, your open-mindedness and how you relate to other students and to teachers. For example, if you are concerned about the environment you might write your assignments on topics related to this area. If you are from a religious family and you don't believe in genetic engineering, you may find yourself in conflict with a biology teacher who pursues this area of research. If you are an empiricist you may have little sympathy for a lecturer who is a postmodern thinker. Examining your world view with its values and assumptions is essential to critical thinking, and learning to think critically is an integral part of university study.

At times your views and values might conflict with your learning. For example, a unit on Eastern religious philosophy may affect your belief in a Western ethic that is goal-oriented. If you have very strong religious beliefs, you may need to learn that statements of faith are not acceptable as evidence in a university essay. You may find yourself disillusioned with the studies required for a long-dreamed-of profession, or with the realities of formal education. Perhaps you are confronted with a challenge to an ingrained prejudice about the superiority of the male sex or of white-skinned races. A new insight into personal relationships can create dissatisfaction with your belief in the nuclear family.

○○○ *How would you complete the following sentences?*

'I believe that humans are essentially . . .'

'I believe that our society should be organised so that . . .'

'What I believe about humans and our society is based on the assumption that . . .'

How does what you believe and value affect what and how you learn?

- Try to work out which beliefs are most important to you, and to identify their source, including those embedded in your upbringing.

- If a conflict of beliefs and values is seriously affecting your study, talk it over with a close friend, a parent or a counsellor. If this conflict is related to material covered in a unit, talk to a teacher if possible.

- Think about the beliefs and values of the people with whom you have frequent contact—consider your friends, your parents, a partner, your teachers, and fellow students. Try to work out why their beliefs differ from or are similar to your own.

- You may want to take a unit in critical thinking to help you clarify the place of values and assumptions in academic argument (see 'Critical thinking', Chapter 3).

Your goals

> Most people most of the time [do not] act the way they do because they are trying to achieve goals, but . . . when they do so, they experience a sense of control which is absent when behaviour is not motivated by consciously chosen goals.   MIHALY CSIKSZENTMIHAYI

Your life goals will be closely related to your beliefs and values, and your study aims will be linked to how you think about learning and education. Being clear about your goals and possible deadlines for achieving them gives you a sense of purpose and direction. This applies to work or leisure, with family or friends, alone or with others, on small or large projects, and in all aspects of your study. It is this sense of purpose that, as a student, keeps you motivated if your interest flags or if the going gets tough; it enables you to use both positive and negative feedback effectively; it focuses your attention, and helps you strive to develop new skills and refine existing ones. As Csikszentmihayi says, you will experience a feeling of control over your studies. It will help if you are clear about any broad goals in your life and how these relate to your study aims.

Sometimes it can be difficult to be clear about specific aims. If, for example, you are going through major changes in your life, you may know that you want to be at university but you have only broad reasons for this. In such situations, focus on making the most of your study, and allow some time to reflect on what your specific aims might be.

○○○ *Do you have any clear goals for the next five to ten years of your life?*

What are your aims for your university study?

How do your study aims relate to your other life goals?

How committed are you to your goals?

- Your goals are your overall reasons for doing something. Within these goals, set yourself well-defined aims that you can act on and achieve within a certain time frame.
- If you have goals but have never taken the time to articulate them, do take some time to write them out clearly. If you are unclear about your goals it can help to write down your thoughts about possible future directions.
- If you are studying because someone else thinks you should, and you have no clear study goals of your own, you probably need to spend some time working out if you are doing the right thing right now.
- Your goals should be specific, measurable, achievable, realistic and time-specific.
- Make your goals challenging but not unrealistic. Remember, your goals need to be flexible so that you can alter or adapt them in the light of experience and information.
- Set yourself realistic deadlines for reaching your goals

Your social self

Your relationships with the people in your life have an impact on your study and learning, so it is useful to reflect on the influence on your study of the people at home, at work and those that you see socially in both your real and virtual world.

Stop for a moment and think about the important people in your life, in your wider society and then within your tertiary institution.

The people in your life

> On Mondays mum has a tutorial, so I have to go around to Grandma's place for tea. That's all right. She lets me watch television. 8-YEAR-OLD GIRL

In your household, the time and energy you have for study can be dramatically increased if you manage to work out a satisfactory living pattern with the other people. This usually takes time and even if you have a comfortable arrangement, there will be difficult periods as you all adapt to the inevitable changes in your lives. However, any time and effort in this direction is well spent when it increases your enjoyment of formal learning. If the people you live with cooperate in making your study effective, you will have more energy and enthusiasm for study.

Do you live on your own, or with others such as parents, relatives, friends, other students, a partner/spouse, or children? Does your 'household' extend to daily contact with people who live in a different location, such as an elderly parent or a close friend?

Do your working hours coincide with those of the other people in your house? Are the others also studying, or do they have some idea of the demands of being a student? Are they considerate of your study needs? Do they resent or support the time you spend studying? How do you arrange time with them and time to study?

Do you have responsibilities in your household, such as domestic chores, financial burdens or caring for young children or a sick relative? Do these responsibilities leave you little time and energy for study? How might they be reallocated?

Are you under pressure from people such as your partner or your parents to succeed in your studies? Why? Are their criteria for success the same as yours?

Are you living away from your family for the first time? If so, how is your time for study affected by the time you need to spend on practical tasks such as cooking and cleaning?

- If there is a persistent or major problem in your living arrangements or personal relationships which makes it difficult for you to study, talk about it as soon as possible with the person or people concerned. Describe how you feel about the problem and suggest ways it might be handled, particularly what you can do about it. Listen to suggestions from the others concerned and see if you can come to a workable compromise. If compromise doesn't seem possible, think seriously about the priority that formal learning has in your life (see 'Tracking your use of time', Chapter 4).

- You may have friends who don't understand that study means you have less time for socialising and who think that because you are at home you can be interrupted. If so, be firm until they come to understand that you now have to program your social arrangements. Ask friends to call or message and not just drop in.

- If you are the first in your family or the first in your peer group to go to university, work out how these people are reacting to your new life. Find out if they are supportive of or excited by your efforts, anxious about or threatened by your new role, uncertain how to react or unsure how to support you. If the people are not supportive of you, seek out knowledgeable supports within or outside the university.

Social groupings

It isn't the work that is going to be hard in college. It's the play. Half the time I don't know what the girls are talking about; their jokes seem to relate to a past that everyone but me has shared. I'm a foreigner in the world and I don't understand the language. It's a miserable feeling. I've had it all my life. At the high school the girls would stand in groups and just look at me. I was queer and different and everyone knew it . . .
JEAN WEBSTER

Think back for a moment to times in your life when you have been the only different person in a group; for example, if you were the only young person in a group of older people, or when you were with others who all spoke a different language, or when the others all had different beliefs from yours.

- If you feel different and isolated from other students, find someone who understands how you feel and share with them your experiences and your problems with learning. At the same time, remember that you have much to offer to other students and contribute your perspectives in formal and informal discussions.

- If you have rarely thought about what it is like to be on the outside, the chances are that you are part of a particular majority group. Make an extra effort to listen to and learn from students from different backgrounds, especially those who are part of a minority group. Show respect for their opinions and experiences.

- Take advantage of the richness and variety of experiences available in the diverse cultural and social groups within the student body. Being open to different world views and new ideas and perspectives, perhaps through informal social interactions with other students, is an important part of your formal learning and is essential to thinking critically.

If you are a full-time student whose friends frequently drop by, your approach to studying will differ from that of a parent with young children who is studying part-time and taking evening classes, or that of a distance education student who lives and works on a farm.

Your virtual social self

> . . . the computer has become even more than tool and mirror. We are able to step through the looking glass. We are learning to live in virtual worlds. We may find ourselves alone or we navigate virtual oceans, unravel virtual mysteries, and engineer virtual skyscrapers. But increasingly, when we step through the looking glass, other people are there as well. SHERRY TURKLE

The explosion of social media sites and their popularity means that you can have a social self in the virtual world. It means that you can interact and be involved with individuals and with groups without ever meeting them face-to-face; and this might include being involved in social movements or in serious game playing. This virtual life can enhance or detract from your effectiveness as a student in much the same way as your other social interactions.

Do you have a particular study friend or study group who you interact with online? Do you also meet these people face-to-face? If so, does your online relationship with them enhance or detract from your face-to-face meetings?

How much time each day or week do you spend on social media sites? What types of social media sites do you use, for example, microblogs, photo sharing sites? Do you keep a blog? Could you set up similar sharing interactions to help with your study?

What is the nature of your online social interactions? Are they to catch up with others or to reflect on events or to share information? Are they to be involved with organising events? How might you translate this to your study activities?

Do you use social media sites to share information, such as links, photos, news, ideas about study? Are these interactions with like-minded people or do you use social media to challenge others or to stir discussion and debate?

Do you find it easier to 'talk' online than face-to-face?

Are you in a group that plays collaborative virtual games?

Do you access social media sites to enhance your study? Or does this detract (or distract you) from your studies? In what ways?

- Keep track of the time you spend online with friends each day or over a week. Assess the degree to which this enhances or detracts from your study.

- You might want to join or start your own online social group with some fellow students, perhaps with a group enrolled in the same unit so that you can use this group to explore your thoughts and to share your ideas.

- If you are an online student, and don't have a social network or support from other students, investigate if it is worthwhile to use social media sites to provide these.

- Perhaps start a blog and use it to get feedback on your writing and study (see 'Blogs', Chapter 13).

The questions and suggestions in this chapter have focused on you because you are central to this book and to why, what and how you learn. Reading and following guidelines that tell you how to make your formal learning more effective is useful only if you adapt these guidelines to your own personality, lifestyle and surroundings.

> This above all; to thine own self be true.   SHAKESPEARE

TEN TIPS

1 Being aware of your body rhythms can help you plan when to study most effectively.

2 Learning how to take a 10–15 minute nap can be very useful for when you are tired but have to study.

3 A balanced diet helps keep your brain and body in shape.

4 Find a physical activity that feels good and is reasonably safe, and do it often to help keep your mind from stagnating.

5 Even a few deep breaths every now and then can help focus your mind.

6 Everyone feels anxious sometimes—find some strategies that help you cope with these times.

7 Try to be aware of what you bring from your cultural background that affects your approach to learning and gives you both strengths and challenges as a student.

8 Seize opportunities to learn with and from people from different backgrounds.

9 Be willing to examine your ideas for possible bias and prejudice.

10 Take time to reflect now and then on the range of reasons why you are studying—these may not all be obvious.

Becoming a university student

2

> . . . *a university education is . . . about inviting students into a larger realm of knowledge than that encompassed by text messages, helping them to discover things that are too complex to be communicated in five minutes. . . . This is the breakthrough moment for students, the point at which they stop being passive consumers of knowledge and become part of the scholarly debate.*
>
> ANN MARIE PRIEST

What to expect from university

Your expectations of university will have been shaped by your prior experience of formal learning, by your knowledge of university generally, by your attitudes to learning, and by the stories that you hear from others or the media. For example, if a family member or friend has attended university, your expectations will have been coloured by their anecdotes. If you are the first among your family and friends to go to 'uni' you may find it difficult to get an insider's view of university and may not have a ready audience with whom to explore your expectations.

University culture

> Academic debate has traditionally been justified, at least in part, by its ability to train students for participation in a democratic society. A necessary component of this claim would seem to be that debate in some way influences the ideology of its student practitioners, giving them training in the tolerance of alternative beliefs and allowing them to see the world from a variety of perspectives.   ROBERT E. TUCKER

Like all institutions, universities have a unique culture, and there are aspects of each university that set it apart from the others. While it is impossible to generalise, one common feature of university culture is a commitment to a way of thinking that includes academic debate and argument. This overarching concept has shaped universities, including the approach to teaching and the expectations of student learning. Once you unlock the key to understanding and applying this way of thinking and communicating you will be well on the way to becoming a fully functioning member of a university community of scholars.

A distinctive feature of universities is that they provide opportunity for scholars to propose theories and ideas, and to defend them, including those that conflict with or are in direct opposition to dominant ideas and current policies or to accepted 'truths'. Through research and scholarship, there is a quest for better explanations and more accurate evidence to support ideas and approaches. Of course, there are heated debates on the different theories and methodologies. Universities can provide an environment within which individuals and groups of scholars put forward their ideas for scrutiny and where explanations and evidence are critically debated. In all university disciplines knowledge is regarded as provisional. Accepted 'truths' remain only while there is evidence to support them. The written and oral forms of communication within the academic disciplines are structured to support these critical debates.

You may be unaccustomed outside university to participating in thoughtful debates about ideas, or you may associate 'argument' with unpleasant conflict. If so, it can be exciting to be in a milieu where debates about ideas are always on the agenda somewhere, and where people can disagree strongly yet remain on good terms. The topics or questions you discuss in your formal learning may be presented to you from only one perspective, or you may be confronted with ideas from many different world views. When you enter into a debate on an issue you too become part of this ongoing dialogue—even if you are a novice in the content and method of the debate, you are still part of that dialogue. When you enter the discussion you do so with your particular view of the world and your particular perspective on the topic. A key part of being at university is to question and test your ideas and opinions in order to become a more independent thinker. The extent of your engagement in the broad learning community of scholars and its sub-cultures, will be influenced by who you are as a student, your commitment to learning, and by factors in your life such as work, financial or family commitments.

University disciplines

Universities are usually divided into faculties, departments or schools, each representing a body or closely related bodies of knowledge called 'disciplines', some of which provide professional training. Some institutions separate—and, it seems at times, even segregate—the disciplines into departments which teach particular subjects and courses of study. The teaching and research in each apparently discrete area of knowledge has an institutional hierarchy with professors, senior and junior academics, and postgraduate and undergraduate students. What constitutes these disciplines is always open to question and change, and new disciplines are always struggling for a foothold.

Each discipline is a culture in its own right with its own discourse—its own language and vocabulary, and its own methodologies for choosing, analysing, critiquing, interpreting, presenting and using knowledge. In some institutions there are opportunities for interdisciplinary or multidisciplinary study, but this has been the exception rather than the rule. So when you start tertiary study you enter not only the overall culture of the institution but the culture of the discipline(s) in which you will study. You learn the current culture of these disciplines partly through immersion in them but also through explicit instruction in the specific content, language and methodology.

Within disciplines where there is conflict about what constitutes 'knowledge', there may be more than one appropriate language or methodology; and at times it may be confusing if you find that the approach to knowledge in one discipline is different from the approach in another. Some students, for example, do very well when writing in one discipline, but not so well when they use the same approach in another.

In your first year you are not expected to be highly knowledgeable in your chosen field or to be familiar with the language or methods of the field; this is part of what you are at university to learn. The way you approached a subject area in secondary school or elsewhere may no longer be applicable at tertiary level. Take nothing for granted and be prepared to ask questions. If you are studying entirely online,

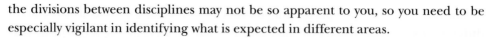

the divisions between disciplines may not be so apparent to you, so you need to be especially vigilant in identifying what is expected in different areas.

> . . . my time is exclusively occupied with study. It's a very bewildering matter to get educated in five branches at once.
>
> 'The test of true scholarship,' says Chemistry Professor, 'is painstaking passion for detail.'
>
> 'Be careful not to keep your eyes glued to detail,' says History Professor. 'Stand far enough away to get a perspective of the whole.'
>
> You can see with what nicety we have to trim our sails between chemistry and history.   JEAN WEBSTER

Understanding and competence in the skills expected for learning in your chosen discipline are aspects of becoming familiar with the field, for example, whether or not there is a strong emphasis on problem solving or collaborative learning. You may find your cultural and social background at odds with the expectations of your discipline (see 'Your cultural self' and 'Your social self', Chapter 1).

The people

> We need scholars who not only skilfully explore the frontiers of knowledge, but also integrate ideas, connect them to action, and inspire students.   ERNEST L. BOYER

The six functions of the university outlined below by Ian Lowe are carried out by *academic staff*, who engage in the scholarship of teaching and research, and general staff who manage, administer and service these functions. As an undergraduate student, your main interactions will be with your teachers and student support staff who help you in areas such as enrolment, using the library, academic skills, your study program or with personal, financial and career matters. There are also people who hold senior positions within the university, such as a Dean or Head of School or a Professor who leads a discipline area. You may only encounter these people at a distance when they deliver a welcome to students or give a lecture, perhaps online. The university leaders include a Vice Chancellor assisted by Deputy Vice Chancellors and Pro Vice Chancellors. You are unlikely to meet the Chancellor, who is external to the university and has oversight of the university's top governing body, the Senate or Board.

As a beginning student your closest contact with academic staff is more likely to be with lecturers, and with tutors who may be part-time or casual, and may be postgraduate students. Across all levels, remember that academic staff are people with a variety of concerns which can include highly specialised research, a lively curiosity about things of the mind and the world in general, and an involvement with teaching; but like all people, they have their share of human bias and ignorance.

Most of your time with other people at university will be with other *students* who usually manifest interest in learning, but otherwise are impossible to categorise. Students of higher education are culturally diverse, at least on larger campuses, with a wide range of ages, living arrangements, ethnic and socioeconomic backgrounds. Within this diversity you are likely to find others who share your background, world view, values, attitudes and expectations. Interacting with students from diverse cultural backgrounds can be a learning process both within and outside the classroom, if you remain open to this diversity.

> Age, sex, socio-economic background and ethnicity contribute to and shape students' expectations of university, their adjustment to being university students, and ultimately their overall teaching and learning experience and satisfaction with it.   CRAIG McINNIS

Common images of university

> The modern university has at least six distinct functions. It conserves knowledge, through library holdings and scholarship. It transmits knowledge by guiding the learning of students through community education programs. It advances knowledge through basic research. It applies knowledge by applied research and consultancy. It refines knowledge through critical review and scholarship. It also fulfils the role of certifying standards of entry to a range of professions having different levels of commitment to intellectual endeavour.   IAN LOWE

Universities have a mystique and there are a number of images of universities that can shape your expectations of them. *One* common image is that these institutions have little to do with the 'real' world, that they are full of professors who dwell in the hallowed halls of higher learning and who expound and debate esoteric theories. A *second* and somewhat contradictory image is that of superior training institutions where doctors, lawyers, architects, engineers, teachers and the like are prepared for their professions. A *third* image is of a community of scholars, who through their research pursue knowledge and new scientific discoveries for the wellbeing of society, which they impart to intelligent students. A *fourth* image that some staff and students come to hold is that:

> . . . universities have become huge bureaucracies with an academic mind and no heart, careless and ignorant about students and their intellectual needs, organised by managers and managerial professors absorbed in their own pursuits, giving service to the existing social order and dispensing its conventional wisdom, bereft of a philosophy and the social imagination to create a new and compelling conception of their own future.   HAROLD TAYLOR

If you enter university with high expectations, some of these images may be disillusioning. On the other hand, the fourth image may dispel the 'awesome' mystique embodied in the second and third images and help you realise that, sometimes, when you are having study problems, the causes may not lie solely with you. Remember that universities can be intellectually exciting places but they are also bureaucratic institutions like any other large workplace.

There is an ongoing debate about the role that universities should have in the modern world. There is agreement that they should play a role in the social and economic wellbeing of society, and some argue that the purely intellectual role of universities has intrinsic value. Within these debates a *fifth* image of universities envisages their primary role as 'selling' applied knowledge and responding to the market economy and consumer demands. At various times there are attempts to 'streamline' and 'rationalise' higher education and the level of funding varies accordingly. In recent years, government funding for higher education has been reduced significantly and a user-pays approach is now the norm. In addition, funding from international students has become increasingly crucial to the functioning of most Australian universities. These changes will have a direct impact on your studies. Reduced government funding can mean that there are fewer tutorials and lectures and that your teachers are not so readily available to give you individual help. In addition, if the staff are preoccupied with earning funding from outside the university by applying for grants or consulting, you may be left more on your own to learn.

> Imagine learning with peers, expertise, and resources that are available whenever you want or need them. These 'class mates' are from Moscow and Mexico City, New York and Hong Kong, Vancouver and Sydney—from urban centers and rural and remote areas. And they, like you, never need to leave home. You are all learning together not in a place in the ordinary sense but in a shared space, a 'cyberspace', using network systems that connect people all over the globe. Your learning network 'classroom' is anywhere that you have a personal computer, a modem, and a telephone line, satellite dish or radio link. Dialling into the network turns your computer screen into a window on the world of learning.
>
> LINDA HARASIM

It is virtually impossible to predict the future of universities but they will certainly be very different from universities today. With globalisation and the spread of electronic technology, a new and *sixth* image of online universities has emerged. These universities have no physical campus (except for an administrative hub), the teachers and students are scattered across the globe, teachers teach online from their office or from home, students access their courses and units via the Internet, and all communication occurs online. In this fast emerging reality, learning is more flexible, and students can enrol at more than one institution and can take their courses and units online at places and times most suitable for them.

An increasing number of courses and units are readily available via open online access from prestigious overseas universities. These courses are usually free, but in some cases students who are seeking a qualification from the institution need to complete the assessment and then pay fees. Some traditional Australian universities are selecting the best of these open online access units and building them into their courses.

Paying fees

> If a man [*sic*] empties his purse into his head no one can take it away from him. An investment in knowledge always pays the best interest.   BENJAMIN FRANKLIN

In Australia, a 'free' university education has become a thing of the past, and debate continues over whether higher education serves the private or the public good. The 'private good' argument is that students, as individuals, benefit from their education so they should contribute to the cost of its provision. The 'public good' argument is based on a belief that education benefits the whole of society; while the individual does benefit from the education, the whole of society is better off if more people go to university. According to this second position, education should be mostly funded from the public purse, that is, from government revenue. In some countries, students must pay upfront fees before they can begin study. In others, students take out a loan that they repay when they graduate; and elsewhere, as in Australia, students are required to repay their fees once their income reaches a certain level.

The requirement that almost all students pay for their education has altered the way many students think about their enrolment and influences what and how they study. In fact, being required to fund their own education, combined with shifting societal values and expectations, means that today the majority of students are employed full- or part-time, and the need to work alongside study has an impact on their engagement both with their studies and with university generally (see 'Combining study with other work', Chapter 3). So students may be less attracted to study for its own sake and instead seek vocational training which helps assure them of employment. In addition, because they are paying for their education, increasingly students are less accepting of any shortcomings in the education they receive.

Making choices and decisions

> 'Would you tell me, please, which way I ought to go from here?'
>
> 'That depends a good deal on where you want to get to,' said the Cat.
>
> 'I don't much care where—' said Alice.
>
> 'Then it doesn't matter which way you go,' said the Cat.
>
> '—so long as I get somewhere,' Alice added as an explanation.
>
> 'Oh, you're sure to do that,' said the Cat, 'if you only walk long enough.'   LEWIS CARROLL

In tertiary education you make many choices about what, why, how, when and where you learn. Unless you were lucky enough to have teachers and schools that allowed you to develop your ability to learn independently, this may be your first experience of making self-directed choices and decisions about your formal education. Before finalising any choices or decisions, seek advice from others and then reflect on the options before you weigh up the pros and cons of each so that you can justify and explain your rationale for one choice over another.

Why are you studying?

> Even the raven started out in human form, and he fumbled blindly, and his actions were haphazard until it was revealed to him who he was and what his purpose was.
>
> PETER HØEG

You make your first choice when you decide to go to university or college. After secondary school, it should be your goals which determine whether part of your learning takes place within the formal education system. Often there are pressures which seem to give you little choice, but the choice is frequently there if you are aware of it.

Ask yourself:

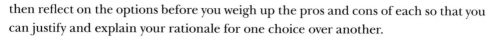 *Why have I chosen to further my education? Is it because my parents want me to? Or I can't find a job? Or I want a better job? Or I want to become an engineer? Or I like discovering new ideas? Or I think campus life will be fun?*

I'm returning to study after some years away from it. Why?

Research on motivations for studying has identified four broad orientations to study:

— vocational, a concern about future employment

— academic, a desire for continuing education

— personal, developing as an individual, and

— social, enjoying the freedom of university life.

Within these four categories some students have an intrinsic interest in study for its own sake, and some have an extrinsic interest, seeing education as a means to an end (Beaty, Gibbs and Morgan 1997). Put another way, some students are intrinsically 'learning oriented' and other students are 'performance oriented', or more concerned with grades (Bransford, Brown and Cocking 2000, 61).

Why you are studying will directly influence how you learn, since your long-term life and study goals will affect your shorter-term specific study aims. Thinking about and identifying your reasons for studying overall and for taking a particular course or a unit can give you useful insights into how to approach your work. For example, you may choose one unit because it is a prerequisite in an area you don't particularly enjoy and your aim may be just to pass at the required level, while another unit may be so intrinsically interesting to you that you prioritise it and do well in it. Being clear about your goals helps keep you going during difficult times, such as when you have peer or family pressures about the amount of time you dedicate to study. You have your own reasons for study and as an adult can make your own choices, but at times you have to justify these choices to others.

Most people let themselves be pushed by chance or other people's expectations into environments of which they make the best, rather than into those which meet their inner needs.
MICHAEL DEAKIN

Consider your motivations for study using the reasons above. Take each of the units in which you are enrolled or are about to enrol, and decide for each whether your reasons are vocational, academic, personal or social and whether or not your interest in each is intrinsic or extrinsic. On this basis determine how you are or will approach your learning in each unit.

Where to study?

The tertiary education landscape is changing rapidly, so be aware of your options. Globalisation and the Internet are largely responsible for these changes and universities have lost their traditional monopoly on post-compulsory and post-secondary education. Government policies now allow competition with overseas tertiary providers, and increasingly students are able to access online courses and units from overseas providers. In today's market place, you have the choice between a university, a privately funded institution or TAFE.

University

The expansion of the higher education system and the range of choice available in a market competition environment has generated a great deal of pressure on students to make informed choices about which course and which university.
MANTZ YORKE and BERNARD LONGDEN

You may see going to a particular university as your only option, but there are many possibilities. Universities are becoming more 'mobile' with multiple sites (satellite campuses), flexible courses and units, summer semesters and new teaching technologies. The rapid expansion of online learning provides new opportunities to study from an overseas or interstate institution. Research your chosen course carefully to see where else it is offered, its availability by open access, and the requirements for fees and credit. You might choose to enrol in an open online course, but be aware that many such courses attract large numbers of students so your learning experience is unlikely to be personalised. Online units vary in quality, so check features such as: ease of access; support systems; integration of real and virtual resources; assessment methods; depth of material; and resources provided. With the plethora of new courses available it is important to examine your life goals and study aims carefully and to evaluate the appropriateness of different institutions and options in meeting these goals and aims.

TAFE

The Vocational, Education and Training (VET) sector offers courses primarily through Tertiary and Further Education (TAFE) colleges or institutes. TAFE courses are increasingly being offered online and articulation arrangements allow students to transfer from TAFE to university, with credit for TAFE courses being used towards a university degree. TAFE institutions are state or privately funded, whereas most Australian universities are federally funded. TAFE institutions are oriented to the needs of the workplace and their primary role is to provide training in a range of work-related fields in trades and professions, such as information technology, business, community development or tourism. Some TAFE institutions are located on and are part of university campuses, many are located in regional areas, and some offer full degrees, or courses are offered through secondary schools.

If your interests are more practical and directly employment-related, and if you prefer a more highly structured form of study, a TAFE course may suit your life goals and your learning style. If so, find out how it might be possible to transfer to university later on. Be aware that while universities offer practical work-related courses, they expect students to take a more theoretical approach to study and expect an independent approach and high levels of skill in critical thinking, research and writing. These differences are particularly important if you transfer into university in second year and enrol in more advanced units, because many required learning skills are taught in first year units.

Private institutions

There are an increasing number of private institutions in direct competition with the government-funded tertiary institutions. Many are international and many offer their courses online. In addition, an increasing number of partnerships are being formed between universities and private providers, on both a national and global scale. These partnerships offer new opportunities for study in different modes and sequences. Before you decide where to study, check out all of the options available to you, and seek information on the reputation of the institution and the course that you plan to take.

> 'I've been to a day-school, too,' said Alice. 'You needn't be so proud as all that.'
>
> 'With extras?' asked the Mock Turtle, a little anxiously.
>
> 'Yes,' said Alice: 'we learned French and music.'
>
> 'And washing?' said the Mock Turtle.
>
> 'Certainly not!' said Alice indignantly.
>
> 'Ah! Then yours wasn't a really good school,' said the Mock Turtle in a tone of great relief.   LEWIS CARROLL

What to study?

When you apply for tertiary study you indicate your choice of courses or discipline areas. Your choices are directed by your long-term goals, your study aims and interests, your previous studies, your skills and the availability of places. Many students enter tertiary study with a clear idea of the course they want to study, and some start out on one track and then change to another. It can be difficult to be sure that you have made the right decision until you experience the course. Even if the course is not ideal, you may choose to stick with it because of what the degree offers once you finish.

Some institutions are flexible and allow for changes part of the way through your time at university. It may not be possible for you to study in your preferred discipline, either because of educational factors external to you (such as quotas or the need to have a high average mark) or because of personal factors beyond your control (such as where you live or the lack of childcare). It is up to you either to accept this, or to find out what steps to take to study your first choice at a later time. In such cases give serious thought to how important it is to pursue that particular course and make plans if you want to do so. Not being admitted to your first choice of discipline is a reason students can be less committed to their studies and may even withdraw from university.

Which units?

Deciding which unit to take depends on why you are studying. Your choice is likely to be influenced by administrative and academic requirements such as prerequisite units, course requirements, or quotas on unit and course intakes. In some situations you will have little choice, such as in a highly structured discipline with many required units, or when confronted with rules and regulations.

To help decide on your units, consult as many sources as possible. Carefully read any information on the university website, but note when this material was last updated. Look through the official handbooks and read any student surveys or guides to units and teachers. Remember that printed handbooks and guides may be out of date as they go to press several months before a unit starts.

Unit descriptions are deliberately brief and usually only provide a short summary of the unit content. While this may help you create a shortlist, close reading of the unit learning outcomes and objectives allows you to determine more precisely the subject matter and skill outcomes the unit coordinator expects you to have achieved when you have completed the unit.

Find detailed information on the likely assignments, assessment methods, and books or materials you are expected to buy. Check the class contact times to see if there is any information on how the unit provides opportunities for interaction with the tutor and other students.

If the institution in which you are enrolled does not offer a unit on a subject you would like to study, ask a staff member in a related subject area if there is some other way you can undertake this. For example, you may be able to pursue it through another institution or an open access online unit, or through an independent study contract (see 'Pursuing your questions in formal education', Chapter 6). For units which interest you, find out who coordinates and tutors them and if possible locate students who have recently taken them. Talk to or email these students as they will also have opinions about the unit and teachers.

For online units, check to see if there is a sample module that you can work through or a discussion list you can access to ask your questions. Check on the website for Frequently Asked Questions (FAQs) and make a list of any other queries that you have. You might have questions about features such as:

— ease of access

— support systems

— integration of 'real' and virtual material

— assessment methods

— depth of material, and

— resources provided.

For unanswered questions contact the coordinator by email. Attend any orientation activities and do any recommended preliminary work. If you can, find out what is expected of you in the first couple of weeks of a unit and start on this. For some units, materials are freely available so that you can audit the unit and only need to enrol formally if you want to be assessed to gain credit.

If you are taking several units, try to calculate your total workload and plan a weekly timetable based on any requirements, such as attending lectures or seminars or listening to online lectures and participating in online discussions (see 'A workable weekly plan', Chapter 4). See if the unit materials indicate how much time an 'average' student should spend each week in both formal and private study. If you have a choice of times and teachers, decide which classes to attend and sign up for tutorials as soon as this is possible. The combination of units you planned may be impossible because of timetable clashes, or difficult because of a high combined workload. These difficulties can occur even for popular or required combinations of units so if you still want to take all of them, check with the organisers if alternative arrangements can be made. Before enrolling in a unit, you also need to make sure the timetable does not clash with your non-study commitments, such as your part-time job or family responsibilities and that, given these demands, you can handle the workload.

Unless your selection of units is very clear, try to delay your final choices until the end of the first or second week of teaching. This is usually not possible for online units but for on-campus study it gives you a chance to listen to lectures and/or attend the early classes and gather first-hand information on the units that attract you, and to meet some of the teaching staff and students. You can't know all there is to know about a unit at this stage, but you can check preliminary information against your own experience in the unit. However, the advantages of delaying your unit choice have to be balanced against the need both to make a commitment and an immediate start on a unit and to make a clear choice before you incur fees.

Which mode of study?

> Online learning is very variable. Some subjects are most rudimentary but others offered by the same university and the same department can be wonderful. So persevere if your first experience is a bit flat. . . . Conversely, if your first experience is wonderful don't be too disappointed if this isn't repeated in every other subject.   GAVIN MOODIE

Increased flexibility in the tertiary sector enables you to decide whether to study full-time or part-time, internally and/or at a distance, face-to-face and/or online. For example, you may have the choice of taking online a section of a face-to-face unit, of mixing face-to-face and online units, or you may be able to take some units from another institution.

Check out options for more flexible and self-directed learning. You can benefit from being a part-time student taking only one or two units at a time, especially if you have a lot of other demands on your time. And if you are a metropolitan student, taking one or two external units in a mostly on-campus course can give you the flexibility to combine study with work. You might include a semester of part-time study in a full-time degree if you find yourself short of money and need to work for a while. If you are a wholly external student, your choice of units may be more restricted than for internal students. Seek information on units as early as possible so that you can enrol in time for unit information and material to be sent to you. Be aware that it is more difficult to engage with the university when you spend less time on campus or only access your units online.

Which teachers?

> Learning grows and develops by the dialogue of teacher and student, becoming sometimes greater than anything an individual, however brilliant, could produce.   F. R. LEAVIS

Sometimes you may have a choice of teachers, although this isn't common for first year students. If you have a choice, sit in on the different teachers' classes, read any handouts they provide and if possible contact them personally. If a student-published guide to units is available, consult this as well as talking to other students. Look for a unit coordinator who clearly sets out learning outcomes, activities, content, workload and assessment, and who is open to your comments and questions. Select teachers who know their subject, stimulate your enthusiasm, encourage you to follow your own interests and are willing to help you improve and extend your skills in studying. A good teacher whose subject areas are only broadly related to your interests can help you follow these interests better than a poor teacher whose interests coincide closely with yours. A skilled teacher whose ideology differs significantly from your own may challenge you to suspend your customary world view.

How well you learn with a particular teacher also depends on how well your teaching and learning styles interact. The lecturer you listen to for several weeks or the teacher with whom you work for a whole unit is important to your learning. If possible, be prepared to change units (but before the census date when fees become payable) or teachers if, after a fair trial, you find you are not learning as much as you would like.

Which technology?

> Many students arrive on campus with increasingly digital lifestyles; accustomed to access to multiple virtual landscapes. SUE WATLING

Computers are essential study tools for communicating with your tutors and other students, for accessing information and research and for preparing and presenting assignments. Electronic teaching and learning also operates via methods such as online lecture notes, bulletin boards, online forums, podcasts and blogs; and you are expected to submit most of your assignments electronically. Although many students are using a range of technology, such as tablets, mobile phones and computers, there are some who have minimal experience with technology and for them adjusting to this can be a challenge. On the other hand, even if you are an avid user of a range of digital technologies, this will not necessarily mean that you automatically have the skills and knowledge for the particular technology required for university study.

There is a wide range of computers and software available and you need to determine which is most appropriate given the computer system you use, the communication system used by the university, and any unit requirements. While a personal computer with fast Internet access has become almost essential for study, most universities provide extensive computer facilities for students who cannot afford the latest technology or whose system is not compatible with what is required. Most universities have a computing centre where students can go for advice on the options, and some provide interest-free loans to enable students to upgrade their technology. Some institutions provide support classes to develop student computer skills and some have digital literacy courses. Such literacy may be a prerequisite for enrolment in certain units.

You might have to buy or lease a computer if you don't have one already, and to connect electronically to your campus you will need to pay any online costs. Because computing hardware and software become outdated so rapidly, carry out some consumer research to determine the best option for your purposes. Avoid believing that you must have the very latest bells and whistles, but be aware that you need sufficient speed and power to access services without frustrating and time-consuming delays. If you have limited financial resources, seriously consider renting equipment but first seek appropriate advice. And ensure that you have sufficient security and backup systems whatever you use.

Getting started

It is in the first year that students are most likely to form lasting outlooks, values and patterns of behaviour with respect to higher education and lifelong learning.   CRAIG McINNIS

Starting university can be bewildering as well as stimulating—you are faced with the triple challenges of becoming part of a new culture, of a new community and of learning independently. So the adjustments you have to make are considerable, in whatever discipline you are studying and regardless of whether your study is full-time or part-time, face-to-face or distance and/or online.

Students beginning university come from a variety of educational backgrounds and with a variety of life and work experiences. Your main experience of formal education may have been recent or in an education system one or more decades ago. It might have been in the structured environment of compulsory schooling where from your first day at school the education bureaucracy and the teachers were responsible for directing what, how, when and where you learned, and where the emphasis was on remembering and reproducing information correctly. You may have attended a private school such as a single-sex denominational school, or a boarding school which structured your study and daily life; or you may have gone to an alternative school where ostensibly you were free to learn what and when you liked. You may have left school before completing a secondary school qualification; you may have studied in a different type of tertiary institution such as TAFE; or you may just be shifting to another course within the same university. Your early learning may have been in a country where questioning a teacher's authority or thinking critically was not acceptable.

The university year

The university academic year is often divided into two main semesters or terms, with breaks in summer and winter, although teaching outside this pattern is common. Within the semesters there are usually non-teaching or study breaks and a study week before exams begin. Each semester is preceded by an enrolment and orientation period. The university academic year will differ for students studying offshore or where there is a different semester schedule, such as at Open Universities Australia where there are four 13-week study periods with no study break and exams in the first week of the next study period. All universities have a census date that occurs a few weeks after semester begins. This date is very important because you can withdraw from a unit up until that date and incur only partial fees, or none.

Before you begin university be aware of the patterns of the academic year and ensure that these are compatible with other major commitments or plans in your life. For example, after completing high school you may want to defer your enrolment for six months or a year to give yourself a gap from study. Or perhaps you need to work to finance your study and you decide to work full-time and begin study a little later. If you decide to do this, explore the options for taking a unit online.

To become informed about how your university is organised and about your studies in general, visit the institution's website; study any pre-enrolment materials; attend orientation days; seek advice from the staff in the areas in which you plan to study; consult a counsellor or study adviser; or read the relevant sections of this book. If studying online, work through any orientation material available to you. Be proactive in this, rather than expecting the information to be delivered to you.

Orientation

Attend any orientation or induction sessions provided, since these provide vital information about the university overall and about a particular school or faculty. Your success with university study is largely dependent on how engaged you are with the university as a whole. Attendance at orientation is one way to kickstart this engagement and provide you with useful contacts with both staff and other students.

All universities, even those online, provide orientation or induction for beginning students. The breadth, depth and style of orientation sessions varies, with some orientation provided partly or completely online. Some provide a wide range of social activities, often organised by student groups, and may include interactive games and competitions both on campus and online. Most orientations are scheduled in the week or days before the semester begins and may extend into the first few weeks of semester.

Orientation programs are designed to:
— orient students to the university
— prepare students for the first few weeks of semester and beyond
— give students confidence in tackling university study
— provide information on the range of support services and facilities available
— induct students into the requirements and expectation of their chosen course of study, and
— foster a sense of community by providing you with social opportunities to meet other students.

Some students begin university with a group from school or from the same country or ethnic background, and the people in these groups often stay together. While there is a sense of security in this, your peer group may not necessarily be studying in your units and it is valuable to expand your horizons by meeting new people. Other students enter university without knowing anyone, which can be a lonely and isolating experience. Take the opportunity to talk to and mix with others at the orientation social events.

You may feel overwhelmed by the information provided during orientation. Try to identify crucial items such as immovable deadlines. Remember, you don't need to know everything in the first week, and some universities provide the information as you need it in a 'just in time' fashion.

The first weeks

You are likely to spend the first few weeks mostly organising your timetable, finding your way around campus and working through administrative requirements. Hopefully, you will have spent some time thinking about and researching most of these things before classes start. During the enrolment period you should have checked if your first year unit enrolments and your study pathway lead to the qualification that you are seeking, but it is a good idea to double check this during orientation, or in the first week of semester. If you have a choice of units, consider those that allow for other study pathways.

During orientation and in the first week, you will begin to recognise faces among staff and students, and may discover some of the social activities that can be part of a tertiary student's life. You will need to focus on finalising your class contact timetable and on becoming familiar with the layout of campus so that you can locate your classrooms, the library, central administration and school- or faculty-based student administration centres. Find and learn about invaluable student support services and centres, such as health and counselling, learning skills, equity, and first-year advisers. Make a note of the names and contact details of those you may need to contact. Join a library tour or take one online, and explore any guides to available online resources.

As the semester progresses you will have other needs. For example, in the first week you are unlikely to need to know how to submit an assignment online or how to use plagiarism detection software (see 'Academic integrity', Chapter 16) or do an in-depth search of a library database. So if you are feeling daunted by initial information overload, put the information on these items aside till you need them. But note who to contact and where to find them if you need assistance later. Asking more experienced students for advice can be very helpful at this stage.

Once you begin university you begin an adventure, a journey that allows you to discover new horizons, explore unfamiliar pathways and learn from a diverse range of people. This can be challenging and unsettling but it can take you on a path that can alter your life in new and positive ways, if you are open to this. The challenge is worth the effort since what you gain depends on what you put into it and how much you choose to engage with it.

TEN TIPS

1   Explore which of the six images outlined in this chapter influence your expectations of university.

2   Reflect on how often you have been involved in debates or arguments with someone who holds a different or opposing viewpoint, and whether you can usually agree to disagree.

3   Identify the discipline in which your chosen course of study is located, and be alert for opportunities for interdisciplinary study which can extend your intellectual horizons.

4   Before you enrol, search on the web for institutions that offer courses the same as or similar to the one you have chosen.

5   Reflect on which of the four orientations to study are important to you.

6   Determine whether or not your technology is adequate and appropriate for your studies.

7   Calculate your overall workload for the semester as soon as this information becomes available.

8   Identify the people you might need to approach for support during the first semester, and list their names and contact details.

9   Make contact with at least two students who are studying the same course or unit.

10 Make the most of orientation activities and information sessions, on campus and/or online.

REFERENCES

Beaty, Elizabeth, Graham Gibbs and Alistair Morgan. 1997. 'Learning Orientations and Study Contracts.' In *The Experience of Learning*, edited by Ference Marton, Dai Hounsell and Noel Entwistle, 72–88. 2nd ed. Edinburgh: Scottish Academic Press.

Bransford, John D., Ann L. Brown and Rodney R. Cocking, eds. 2000. *How People Learn: Brain, Mind, Experience, and School*. Washington, DC: National Academy Press.

Engaging with university

3

Asking critical questions about our previously accepted values, ideas and behaviours is anxiety-producing. We may feel fearful of the consequences that might arise from contemplating alternatives to our current ways of thinking and living; resistance, resentment, and confusion are evident at various stages in the critical thinking process. But we also feel joy, release, relief, and exhilaration as we break through to new ways of looking at our personal, work, and political worlds.

STEPHEN BROOKFIELD

Focusing on your goals and aims

Engaging with others
Getting to know other students
Approaching teachers

Engaging with study
Developing skills and attitudes
Critical thinking
Problem solving
Researching
Collaborative learning
Using learning outcomes to guide your study

Adjusting to being a student
Coping with personal change
Combining study with other work
Seeking help from others
Dealing with difficult situations
Deferring or withdrawing from study

Staying focused on your goals

The more you engage with university the more challenging and satisfying you will find your time there. Being engaged means being involved and active as a student but it also involves feeling and being part of a university community.

Focusing on your goals and aims

Your overall goals and your reasons for study and completing individual study tasks have a direct impact on how you approach your study and how enthusiastic you are about it.

Maintaining your motivation to study is one of the keys to being engaged and thus persisting. What motivates you will not necessarily motivate another person as it is very personal to you and is dependent on a number of factors including:

— the priority study has in your life and in relation to your long-term life goals (see 'Your goals', Chapter 1)

— your short-term aims for completing units and assignments

— your interest in the course and units in which you are enrolled

— your expectations of university and of the course and units you are taking, and whether or not these expectations are being met (see 'What to expect from university', Chapter 2)

— what the university expects from you

— other people's expectations of you, and

— the environment in which you live and study (see 'Where you study', Chapter 4).

Be prepared for your goals and aims to change. Any serious attempt to come to grips with new concepts, especially those that raise questions about yourself, your world and your beliefs, always engenders confusion and suggests new directions to consider. Learning what is important to you changes you, often in unexpected ways. Universities can offer you real learning if you explore what is available and are able to make your own independent decisions about your overall life goals and study aims.

Engaging with others

. . . the social nature of the university experience has the potential for contributing positively to academic performance, and more generally should influence the individual's sense of competence . . . The nature and extent of social involvement is meaningful in its own right as part of the process of personal development and identity formation.   CRAIG McINNIS

Engaging with other students and your teachers is a vital part of academic life and can make a big difference to the depth and enjoyment of your formal learning. Contacting the people in your classes or on campus generally helps you come to know them as individuals, to learn about the real people behind your images and expectations of what teachers and students are like. Adjusting to being a student takes time and practice and often courage. Many of the adjustments involve approaching other people, and it is often up to you to take the initiative to contact them.

Getting to know other students

Universities are social communities and provide many opportunities to interact with other students. In addition to the regular student meeting venues, such as the cafeteria, the pub or the 'learning commons' in a library, there are often university- and school-based events and many student-run clubs and societies. Find out about these and take advantage of the opportunities they provide. Chat with friends after class, go to the student pub at the end of the week, attend a lecture instead of viewing it online or chat casually with others from your class. Provided you balance this social time with your study, interacting with others can help keep you motivated and engaged.

As well as purely social events there are also opportunities in class and online for social interaction with others. Some of these will be included as part of your tutorials, when your teachers organise activities for you to work collaboratively or participate in group work, perhaps involving an assessment task. It is up to you to share your thoughts in class or in an online discussion group or to make contact with the stranger sitting next to you in class (see 'Playing your part during discussions', Chapter 12). Outside of class it will be largely up to you to take the initiative to interact with others. Take advantage of these opportunities to meet and get to know other students who you might then meet socially. If you came to university with a close group of friends, use the security that this gives to get to know students who are more isolated or from other backgrounds.

In addition to socialising with other students, an invaluable part of a student's life is to have at least one or two fellow students with whom you can toss around ideas and share study problems. It can also be a very rewarding learning experience to find another student or group studying the same subjects so that you can regularly share ideas and read and comment on each other's written work (see 'Collaborative learning groups', Chapter 12, and 'Share your writing', Chapter 13). This sharing within the context of your study is particularly important in the current educational climate where teachers are becoming less accessible and have less time for one-to-one contact with students because of large classes and increased workloads. If you have trouble with work or with a teacher, mention it to a couple of students in your class. They may have ideas on what you can do, and if they share your problem you can tackle it together.

> It is anything but easy to enter a classroom full of people whom you feel must be more intelligent than you . . . Still you must persevere. GWEN WESSON

For some people, making contact with others can be challenging. Sitting by yourself in the cafeteria, not knowing anyone in the first weeks of class, not being part of student social life or being an online student can make you feel very alone. If you are a beginning student from the country or overseas, you may feel disoriented without your usual contact with family and friends, and this feeling can be compounded if you are from overseas and English is not your first language. You may find it eases the transition in the first few weeks of university if you maintain contact with those at home so that you can share your experiences with them.

If you find university or college strange, if you have difficulties with your work or if you feel shy with other students, you can be certain that other students feel this way too. Help someone else as well as yourself by talking to the person you sit next to in class, or by contacting another student and not always expecting them to contact you first. Take part in some of the social or academic activities on campus if you can and take advantage of the multicultural campus community (see 'Social groupings', Chapter 1).

It can be helpful to consider what is the worst that could happen when you try to make contact with other students. If they don't seem interested, perhaps they are shy or preoccupied with other things, in which case try another time or approach someone else. Perhaps they don't seemed tuned into your particular study problems— you can find other people you can ask for help. If you continue to have difficulty getting to know a few other students, talk this over with a friend, learning adviser or counsellor. You will find that most students are willing to talk about units or teachers, the test next week or the essay you are supposed to finish in two days' time. To make contact with someone who has taken or is taking the same unit as you, use the relevant university discussion forums, but realise that even talking to somebody studying a different unit can provide you both with invaluable moral support. You won't become close friends with everyone you meet, but you will find some people with whom you enjoy spending time.

As a part-time or online student, it can be difficult to contact teachers and other students, so be prepared for this to take time and energy. If you study online, perhaps it is because of the flexibility it offers or because you enjoy the pleasures of being a solitary scholar and the opportunity to learn independently. However, you might also feel disconnected from a campus because you are geographically remote; are a metropolitan or regional student unable to visit your university; or are an 'open university' student enrolled at more than one campus. Perhaps the isolation partly frees you from the pressures of competing with other students, but you may miss sharing the pleasures and problems of study with other students. This situation may also mean that you miss out on the informal discussions that are integral to what higher education has to offer. Be aware that if no one in your community sees tertiary study as valuable, you may feel particularly isolated.

If you are an online or distance student, you can actually benefit from the opportunities provided by online learning. Participate in online discussion groups and don't be afraid to speak out so that others get to know you. If possible, sit in on the occasional class on campus where you have a chance to meet other students and share your learning with them. If you are nervous at the thought of attending special on-campus sessions, you will usually find that some other students feel the same way. Once you actually meet each other, you are likely to have plenty to say.

Approaching teachers

The main opportunities for engaging with your teachers on campus arise in class, after a class or lecture, during their office hours or by special appointment. Take advantage of these opportunities to ask for the information and help you need. Teachers usually appreciate students whose questions and comments show genuine thought and enthusiasm for learning and, like most people, they take pleasure in discussing their special interest and explaining what they know to others if they have time. Often the students that a teacher comes to know best are those who ask questions, seek advice or are keen to discuss ideas—and it is more satisfying to teach people you know than to impart information to a collection of half-remembered names and faces.

Large classes in universities are becoming much more common so you may have less one-to-one contact with teachers and less feedback from them. It is not always easy to approach a teacher you see once a week in class, to ask a question of a seemingly remote professor or to put forward your questions or thoughts in an email to a unit coordinator. Before you seek information or ask questions from unit teachers or administrators, check that the answer is not already provided in your study materials and be as clear as possible about your questions. This will save both you and your teacher time and effort. It is unlikely that a teacher expects you to be very familiar with a subject you have just begun studying or expects you to write a perfect first assignment.

If you are anxious about approaching a teacher, it can be helpful to think about the worst that can happen when you ask for help. Perhaps you persistently have trouble finding them. If so, try to arrange an appointment or leave a message. If the teacher is busy at the time, make an appointment for another time. Remember that tertiary teachers have responsibilities for research and administration as well as for students. Recognise also that teaching staff may also be employed on a casual basis for a limited number of hours and thus have less capacity for student interaction. Perhaps you won't receive a helpful answer to your question. If the teacher is not skilled at providing clear explanations, look to a book, an online source, a student or another teacher for your information.

Perhaps the teacher you approach is abrupt or seems unwilling to help. If so, maybe he or she is having a trying day, so ask if you can come back another time. Perhaps you find the teacher inadequate as a teacher. Nevertheless, teachers are paid to help you learn, so if you want to, persist with your request. If you don't want to persist, look elsewhere for help. There are always one or two friendly, helpful advisers or teachers on campus who can help with your study and, in some cases, with your personal problems.

If you study online, as soon as you have access to your unit materials set aside some time to become thoroughly familiar with any information on the organisational, assessment and practical details, such as ordering books. And if you have questions for the unit coordinator, only ask after you have done this. Many teachers like to receive communication from you apart from the assignments you are required to submit—just don't expect an instant response. Send an email to tell your teacher a little about yourself. Ask about comments on an assignment or thank your teacher for help. Message them about ideas not covered in lectures or to discuss your concerns about your work or unit requirements, keeping what you want to say as specific and focused as possible. If you can arrange to visit your teachers on campus, you will be able to visualise the place and person to whom you are sending your work, rather than simply delivering it up to the online assignment delivery box, and an unknown person with a red marking pen.

These personal contacts help your teachers come to know you as an individual, and enable them to provide feedback on your work that is directed to your individual strengths and needs. Your teachers may also be encouraged to make more detailed comments and to return your assignments promptly.

Engaging with study

> Engagement has come to refer to how involved or interested students appear to be in their learning and how connected they are to their classes, their institutions and each other.
>
> RICK AXELSON and AREND FLICK

Developing fundamental university skills and attitudes and fully utilising your unit learning materials can help you to engage fully with your study. This development takes time and practice. You need to develop the skills of critical thinking, problem solving, researching and collaborative learning in conjunction with your other learning skills—particularly those involved in reading, listening, oral and written communication, self-directed learning, and time management—and to do so within the disciplinary context of your studies. In addition, your learning materials provide statements of learning outcomes which outline what you are expected to learn, so use these to guide your study and thereby enhance your engagement.

Developing skills and attitudes

> While generic attributes might at first glance appear to be relatively innocuous and uncontentious outcomes, . . . they have their roots in the contested territory of questions as to the nature of knowledge and the nature of a university.
>
> SIMON BARRIE and MICHAEL PROSSER

Traditionally, specific content knowledge and skills have been the major focus of most university degrees, with little explicit teaching of learning skills or the development of attitudes. While you are expected to focus primarily on developing subject knowledge, you are now also expected to develop generic skills and attitudes which equip you as an independent thinker capable of self-directed learning. The skills and attitudes are considered 'generic' because it is argued that, in higher education, they should be systematically developed in all students in all disciplines, as the skills can be transferred to many contexts in learning and are fundamental for graduates in any future workplace. While there is debate about whether such skills are generic or context-specific, it is intended that you should develop these skills throughout your formal study and continue to develop and use them in your work and throughout your life.

Generic skills are variously called 'Graduate Attributes' (or Qualities), which foregrounds their importance to graduating students, or 'Core Capabilities'. Many universities, in their handbook or on their home page, have published lists of the qualities they wish their graduates to acquire. You may find it useful to see if your university has such a list, and to use this as a checklist or benchmark for your own development throughout your studies.

Critical thinking

> Critical thinking is a lived activity, not an abstract academic pastime. It is something we do, though its frequency, and the credibility we grant it, vary from person to person . . . the ability to think critically is crucial to understanding our personal relationships, envisioning alternative and more productive ways of organising the workplace, and becoming politically literate.   STEPHEN BROOKFIELD

Critical thinking is fundamental to academic debate and to university culture (see 'University culture', Chapter 2). It is a generic skill that you are expected to acquire in your undergraduate education and transfer to your everyday life and paid work. Such critical thinking is designed to encourage you to identify and question your world view with its values and assumptions and contradictions, to be open to other views, to develop a position on topics under discussion and to construct cogent arguments in both your writing and your discussions (see 'Beliefs and values', Chapter 1). Although critical thinking is highly valued by most academics, few of your teachers have the skills to systematically and explicitly help you develop critical thinking skills and attitudes. Indeed, definitions of what it means to think critically vary from discipline to discipline and in some cases from teacher to teacher within a discipline. For a fuller understanding of critical thinking processes, you might usefully undertake one of the self-contained critical reasoning units that are usually offered through the discipline of philosophy.

When anyone presents an argument, in fact when anyone communicates or even thinks at all, he/she does so from within a world view. This world view is a set of assumptions about the world, along with values, attitudes, standards and so on. Some of these world views are rigid and closed. . . . Other world views are open and flexible, valuing tolerance of other people's positions, though still striving for coherence.

PAUL JEWELL

Many of your teachers at university will use terms such as 'criticism', 'argument', 'logic', and you may be told to 'be more critical in your approach' or to 'argue your case'. The definition of critical thinking used in this book is 'reasonable, reflective thinking that is focused on what to believe or do' (Ennis 2011, 1). Some of the elements of critical thinking that are pertinent to your studies are outlined below.

- The presentation of *arguments* to persuade or influence others is central to critical thinking. Academic arguments have two parts: a thesis, and reasons or premises to support the thesis. In your reading and listening it is important that you learn to identify the thesis and supporting premises, and that when you write argumentative essays you develop a thesis through your choice of main points.

- Critical thinking involves *debate* and negotiating positions, resolving conflict and dealing with difference and opposition.

- *Reflection* is crucial to critical thinking. Thus, every time you reflect on and question what you do or think in your life and studies you are thinking critically.

- Although critical thinking is partly something we all do privately, it is also a *communicative* activity. In a sense, every time we are involved in a debate or discussion with others who hold different opinions we are involved in critical thinking, if we are prepared to question what we believe or are told. Similarly, every time we read and question material that presents us with different arguments on a topic, we are involved in critical thinking.

- The outcome of critical thinking is making a decision and *acting* on what you have come to think and believe.

- Critical thinking involves *emotion* as well as reason.

- Critical thinking requires an attitude of *openness* to different viewpoints.

Problem solving

Knowledge, like nature, is revealed not in itself but through our methods of questioning. Those methods have, over time, become more and more highly differentiated, more and more specialised. Within the university these different ways of questioning can be identified with the disciplinary foundations of knowledge. The disciplines are marked off from one another less by the uniqueness of the area of reality or experience they set out to investigate than by their distinctive methods of investigation—their distinctive modes of analysis.

BRIGID BALLARD and JOHN CLANCHY

Problem solving means different things in different disciplines, as does critical thinking. Problem solving is used extensively in the sciences and is the basis of 'problem-based learning'. It requires many of the same skills and attitudes as critical thinking, and some educators consider problem solving to be a subset of critical thinking. Students, particularly in their early undergraduate years, may be required to follow guidelines or 'recipes' on how to solve problems in a particular context. These guidelines vary in the disciplines but basically follow the same six steps:

— exploring the problem

— defining the problem

— generating possible solutions

— deciding on a course of action

— implementing the solution, and

— evaluating the solution.

(See Chapter 15, 'Writing scientific reports', for the relationship between problem solving and the process and genre of scientific report writing).

Researching

> Programs should induct students into the role of research in their discipline and present knowledge as created, uncertain and contested.   M. HEALEY

The research process begins when you ask your own questions and seek answers, whether in your everyday life you ask a question and go to the Internet for an answer or whether you ask an academic question that requires you to conduct an experiment in the field or laboratory or carry out an advanced literature search.

The process of research (Willison and O'Regan 2007, 402–403) can be considered in phases that include:

— asking a question, either one given by a teacher or one that you devise yourself (see Chapter 6, 'Asking your own questions')

— finding information, ideas or data using methods appropriate to the question and the discipline (see Chapter 9, 'Using information sources')

— critically evaluating the knowledge you find (see Chapter 8, 'Researching a topic')

— organising the ideas and information (see Chapter 8)

— analysing and integrating the knowledge (see Chapter 8), and

— communicating the knowledge to others (see Chapter 13, 'Developing your writing', Chapter 14, 'Writing essays', and Chapter 15, 'Writing scientific reports').

> Research and experimental development (R&D) comprise creative work undertaken on a systematic basis in order to increase the stock of knowledge, including knowledge of man [*sic*], culture and society, and the use of this stock of knowledge to devise new applications.   OECD, FRASCATI MANUAL

One of the key functions of the university is to advance knowledge through research and to disseminate this knowledge, and most of your teachers divide their time between teaching and research. The different types of research in which your teachers may be involved include:

— pure research, to discover new theoretical knowledge without a specific practical objective

— applied research, which carries out an original investigation and looks for a practical outcome, and

— experimental work on materials, products or devices, or on processes and systems.

In lectures and tutorials your teachers may present you with the findings of their own and other academic research so that you are aware of research in your discipline. To develop your understanding of research, you will probably be introduced to research methodologies and how academic knowledge is produced. As you become more advanced in your study, you may also be given the opportunity to participate in actual research projects.

As a beginning university student you are not expected to be an expert researcher. You develop these skills as an undergraduate and apply them with increasing autonomy and increasing sophistication and depth as you progress through your study as preparation for research in postgraduate study and the workplace.

Collaborative learning

> Individual commitment to a group effort—that is what makes a team work, a company work, a society work, a civilization work.   VINCE LOMBARDI

Learning in teams has recently been acknowledged as a generic skill that is important for all students to acquire before they graduate. Increasingly, employers are seeking graduates with demonstrated ability to collaborate with others and who have basic skills in teamwork, negotiation and conflict resolution. In fact, job advertisements and interview panels increasingly request information on experience in thoughtful social interaction and leadership.

Although universities have always provided opportunities for students to interact with others through tutorials and seminars this has not been a consistent feature of all disciplines. The development of this skill is required as a Graduate Attribute in all university courses, so many units set up collaborative learning groups. These formal groups are usually student-led and organised; they may be face-to-face or online; and they may be short-term or a major part of a student's workload. The groups vary in size but usually consist of three to ten students. They might involve a group written project and, possibly, group assessment of the discussion process and any work produced (see 'Playing your part during discussions', Chapter 12, for more on collaborative learning, and 'Peer evaluation', Chapter 17).

Using learning outcomes to guide your study

> When we mean to build
>
> We first survey the plot, then draw the model.   SHAKESPEARE

Each unit has a place within an overall plan to instruct you in the disciplinary subject area and to develop certain skills (see 'Developing skills and attitudes', Chapter 3). Your unit materials should contain a statement of what your teacher wants you to gain from the unit and from each assignment you complete. This is set out as objectives or learning outcomes.

TABLE
3.1   **Learning outcomes and objectives**

Learning outcomes = content = learning tasks or activities = assessment

Learning outcomes	**Learning objectives**
These:	These:
— are very specific	— are usually expressed in very general terms
— outline skills and particular knowledge that you should be able to demonstrate when you finish the unit	— are broad statements outlining what the unit coordinator plans to achieve
— are described using verbs	
— describe actions that you must be able to perform to prove your learning	
— can be tested	
For example:	For example:
— to identify and analyse opposing theories on a topic	— to prepare you for second year mathematics
— to apply a particular research methodology	— to help you understand how people from all classes of society lived in the Middle Ages
— to write clearly and logically	
— to critically examine . . .	— to acquaint you with an issue central to a subject area
— to translate . . .	— to stimulate you to think critically
— to participate in . . .	— to question your attitudes
— to write a report . . .	
— to calculate . . .	

Outcomes can be very useful to you if you pay attention to them. They can help you, for example:

— to focus your assignments more clearly

— to anticipate what will be in exams, and

— identify skills you need to develop.

Outcomes and objectives should dictate all aspects of a unit; they align with the content and skills that you learn, the tasks and activities in which you participate, and the unit assessment. These statements clarify what is in a unit and what you are expected to learn. If the unit outcomes are not provided, ask for them.

There are a number of ways in which you can use outcomes to guide your study.

- Locate the unit outcomes in your materials and keep a copy of these handy so you can refer to them during the semester. For example, if the skill of critical thinking is a stated outcome, consider if you are applying this in your reading.

- Discuss the outcomes with other students and with your teachers. For example, how do the objectives for your first assignment relate to the overall unit outcomes?

- Examine the outcomes in relation to your own learning aims. Do the outcomes correlate with your study aims? For example, if one of your aims is to improve your writing, is this included as a unit outcome? If the outcomes are not compatible with your aims, do you need to adapt your aims? For example, an outcome might focus on a specific genre which is new to you. Or when choosing an elective which interests you, look closely at the outcomes for more detail on the knowledge and skills you are expected to achieve.

- Once you are clear about the outcomes and their relationship to your aims, use them actively to guide your study. Part-way through the semester check back over the learning outcomes and see if your studies are on track with them. For example, when final assessment is near, revisit the outcomes to remind yourself what you need to focus on for the exams.

When teachers don't set out clear outcomes, it may be because they have not fully thought these through. Although all of the outcomes may be clear in the teacher's mind they have neglected to put them in writing for you. Occasionally a teacher may choose to conceal their learning outcomes for particular activities. For example, early in a unit you may be given a short written assignment to introduce basic knowledge and at the same time to diagnose your writing abilities. To test your writing ability more effectively, you may not be told about the second objective.

Adjusting to being a student

> The act of engaging in higher education, for most students, is indicative of their commitment. They want to be successful, and most persevere in the face of considerable adversity . . . perhaps because of factors . . . such as motivation . . . and whether the student has a sense of belonging (both academically and socially) in an institution.
>
> MANTZ YORKE and BERNARD LONGDEN

Becoming a student in a new culture entails practical and emotional adjustments in your life. (Some aspects of your self and your surroundings which influence study are presented in Chapters 1 and 4.) If the people you are close to support you as a student, the changes are easier and you can relax and explore what your new life has to offer. Even with the support of others it is valuable to have strategies to deal with the changes as you establish a new lifestyle as a student, as well as developing new academic skills and attitudes.

Coping with personal change

> I don't feel it is necessary to know exactly what I am. The main interest in life and work is to become someone else that you were not in the beginning. If you knew when you began a book what you would say at the end, do you think that you would have the courage to write it? What is true of writing and for a love relationship is true also for life. The game is worthwhile insofar as we don't know what will be the end.
>
> MICHEL FOUCAULT

For some students the changes wrought by higher education are secondary to the other events in their lives. For others the educational process stimulates ideas that force them to question their life and view of the world (see 'Beliefs and values', Chapter 1). This in turn can lead to the desire, perhaps accompanied by excitement or by difficulties and fears, for a life that is more in keeping with their changing world view and values.

For example, many mature age students enter university at a time when they already perceive the need for change. For a woman living in a nuclear family relationship with a husband and children who expect her to fulfil the role of 'housewife' and 'mum', a unit in sociology studies can raise stimulating and confusing questions about her roles. A student from overseas faces educational challenges as well as adjustments to living in a new culture away from many supports and expectations at home. For some students, changes occur that are independent of their studies, such as moving house, starting a new relationship or a sudden bereavement in the family. If you are a school leaver starting tertiary study at 18 or 19 you are probably facing a time of intense personal growth; this can be a time of leaving home and finding your own social niche. These changes impinge on studies and there is a two-way interchange between learning and the rest of your life.

It may help to ask the following questions:

○○○ *Is my education stimulating me to think about issues that make me want to change the way I live?*

When the changes in my life create stress, how do I cope with my studies?

Where do I go for help when I am stressed by such changes?

How do I usually deal with change in my life?

Do I have a friend or acquaintance who will help me explore new possibilities and listen to my problems?

Do I think I need to seek professional help to deal with these changes in the most positive way?

How are these changes affecting the people close to me?

In the quote above, Foucault aptly points to the uncertainty of where life can lead and reminds us that change can be seen as opening new possibilities rather than as something of which to be afraid. However, too many major changes all at once can be unsettling. But if you are seeking certainty in your life and do not want to change your views and values, many of the courses and units offered in higher education may not be the best place for you.

> He believed to the end exactly the same things he started with. It seems to me that a man who can think straight along for forty-seven years without changing a single idea ought to be kept in a cabinet as a curiosity.   JEAN WEBSTER

Combining study with other work

Being a university student is no longer the only focus in most students' lives. It has become the norm for students to work in paid employment, and the proportion of full-time students who need to work has increased significantly. Furthermore, students are working longer hours and often in irregular casual jobs. This work might be to cover basic essentials such as rent, food and textbooks; to maintain a chosen lifestyle which includes socialising, travel and up-to-date technology; or to pay fees if these are not, or cannot be, deferred. Fewer student allowance schemes have also increased the need for students to take on paid work.

Whatever your reason for working, you need to plan how to combine your study with paid work. How you do this so that work and study mesh as productively as possible is one of the big adjustments you need to make as a student. Your employment, however much and whatever it is, will mean that you regularly need to consciously re-focus on your study. Ask yourself the following questions.

○○○ *Is my job directly related to my subjects?*

Does the amount of energy I put into my job affect my study? How? How can I change this?

Do I find my job stimulating/challenging/physically exhausting/emotionally draining?

Does my job mean that I am able to spend less time on campus than I would like?

How might my work affect my study timetable and which units I can take?

Is online study the only practical option for me?

- Spending less time on campus may be ideal if, for example, you are a student with multiple commitments outside study. Often mature age students with major work or family responsibilities spend less time on campus than they would like, but this is also increasingly difficult for younger students in paid work.

- If your job is directly related to the subjects you are studying you can engage more with your studies and have opportunities to transfer skills and knowledge from one context to another. For example, you may be a veterinary student working part-time in an animal clinic, or a parent studying children's literature. Even if your work isn't directly connected with the content of the subjects you study, it may require you to use your mind imaginatively to solve problems and grapple with new ideas. In this case, these existing skills stimulate your brain so that it feels less rusty when you tackle formal study. Useful connections between your employment and your study can be particularly important if you are a distance or part-time student with little opportunity to discuss your learning with teachers or other students. However, close connections between your work (paid or unpaid) and study can sometimes create problems if, for example, you are also a teacher and you read a textbook that criticises the teaching methods you use, or if units you take for further job qualifications come to seem irrelevant.

- The amount of energy you put into your job affects your energy for studying. A job that isn't satisfying but is financially necessary may demand a lot of your energy. If you do heavy outdoor physical work or spend your day looking after children, sometimes you will be too tired to study; at other times you will welcome the change to mental exercise. The high level of energy and creativity which you devote to a satisfying job can carry over to your studies. But if your studies are less stimulating than your work, you may rapidly lose interest in them.

- If you work in a high-speed job, you can find yourself impatient with the leisurely pace of some units, especially if you have only limited time off work for classes. If a unit doesn't regularly require work to be handed in, the apparent aimlessness of your study may be frustrating. However, study can provide you with a relaxing change from a high-pressure job—and the workloads in most units become demanding soon enough.

- Financial decisions affect your study, and it will be up to you to balance how much you work in relation to your needs and your study goals. If you need to work part-time to finance your education, you will have less time for study itself. If you have been a secondary school student or homemaker without an independent income, you may have to justify your desire to study to the person whose income will now support you. You may feel under pressure to 'succeed' or to choose vocational courses, particularly if your study calls for extra money to pay for books or travel or childcare.

Seeking help from others

One of the first steps in dealing with change, both positive and negative, is to talk with other people. If your family and friends support you as a student, the changes will be easier, and while other people can't live the changes for you, you don't have to deal with the situation completely on your own. Look for someone who can pass on handy hints and provide a listening ear to help you sort out how you want to handle the changes. Even if you do feel alone now, share these changes with:

— other people who are going through similar changes or have done so in the past

— friends who care about you achieving your goals

— a learning adviser, counsellor or sympathetic teacher who has seen other students going through similar experiences, or

— a virtual friend or members of an online discussion group.

You may find that you look to one person or group to discuss your changing views of society, to another to help deal with the repercussions at home of your changed lifestyle, and to a third person or group for moral support when you have to write your first tertiary-level essay. Think creatively and stay open to all sorts of possibilities for help—words of wisdom and warm support can often come from unexpected sources.

Dealing with difficult situations

As a student you will inevitably find yourself in situations that are difficult and cause anxiety. One technique which many students find useful to cope is the '*imagine the worst . . . and then . . .*' approach.

> When things are really bad . . . I picture a black tunnel in front of me. I go up to it . . . I know a train is coming . . . I go to meet it . . . I know that inside the tunnel, underneath the wheels, down between the sleepers, there is a little spot of light.   PETER HØEG

Now stop, and think of a situation that is worrying you at present.

Imagine the worst that could happen, *then imagine yourself coping with it.* What are your alternatives after the worst has happened? Which ones seem most viable? Think about why you are worried and what you can do to deal with the causes of your worry. Share your anxieties with others and see what they have to suggest. And perhaps most important of all, don't accept that you have to be worried. Is it really a matter of life or death?

For example, are you anxious that you seem stupid in a discussion group? Imagine this happening—*then go on* to imagine yourself handling the situation. Think about why you are anxious and what you can do about the causes of your anxieties. Do you need to prepare more thoroughly for the group so that you feel more confident about contributing to the discussion? Getting to know a couple of other group members outside the discussion time might make you feel that you have sympathetic listeners for anything you say during a discussion, and enables you to share your feelings and experiences in collaborative learning groups and other learning situations. Sharing will probably lead you to discover that you are not alone in your anxieties. Other students may have helpful advice on how to cope with a situation that is worrying you. If several of you are worried, try 'imagining the worst . . . and then . . .' together and see what alternatives you come up with (see 'Playing your part during discussions', Chapter 12).

Deferring or withdrawing from study

The majority of students find university satisfying and challenging and complete a degree. However, practical circumstances (such as the need to earn an income) can mean that you might consider deferring study or possibly even withdrawing from university. At times you may question whether or not you have enrolled in the right unit; whether a course is the one you really want; or whether you should be at university at all. Perhaps you find your study goals and aims are no longer a priority for you, you have developed other interests, or you don't find your studies sufficiently stimulating. Feelings of self-doubt are not uncommon and may be fleeting or persistent. If they persist, revisit your goals and clarify them, talk to others, and think through what your alternatives would be if you withdrew.

> I left the woods, for as good a reason as I went there . . . it seemed to me that I had several lives to lead, and could not spare any more time for that one. It is remarkable how easily and insensibly we fall into a particular route, and make a beaten track for ourselves.
> HENRY JAMES THOREAU

Before you finally decide to defer or withdraw, ask yourself the following questions.

Do I basically dislike studying at this stage in my life?

Do I want to change to a different unit or course? If so, which one? Is this feasible at this stage of the semester?

How will withdrawing from a unit impact on other areas of my study? Is the unit required, and if so can I take it at a later date? What are the alternatives?

Are there factors in my life at present that make it untenable or difficult to continue studying?

If I decide to defer studying for a time, will I consider returning at a later date? If so, when? Will withdrawing now influence my chances of returning?

How might withdrawing from study impact on other areas of my life? Will friends and family approve or disapprove? Is this a reason to continue? If not, how will I explain my decision to them?

What emotional impact will withdrawing have on me? Will I feel relieved or will I feel that I have failed? How will I deal with this?

The decision to leave a programme before the end is rarely taken lightly, and is often anguished . . . The decision once made, there was often a sense of relief.

MANTZ YORKE and BERNARD LONGDEN

If you are seriously considering deferring or withdrawing from a unit or an entire course, there are some practical steps you need to take. Find out the 'census date', that is, the date before which you can withdraw from a unit without penalty, without a 'fail' grade showing on your academic transcript, and without paying full fees. And before you defer or withdraw, find out what you need to do in case you later want to return.

Staying focused on your goals

Coping with change involves taking time now and then to focus in depth on why you are studying. When confronted with confusing changes and the decisions which go with them, it helps to be clear about the core reasons why you are studying and what you hope to achieve, and then to stay open to ideas on how to achieve this.

Imagine, for example, that you are studying because you want to work with people, so you have enrolled for a psychology degree. However, you find that the way that psychology is taught at your institution does not seem to coincide with your vision of how you would work with people. You then need to define as clearly as possible the essential characteristics of your goal or dream. Do you want to work with people with severe problems or people who are having temporary difficulties? Do you want to work on your own, in a small team or in an institutional setting? Is your orientation towards a particular school of psychological thought because of its views of human nature?

With these essential characteristics in mind you can then brainstorm to see, first, what your current psychology degree program offers you and, second, what other avenues might be open to help achieve your goal. Of course, your goal itself may change with time and with changes in you. It is important to keep refining the essence of what you want, and not to mistake the means of achieving this for the dream itself.

Have a broad picture of the place of tertiary study in your education rather than automatically thinking of it as the be-all and end-all. 'Lifelong learning' has become something of a catch-cry and is a term with a multiplicity of meanings covering formal and informal learning. Some decades ago, relatively few people went on to tertiary study, and secondary school to the age of fourteen was seen as the end of formal education; now there is an increasing likelihood that you will need and be expected to continue your formal education and training beyond a degree or diploma. You may, for example, be required to update or broaden your professional knowledge, or to acquire knowledge to enable you to move into a new field or to specialise in a particular area. You may have to acquire new skills for accessing and selecting up-to-date information in your field.

Allow yourself time to discover what being at university is like for you. Expect to feel both confused and excited in the first six to twelve months while you settle in. Begin to understand what is expected of you and to define some of your aims. During this time, as well as trying to pass units, put some energy into learning how to learn and into making contact with staff and students. Remember that, outside school, you acquired knowledge and skills that you can transfer into your formal learning. Have confidence that you do know how to learn when you want to.

As well as any further formal education you undertake, your informal learning will be lifelong. Hopefully persisting with formal study, whether undergraduate or postgraduate, will enhance your ability to learn and discover future directions you want to pursue both informally, and in further education and work. Whatever directions your learning takes, remember to ask yourself 'What are my goals?', 'What is my aim in wanting to learn this?' and 'How can I best engage with and share my learning?'.

TEN TIPS

1   Be proactive in making contact with other students in class, over a coffee or online.
2   If you have questions for a teacher, first check that the information you want is not provided in unit materials, and then make your questions as clear and specific as possible.
3   For each unit, print out the learning outcomes and objectives and keep these in a place where they are easy to refer to.
4   Find out what your university considers to be generic learning skills and necessary graduate attributes, and look for opportunities to develop these in each of your units.
5   Reflect on when, in your everyday life, you engage in thoughtful discussions with others who hold different views, and whether you are trying to extend your understanding rather than win an argument.
6   Think about when in your everyday life you apply the six steps of problem solving.
7   Identify the strategies, no matter how small, that you find most useful in combining study with other major responsibilities.
8   Practise using the 'Imagine the worst . . . and then . . .' strategy in a range of potentially anxiety-producing situations.
9   Think of three key practical changes you need to make as you adjust to university study.
10 Take time to think through your responses to the questions in 'Coping with personal change'.

REFERENCES

Ennis, Robert. 2011. 'The Nature of Critical Thinking'. Academic paper. http://faculty.education.illinois.edu/rhennis/documents/TheNatureofCriticalThinking_51711_000.pdf.

Willison, John., and Kerry O'Regan. 2007. 'Commonly Known, Commonly Not Known, Totally Unknown: A Framework for Students Becoming Researchers.' *Higher Education Research and Development* 26(4). http://www.tandtonline.com/doi/abs/10.1080/07294360701658609.html.

Planning your study

4

. . . time is not something you have lost. It is not a thing you ever had. It is what you live in.

JAMES GLEICK

If you are a full-time student, you have the opportunity to be involved in academic life and campus activities. These involvements might enhance your learning—for example, if you are a keen athlete taking human movement courses or a parent studying child psychology. Possibly these activities conflict with your study—your family may expect you to put their needs first, or a close friend might not understand the demands of study.

Most students today spend less time on campus than a couple of decades ago, when full-time student life often centred around university study and campus life. This situation may be ideal if, for example, you are a student with a well-established life outside study who visits campus to attend a few classes to upgrade qualifications.

Some students wish they could spend more time on campus and on their study, but cannot do this because of other commitments. This often applies to mature-age students with major family or work responsibilities, but other students can also have difficulties getting to campus. The proportion of full-time students who need to undertake paid employment has increased significantly and they also work longer hours. Irregular casual work can compound the problem of allocating regular time to academic life (see 'Combining study with other work', Chapter 3).

Spending less time on campus and on study can be a problem as you try to juggle the different parts of your life and stay sane. Yet it can also mean that out of necessity you develop the skill of focusing on what needs to be accomplished in a limited number of hours. Some planning ahead is essential to this, rather than relying on serendipitous encounters. For example, make appointments to see teachers rather than hoping to catch them, and set aside regular time for online work.

You make the main decisions about your study timetable—and you may be surprised how much work is involved in being a purposeful tertiary student. The time you are expected to spend in formal face-to-face or online class contact varies, as does the amount of time you need to spend on a unit overall. For example, architecture students usually spend much more time in class than social science students, while units without a large component of practical work usually require more time outside class for research and writing. Whether or not you attend a class, read a book, or hand in an assignment early depends on your enthusiasm for a subject, your desire to pass at a particular standard, your response to teachers, and your other commitments. Some teachers and units are more flexible about these matters than others. The standard you hope to reach depends on your study goals and motivation. Except for formal class time such as lectures, discussion groups and laboratory sessions, it is usually you who decides whether to access library services during the day or at home in the evening, to work at a job or to be with your family, or to sit in the cafeteria or the local student pub talking to other students.

Whatever your connection to a campus, learning can be creative and satisfying. That said, there are inevitably times in your formal learning when you have to make yourself work: when you are not interested in a topic, when you have difficulty with an assignment, when you have other things on your mind, or if you feel your chosen field of study is not what you expected and looked forward to. Planning how to spend your time can give you the opportunity to explore the pleasures of using your mind, and help you cope with occasions when it is difficult to study.

All **first year** students are taking an 'invisible unit', that of learning about university culture—what's expected of you, what your chosen field of study is like, and what learning at university might offer you personally. In addition, students from non-Australian cultural backgrounds are learning how to operate in Australian society. How you might best use your time is part of such cultural understandings. It involves such things as learning how to manage your workload as effectively as possible, how to balance study and the rest of your life, and how to set aside time for reviewing what you've already covered.

In your first month at university, you are likely to have a mix of feelings such as excitement and anxiety. School leavers—particularly those with a high entry score—may mistakenly see university workloads as easier than their demanding final school year, because in the first few weeks no one is asking you for major assignments or allocating constant homework. In contrast, it is not uncommon for apprehensive mature age students to feel 'It's a mistake they let me in and they'll find out when they see my first assignment'. This fear drives some older students to work long hours, but they may not use that time effectively.

While it is important to develop new time management skills, in your first year you will almost certainly have to examine and unlearn patterns which are no longer helpful. Everyone has habitual ways of using time that if you stop and think about, you realise are just not working any more. Does it always have to be Thursday nights that you get together with mates? Will you really lose friends if you drop out of contact for a couple of hours now and then to focus on urgent study? Does the essential housework need to be shared around a bit more?

Why plan your time?

Time management techniques are sometimes presented as though their main purpose is to enable you to squeeze more into your days or to become a 'better' person (slimmer, wiser, fitter, smarter, richer or . . .). Such approaches often only serve to make us feel guilty or anxious if we don't live up to them perfectly. However, our lives are not commodities which can be neatly packaged. Inevitably the unexpected happens, and even careful planners can find their lives thrown into disarray.

> The experts who write these [time management] books reveal confusion about what it means to save time . . . They offer more time, in their titles and blurbs, but they are

surely not proposing to extend the 1,440 minute day, so by 'more' do they mean fuller or freer time? Is time saved when we manage to leave it empty, or when we stuff it full of multiple activities, useful or pleasant?   JAMES GLEICK

Since being a student is not a 'nine to five' job, one of the challenges is that at almost any time in the day or night you could be studying. And regardless of how much support or advice you receive or find, getting the work done is up to you. Yet planning what to do, and when, can help minimise crises and stress. One of the first steps is to set some priorities—to distinguish between what needs to be done now and what can wait. Prioritising enables you to focus with more attention on what you are doing at present. This improves the chances of producing better quality work and of finding that work more satisfying, or at least getting through unwanted work more quickly. Setting priorities also helps to avoid the feeling that with all this work hovering, somehow you should be tackling all of it now. Even if you prefer to live life more spontaneously, some realistic planning ahead can help you to see when you will need periods of concentrated effort and when your time is more flexible. And for people who have many commitments in their life and can barely manage to fit study in, prioritising is an essential survival skill.

The good news is that worthwhile time management is also about building into your life activities which give you joy and satisfaction and replenish your energy. It is not just about the things you 'should' do. Sometimes conscientious students spend yet another afternoon driving themselves to work on an assignment and not getting very far because they are too tired to be effective. If this applies to you, you might be more effectual if you first take an hour to do something you love but have given up because you feel you must study at every available moment. Curling up with a trashy novel, going for a walk on the beach, spending time in the garden, dancing to a favourite piece of music, playing in the park with your small child—you'll have your own favourites.

The bad news is that time management techniques are not magic bullets. Competent time planners know that sometimes there is no substitute for willpower. If you feel overwhelmed by the amount of work you have to do, actually sitting down straightaway and doing just an hour's work can give you a sense of achievement and relief—and at least you are an hour further on than you were before.

As a student, down-to-earth time management can help you:

— avoid the nasty surprise of discovering that an assignment you thought was weeks off is in fact due next week

— manage your overall workload

— clarify the quantity of work expected at university and in specific units

— achieve higher grades if these are important to you

— practise working out the stages that lead to final versions of assignments and how long each of these stages usually takes you

— take a reality check on just how much time you can spend on each stage of an assignment

— balance your study and your personal life, and

— develop skills that will be useful for the rest of your life.

Many persons believe that either you were born organized or you weren't—and that if you weren't, you're doomed to a lifetime of mismatched socks and disappearing file folders. Nothing could be further from the truth.   S. SCHLENGER and R. ROESCH

There are three parts to practical time management—making plans, sticking to them, and recognising which approaches to managing your time work best for you.

When to study

Before you can decide on priorities or when you are going to tackle various tasks, you need to have a clear idea of what needs to be done.

A semester overview

You need an overview of what work is due in a semester, even if you are averse to planning. Even if you use an electronic diary, it is more effective if you make this plan on an A4 or A5 single sheet that you can pin up in your study area or carry with you, rather than simply entering items in a week-by-week diary (electronic or paper) and having only a hazy idea of what is due when. Keep your plan somewhere visible, such as in the folder you always carry.

1   To make such a plan, use a calendar (or your own template) which shows all the weeks of a semester, including exams and any break weeks. Fill in and highlight due dates for assignments, along with percentages and word requirements.

2   This calendar will be much more useful if you also work out the stages leading to each assignment, allowing more time for work that is worth a greater percentage of marks. Some people find it easier to work backwards on this—to look at each deadline and think about what needs to be done in the week before, and then in the week before that. For example, in the week before an essay is due you might aim to produce a rough draft, and in the week before that to complete your research.

3   While deadlines are generally not under your control, when you do the work leading up to the deadlines often is. Look at your overview to identify the weeks where your workload is heavier or lighter. Try to adjust when you will work on the various stages of assignments (and personal commitments) so that you distribute the work more evenly.

4   Once your plan is complete, work back from where you want to end up (the due date for an assignment, for example) and think about what it all means for

the specific small tasks you need to do in the next week; and list these tasks as precisely as possible. For example, write 'make notes on two articles for Monday class' rather than 'class reading'.

5   In an overview plan, you can also build in major non-academic commitments (e.g. running a marathon, school holidays, a workplace conference, an important birthday) and use the same approach of highlighting deadlines and planning stages. Do this to balance the different aspects of your life.

6   Allow some 'just in case' time—just in case you break an arm, win the lottery, fall in love or have a major computer malfunction.

7   As a final step, build in some rewards, even small ones. You could also schedule a heavier work period to end just before the reward of a pleasurable commitment such as a weekend away.

It is impossible to enjoy idling thoroughly unless one has plenty of work to do.

JEROME K. JEROME

When semester starts you will be given lots of information about what is expected and when, and you need to pay attention to this. If you don't pick up on such information you may well waste time on work which is not what is wanted. It is likely that there will be more information than you can absorb all at once, so invest some time in reviewing unit guides in the middle of the semester and again just before final assessments are due. And be alert for information given at the start and end of lectures and other classes, and for additional handouts or online instructions.

A workable weekly plan

To decide what to do and when, it is valuable to have a reasonably realistic estimate of the time available. Sometimes students feel guilty at the end of a day about not tackling many of the items on a 'To do' list, when in fact there simply wasn't enough free time to complete them. If you dislike planning, try setting aside and using a regular time each day or week for concentrated study. Combine this with making and using an up-to-date list of 'Things to do'. Your reality check will be provided by whether or not you complete everything you must definitely do.

For those who find that a moderate amount of structure helps to reduce stress and increase satisfaction in their work, the following method is probably most useful on a weekly basis but can also be used to make monthly and/or daily plans.

1   Using your own template for a week, or a page with plenty of space in a week-to-a-page diary (electronic or paper), enter any *essential commitments* you have at definite times. These commitments may be academic such as attending lectures or a meeting with a tutor, or non-academic 'appointments' such as paid work or childcare. Many people find it helpful to create a visual representation for their week by blocking out the slab of time needed for each commitment, rather

than just writing the name of the appointment next to its start time. As part of your time-definite commitments, incorporate regular activities such as travel and many practical necessities, including preparing meals and getting ready in the morning. These times are not available for study, and not including them as commitments is one reason why people overestimate the amount of disposable time available.

2 The next allocation of time is for *floating activities* which are not tied to a particular time. These include:

— tasks which must be completed during the week, such as handing in the final draft of an essay to avoid late penalties, and

— activities which you definitely want to complete, such as the discussion section of a report while the research is fresh in your mind.

If you are doing this on paper, you may want to pencil in these activities so that you can move them around during the week if necessary.

3 The remaining time is likely to be a combination of segments of up to 30 minutes and larger chunks of over an hour. This time is at present 'free', although part of it will be occupied by unexpected events, both big and small.

4 Once you have a reasonable estimate of the *disposable time* in your week, what are some strategies for making best use of the time available?

● Don't fill in every spare moment—your plan needs some flexibility to cope with the unexpected.

● Keep an ongoing list of brief tasks that you can dispose of in the small time segments.

● Perhaps a lot of your time is spent skipping between various electronic devices. But it takes much longer to complete large assignments if you only do them in small bits and pieces, so create some chunks of a couple of hours in which you can focus on such tasks.

● Allocate the longest chunks of time to activities which require your sustained concentration—don't fritter these thinking spaces away on small practical tasks.

● Plan relaxation and social activities so that they complement your studies.

A quick reality check of your week

At the end of the week take five minutes to think back on how your week has resembled your plan. Don't expect to keep absolutely to your schedule—instead examine why your week differed from your expectations. For example, if you find you are spending many hours in front of a computer screen, pause to reflect on whether this time is directed to your purpose at hand—the Internet provides many distractions. Or if you frequently find it difficult to meet study deadlines because others think that the needs of your extended family network or your domestic responsibilities should take precedence, discuss ways of handling this with a friend, teacher or student counsellor.

As you become more practised in realistically estimating your time commitments, you will also find yourself monitoring which tasks usually take up more of your time and which you can complete more swiftly. For example, students who are not avid readers may find research time-consuming, whereas other students may read quickly but labour over writing. And in your early days as a student you may underestimate how long it takes for activities such as choosing and defining an essay topic. You develop a more accurate picture of the quality and quantity of work you can produce in the time available when you:

— learn more about university expectations (see 'What to expect from university', Chapter 2)

— increase your knowledge of your particular strengths and weaknesses, and

— combine these with a more accurate picture of the time available in your week.

Time is like money. If you have lots of it to spare, you have more choice about how you spend it. If it is in short supply, knowing where it has gone can help you budget for the future.   ANON.

Tracking your use of time

To become more aware of how you actually use your time, apply the questions in Table 4.1, 'Timetracking'. Since the exercise concerns a short period, it is only an indicator of your time use. Nevertheless it can help you realise the priority that study has in your life; how other activities help or hinder your study; and where your time 'vanishes' to. For example, timetracking was useful to a student who was concerned about putting in hours every day on study but always completing assignments in a last-minute rush. When he examined an accurate record of his week, he discovered that a significant part of what he had thought of as study time was spent on lengthy chats with friends about his assignments, playing with the dog, and procrastinating about study by making elaborate timetables about how much study he was going to do. Yet because he felt he was working so hard, he had also been taking a lot of time to recuperate in front of the TV.

There's lots to do; we have a very busy schedule–
At 8 o'clock we get up, and then we spend
From 8 to 9 daydreaming.
From 9.00 to 9.30 we take our early midmorning nap.
From 9.30 to 10.30 we dawdle and delay.
From 10.30 to 11.30 we take our late early morning nap.
From 11.30 to 12.00 we bide our time and then eat lunch.
From 1.00 to 2.00 we linger and loiter.

From 2.00 to 2.30 we take our early afternoon nap.

From 2.30 to 3.30 we put off for tomorrow what we could have done today.

From 3.30 to 4.00 we take our early late afternoon nap.

From 4.00 to 5.00 we loaf and lounge until dinner.

From 6.00 to 7.00 we dilly-dally.

From 7.00 to 8.00 we take our early evening nap, and then for an hour before we go to bed at 9.00 we waste time.

As you can see, that leaves almost no time for brooding, lagging, plodding, or procrastinating, and if we stopped to think or laugh, we'd never get nothing done.

NORTON JUSTER

TABLE 4.1   Timetracking

1 Examine how you spend your time

For several days or a week, preferably near the beginning of semester or term, keep a record of how you spend your time. Be honest with yourself. Do this about every half to one hour, since this makes it easier to note down accurately what you did. Make sure your record is accurate— recording three hours' work on statistics is misleading if you spent part of that three hours messaging friends, on the phone chatting to a friend, shuffling desktop files or watering the garden. Log how much time is occupied by:

- compulsory formal classes at set times
- other required unit activities and tasks
- independent or private study
- paid or unpaid employment
- relaxing alone and/or socialising
- social media time or game playing
- active recreation and exercise
- face-to-face time with friends or family
- practical necessities such as washing or buying food
- domestic chores and family activities
- travelling
- sleeping and eating.

You might find it helpful to indicate the times during your private study when you concentrated at your best.

At the end of the week, estimate the number of hours you spent in each of the areas listed above, and ask yourself the following questions about your data.

continued

TABLE 4.1 **continued**

- Were there times when I studied more effectively, such as early in the morning or when I had half the entire day to study? Why?
- Did I work more effectively in some places than others, such as in at the library or at home? Why?
- Did I get more work done on my own or with other people?
- How did the amount of time I spent in required tasks compare with the time I spent on independent study out of class?
- Did I have a particularly heavy workload during this week?
- Did I usually work more effectively in short periods and then lose my concentration, or did it take me a while to settle into study so that I needed longer periods for serious work?
- When I set aside time for study, is there any evidence to show that I actually used that time for focused work?
- Is my study connected with any of my other activities?
- Did I prepare myself for long periods of serious study? How? Was this effective? Did I relax afterwards?
- Which activities took up a lot of time? Are these time traps, such as watching TV, logging into social media, or surfing the Net?

2 Give study the priority you want it to have in your life

Now that you have some data on how you spent a few days or a week, are you happy with how you spent your time? Would you like to make any changes? If so . . .

- List four activities which take a lot of time and energy in your life at present. List four activities which you think should take the most time and energy, and four on which you would like to spend the most time and energy. Compare your results.
- Ask yourself whether you spend enough time studying effectively. Do your non-academic activities and interests leave you sufficient time and energy for formal learning, and do they increase or decrease your satisfaction with that learning?
- If other involvements prevent you from learning as well as you would like, consider limiting these involvements, reducing the number of units you are taking, or reducing the time and effort you put into a unit.
- If there is a significant difference between your current involvements and those you feel you should or would like to have, consider changing your priorities. Think about why you are at university, and how important your formal learning is to you.

Weekly priorities

One simple way of identifying priorities is to consider the consequences if you do or don't do certain things. You can then sort activities into categories such as:

— items you must do if, for example, you are to pass a unit or have food to eat

— items you definitely want to do if, for example, you aspire to a higher grade or a deeper knowledge of an area, and

— items you would like to do because, for example, they would give you satisfaction or pleasure or relieve stress.

This approach, while quick and useful, mostly rates activities on their relative urgency. Most time management literature now includes another approach which emphasises creating time for activities which are *not urgent*, but which are *important* in helping us to minimise crises and live more satisfying lives. For example:

— spending time on maintaining your health helps to avoid major illness

— taking time to set up an effective filing system saves time and panic when looking for files later on

— developing a semester plan of your workload helps give you time for more interesting research

— developing new skills such as previewing helps to make your reading more effective, and

— building in time each week for coffee with a friend provides you with relaxation and helps to maintain a close friendship.

This 'Is it important and/or urgent?' approach suggests that you also minimise time spent on activities which are neither important nor urgent in your life at present. These activities include:

— timewasters, such as lots of shopping or screen time, which you may resort to as an escape valve if you are spending much time in crisis mode

— procrastinating, which actually consumes time and emotional energy, and

— being a perfectionist so that, for example, you spend another day on polishing what is already a high-quality essay instead of starting on a report due in a week.

Constructing an overview of your semester, developing a workable weekly plan, being realistic about the time available and prioritising all contribute to an effective plan for managing your time. However, even the most thoughtful plans can come unstuck.

Sticking to a plan

The road to hell is paved with good intentions.   WESTERN PROVERB

Problems in keeping to time management plans have a variety of causes.

- You may make your plan too inflexible, so that the slightest unexpected event throws the whole plan out of kilter. The unforeseen can occur:
  - first, because you know that problem X will occur but not when, for example, you are likely to have computer problems but you can't usually predict when they will strike, and
  - second, there are totally unforeseen major emergencies such as a car accident.

  Allow for some 'just in case' time in any plan. If you don't need it for the unexpected, it's yours to play with.

- You may have made a plan but it is one that mostly schedules in things that you basically do not want to do. Every major aspect of your life, including study, is likely to have parts you would rather not do (for example, having to write an essay on a topic you see as boring). However, if your lack of motivation arises because you don't want to be at university, then making time management plans is of limited use. Whether or not you like to plan your time, examining your reasons for studying is worthwhile (see 'Why are you studying?', Chapter 2).

- You may be working on what you'd planned but find that it is taking longer than anticipated. For example, being stressed and anxious about what you are doing can slow you down; or you may still be learning just what is involved in university research and writing; or you may be a perfectionist. The reality checks outlined in the previous section can be useful here, as can asking for help.

- You want to get to work and are trying to do so, but your concentration is disrupted by people in your life—a demanding three-year-old, a family who sees you as the household organiser, friends who can't understand why you now restrict your social life (see 'The people in your life', Chapter 1, for suggestions on negotiating a workable arrangement). Develop strategies for saying 'no' firmly but tactfully. And set aside some time to think through what sort of practical arrangements you might need to put in place, such as exchanging childcare with another student.

Procrastination

What sort of things do you put off doing in your everyday life? Why?

In your study are there particular tasks that you usually postpone?

We all procrastinate at some time or other. Sometimes putting off doing certain tasks is a sensible choice—you consciously decide to give other matters higher priority. In such situations, instead of relegating the activity to a 'sometime' list, plan in a specific time when you can get back to it. To avoid expending time and energy in procrastinating, it's useful to become aware of signs that you are delaying; to reflect on why you are choosing to act like this; and to have some strategies you can use to overcome the situation (see Table 4.2, 'Managing procrastination').

If you stop and think about it for a minute, you can probably identify behaviours which show up when you are avoiding a task. For example, you may suddenly feel the urge to weed the garden or clean the oven or do your tax return—jobs which consume time and which would not normally fill you with enthusiasm. Or perhaps you feel compelled to go for a walk 'to clear your mind'; or you sit down to start work but immediately get up and go to get something to eat. You might also tell yourself you've started serious work but are actually busying yourself with lots of low priority tasks. Or you might welcome interruptions from other people, especially if they 'need' you to do something which takes up time.

When you actually get down to working on something you've been delaying, it's not uncommon to feel both relief and 'That wasn't as bad as I thought it might be, why didn't I do it earlier?' Congratulate yourself on what you've achieved, and enjoy your planned reward. Use the time and energy you haven't spent on procrastinating to instead do something you love.

> Efficiency concerns the best ways of doing an assigned job. Effectiveness, on the other hand, concerns the best use of time—which may or may not include doing the particular job in question.   EDWIN C. BLISS

Both your long-term and short-term study plans need to combine flexibility and a commitment to realistic and challenging goals. You can best use your plans by reviewing them several times during a semester. Adjust them according to your current study aims and goals, and to take account of other changes in your life.

- At the beginning of a unit you need to explore and familiarise yourself with the unit outcomes (for content and skills), and you probably spend a high proportion of study time in research and in classes.
- Halfway through a unit you are likely to be relating new materials to what you have already learned, and to be planning and producing written work as well as attending classes and doing research.
- Near the end of a unit you spend your time reflecting on and reviewing what you have learned, and are probably involved in completing major assignments and preparing for exams.

TABLE
4.2　**Managing procrastination**

> Procrastination is the art of making the possible impossible. ANON.

1 Reflect on why you might be avoiding what has to be done

We all have thought-stories we tell ourselves as perfectly valid 'reasons' for not getting down to what we need to do. Some common stories include:

- I work best under pressure.
- There's plenty of time before it's due.
- I'm just the sort of person who is always late.
- I'll relax for a bit and then get started.
- I don't have the big chunk of time that this needs.
- Maybe something will come up and they'll give us an extension.
- Perhaps I could come up with a good excuse and get an extension.

And there are usually feelings involved—you may be anxious or confused or overwhelmed. For example:

- I'm not clear on what's expected.
- I'd like to do this but I don't know how.
- This all just feels too big and I have no idea where to start.
- I don't know if I've done enough research to get started.
- I'll probably fail at this.
- It needs to be perfect.
- If I put down my ideas for someone to read they'll find out I'm no good at uni work.
- I'm no good at writing (or reading, or doing research, or this subject, or . . . the possibilities are considerable).

Or perhaps you are angry. For example:

- I don't really want to be at uni so I shouldn't have to do this.
- Did they have to pick the most boring topic they could think of?
- It's not fair that they expect us to do all this work.

2 Plan how you will minimise the delay

There are two aspects to consider in successfully conquering procrastination. If the main difficulty lies with how you feel, ask yourself what could be genuinely helpful advice to give a friend in the same situation. For example:

- Look for moral support from someone who'll be sympathetic but at the same time firmly encourage you to go ahead.

- Find out who can give you reliable practical help in the areas where you feel unsure.
- Carefully re-read any assignment guidelines or requirements—there may well be a crucial piece of information you missed that is just what you need to know.
- Aim for a 'good enough' outcome—no teacher expects 100% perfection.
- Recognise that with producing work sometimes you just have to persist even if what you're generating is not very good, until you get a breakthrough and the ideas start to flow.
- Use peer pressure—ask someone to check upon how much work you've done.
- If the problem lies mainly with the task itself and how you see it, you might:
  — turn a mountain into molehills—break down a big task into manageable small steps, with a reward planned after each one which matches the size of the task.
  — get some serious work done straightaway to fill your mind with the topic—it can be surprising how having the particular task started in your mind helps you take the next step.
  — identify a few small steps which need doing very soon, and set a specific time to do them.
- Block out a specific time slot tomorrow when you will spend a decent amount of time on one high-priority task.
- Make it a challenge to find three interesting aspects to a task which initially seems boring.

How to study

Planning when to study is a beginning. To make full use of the time you have set aside, also think about how to study.

Knowing what works for you

Since there is no one right way to manage your time, it makes sense to look for a range of techniques and try out those that you think might work for you. Other students often understand your situation and can provide valuable ideas, as can student learning support centres or counsellors. As you expand your repertoire, give yourself credit for the time management skills you already practise. Often students concerned about time management look mostly at their deficiencies and overlook the skills they take for granted, seeing themselves as poor time managers when this is not the case. Simple strategies such as making sure your car always has enough petrol, using a reliable method of waking up in time to get to class, or packing everything you need into your bag the night before—these are all smart time management tactics.

In addition to developing a repertoire of strategies, managing your time effectively requires some self-awareness about you as an individual and as a learner (see Chapter 1, 'You'). Do you find writing relatively straightforward? During the day, when are you likely to be most mentally alert? Do you work best in bursts of intense activity for several days or weeks, with periods of relaxation in between; or do you prefer a regular daily or weekly work session?

Each style of working with time has its strengths and weaknesses. For example:

- If you basically prefer not to plan, decide on the minimum standard that would satisfy you in your study. Then find some strategies which make it possible for you to reach this standard while maintaining maximum flexibility in your life. Make use of the lateral thinking which can come with living with unpredictability.

- If you like to make multiple lists, be clear why you are doing this and whether your list-making takes up time which could be more usefully spent on study. If you make lists because you are anxious about the amount of work to be done, break large tasks into small manageable stages; and consider replacing some of the list-making time with learning an effective relaxation technique. If your lists help you to achieve a lot in your life, give yourself a pat on the back—you might even make a list of your accomplishments!

- If you believe that you work best under pressure, experiment with completing just two pieces of work a week or so ahead of the deadlines and see how this feels and what you learn. And when you are not studying, use your time to do something else that is really important to you instead of just letting the days drift by.

- If you are a mature age student who brings solid time management skills to your studying but is still anxious about 'what's expected', congratulate yourself for having the courage to take on the role of a beginner again. Sort out which of your existing skills are most valuable when studying, and realise that academics enjoy having responsible students like you in their classes and so are more likely to be willing to help with any questions you might have.

- If you are just out of your final year at school, you might be accustomed to not being able to plan even a couple of weeks ahead because you were often given extra work at the last minute. At university, you are usually told well ahead of time when work is due. So since you are expected to be an independent student you need to plan how you are going to complete your assignments.

Once you have a plan and a style of study that works for you, to make the plan work you need to be able to focus in on one specific task at a time, and to sustain that focus for long enough to get the job done.

Focusing

Depending on our habits, our circumstances and our interests, we vary in our ability to focus for more than a few minutes on just one thing at a time, and then to stay with that chosen focus.

From flicking to focusing

You may be used to moving quickly from one brief activity to another, such as checking multiple electronic devices more or less at once, or as a parent preparing a meal and planning a shopping list while coping with a tired and hungry toddler. Such quick switches can look like multi-tasking, but in fact your brain is moving very quickly from one activity to another. Unless one of your activities is an ingrained habit (such as a way of brushing your teeth), your brain uses part of its working memory to rapidly swap tasks.

Such speedy serial tasking can be useful in study if you do it with a particular purpose in mind, for example, if you have limited time to scan a series of journal abstracts to pick the most useful ones, or to check a list of terms to find the unfamiliar ones. And being able to move quickly between different items may enable you to pick up less obvious links or to identify possible patterns. However, some people who consider themselves to be accomplished multi-taskers—because they are usually jumping between activities—are simply people who are easily distracted.

If much of your life involves flicking from one thing to another, when it comes to study you need to practise choosing to work on one thing at a time. The reward for doing this is that your brain can then work much more effectively on more demanding tasks, so you need less time to produce an assignment; you are less prone to mistakes; and you'll find it easier to recall material if you pay more attention to it in the first place. Imagine how little you'd accomplish and how your mind would feel unsettled if you were working in a job which constantly required you to switch from one fleeting activity to another but also expected you to complete big projects.

> Last night I had to write a book review and it honestly should have only taken me a couple of hours. By the time I'd actually logged on to start writing it, I'd already checked my Facebook, my Twitter, my blog, chatted to people about what I was writing and then eventually at four in the morning I wound up finishing it.   A STUDENT

To be able to focus on one task, students have always needed to deal with distractions around them. But extra challenges now come from distractions within your computer and from other communication devices you have nearby. Perhaps you 'just' check a non-study link while waiting for a download of study material, and find quite some time later that you are still immersed in a web trail irrelevant to what you have to do.

Or you might start checking for personal messages because you are procrastinating about study, but then find that such checking becomes a regular habit, a set of tasks that you feel you 'must' do alongside study.

How might you go about choosing to pay attention to just one task for up to 15 minutes?

- Start by thinking about instances in your life where you regularly concentrate on one activity at a time. How do you manage this? What motivates you? Can you transfer this skill and motivation to the study you need to do?

- Reflect on how you feel when you imagine paying attention to one thing at a time for even 10 minutes—comfortable and looking forward to it, or perhaps anxious at the prospect, or already bored? Is this true for most activities in your life, or mostly for studying?

- And how do you feel when you remove all possible electronic stimuli from your surroundings? If much of every day is spent on social networking, try to remove your primary mental focus from your 'technology tasks' by taking 15 minutes where you mute your phone, put your devices away, and do something which feels noticeably different (going for a quick walk, sitting outside in a favourite spot, playing with the dog or a guitar). If 15 minutes is too much of a challenge initially, start with five minutes and build up. What you are aiming for is to be able to choose one study task on which to focus and to stay with that task for at least 15 minutes. You are laying down new pathways in your brain—keep at it.

Time away from digital media is not only no longer our default state; it is something we cannot experience without explicitly aiming to do so.   TOM CHATFIELD

When you are practising trying to focus, your mind may well keep wanting to jump elsewhere, so as with learning any new skill you need to allow a little extra time to get work done. Luckily, our brains are quite malleable, so just because you've always done particular activities in particular ways doesn't mean that you can't lay down new neural pathways. In the longer term, you might want to take on an activity like meditation or Tai Chi in which you repeatedly practise stilling your mind and body (as well as deriving many other benefits which help you study). But there are short-term strategies you can use.

- Check how your body feels when you try to focus—if you are fidgety it's difficult to stay mentally focused, so take time to calm your body. Deliberately breathe and move slowly for a couple of minutes.

- Is your task one that can be accomplished while you walk around, listening or watching? Can you go for a walk while listening to a podcast, or stroll around your room while staying focused on an online video? You could do some routine physical task, as long as it doesn't require thought.

- Put your inclination to flit to good use. Recognise that you are used to skimming and searching and making choices about what to follow up. But instead of random browsing, decide on a purpose for it (for example, to identify new information or views that differ from yours) and stay with this focus. If you have a long task to get through, set a time limit for any deliberate scanning—perhaps use it as a warm-up activity.

- If you are reading written material which includes features such as boxes of text, graphs or illustrations, it can be tempting to jump away from the text. So start by previewing these features carefully to see what they suggest the whole item might be about. This is a useful study warm-up tactic, and it enriches your reading because when you move to a new page of written text or scroll to a new screen the features suggest the likely content of the material.

- If you need to absorb longer material which is mostly in paragraphs of text and you are unused to this, your mind is more likely to wander. Set yourself the goal of focusing on just one section (1–2 pages), and when you reach the end of the section ask yourself, 'What is the main idea or information in what I've just read?' Then decide on the next section to read, and repeat the strategy.

- Underline and maybe annotate key parts of the text as you read—this means that your mind is checking out and evaluating text and provides a small level of physical activity (see 'Notemaking and/or underlining', Chapter 10).

Focusing for a sustained time

To imagine prolonging your focus for over an hour or more, envisage becoming a skilled deep sea diver rather than simply swimming about on the surface. Such sustained focus is necessary for exams, as well as being a very useful life skill if you really want to achieve something substantial. Stories about young inventors and creators often give the impression of very bright people who have lots of fun coming up with new quickfire brilliant ideas. But the stories don't always portray the sheer hard work and persistence that followed as at least some of the ideas were explored and tested and followed through over a considerable period of time.

If your brain is always occupied with potentially being connected, always anticipating the next message or feeling phantom vibrations from your phone, does this mean that you find life boring if you are not always being stimulated and entertained by switching to something new? If frequent flitting is your dominant brain mode, you will need to train your mind to enjoy the satisfactions that come from engaging in one task for at least an hour or two; and to apply this ability to studying.

To practise focusing for longer periods:

- Before you start studying, give yourself a time limit of five minutes to check in with your social media before you spend ten times as long on studying.

- Or do it the other way round—reward yourself after an hour of study by allowing five minutes to check in before going back to study.

Creating brainspace

As well as focusing in, we need the capacity to expand our thinking out, to use our brain in different ways. Much of the discussion about social media has been on how they might change our relationships and connections with other people. This has obvious implications for how you study, for example, how much and how often and how you connect with other students. As a student, it's also worth thinking about how having social media as a constant part of your life might affect how you think, and how much room there is for reflecting on your thoughts.

If we spend time constantly connecting (actively or passively), does it reduce the likelihood that intuition and subconscious brain activity can happen? Many thinkers and writers have spoken about the vital role that random insights have played in their work, or about the benefits of doing some really focused work and then setting it aside and allowing their subconscious mind to go on working away at the task at another level. You may have had the experience of completing part of a piece of writing, setting it aside while involved in quite different activities, and discovering when you pick it up again that you can see clearly how it can be improved.

> The kind of thoughts that can emerge in 'empty' time in our lives—on a train, in the bath, walking, glancing out the window between turning the pages of a book—are impossible to reproduce either through dedicated digital planning or carefully arranged offline sessions.   TOM CHATFIELD

Create some brainspace for yourself so that your intuition, inspiration and your subconscious have a chance to come into play. Build some fragments of 'slow time' and contemplation into your life now and then, where you are still active but moving at a different pace and engaging fully with what you are doing by paying attention to your senses. (If you shut your eyes for a couple of minutes right now, how many sounds can you hear? What is the quietest sound you can pick up?) We might experience this engagement when on holiday, but you don't have to leave your everyday life to have moments of slow time—think of sitting watching a sunset, or savouring every single mouthful of your favourite food.

Concentrating

> 'How can you go on talking so quietly, head downwards?' Alice asked, as she dragged him out by the feet, and laid him in a heap on the bank.
>
> The Knight looked surprised at the question. 'What does it matter where my body happens to be?' he said. 'My mind goes on working all the same.'   LEWIS CARROLL

Keeping your mind on a task is not always something you have to work at—if you really want to know or do something you can concentrate easily, possibly for a long time. When concentrating fully you are so absorbed in what you are doing that you are unaware of time passing or of what is going on around you. Watch a small child building a sandcastle, or two friends involved in an intense debate.

However, if you are required to learn about a topic which doesn't particularly interest you, or to study for a purpose which doesn't coincide with yours, or if you have to study at times or in ways which are difficult for you—then you have to make an effort to focus and sustain your concentration. Have you ever noticed that during a lecture many of the audience suddenly become restless, or that shortly before the end of a lecture many people change position, check the time and prepare to leave? The length of time for which you can fully concentrate depends on factors such as your enthusiasm for what you are doing, your skill at a particular task, your emotional and physical state, and your surroundings at the time.

You don't have to assume the position of a Zen Buddhist or Rodin's Thinker or sit at a desk with pen in hand to concentrate. Why not let your ideas sort themselves out while you surf, watch the sunset, walk, or travel to college? When you do read and write, concentrating is not simply the act of reading every word on a page or putting lots of words onto paper or screen. Full concentration involves actively questioning and critically evaluating your material and integrating some of it into what you already know. This questioning, evaluating and integrating helps you understand what you read and organise what you write; it also helps you when you share your ideas and knowledge with others.

This section suggests a step-by-step process for concentrating more effectively in study sessions of at least an hour. These sessions might include reading, notemaking, writing, working on a spreadsheet, organising or editing material, or listening to an online lecture. Concentration during class or while working with other people involves similar principles.

> Experience as a mother has taught me a lot. Gone are the days of spending uninterrupted hours writing an essay or compiling a report. I'm lucky if I get half an hour now. But this maternal conditioning has its advantages. I'm now capable of making the maximum use of the time that is available and then switching off when family demands become pressing.
>
> Learning to use the available time to maximum advantage is one of the main secrets to success of the part-time student mother.   VIVIENNE

Have you consciously thought about your study habits—when, where and how you prefer to study? How do you settle down for a study session? For how long can you usually concentrate fully? What do you do when you find it difficult to concentrate? There will be times when you can only concentrate for short periods, or when you can't concentrate at all.

However, you can concentrate for longer periods and more effectively if you know how to cope with the distractions that arise at certain points in your study. While you are warming up or preparing for concentrated study you might be prone to procrastination, and your mind could be partly elsewhere. After you have been concentrating intensely for a short time, you might suddenly become impatient with your task, be unable to capture a particular thought or think through a specific problem clearly, and you might begin to feel stiff from sitting still. After sustained concentrated work, when you are reaching the end of your concentration span for a particular subject you feel less mentally alert. When you can no longer concentrate at all, outside thoughts or events intrude and you feel generally tired.

Warming up

Demanding physical exercise requires a warm-up session; so does sustained mental exercise and intense study. You can begin this mental warm-up during your previous activity. When travelling to the library, you can plan what you will research; while doing household chores you can mull over ideas for an essay; while finishing a non-study task, visualise yourself sitting down at your desk with a hot drink and beginning to study. When you actually sit down at your study place, deliberately preparing your mind for study can motivate you, help eliminate conflict or anxieties from your mind, focus your thoughts on the task at hand, and increase your ability to understand what you learn so that you remember it more easily (see 'How you learn to remember', Chapter 5).

If you have difficulty settling down to study, the following suggestions may help.

1   Consider how you feel emotionally and physically. If you feel good, direct this energy to learning. If you are definitely not in the state of mind for studying, decide whether you need to study at this particular time. If you don't need to, plan another specific time to work. If you do need to, use techniques that help you set your problems aside (see 'Emotions', Chapter 1). Try a brief energetic walk, a run around the block, a cup of tea, or a very short chat with a friend.

2   Turn off any electronic devices which are not directly related to your study and put them out of reach. The world will still be there when you return. If not being near them makes you anxious, keep them hidden nearby and on silent.

3   Seat yourself comfortably, with everything you need at hand—books, blank paper, a drink, disks, or lecture notes (see 'Where you study', below).

4   Decide on your time limits for this study session. Take into account your non-study commitments, then set a minimum study time to become involved in your subject. Set a maximum time, so you don't feel overwhelmed by apparently endless work and so you can focus your energy fully. Don't make these times so inflexible that you feel you must stop work precisely at the time planned. Plan to reward yourself after you have completed your study by doing something you particularly enjoy—go to the beach, visit a friend, watch a special video or prepare your favourite snack.

5   Decide what to study while your mind is fresh. Will you start with the subject or activity you find easiest? Will you tackle an assignment that has been worrying you or which you have been intending to do for a long time?

Think about the study activities from which you have to choose. You might, for example:

— read for a tutorial paper or an essay

— find and bookmark an appropriate website

— edit the final draft of an assignment

— write the first draft of an assignment, a lab report, a short story or a journal entry

— prepare an annotated bibliography or graphics for an assignment

— listen to an online lecture, or

— interpret information from a graph.

Set yourself a clear specific target. If you have a large task, planning to tackle it in stages, one section at a time, makes it easier.

6   Begin your study with a *brief* warm-up task which helps you to concentrate. Use this task only if it is necessary—not if it is a form of procrastination.

● Do a couple of short routine tasks which are part of the subject, such as filing lecture notes or compiling a list of important vocabulary.

● Revise previous work in the area—for example, summarise notes or write comments on a discussion. This revision brings ideas to the front of your mind and can give you a sense of achievement if you are overwhelmed by the study before you.

● Foreshadow a topic by asking yourself 'Why am I studying this particular topic?' 'To whom do I want to communicate my ideas?' For example, are you studying to clarify ideas for your own benefit, or to prepare for a discussion group? Brainstorm your topic by jotting down as many ideas on it as possible—don't worry about the order of these ideas or how far-fetched they seem. Fill your mind with the subject.

● Preview a book you will use (see 'Previewing', Chapter 10), or read a section of the book and try to identify the central idea (see 'Reading for an argument or theme', Chapter 10).

If you still have trouble concentrating, ask yourself why and what you can do about it. What must you change to help you concentrate better? In the next section there are suggestions for coping with problems such as tension or a noisy study place.

Sustaining concentration

'Fan her head!' the Red Queen anxiously interrupted. 'She'll be feverish after so much thinking.'   LEWIS CARROLL

Some people study mostly in short, intense bursts with frequent breaks in between; others need to study for long periods to become fully immersed in their task. Your concentration span also varies for different activities and how engaged you are in what you are doing.

- When studying intensely, you occasionally become aware you are distracted by something and feel impatient with your work. Set yourself another five minutes in which to work. Then if your impatience still persists, give in to it. After the five minutes, take a short break while you physically loosen up—stand up and stretch, walk around, and consciously relax. Leave your study spot for five minutes or so—get a drink, glance through a newspaper, or organise your desk. Don't take a break for too long or you may require another warm up.

- If something from your personal life keeps intruding, jot down a quick note about it and tell yourself that you can come back to it when you've finished a solid burst of study.

- When you've been studying for a long time so that your concentration is diminishing and can't be rejuvenated by a short break, you need to recharge mentally. Remotivate yourself by reviewing the material you have just covered and trying to get an overall picture of it. This often gives you a feeling of achievement as well as reminding you why you are studying a particular topic.

- Look ahead at what you intend to do next. Preview the rest of the book or chapter. Jot down or voice-record ideas for the next section of an assignment. Switch to another subject and work on that until it becomes stale, then return to your first subject or go on to a third.

Losing concentration

Try to recognise when you can't concentrate any further. There is no point in believing you are still studying when you are simply staring at the words on a page, when you repeatedly can't find the words you want, or when your mind is far away.

- When you feel you are losing concentration, quickly review what you have been studying. If your task is part of a large piece of work, reflect on where the part fits into the whole and which part you will tackle next.

- Write down a few small very specific tasks you need to do when you come back to the subject. This is a simple but effective strategy for getting started next time.

- Decide when you will study again—in an hour's time, the next morning, or a day later.

- Then stop studying and relax. Reward yourself—enjoy that special reward you promised yourself earlier.

> I do not happen to be a believer in the cliché that 'Virtue is its own reward.' As far as I am concerned, the reward for virtue should be at least a chocolate sundae, and preferably a cruise to the Bahamas.   BARBARA SHER

Where you study

We can study better in some environments than others, and almost certainly find that we can complete particular types of tasks more effectively depending on where we are.

Location

Where do you prefer to study? Why? Does a relatively impersonal environment such as a library help?

Are the materials you need readily available where you study?

Are there other people around where you study? Are they also studying? Do they help or hinder your learning? Why?

- Decide whether you study more effectively at home or elsewhere. If necessary, try to reorganise your time so that you can study in the location where you learn most effectively.

- If you have to study in a particular place—for example, because that is where you have free time online—it is important to make this environment as conducive to study as possible.

Study spots

You say I'm well read.
Thank you but—
I owe my deep and liberal knowledge
To the 100 watt bulb
in the loo
And not college.

MARGARET NORTON

The association of one place with a particular study activity helps you settle down more quickly and also enables you to leave it behind when you finish. You might choose a comfortable chair to read a book, but prefer a library workstation when organising essay research notes. If you have a room of your own, you will organise study sessions differently from a person who works at the kitchen table or in a shared bedroom, or in the library. It is not essential to have ideal surroundings before you can study effectively, but often you can make changes that improve your study situations considerably.

If you don't have a quiet study place at home where you can leave your work spread out, can you arrange one? How?

What objects on your work space help you study—a favourite pen, lots of scribble pads, a bunch of flowers? Why?

Can you study effectively outdoors?

- If possible, find or create one or two places where you can regularly study—a desk in your bedroom at home, a corner table in a library, or a chair in a quiet room at a friend's house. You may be able to screen off a corner of a room or move a table into one corner of a backyard workshop.

- Have any technology you need well set up—you don't need technical interruptions.

- Create a work space which includes objects that prompt you to study and is organised according to your needs for space and order. Having your own work space, no matter how small, is preferable to packing away your papers and books each time after you use them.

Comfort

You concentrate better on studying if you are physically relaxed (but not too relaxed!), for example, if you are sitting in a comfortable position, with lighting that cuts down eye strain, and without distracting noise.

Are you more comfortable when studying at a table or desk, or when sitting on a couch or bed? Do any of these positions help you study for a sustained period?

If your study places are too warm, too cold or too stuffy, how can you alter this?

What type of noise distracts you? How long can you concentrate fully with 'background' music playing?

Do you know which exercises help you loosen up after a stint at the computer?

Do you have ergonomically appropriate furniture?

- Prevent eye strain by avoiding glare or uneven lighting on a book or work surface. Light the whole room as evenly as possible, and adjust your position and lighting depending on whether you are reading a book or screen. Prop up your book or screen at a constant angle so that your eyes don't have to keep adjusting to different distances, and every so often rest your eyes by looking at something further away or outside a window.

- To reduce noise distraction, avoid irregular noise, use ear plugs or headphones or white noise, or study when your household is at its quietest. If you like to study with music on, be honest about which music helps you concentrate and which actually distracts you. For example, check if music with lyrics makes it difficult to pay attention to the words you are reading. Try studying sometimes without any music at all.

- If you are cold, put on an extra layer of clothes, wrap yourself in a blanket or turn on a heater at a low setting rather than attempting to study in a stuffy overheated room. If the weather is hot, study at the cooler times of day or find an airconditioned place.

- When using a computer, most of us inevitably slump. Check an online video for tips about how to sit so that you are comfortable for as long as possible, and every so often get up and loosen up. This is particularly important if you are using a laptop for prolonged periods.

- There is appropriate study furniture available such as ergonomic chairs. If you can't afford these, check them out so that you can improvise something similar with what you already have.

It takes time and practice to become aware of and create your own study patterns and to discover the concentration techniques that you find most helpful. Being mostly in control of when and how you study is crucial to learning independently.

TEN TIPS

1   Approach time planning as a practical tactic to make your life easier, not as something that will only make you feel guilty or anxious if you don't live up to it perfectly.

2   Make a habit of doing a reality check of how much time you actually have available after planning in appointments and other essentials.

3   For each day, identify one key task for the morning, one for the afternoon and one for the evening, choosing tasks which are important and preferably not urgent. Make these the first things in any daily plan and allow enough time to complete them.

4   Allow for 'just in case' time—the unexpected will happen.

5   Breaking big tasks down into small stages helps you work out realistically what needs to be done when; and small tasks feel more manageable.

6   Have a list of ten-minute tasks you can tap into at any time to give you a feeling of achievement.

7   If you spend much of your day flicking from one electronic tool to another, training your brain to stay focused on one task for a sustained time will mean that you get work done more quickly and with fewer mistakes.

8   If a crisis comes up or you are suddenly feeling overwhelmed, try the following. Stop whatever you are doing. Grin. Deliberately go s-l-o-w-l-y for just 5 minutes—breathe slowly, speak slowly, move slowly.

9   If you are feeling generally inundated with the amount of work to be done, actually doing an hour of work can make you feel better.

10   Any good time plan should have special rewards built into it.

Learning and remembering

5

Oft in the stilly night,
When the mind is fumbling fuzzily,
I brood about how little I know.
And know that little so muzzily.

OGDEN NASH

○○○ *Why do you remember the things you do?*

Why do you forget?

If you want to know how to ride a bicycle, you practise with great concentration and persist with your riding despite the occasional spill. Once you can ride with skill, even if you sell your bicycle you always remember how to ride one.

A small child who wants to learn how to build a tower of blocks concentrates intensely while trying various ways to make the blocks stay put one on top of the other. After repeated attempts, she comes to understand the most effective way to build a tower of blocks. This skill is later remembered and transferred to a new context to build other towers of toys, books or cushions.

If you concentrate while learning what you want to know, you are more likely to understand and be able to use it. Remembering what you learn well enough to use it depends on why and how you learn. If you learn to ride a bicycle because you want to, and if you learn at your own pace, you easily recall the skill. You are less likely to remember it if you learn because someone else decides you should and teaches you in the way they think best. Whether or not you want to learn depends on you—what you already know, how you learn, your current interests and how you feel at the time.

Filters on what you learn and remember

> The past which we remember is partial and distorted; it has been edited by the censors to exclude events which are disturbingly painful or disturbingly pleasurable . . . The history we recall tends to be propaganda which preserves the status quo of personal identity.   SAM KEEN

Your mind and body unconsciously select and interpret what you learn and remember from your daily life, and what you remember changes with time. Five people who witness the same car accident give five different versions even if asked shortly afterwards to describe what happened, and a year later each person will have yet another version of the episode. They may even 'recall' things that didn't actually happen—events that could have been expected to occur but didn't, or details of a 'long argument' between the drivers that was in fact only a couple of remarks. What each of the five recollects is their personal experience of the accident, modified by their experiences in the meantime.

○○○ *What do you remember about today?*

What immediately comes to mind?

Try recalling in order everything that has happened since you woke up.

What do you remember from yesterday?

What do you remember from last week? Why?

What memories do you have of your last birthday?

Do you remember your first day at school?

What is your earliest memory?

Spend about half an hour answering these questions. If you finish in less time, go back and see how much more detail you can recall. Can you work out why you recalled what you did?

Share the questions with someone else. How do your memories differ from theirs? How are they the same? Why?

> 'I could tell you my adventures—beginning from this morning,' said Alice a little timidly; 'but it's no use going back to yesterday, because I was a different person then.'
> LEWIS CARROLL

○○○ *Now stop for a moment, and let yourself become aware of everything your senses are telling you. Of what are you most aware? Smells? Sights? Sounds? Tastes? Touch?*

After your first sense impressions, what else do you begin to notice?

What thoughts are running through your mind?

Trying to be fully aware of even one fleeting moment makes you realise how much you forget, perhaps for a short time, or perhaps for all of your life. Some things you need to 'forget', in the sense of taking them for granted. Imagine if you wanted to be fully aware and decided to consciously breathe every breath. You would soon give up because you wouldn't have time for anything else. Other things you 'forget' by pushing them below the surface of your mind—items that have little interest for you, that have unpleasant associations or that don't fit with your view of the world.

> A world view is a paradigm. It is all of the assumptions that you hold that all build up, and it is like a framework that we have in our heads, and then whatever we see out there we filter through that framework.
> JULIA HOBSON

Sometimes you forget things you would like to remember. Have you ever read a childhood autobiography and marvelled at the amount of detail the writer recollects? Few people remember such detail without making a conscious effort to do so. Keeping a diary or blog or taking photographs can make you more aware of your surroundings and help you remember them. Photos or diaries also help you realise how much you forget. Have you ever read back over a diary or blog entry from some time ago and been amazed at how your memory of that time has changed and how much you have forgotten?

○○○ *Try it now. See if you can find a letter, a poem or a diary you wrote, or a photograph you took. Look at it and conjure up your memories of that time.*

Remembering isn't just something you set your mind to do—**your senses** are involved too. Do you have a good memory for faces? For phone numbers? Or for jokes? Some people remember mostly what they see, and can recall how to spell a word after seeing it once; others remember what they hear and can repeat verbatim snatches of dialogue from a movie (see 'Senses', Chapter 1).

Your background, experiences and world view lead to knowledge and beliefs about yourself and your world which influence your awareness at any moment. If you have been a keen surfer or sailor for several years, you are more likely to know and remember how the wind and waves change from one season to another than will someone who plays cards for their recreation. If you have worked as a carpenter, you can pick up and remember new information about the craft because of your previous knowledge.

Your active interest in a subject increases what you remember about it. A football fan can tell you in detail about the previous wins of her club, but if she is not interested in horseracing she may have no idea who won the Melbourne Cup. If you are concerned about the role of women in Australian society, you will remember facts from a history of Australia which others without your concern wouldn't notice. Interest in a topic can be kindled by another person's enthusiasm. You may remember a conversation with someone you met at a party because you were entertained by them. Skilled teachers who care about their subjects can hold your attention so that you remember far more than expected.

How you feel emotionally and physically also influences what you learn and how vividly you remember it. If you are alert, perhaps because you are feeling exuberant or uncomfortable, your chances of remembering that particular time more fully increase. Your surroundings influence how you feel and are part of what you remember. Have you ever picked up a book that you once read and been reminded of when and where you read it? And items you can recall in one situation you can't remember at all in another.

Reflection is a vital component of learning and remembering. If following an experience you take the time and create personal space to reflect on that experience— to let your impressions, feelings and ideas about it gel in your mind—you are more likely to remember the experience and to be able to draw on it in a new situation. If we are busy we often fail to make sense of our learning, or we lose much of it because we don't take the time to reflect.

Your background and experiences, your interests and world view, your senses and current state of being act as filters on your life, both past and present. They affect what you are most aware of and what you reflect on and learn, and so influence what you remember from the information you are offered.

Why remember?

Memory is the mother of imagination, reason and skill . . . This is the companion, this is the tutor, the poet, the library with which you travel.   MARK VAN DOREN

Remembering enables you to learn more about yourself and your world. Newborn human babies seem to operate mostly by reflexes rather than by consciously knowing and remembering. But toddlers in their second year are able to call on what they have learned, and can form a concept such as 'dog-ness' by remembering the characteristics of dogs that aren't present and comparing them with a dog that is. As an adult, the more you can remember, the less you have to re-learn. The more you can remember concepts, the more you can solve problems and cope with new situations and ideas. If you can recall the fundamentals of Darwin's theory of evolution, you can move on to further related knowledge without repeatedly relearning the theory.

When you find **pleasure** in what you learn, you probably want to remember it. Perhaps you do this unconsciously because your senses and curiosity are more active, or perhaps you deliberately heighten your sense of awareness. You may relive the experiences in your mind, in a diary or through photographs. You may learn by heart the words of a song that please you. Maybe you want to remember an intriguing idea, so you can contemplate it further.

If you **apply what you learn**, you are more likely to remember it. To cross the road without having an accident, you learn and use an array of skills that become habits, or unconsciously recollected knowledge. If you need to prune fruit trees, you have a reason for using and remembering what you learn about pruning. If you want to use an idea in a discussion paper, you try to understand the idea and its links to your topic so that you remember it fully enough to explain it to others.

Some things you are required to remember for **reasons not directly your own**. You might enjoy learning the manual skills of flying an aeroplane but not want to study the navigation theory required for a pilot's licence. Although it is important to know where and how to find information, in exams you will have to remember the information yourself. In your formal education you are expected to remember material so that you demonstrate that you have achieved the learning outcomes and so that your progress towards unit objectives can be evaluated and recorded according to tangible criteria. For example, you may be required:

— in an exam, to show that you remember and understand the rudiments of a particular subject

— in an essay, to recall information well enough to argue your position

— in a report, to remember and describe a sequence of steps in an experiment

— in a tutorial, to review and present a summary of your reading on a topic

— for a seminar paper, to remember material in the short term, such as dates or data, or

— to remember information and skills for long periods so that you can take a final exam, or transfer them to a subsequent unit or a future job.

These requirements are based on the assumptions that in formal education there is certain knowledge worth having, certain learning skills and abilities worth acquiring, and a specific sequence and time limit in which this learning should be acquired. These assumptions shape why, what and how you learn and remember. Even if you disagree with these assumptions, they will still influence your learning and remembering if you decide to accept them as a means to your own ends. For example, even if some unit material doesn't interest you, you may study it for an exam, because you accept the exam as necessary to acquire a qualification you want.

How you learn to remember

'But what did the Dormouse say?' one of the jury asked.
'That I can't remember,' said the Hatter.
'You must remember,' remarked the King, 'or I'll have you executed.'   LEWIS CARROLL

We have short-term and long-term memory. **Short-term memory** lasts less than a minute and enables us to process information, but there are limits to how much material we can hold in this working memory. Sometimes to process essential information, we need to limit the amount of information coming in. We choose to do this in situations such as when we suspend a conversation to focus on safely crossing a busy road, or when we screen out background noise in order to concentrate on understanding a key article. One of the disadvantages of being constantly connected to electronic devices is that part of your brief working memory can be occupied in anticipating a message or a call. To help keep information in your working memory, you can repeat it several times (such as a phone number). You can also manipulate the information to look for structures, construct patterns, detect sequences or separate main points from details.

Our **long-term memory** involves two types of knowledge. One is implicit or 'procedural' knowledge, or knowing *how* to do things. Once skills such as how to ride a bicycle or preview an article are learned well, we can use them without consciously having to recall what to do. Explicit or 'declarative' knowledge is like our personal encyclopedia, a knowing *that* certain information is 'true' or 'real', for example, facts (such as the population of Australia) or concepts (such as the definition of 'epistemology') and experiences (such as a broken elbow at age five or an apple eaten for lunch).

Each computer and device may be unique, and have a unique history, but it is not this uniqueness that makes them what they are. Often, they function despite their histories, as anyone familiar with the symptoms of operating slowdown will know . . . Classifying information neatly and keeping the operational sector clean is best. It's a fine lesson for the realm of work and productivity—but the exact inverse of what it takes to develop a well-stocked mind.   TOM CHATFIELD

You are likely to remember what you learn if your curiosity about a subject remains alive. To sustain your curiosity and to transfer material from your short-term to long-term memory, there are certain prerequisites for learning.

What is important to you

You need to learn according to who you are—your purposes, your background and experiences, your interests, your world view, your questions (see 'Beliefs and values', Chapter 1). You are much more likely to recall information to which you pay close attention in the first place.

When you are ready

You need to learn at a time and place and in a way that makes sense to you, at 'the moment of readiness'. You are not always ready to learn during specified hours each week in a lecture theatre or when you have free time after a busy day. If you are not ready, it is more difficult to concentrate on and to understand what you are supposed to learn, and you are more likely to forget what you do learn unless you use memory techniques such as those mentioned in this chapter (see also 'Concentrating', Chapter 4). One advantage of studying your units online is that you can often learn at times and places that suit you.

A way that suits you

> I never was from boyhood one of those for whom skill came easily. The throwing of a stone at a mark was a conscious effort of concentration rather than an instinctive fling. It was the same with fishing. Every cast was the result of drill, theory and earnest business.
> PATRICK O'BRIAN

If you have some insight into how you learn informally, your formal learning can be enhanced. Some people have strong visual memories, some learn by doing, others learn by discussion, others by reading and making notes. Which ways suit you best? If you want to find out about kangaroos, do you go to look at them in the zoo or try to study them in their natural habitats? Do you ask other people about them? Do you read books on the subject? Do you take a course in marsupial physiology? Do you search the Internet for information? Learning in a way that suits you enhances your ability to remember.

Building on what you already know

> I can give you nothing that has not already its being within yourself. I can throw open to you no picture-gallery but your own soul . . . I help you to make your own world visible. That is all.
> HERMANN HESSE

You need to learn by building on your prior knowledge, skills and experience, on the patterns and beliefs that shape your world and your language. Even if you know only a little about a new area, having a context in which to understand this new field helps you remember it more clearly. Have you ever attempted to read a book you don't understand and then some time later read and remembered it more easily? By the second reading you have acquired new knowledge to which you can relate the book's contents.

If you are required to reproduce facts that you can't relate to something familiar, you may have to resort to rote learning and mnemonics, acrostics and rhymes such as '30 days hath September, April, June and November'. But to transfer information from short-term to long-term memory we first need to link it in a meaningful way to knowledge we already have. Then it becomes possible for the new knowledge to be consolidated and stored for future recall. Some examples follow.

- Learn the principles which underlie a good book review before reviewing a book on a new topic, and your recall of the book will be more thorough.

- To help you remember the intricacies of Darwin's theory of evolution, test it against species' differences with which you are familiar.

- When learning and remembering new material, use analogies, similes and metaphors based on comparisons with familiar ideas and information. For example, the metaphor 'the body politic' helps you think about a political system in new ways by comparing it with your own body; so what you learn from such a metaphor is likely to stay in your mind.

Suspending previous knowledge and beliefs

Unless you are self reflective, you don't recognise that no matter who you are, you're operating within a particular conceptual framework, a particular way of seeing and way of doing. PATSY HALLEN

There may be times when you are required to suspend your previous understanding, and to think about and reassemble information in an entirely different way. This can be disorienting and it can be difficult to learn and remember the reshaped information. For example, you may have first learned about the causes of drug addiction in a psychology unit based on a paradigm that centred on changing the individual addict. If you then take a sociology unit which examines the social construction of individuality and posits that individuals change through shifts in society, you will need to reorder your information and ideas within this new framework. Making shifts like this requires you to reflect on and question your world view. Although it is tempting and comforting to hold on to your entrenched view of the world, making an effort to understand, accept and remember different and possibly conflicting views is very challenging but can be rewarding. Being aware of the influence of your personal view and being willing to accommodate different perspectives, is crucial to thinking critically (see 'Critical thinking', Chapter 3).

Frameworks are not given; they are not uncontroversial. We can always step outside the framework in which a position has its natural home and we can try looking at the phenomenon from a different point of view. Our understanding can be challenged; and radically so.

This is a characteristic of genuinely *higher* education. Are students encouraged to recognise that what counts as truth can be viewed and evaluated from a number of perspectives?   RONALD BARNETT

When you come to learn about a new topic in a class, study session or assignment, start by spending some time considering what you already think you know about it. Think about what you want to learn on the topic and, if you have a choice, how you want to learn. This preparation provides reference points or a framework for your learning and enhances your ability to remember.

Selecting what to learn

. . . Funes not only remembered every leaf on every tree of every wood, but even every one of the times he had perceived or imagined it. He determined to reduce all of his past experience to some seventy thousand recollections, which he would later define numerically. Two considerations dissuaded him: the thought that the task was interminable and the thought that it was useless.   JORGE LUIS BORGES

Even if you are able to learn what, how and when you want, you can't possibly remember everything. Every minute you 'learn' a great deal of information, but most of it you remember only if prompted. To retain some things, you need to 'forget' others, focusing your conscious awareness to select what you take in and learn. To remember what a teacher is saying, focus your attention on just that and let go of other thoughts which impinge on your awareness, such as what the teacher is wearing.

It is essential that you consciously select what you want to remember. As a student you are confronted with large amounts of information, and your research in libraries or on the Internet is likely to yield more information than you can possibly use or absorb. You quickly discover there is little point in trying to remember it all and that some time needs to be spent:

— clarifying why you need the information

— selecting what you need to remember, and

— deciding how to record and retrieve it (see 'Recording and filing references', Chapter 8).

In your written work and discussions, for example, your time needs to be spent selecting central points to remember; and you might choose to remember a particularly striking example to illustrate a point when several other examples would have been just as valid.

How much material you need to concentrate on and remember for tests and exams varies according to unit learning outcomes and objectives and the preferences of individual teachers. Find out from your unit coordinators and teachers how much detail you need to learn and remember (see 'Using learning outcomes to guide your study', Chapter 3). Generally, you will need to remember frameworks, concepts, theories and ideas developed in a unit, and be able to recall sufficient detail to explain them. In a biology unit, for example, if the 'greenhouse effect' has featured in discussion, essay topics and readings, you would be well advised to learn and remember the basic principles underlying the effect. Similarly, if the concept of 'power' has featured prominently in a social science unit, it is wise to study and remember the different meanings of this concept and to concentrate on the way it is used in the unit. In an exam you may need to write an essay showing you understand the concept or you may need to apply it to a real-life situation.

Learning thoroughly

> Our memories have been impaired by print; we know we need not 'burden our memories' with matter which we can find merely by taking a book from the shelf. When a large proportion of the population is illiterate and books are scarce, memories are often tenacious to a degree outside modern western experience.   J. CHAYTOR

Once you have selected what you want or have to learn, you need to learn that material thoroughly. Even material you thought would be dull or difficult can be unexpectedly interesting when you set out to learn it thoroughly, particularly if you turn the learning into a game or challenge.

Different ways for the same material

Take in the same information in as many ways as you can. In your learning utilise as many of your senses as possible, especially your strongest sense. If a friend explains to you the differences between a ketch and a schooner, you are more likely to remember these if you also see a diagram of each and then sail on them. If you read about a topic as well as discuss it and listen to a lecture on it, your recall of what you have learned will be greater. This approach is particularly important if you are trying to remember complex material like the elements of existentialist philosophy or the intricacies and implications of Einstein's theory of relativity. For some people, such material can only be understood and remembered after different and repeated encounters.

Patterns and principles

> Previously we learned more and more about less and less. In future people will need to know in a very real sense less and less about more and more. The basic required skills will be to understand patterns quickly and to make sense of their meaning in specific times and places, rather than to solve problems within previously understood approaches.   ROBERT THEOBALD

If you learn by comprehending the patterns and principles, the structures and relationships which link individual ideas and information, it is easier to remember these items than trying to do so bit by bit. Learning in patterns also makes it easier to recall information you thought you wouldn't need, since you can search for it by reconstructing the patterns in which you learned it. Use patterned notes, concept maps, flow diagrams or charts with different colours to summarise information from a lecture, a chapter of a book, a section of a unit or a topic. Convert numerical information embedded in text to sketch graphs or tables, and vice versa. Depending on the way you remember information, colourful mind maps can make recall easier because they show at a glance central concepts or ideas and the links between them.

The form of argument used in critical thinking, with its thesis and supporting reasons, provides a pattern or structure into which you can organise much of the material you need to learn (see 'Genres', Chapter 7). Patterned notes can also be used to clearly separate a thesis from supporting premises, a theme from supporting material or main points from details (see 'Notemaking and/or underlining', Chapter 10).

Before, during and after classes and study

'—but there's one great advantage in it, that one's memory works both ways.'

'I'm sure mine only works one way,' Alice remarked. 'I can't remember things before they happen.'

'It's a poor sort of memory that only works backwards,' the Queen remarked.

LEWIS CARROLL

Thorough learning from a class or study session partly depends on what you do before, during and afterwards. Many of the chapters in this book use this principle as their framework, and you will remember more of what you learn if you use the approaches they describe. 'Concentrating' in Chapter 4, for example, describes warming up, concentrating fully and concluding a study session. Chapter 11 on lectures discusses how to make the most of a lecture by preparing, questioning as you listen, and reviewing and using the material soon afterwards.

Study session techniques

There are techniques you can use in a study session to enhance your ability to remember what you learn.

- Vary the length of your study sessions according to the material. Your mind can only take in so many statistics at once, while in contrast you need time to understand a philosophical argument well enough to remember it.

- Learn from the general to the specific. Take in the big picture by previewing for the thesis or main idea, and then focus on the supporting reasons or specific details.

- Break the information into manageable chunks and focus on them one at a time. This is particularly useful if there are no obvious patterns or principles to the material or if you are having difficulty remembering new material.

- When learning details from two similar subjects, study a contrasting subject in between so you don't confuse information. This applies, for example, if you are trying to remember dates from two similar history courses, or studying verb tenses in Spanish and Italian. Avoiding interference between subjects is especially important in the early stages of learning and for long-term recall.

- When trying to remember concepts, studying related subjects creates associations, because the differences and similarities between them enhance your understanding of each. For example, this approach can help when studying concepts of human nature in Rousseau's philosophy and in humanistic psychology.

- Use your body as you study. Get up and move around. Gesticulate. Read aloud. Talk to yourself. Pretend you are debating with someone. Explain the information to a fictitious person.

Memory keys

One way of consciously remembering is to précis the essential chunks of what you have selected to learn, and then find memory keys for each of these parts. These keys can then be used to unlock your memory of each part and its associated details. You unconsciously use such keys when an unexpected memory is evoked because you hear a particular piece of music, walk past a certain street or drink a once favourite drink. In your formal learning you can use memory keys consciously, for example, to recall the discussion in a seminar. Summarise the argument and structure of the discussion, represent these by key words, phrases or images, and use these keys to review and recall the discussion.

What would you choose as memory keys to help you remember each paragraph in this section on 'Learning thoroughly'?

Transferring and using what you learn

What is . . . central to a properly educative endeavour is the identification of what is involved in transferring . . . knowledge, learning, understanding or skill gained in one cognitive domain and/or social context to adapt, modify or extend it in such a way as to be able to apply it in another.   DAVID BRIDGES

Transferring the knowledge and skills that you learn in one context to another context is crucial to your learning. You will rarely use information in the same context as that in which you learned it. You need to assess a situation and transfer and adapt your prior learning to the new context. When you begin higher education you will bring knowledge and skills from your previous studies, work and life that are transferable to your learning. For example, if you worked in an office you will have developed organisational skills that you will be able to use in your studies.

As you progress with your studies you acquire knowledge and skills that you transfer and use in future units. For example, if you learn to write an argumentative essay in a first year unit, it is important to transfer (and build on) what you learned to other first year units and to your second and third year studies. Similarly, the knowledge and skills that you learn during your degree studies are designed to be used and transferred into other contexts and into your life generally.

Unless you continue your learning by recalling it, you forget even things you wanted to learn. Going over your day helps fix it in your episodic memory, and recording the day in a journal or blog makes it available for you to relive, to 'use' again. Discussing the ideas from a lecture with other people who have shared it has a similar effect, with the added dimension of the others' perceptions now becoming part of yours. And when you think back over an event from your day, what you remember depends on what has happened to you in the meantime, even if that time has been very brief. For example, if you describe an event in your journal, your description of the event is influenced by the surroundings in which you write and these too become part of your memory.

Use what you learn as soon, as often and as widely as possible if you want to remember it. You recall the alphabet easily because you have used it over and over again in different situations. When you first learn to ride a bike, if you practise every day and in many different conditions you are likely to remember the skill more quickly than if you practise once a week and have to spend some of that weekly time in relearning. Unless you have an exceptional memory for figures, you are unlikely to remember statistics such as the population of Singapore unless you use them frequently. If you want to remember an important idea, write it down and try it out on various people. You will come to a new understanding of it each time and remember the original idea more fully. To remember material for long-term use (perhaps for exams or future employment), use it by revising it periodically and relating it to new knowledge you have acquired.

Exams

You are likely to need to remember material in exams and tests. Your memory in exams depends as much on being prepared for the exam situation as it does on learning material well. Even if you know the material, you may be unable to recall it effectively if you become very anxious in an exam room or if you have a learning disability which means you tire easily. 'Dealing with difficult situations' in Chapter 3 suggests a technique that can be applied to exams.

Imagine yourself in an exam room, faced with a question that requires an essay answer. You have the sinking feeling that all you know on the topic could be expressed in a few sentences. What do you do? Panic instantly? Start scribbling furiously in the hope of inspiration? Leave the exam room? Most students worry about not being able to answer exam questions and imagine themselves in this situation. But their imagination stops there. You can help yourself cope with this problem ahead of time by also imagining what you will do about it.

Now continue imagining that you put down your pen, sit back, stretch a bit, and take several deep breaths. You read the question again, slowly and carefully. You pick up your pen and start to jot down anything which comes to mind on the topic. You don't try to order this knowledge, but concentrate instead on recalling as much of it as you can. If you start feeling rushed, you pause deliberately for a few moments and then continue. When you feel you have all your knowledge before you, you check that each item is relevant to the question. You then organise the information into two or three main points. When this is done, you start writing, concentrating on saying what you want as clearly as you can. You avoid the temptation to pad your answer with irrelevant facts, long-winded sentences or complex language. If at any stage you find yourself feeling rushed, you stop for a minute and concentrate on relaxing. You may just sit and look out the window as a way of relaxing. When you have finished saying what you want to, you sit back and feel pleased at knowing more about the question than you thought you did. Then you check over your essay carefully to make sure it answers the question and is clearly expressed. Finish.

Imagining the worst *and* imagining how you will handle it cannot guarantee you will answer the question successfully. Nothing can. However, it does make that outcome a lot more likely.

Part of the 'imagine the worst' approach is to think beforehand about why you are worried about an exam. Is it because you might fail a unit, of which the exam is part? Imagine yourself failing the unit, and then go on to imagine other possibilities once you have failed. Can you sit for a supplementary exam, or repeat the unit? Think about why you want to pass the unit. Can you realise your aims in other ways? It can be invaluable to realise that there are often alternatives to some of the difficulties you face. If you know that you always panic in exam situations, despite knowing your subject well, it may be possible to arrange with your teacher for alternative forms of assessment. You may be able to select a unit where exams don't count for all or most of your final assessment.

Look at Table 5.1 'Exam techniques' to help you remember what you have learned when you read the questions in a limited-time, 'closed book' exam. And whatever else you do, make the most of what you remember by reading and analysing each question very carefully. You can know your subject well but you will not get a good grade if you misread a question or answer only part of it.

Look back at the section on 'Why remember?' What do you remember from this section?

Why do you recall this material?

How could you remember this section more effectively?

Without remembering, each day, each event, each moment would be a totally new experience. How fully you remember depends largely on how thoroughly you learned in the first place, and the material you recall is as unique to you as is why, what and how you learn. As you learn in your formal education, think about how you can learn in order to remember more effectively.

TABLE
5.1   **Exam techniques**

a   If you are uptight before an exam, try to relax (see 'Tension and relaxation', Chapter 1).

b   When you are given the exam paper, before you start writing, take the following steps.
- Carefully read the instructions which should tell you how you are expected to answer the paper, how many questions you should answer and the value of each.
- Read through all the questions.
- If you have a choice, decide which questions you will answer or at least which questions you will do first.
- Decide how much time you will need to spend on each question because of its value and according to how thoroughly you can answer it.
- Decide on the order in which you will answer the questions. Answer first the questions you know most about and that are easiest. Then if you run out of time, at least you do so on a subject that will earn you fewer marks.

c   When you are allowed to start writing, jot down any thoughts or ideas you have about each of the questions you will answer. These jottings can be useful memory triggers when you actually come to answer the question.

d   For essay questions, analyse the wording of the question and plan your essay. Include your plan in your exam booklet.

e   Write as quickly and as clearly as you can.

f   For multiple-choice questions, don't waste time over questions you can't answer. Be careful about guessing answers if points are deducted for incorrect responses.

g   When answering mathematical problems, include all your calculations. Even if your answer is incorrect, the examiner can see where you went wrong and you may gain some points for your method.

h   If you have a memory lapse in the middle of a question, leave a few pages, go to another question and later return to the previous question.

i   In an essay-type exam, answer the required number of questions. Answer fully the questions you know well and write as much as you can on the others. Make sure you write on the set question.

j   If you run out of time, jot down the main points you were going to make.

k   Try to leave time at the end of the exam to read over your answers. Correcting poor expression or spelling or checking your calculations can make an important difference.

TEN TIPS

1   Try to identify the sort of things you usually remember easily and what you find difficult to recall.

2   If you can't recall a piece of information, think back on how much attention you paid to it at the time.

3   If you easily recall visual information, such as images, graphs or flow charts, try creating mind maps of the knowledge you need to remember.

4   Learn about how short-term memory functions and what it is needed for.

5   Become familiar with strategies to transfer learning from your short-term to long-term memory.

6   Prepare your mind for absorbing knowledge on a new topic by first taking five minutes to call up information that you think you already know about it.

7   Look for underlying connections and patterns and frameworks to link items of information and make them easier to recall.

8   Identify knowledge that you are likely to need to recall for discussions or exams.

9   Identify material that you will need to find again quickly, and record specific details of its location.

10   Practise using the 'Imagine the worst, and then . . .' technique in your everyday life so that you can use it during exams.

Asking your own questions

6

Asking questions is a constant taking apart, putting back together, and reshuffling into new creations. At their highest level, questions probe, discover, explore and manipulate information. They constantly seek new and stable ways to understand information.

CRAWFORD LINDSEY

What questions might you ask?
Why do I want to know?
What do I want to know?
How do I know that . . .?
Why?
When? Where? How? Who? What?
What happens when . . .?
What if . . .?

Pursuing your questions in formal education
Independent study

You ask questions all the time, both consciously and unconsciously. When you walk, as you take each step your foot is seeking out information to relay to your brain. When you pause at an intersection and glance both ways, you are checking the traffic. You learn when you have a question in your mind, whether as a small child continually asking 'Why?', or later as you learn about dinosaurs, gardening, jet aeroplanes, philosophy or toxicology.

You learn when you are curious, and when you want or need to know. Sometimes you may express your curiosity as interest in a field of study such as ancient history, modern music or marsupial reproduction. Turning your curiosity into a series of questions focuses your explorations in the field. In your study these questions drive your choice of topic, direct your research, and determine how you approach your assignments.

In formal education, usually teachers ask the questions and you provide the answers. Much of your primary and secondary education would have asked questions that began with 'What . . .?' and you would then have been expected to give correct answers that showed an ability to remember and reproduce information. In tertiary education, while 'What . . .?' is a valid question, you are expected to ask questions that lead you to be more analytical and critical. These questions begin with 'Why . . .?' 'How . . .?' 'How important . . .?' or 'How valid . . .?' Asking 'What if . . .?' or 'What might happen if . . .?' are higher-order speculative questions intended to lead you to reconsider your assumptions and beliefs.

In tertiary education, it is usually the teacher who formulates the questions that you discuss in tutorials or write about in your assignments and examinations. Some teachers will help you to formulate your own questions when you lead a discussion group, write on a topic of your own choice or undertake some form of independent study. Throughout your education many of your teachers will be committed to leading you to asking questions and exploring knowledge, teaching you to think critically, and trying to lead you to understand that there are no correct and definitive answers.

> There is something paradoxical in the idea of questioning knowledge in an institution dedicated to the continuation of knowledge and at times universities become the means of maintaining the status quo rather than questioning it. When it becomes impossible to question the paradigm of what is taught, when norm paradigms become dogma, when radical thinkers have no place, then the idea of the university dims, and they become mere institutions, universities in name not nature.
>
> JOHN TIFFIN and LALITA RAJASINGHAM

Some questions you ask constrain you and stop the learning process. Other questions enable you to ask further questions, perhaps by generating initial answers that lead on to questions that enable you to analyse and evaluate critically. As a higher-education student you need to ask questions that explore your relationship to learning, questions that help you understand, criticise, evaluate and analyse what you learn, and questions that help you to integrate what you learn with your previous knowledge and ideas.

What questions might you ask?

Just before she died she asked 'What is the answer?' No answer came. She laughed aloud and said: 'In that case what is the question?' Then she died.

Last words of GERTRUDE STEIN, quoted by DONALD SUTHERLAND

○○○ *What questions do you have on your mind right now? Questions about your work, your personal relationships, your ideas, who you are?*

A **simple question** such as 'Should I cook spaghetti or a stir fry for dinner?' or 'Did I leave my glasses behind?' can be answered without much imagination, perhaps with a 'Yes' or 'No'. Questions such as these close off other possibilities and leave you with only a limited answer. This may be adequate when checking if you know a fact, such as 'How many grams in an ounce?' or 'Where is my clavicle?' If you are looking for information on a topic such as basic human needs, to ask 'Do humans need food to survive?' is asking a closed question, while asking the more complex question 'What types of food do humans need to survive?' opens many possibilities.

Complex questions demand time and careful thought when you attempt to answer them. Some complex questions can never be answered fully. 'Am I making the right choice?' 'What would have happened if I hadn't gone to university?' But it can be tempting to believe that there are absolute 'yes/no' answers to questions that can't be answered so simply, and perhaps you check your horoscope or consult tarot cards in an attempt to find definite answers to such questions.

What men [*sic*] really want is not knowledge but certainty.   BERTRAND RUSSELL

One of the most unsettling aspects of university study for some students is realising that knowledge is relative, and that many taken for granted or seemingly common sense notions are not necessarily right or true. Often an answer that is right today may be wrong tomorrow, or an answer which makes sense in one culture may be a mistake in another. Are there any answers that are always right? Much of what you are told is true later turns out to be not quite the whole truth; and many so-called 'objective facts' are actually the results of a consensus of the subjective opinions of the people concerned. The same question can generate many different answers depending on the position you take, and the positions available to you will depend on your culture and world view (see 'Critical thinking', Chapter 3).

The way in which you ask questions shapes your answers. If you ask 'Is intelligence determined by genes or by environment?' you have precluded the possibility that both factors may contribute, and you may also have overlooked the possibility that other factors beyond genes and environment may play a significant role. Such 'either . . . or' questions are examples of how language limits your exploration of a topic and encloses what you can learn.

Every language conceals within its structure a vast array of unconscious assumptions about life and the universe, all that you take for granted and everything that seems to make common sense . . .   N. J. BERRILL

When you are curious about a subject, there are some basic questions you can usefully ask. As you read the questions suggested here, apply them to a topic that interests you or a topic you are researching for an assignment and make notes on the answers and further questions that arise. (See 'Analysing a topic and developing a research question', Chapter 7.)

Why do I want to know?

Tiger got to hunt,
Bird got to fly;
Man got to sit and wonder, 'Why, why, why?'
Tiger got to sleep,
Bird got to land;
Man got to tell himself he understand.   KURT VONNEGUT Jr

Asking why you want to know about a topic can clarify what you want to find out and how to go about your search. How did you become curious about the topic in the first place? What is *your purpose* for seeking the information? Perhaps you want to share it with others, use it to pass an exam, complete an assignment or progress through a sequence of practical skills. If you need to remember information for a short while, such as for a seminar paper next week, how you go about learning it will differ from your approach if you need the information for long-term use (see Chapter 5, 'Learning and remembering').

What do I want to know?

What do I want to know? What interests me about this topic? What seem to be the most important aspects? These are some of the *first questions* to ask yourself when you want to find information on a topic. For example, if you are interested in convicts in eighteenth–century Australia, ask yourself 'What do I want to know about this subject?' You might have questions about who the convicts were, why they were transported, how many were women, their living conditions, the number of convicts who were political prisoners, how they were organised and used in the colonies, and their role in the economy of the new colonies.

How do I know that . . .?

Artists can colour the sky red because they know it's blue. Those of us who aren't artists must colour things the way they really are or people might think we're stupid.

JULES FEIFFER

Perhaps you 'know' that the sun will rise tomorrow because in your experience it always has. Perhaps you 'know' the grass is green because your eyes and the labels available in your culture tell you so. Perhaps you 'know' that Marie Curie discovered radium because you read that she did.

What are the *sources of your knowledge*? The first-hand evidence from your senses is one source that can be deceptive—for example, if you relied solely on your senses, you would most likely believe that the world is flat (see 'Primary and secondary sources', Chapter 9). Much of what you know is not from first-hand experience. Much of your knowledge comes from your cultural and personal biases, many of which you may be unaware of, such as the belief that technological progress is always desirable or that women don't make good business managers. Much that is believed to be 'common sense' in your culture is not thought about or questioned (see 'Your cultural self' and 'Your social self', Chapter 1). It is therefore crucial to question the nature and reliability of your sources of knowledge. Can you prove that Marie Curie discovered radium or that the sun will rise tomorrow? Even if you can't prove it, it may still be true, but you need to consider and draw on supporting evidence before you assert its truth.

On the topic of convicts in eighteenth–century Australia, ask yourself 'What do I already know about this topic, and where does my knowledge come from?' Do you 'know' that most convicts were petty thieves or that women convicts were prostitutes, or have you assumed this? Asking yourself how you know these 'facts' should lead you to examine whether or not they really are facts.

> People who are reflectively sceptical do not take things as read. Simply because a practice or structure has existed for a long time does not mean that it is the most appropriate for *all* time, or even for this moment. Just because an idea is accepted by everyone else does not mean that we have to believe its innate truth without first checking its correspondence with reality as we experience it.   STEPHEN BROOKFIELD

Academic debate is fundamental to university education and provides you with a chance to examine your most cherished beliefs. By doing this, you may modify them, reject them, or end up still holding them but with a deeper understanding of why you believe what you do.

Why?

> . . . and books that told me everything about wasps except why.   DYLAN THOMAS

'Why?' is one of the most important questions you can ask, especially if it enables you to *identify assumptions* that may be hidden. For example, debates about education frequently ask 'How can we do this particular thing better?' while the question 'Why are we doing it in the first place?' is not dealt with. It might be more useful to start by asking 'Why are teachers trained?' instead of 'How can teachers be trained better?', or to ask 'Why am I going to write this report?' before you ask 'How can I best go about writing it?'

If you have a problem to solve, you might only ask how to solve it. For example, you might ask which methods you should use to remember material for exams. If you also ask why the methods are effective, you can decide whether they suit you and you will find it easier to remember how to repeat them and use them in different exam situations. On the topic of convicts in Australia, asking why convicts were transported will uncover further questions about the social, political and economic conditions in England in the eighteenth century.

When? Where? How? Who? What?

Asking these questions one after another is a *brainstorming* exercise allowing your mind to generate ideas without having to justify their immediate relevance. It is a useful way to stimulate your initial thinking about a topic and to provide new directions if you become stuck while researching. For example, given the adage 'Know thyself', you could ask questions such as the following:

- Who said this?
- When?
- Where was it first used?
- What was its original context?
- How has it been interpreted?

What happens when . . .?

'What happens when . . .?' is the *cause-and-effect* question that experimenters ask, whether the experimenter is a three-year-old child pulling a cat's tail or a professional researcher testing a hypothesis or solving a problem. Experimenting involves manipulating your environment to see what happens, sometimes predicting what is likely to happen, and then describing what actually happened. Here are some examples:

- What happens when you drop a piece of paper and a heavy lead weight from the top of a high tower?
- What happens when you write an assignment as a dialogue instead of in prose?
- What happens when you stop drinking coffee?

Asking this question in the past tense, 'What happened when . . .?' can be useful to understand a *sequence* of events as in the following examples.

- What happened when hydrochloric acid was added to the test tube?
- What happened when Marie Curie invented radium?

What if . . .?

Why, sometimes I've believed as many as six impossible things before breakfast.

LEWIS CARROLL

Imagine living in the sixteenth century and asking yourself, 'What if the sun rather than the earth is the centre of our universe?' What answers might you arrive at if you ask 'What if fossil fuels are no longer available by the middle of this century?', 'What if Robert Ardrey's theory that human animals are predatory killers is true?' or 'What might have happened if men were the sex that had babies?' These *speculative questions* require you to transcend your customary frameworks for viewing the world. Using your creative imagination and suspending disbelief enables you to look at the world through new eyes, which is essential for critical thinking and problem solving.

> Critical thought . . . has an epistemological edge. It places its object. It sets it in a framework. Critique asserts that no framework has priority, even if we cannot but place our observations in a framework of some kind. Critique, and a higher education founded on critique, obliges us to take the responsibility for the frameworks we employ. Critique points up the epistemological insecurity of any truth claim. It denies the pretentiousness of knowledge represented as Knowledge. RONALD BARNETT

You don't need to ask all of the above questions in a particular sequence; you are more likely to move backwards and forwards among them. What you want to know and the questions you ask will be influenced by how much you already know about a topic. For example, when confronted with a new topic you can immerse yourself in it by asking **basic questions** that uncover fundamental information about your topic, such as 'What is evolution?', 'What is Freud's concept of the unconscious?', 'What is carbon bonding?', 'What is Wall Street?' or 'What are marsupials?'

In contrast, when familiar with a subject you can ask **higher-order questions** which lead you to evaluate this information. For instance, 'How was Freud's theory of the unconscious applied in late-twentieth century psychoanalysis?' If you already know something about marsupial reproduction you might then ask if the reproductive process in kangaroos is an adaptation to the Australian environment. (Chapter 7, 'Choosing and analysing a topic', suggests a systematic way of analysing a question or topic.)

Pursuing your questions in formal education

> The teacher's work, therefore, begins when that other person asks a question . . . If you ask me a question all I can do in my reply is try to put into words a part of my experience. But you get only the words, not the experience. To make meaning out of my words, you must use your own experience. JOHN HOLT

Without curiosity, learning is dull and mechanical, if it occurs at all. Wanting to know, enjoying stretching your mind, feeling wonder or delight at a new experience or idea—all these need a mind that is receptive and questioning.

Unfortunately, the crucial part your curiosity and questions play in learning is often forgotten or disregarded. Formal learning is frequently based on a model that assumes there is a body of knowledge to master, and a particular way to master it; and the proof of your mastery lies in answering set questions correctly. This model of learning is most evident in the types of questions set in exams but can also underlie work such as essays, tutorial papers and laboratory reports. If you are given a question for a tutorial paper, do you approach it by asking your own questions, or by doing what you think your teachers expect? If you read a lot for an assignment, but feel uncertain about what to write on the topic, perhaps you are trying to guess what you are expected to write, rather than reading and writing about what seems most relevant and interesting to you. In a discussion group, are you hesitant to take an active part because you fear you might say the 'wrong' thing, or give the 'wrong' answer?

> Knowledge is a process in the minds of living people. It is what we do as we try to find out who and where we are, and what is going on about us.   JOHN HOLT

No teacher can tell you why and what you want to learn, but he or she can help you discover this. Teachers with an active curiosity who are interested in you as a learner can stimulate your curiosity in new ways; they can help you articulate your questions, guide you to ask more sophisticated questions, and steer you to appropriate research methods. Such teachers also help you rediscover the confidence and skills needed to pursue your own questions in formal education. Obviously, some teachers and assignments allow you more scope than others for asking and finding answers to the questions that interest you. If your learning is to be satisfying and meaningful to you, you need to ask your own questions, even with teachers who prefer you to answer theirs.

Independent study

> Students are partners in learning and they have a responsibility to contribute to their university experience. Most realise this and want to take charge of their learning. In some instances, however, they are denied the opportunity by the structures of courses, restrictive assessment schemes and the 'firehose' approach to teaching taken in some courses—which seems to operate on the principle that teaching involves the transmission of vast amounts of information. The overloaded curriculum is a particularly insidious obstacle to independent learning.   CRAIG McINNIS

The basic questions of what, why, how and when you learn apply to any independent learning, and can be applied to an individual assignment, to a research project or to your formal tertiary education as a whole. If you want to be a more self-directed, autonomous learner, think about who is determining the direction of your goals and aims. Becoming an independent learner requires thinking about and formulating your own goals and aims. It involves studying a subject of your own choosing, on your own initiative, and making your own decisions about how and when you study it and with whom. Independent study that is fully self-directed differs from 'individualised' learning. In the latter, although you study alone, you have limited choice of what and how you study, and how you study is controlled by the unit objectives and learning outcomes. Your own learning aims are more likely to be based on these unit objectives.

Studying independently entails asking yourself the following questions:

- What do I want to study, and in what depth and breadth?
- Why do I want to study this particular topic? Your goal might be to explore an interest more fully, acquire specific skills or examine previous work in a new context.
- How will I study the topic? Perhaps you want to conduct library research, interviews or laboratory experiments, or to undertake field work or to read extensively.
- How do I want my work to be assessed? You need to decide what work to produce specifically for recorded assessment, and who will assess this work and by what criteria (see Chapter 17, 'Learning from evaluation').
- How much time will I spend on this study?
- With whom will I discuss my work?

If you usually rely on material from your teachers for the 'right' answers, without questioning their information or assumptions, you may find it frightening to consider asking your own questions. Perhaps you have become so accustomed to teachers asking you questions that you have largely forgotten how to ask your own, or have lost the confidence to ask them. Even if a teacher encourages you to approach a topic in your own way, you might be so unaccustomed to this that you prefer to retreat into the safety of looking to the 'experts' for the answers. In this case you are probably assuming that your task at university is to meet the requirements of units and teachers, rather than seeing them as resources enabling you to move towards your goals and aims and to think about your questions. So perhaps the first questions you should ask yourself are 'Why am I at university or college?', 'What are my goals?', 'What are my study aims?' and 'What are my questions?'

A few universities and colleges allow you to complete part of your undergraduate course independently. Sometimes, you can obtain credit for exploring a topic or question in depth through a study contract. If independent study appeals to you, explore the possibilities for this method of learning within your institution or through cross-crediting from another institution, perhaps online (see 'Which units?', Chapter 2). If you develop a serious academic interest that you want to explore further, you may decide to go on to honours or postgraduate study.

Within a unit, the extent to which you are allowed to work on your interests varies. Most units, particularly in first year, allow you little scope for independent study; the work you do is assigned by teachers and you are told what to read, what experiments to conduct and how to present your written work. As a beginning student you need to accept this and allow the teacher to help you build your knowledge, develop skills and induct you into university culture. In some units you will be able to spend time exploring your interests with or without close supervision. However, when you do have the opportunity for independent study within a unit, it often takes the form of an individual or group project based on your choice of topic and methods of research.

Often your learning becomes largely a matter of asking more exact or more intricate questions, rather than finding answers. It is impossible to learn all there is to know about any subject, so when pursuing your own questions, you will quickly realise that the more you know, the more there is to learn, which leads you on to further questions.

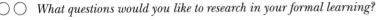 *What questions would you like to research in your formal learning?*

TEN TIPS

1   Know the difference between questions which are open-ended and those which close off possibilities.

2   In your everyday life pause every now and then and ask yourself, 'Where did this piece of knowledge come from?'

3   Asking 'Why?', and then asking 'Why?' again about a response, is one of the most useful habits that you can acquire as a student.

4   Try asking questions that start with 'When?', 'Where?', 'How?' 'Who?', 'What?' in connection with a couple of current unit assignments and see what you come up with.

5   Enjoy playing with speculative 'What if?' questions.

6   Distinguish between questions that concern facts and those involving complex concepts and ideas.

7   Reflect on where and when you feel most confident to ask questions, and why.

8   Reflect on where and when you feel least confident to ask questions, and why.

9   Be on the lookout for teachers who encourage you to pursue your own questions.

10 Find out about any opportunities in your institution to undertake independent study as part of a unit or course.

Choosing and analysing a topic

7

Research is motivated by a need to know about, or a curiosity about, how things are, and what things do or may do. This initially requires no specially developed skills, just a capacity to wonder . . . To research, we embark on a voyage of discovery launched by curiosity or need. Children have this capacity to wonder early in life. However, to be maintained, this desire to embark on inquiry needs to be nurtured. The education of students should lead them to ask research questions of increasing sophistication, specificity, depth and breadth, that set them on a journey towards making the unknown known.

JOHN WILLISON and KERRY O'REGAN

As a student in a tertiary institution, most of the work you submit for assessment is in the form of assignments in which you communicate your knowledge and demonstrate your skills. These assignments are usually written (essays, discussion papers, reviews, exams, projects and reports) or oral seminar or tutorial presentations, and occasionally use other media. In some units teachers require web-based assignments, such as developing a website, keeping a blog or building an e-portfolio. In addition to assignments, you are expected to assemble information for lectures, discussion groups, practical sessions, field trips and exams (see Chapter 8, 'Researching a topic'). Most of this work you undertake on your own, but it is also worth being aware of any opportunities to work collaboratively with other students.

Purposes for assignments

'Why, if a fish came to me and told me he was going on a journey, I should say 'With what porpoise'?'

'Don't you mean 'purpose'?' said Alice.   LEWIS CARROLL

Your aims

Your aims for a particular assignment should ideally reflect your reasons for enrolling in the unit and, on a broader level, your reasons for being at university. You might enrol in a unit to complete a prerequisite or to follow up an interest or to work with a particular teacher. Your aims for an assignment might be to:

— obtain background information for your main area of study

— complete a section of a unit that you know will be on the final exam

— increase your knowledge in a new area or read more in an area of interest, or

— practise communicating your ideas in writing and receiving feedback on them.

It is useful to write down these aims and refer to them as you do your research. If you have trouble articulating your aims, ask yourself the following questions:

What knowledge do I want to acquire?

What aspects of the question stimulate my curiosity?

What do I hope to accomplish by producing this piece of work?

What skills do I want to learn or improve?

What aspect of my learning and writing do I most need to improve?

There may be times when your aims for an assignment differ from what is expected of you in the unit or by the teacher. You may be expected to give a seminar paper on a topic that doesn't interest you, or to present a written report when you feel that an interactive presentation would be more effective. When such conflicts arise, ask your teacher if you can choose an alternative. Some teachers welcome such initiative and may allow you to pursue your own topic and form of presentation. If no alternative is possible, your discussions with the teacher should at least give you a clearer idea of the objectives of this particular assignment. If you can't use the assignment to achieve your own long-term goals or short-term aims and questions, you may need to find an alternative way of pursuing these (see 'Independent study', Chapter 6).

If you are working with other students on a group project, it is necessary in the initial stages to clarify how each of you interpret the objectives and outcomes for the assignment, and what each of you wants to learn during work on the project. Making your aims and expectations explicit is a vital ingredient for a harmonious working relationship and for achieving a satisfying end result (see 'Setting up discussion groups', Chapter 12).

Learning outcomes and teachers' objectives

Each assignment has a place within an overall unit plan to familiarise you with the disciplinary subject area and to develop certain skills (see 'Developing skills and attitudes', Chapter 3). A unit coordinator has several objectives and learning outcomes in mind (see Table 3.1, 'Learning outcomes and objectives') and these should be clearly articulated in unit materials and in class. However, if you think your teacher has not 'unpacked' everything they seem to expect from you, ask them to make their objectives and the outcomes more explicit.

Expectations of assignments

Expectations is the place you must always go to before you get to where you're going. Of course, some people never go beyond expectations . . .   NORTON JUSTER

Before you begin writing an academic assignment, as well as being clear about your aims, it is important to clarify what is expected in your work. These expectations come into play at different levels.

Tertiary study

At a macro level, there are the overall expectations of tertiary study, and fundamental to this is learning to participate in academic discourse (see 'University culture', Chapter 2). Arguing your position in an essay or seminar, or showing how you solved a problem in a scientific report, are intrinsic to learning to participate in university culture and the disciplines within it. This partly accounts for the predominance of essays and seminars in the social sciences and humanities, and report writing in the sciences. In addition, there are skills and attitudes you are expected to develop as part of your university education (see 'Developing skills and attitudes', Chapter 3). The generic skills pertinent to your written assignments include:

— researching

— planning and organising

— summarising and paraphrasing

— analysing and critiquing information

— presenting a reasoned argument

— communicating clearly and concisely, and

— using formal writing conventions and appropriate referencing conventions.

Most importantly, your teacher will expect you to fulfil any explicit requirements for the assignment, to address the set topic, and to do this in the genre required.

Disciplines

You need to be aware of the expectations, methodologies and conventions expected in your discipline, and the units within it. The essays you write in one discipline, such as history (or economics or philosophy) will differ in significant ways from those in another discipline, such as politics (or law or media studies). Similarly, the expectations of a written report in psychology are different from those in the physical sciences, and scientific report writing in chemistry differs from report writing in biology.

> The knowledge of law is organised by the institution of law so that when particular forms of social practice come into the domain of the law, it talks about them in certain kinds of ways and not other kinds of ways. For example, if my neighbour and I have an argument over the back fence which has deteriorated in a particular way then this is talked about by my wife and I in a certain kind of way, but when we go to see the lawyer it gets talked about in a different kind of way. And this is what I mean by discourse. Now discourses are important in schools, particularly in secondary and tertiary education, because the organisation of knowledge becomes more and more specific to the disciplines which a . . . student enters into. Thus you have particular ways of writing which correspond to the ways of organising knowledge within particular disciplines.
> GUNTER KRESS

Genres

You will be required to write in certain genres and to use the conventions of that genre. The predominant genres in academic writing include essays, reports, reviews, presentations and discussion papers, and each conforms to certain rules (see Table 10.4, 'Writing a review'; Chapter 14, 'Writing essays'; and Chapter 15, 'Writing scientific reports').

Many students coming from secondary school assume that what is expected of their writing at university is similar to what was expected at secondary school. This is not the case. The defining feature of a university essay (and an academic debate), even if not explicitly stated, is that it should have an argument or a theme. Essays should not consist purely of description. For example, whereas it might be acceptable in a school essay to do a small amount of research and then describe much of what you have read or been told on the subject, in a university essay your research needs to be extensive and you need to choose specific aspects on which to focus. And in tertiary study, it is usually only students in creative writing and other highly specialised units who have the opportunity to experiment with purely descriptive writing or with fiction.

You are expected to build on your ability to organise and express ideas and information. However, unless your prior learning has encouraged you to think critically, rather than simply to reproduce given information, some of the advice you were previously given or the approach you have previously taken is not applicable in tertiary study. Similarly, much that you are told in one discipline arises from the conventions and methodologies of that particular discipline and does not apply to another. It is important to read very carefully any unit materials that provide instructions on research and written work. These should outline the objectives and outcomes for assignments and how to present them. If in doubt, ask your teacher before you choose your topic.

What is expected from an essay that is intended to persuade will differ from one that is primarily intended to be informative. This difference influences how you organise the information that you present in your essay.

In an **informative** or **expository essay**, you choose material according to a *theme* that frames and limits your choice of ideas and information. You then choose *main points* that explain, describe, define or illustrate significant aspects of your particular topic or question. For example, if your topic is to explain the different treatments of capital and income under tax law, you choose the three main points that seem to you to be the most significant in explaining these differences. In your introduction you justify why you have chosen these three main points and not others. Note the directive verb is 'explain' which indicates an expository essay.

In an **argumentative essay**, you must have an argument that consists of a *thesis* that is supported by a number of *reasons* (or premises), and each of these reasons will form a main point in the essay. The thesis you choose to develop will depend on your position, your interests and world view. It is the thesis, and the reasons you choose to support this thesis, that help to make the essay distinctively yours. For example, you choose a topic that asks you to critically discuss deep-sea fishing and you hold a conservationist position on the question. Your argument consists of the thesis that fishing quotas should be implemented; and your reasons are declining fish stocks and the impact on the food chain. (Your thesis should be able to be expressed in a full grammatical sentence.) You support your reasons with evidence and examples (see 'The body of your essay', Chapter 14). The way you sequence your reasons and the weighting you give to each one are central to developing your argument. In some essays, you need to make sure that you account for arguments that oppose yours and demonstrate why these arguments don't carry weight. Developing your skills in writing argumentative essays will help you partipate in academic scholarship (see 'University culture', Chapter 2).

Sometimes you may find it difficult to identify your position on a topic. Usually this is because the position seems so self-evident to you that you are unable to recognise it as a position. In such a situation, remember that there is always more than one possible stance on a topic and you are expected to make yours explicit and argue for it.

Individual teachers

Your written academic assignments are normally produced for only one person and for assessment. You should be told the objectives and outcomes of an assignment and how you are expected to present it. In some units, a list of criteria (used by teachers as a marking guide) with weightings for each criterion is provided. If these are not included in your unit materials, ask for them. You cannot be expected to second-guess what your teachers expect, and if you try to do so your assignments are likely to be cautious and dull. It is, of course, difficult to imagine everything that a teacher expects from you and impossible to understand fully what they know. You are not an expert in your field and as yet you are not expected to be. However, it is your aims, interests and views that make the assignments distinctively yours, so spend your time researching and presenting these interests and views as effectively as possible. Most teachers prefer a well-researched and well-argued original piece of work that expresses your position and addresses a precise research question, rather than a rehashing of familiar textbooks or their own lectures.

Topics and questions

Before you choose, analyse and research a topic, you should define your aims and clarify the outcomes set for the assignment. You will usually be given one topic or a list of topics, and sometimes you will be free to devise your own.

You may be given either:

— a *general* topic, such as 'The ecology of eucalypt forests', 'Romantic literature', 'British journalism', 'The French Revolution' or 'Scientific method', or

— a *specific* topic that may be worded as a directive sentence, for example, 'Discuss the Hindu ideas of forgiveness and tolerance', 'Analyse the distinguishing characteristics of university culture', and 'Critically examine the likely effects on the local flora and fauna of the freeway proposed for your capital city'.

In this chapter, 'topic' is used for a general content or subject area, while 'question' refers to a focused research question that arises from your analysis of the topic and is used to guide your research. Your teachers may use either 'topic' or 'question' when referring to essays and other assignments.

Choosing a topic

Deciding on a topic can seem deceptively simple—a matter of choosing from a list of suggested or set topics, or selecting a topic from within the subject matter of a unit. However, your decision also involves analysing possible topics. Start making your choice by thinking about the possibilities of each. Explore a couple of options and choose between them as you analyse them in some detail, or decide on one at the start and change your mind if your initial exploration suggests that it has limited possibilities. Often a topic which at first doesn't seem very interesting may become attractive as you explore it.

- Your choice of topic is affected by *what you already know*. If you are given a list of topics and are uncertain which to choose because some of them are unfamiliar, find out more about these options from a source such as an online encyclopedia, a unit text or an expert. If you have limited time to gather information, choose a familiar topic. If you have ample time, decide whether to explore a previous interest further or to learn about an unfamiliar topic.

- *Your enthusiasm* for a topic also affects your choice. For example, if you are interested in women's history you might choose a topic such as the suffragette movement. If you are an athlete, you might write on the physiology of marathon runners.

- Your choice of topic is often influenced by *the information sources available.* Skilful research into sources can increase your choice of questions (see Chapter 9, 'Using information sources').

Unless your choice of topic is quite clear from the start, or you have little time in which to choose, keep several options in mind. Allow yourself time to analyse their possibilities further, and to find out if the resources you need are available.

Personal opinions

> The trouble is that essays always have to sound like God talking for eternity, and that isn't the way it ever is. People should see that it's never anything other than just one person talking from one place in time and space and circumstance.   ROBERT M. PIRSIG

Your approach to a topic is always subjective to some degree. Even a set specific topic can be tackled in a variety of ways, and your particular approach is reflected in what you include and omit from the possible material. Even if you are presenting a report in which you try to eliminate as much subjectivity as possible, the words you use carry with them personal associations for you and your audience. So the most useful question to ask is not 'Shall I take an objective or subjective approach?' but rather 'What role might my personal opinions play in this assignment?' For example, are your views influencing the research sources you choose, or do they lead you to assume that there is only one way of responding to the topic? Examine your biases and preconceptions so that they distort your research as little as possible. (See the Appendix, 'Discrimination', for examples of bias.)

In an assignment such as a laboratory report you are required to report only what you see as 'facts' and to provide personal input only in your critical interpretation of raw data. In other assignments, such as a philosophy essay, you will be required to present an argument based on your current knowledge. However, remember that no two people will choose to report facts in the same way or in exactly the same language.

Your scope for presenting a personal position often depends on the conventions of a particular discipline and the personal preferences of your teacher. If you feel unsure about including your opinions, even when asked to, remember that practice in communicating your knowledge and arguing from a position is a vital part of learning—and, given practice and some encouraging feedback, it does become easier. Usually it also makes your assignments more interesting to read. But remember that an outpouring of unexamined assertions and prejudices is not acceptable.

> . . . my purpose is to employ facts as tentative probes, as a means of insight, of pattern recognition, rather than to use them in the traditional and sterile sense of classified data, categories, containers.   MARSHALL McLUHAN

Analysing a topic and developing a research question

The research for your essay will be much more effective if you have a clearly defined topic, and if you can turn this topic into a research question. When devising your own specific question, it needs to be clear and accurate. In the early stages of analysing a topic, you are unlikely to be ready to decide on the specific wording of such a question, but keep in mind that this is what you are working towards. As you proceed with your analysis, revise the wording as necessary.

If you are given a *general topic* you need to limit it to a specific topic that will help you devise a research question. In an argumentative essay this will enable you to decide on an argument, and in an expository essay, your theme (see 'Genres', earlier in this chapter). For example, in the general topic 'Discuss the French Revolution' you might narrow the topic down to three main causes of the revolution. You might then argue from a Marxist position the thesis that the economic situation in France caused the revolution and give reasons to support this.

If you are given a *specific topic*, the wording will help define how to develop it as a question. For example, in the specific topic 'Analyse the distinguishing features of university culture' your question might be 'What are the main distinguishing features of a university culture that differentiate it from the features of another culture?'

The points listed below are designed to help you with the process of analysing an essay topic and developing a research question. They should lead you to a written statement that outlines a possible argument or theme and suggests a structure for the essay.

When writing an assignment or exam answer, it is extremely important to address the set topic. It is common for students to read a topic and to quickly decide what it is about—before heading off on the wrong track. Rigorously analysing a set topic is a fundamental prerequisite to answering it, and failure to do this is one of the main reasons that capable students do not produce work which reflects their abilities. Re-read every single word in a set topic at different stages of producing your essay.

Apply each of the suggestions below to your essay topic before you begin your research and writing. It is not necessary to apply the questions in the order given here. It will help if you make notes as you go, and you will be surprised how much you already know.

1 What is the topic about?

- Think about the *exact wording of the topic* and of any guidelines so that you understand more clearly what you are expected to write about and the possibilities that the topic offers. It is very useful to write out the exact topic in full to help cement it in your mind, and keep it somewhere visible so that you can refer to it as you write.

- List terms and concepts in the topic and their possible meanings. Does the topic contain terms and concepts you don't understand? For example, the possible uses of the word 'culture' in the topic 'Analyse the distinguishing features of university culture' may not be clear.

    To help with this, check in any unit materials for a definition; and run some online searches to explore possible meanings within the relevant discipline. Ask your teacher to explain terms you don't understand, or if a topic isn't clearly worded, to explain it more fully.

- Ask yourself 'What assumptions seem to underpin the question?' For example, the topic, 'Discuss the most effective way to apply Piaget's theory of children's developmental stages to teaching mathematics in primary schools' assumes that Piaget's theory should be applied in this case.

2 What do I already know about the topic?

- Jot down any ideas or knowledge which come to mind.

- Use any available lists of study questions on the subject to start your mind ticking over.

- Brainstorm the topic by asking 'Why?', 'Who?', 'What?', 'When?', 'How?' and 'Where?' about it, or ask 'How do I know that . . .?' to check the validity of your existing knowledge. (See 'What questions might you ask?', Chapter 6, for more questions to start you thinking.)

- Compile a list of subject headings that could be used in your research.

3 How much breadth and depth can this essay have?

Given the requirements of the essay (such as length or format) ask yourself the following questions:

- Should I concentrate on presenting a broad overview of the topic, or on exploring one or two facets of it in depth?
- How many main ideas can I convey?
- How much information can I present?

Most topics could be the subject of a book but your assignment is of limited length; so you will need to restrict the scope of your assignment to what you see as the most significant points from your research.

For example, in the topic 'Scientific method' you may focus on the question 'Is there a scientific method?', arguing that scientific method depends on time and place. You might do this by contrasting the ideas of Paul Feyerabend (who argues that there is no single scientific method) with the views of John Kemeny (who posits that there is one basic method common to all scientific activity). You argue your case using only these 'experts' because the length and time set for the essay don't permit you to look at many writers in detail, and because you want to contrast two theories related to the question.

4 What might my thesis or theme be?

- For an argumentative essay, ask how you would complete the sentence '*In response to this topic I will argue that . . .*'.
- At this stage keep in mind that the reasons to support your chosen thesis constitute the main points in your essay. Your thesis may be only tentative at this point and you may have to revise it several times.

5 What are the possible main points?

- Ask yourself the following questions as a starting point:
  - Which aspects of the topic do I most want to explore?
  - What seems most important about the question?
  - What differences of opinion might the topic generate?
- Compile a list of points that seem to be central to the topic, in preparation for your research.

  In a set specific topic, you may be given an indication of some main points. Briefly describing your understanding of central terms or concepts is likely to form an early part of the assignment. So in the Piaget topic, as your main points you would need (a) to describe Piaget's theory of child developmental stages, before (b) discussing its possible applications to maths teaching in primary schools. Otherwise, possible main points are likely to come from your background knowledge, from unit materials or lectures, from recommended reading or from class discussions on the topic.

- For an argumentative essay, ask 'What key reasons might I use to support my thesis?' For an expository essay, ask 'Which main points seem to be central to the theme?' (See 'Genres', above.)

Make an initial list of key terms for each likely main point. Search subject dictionaries or a thesaurus or specialist wiki to look up these terms and to find related terms. To find references to the changing composition of the workforce, you may need to look up 'Unemployment', 'Trade unions' and 'Women, working', as well as the obvious heading 'Workforce'.

6 Which sources might I use?

Given the requirements of the essay ask yourself the following questions:

- Do the instructions on the assignment specify the number and type of references that I need to consult during my research?
- Am I expected to use mostly suggested references, or to locate my own? What proportion of each is acceptable?
- How much scope do I have to research beyond the suggested references?
- Will my research be based on books, articles, the web or other sources? What proportion of each is appropriate?
- Am I expected to use peer-reviewed journal articles?
- Are there any limits on using unit materials such as textbooks or lectures?

7 How might I structure my response to the topic?

Many topics include 'directive' or 'process' verbs, such as 'criticise', 'discuss' or 'evaluate', which help to shape the type of essay you write and its structure (see Table 7.1, 'Directive verbs'). In assignments such as expository essays, which do not require you to develop an argument, these directive verbs determine the task you undertake in your written work.

- Decide which words are 'directive' verbs.
- Work out how many parts there might be to the topic.
- Decide if the essay is to be argumentative or expository. For example, if the topic includes the words 'discuss' or 'critically', an argument will be expected.
- Analyse the directive verbs to determine how they will shape the assignment structure. Then choose among options such as:
  — whether the topic involves description and/or analysis of this description
  — whether to compare two different aspects of a topic, or instead to clearly define all its components, or
  — whether to argue a case for or against a particular controversy relating to a topic, or to review the range of opinions on it.

TABLE
7.1 **Directive verbs**

'When I use a word', Humpty Dumpty said, in a rather scornful tone, 'it means just what I choose it to mean—neither more nor less.'   LEWIS CARROLL

Analyse	Show the essence of something, by breaking it down into its component parts and examining each part in detail.
Argue	Present the case for and/or against a particular proposition.
Compare	Look for similarities and differences between propositions.
Contrast	Explain differences.
Criticise	Give your judgement about the merit of theories or opinions about the truth of facts, and back your judgement by a discussion of the evidence.
Critique	See *Criticise*.
Define	Set down the precise meaning of a word or phrase. Show that the distinctions implied in the definition are necessary.
Describe	Give a detailed or graphic account.
Discuss	Investigate or examine by argument, sift and debate, giving reasons for and against.
Enumerate	List or specify and describe.
Evaluate	Appraise and judge different perspectives; include your opinion.
Examine	Present in depth and investigate the implications.
Explain	Make plain, interpret, and account for in detail.
Illustrate	Explain and make clear by the use of concrete examples, or by the use of a figure or diagram.
Interpret	Bring out the meaning, and make clear and explicit; usually also giving your judgement.
Justify	Show adequate grounds for decisions or conclusions.
Outline	Give the main features or general principles of a subject, omitting minor details, and emphasising structure and relationship.
Prove	Demonstrate truth or falsity by presenting evidence.
Relate	Narrate/show how things are connected to each other, and to what extent they are alike or affect each other.
Review	Make a survey, examining the subject critically.
State	Specify fully and clearly.
Summarise	Give a concise account of the chief points or substance of a matter, omitting details and examples.
Trace	Identify and describe the development or history of a topic from some point or origin.

Source: Adapted from Maddox 1967, 119–120.

8 What role might my personal opinions play?

- The essay argument and structure will be your own, developed by engaging with relevant materials. In an argumentative essay you will decide on the thesis and main points.

- Check any available guidelines and note how much personal opinion you are able to include. Can you use 'I' in your essay?

- Think critically about any preconceived ideas or biases you may have in relation to the topic. How might you minimise the effect of these and remain open-minded as you develop a possible thesis or theme? For example, in the question on the changing nature of the workforce, perhaps you are ideologically opposed to trade unionism. How might your approach to the topic differ from someone who is an avid trade union supporter?

- Are there strong opposing ideas to the ones you hold? If so, account for these in your research and writing.

9 What is my initial research question?

With a vast array of online information to select from, it speeds up your research if your analysis of the topic leads to working out a clear question which defines just what you want to find out. For example, if you know by now that your topic is 'Genetic variations in Amazonian butterflies', you might do an initial search by combining a few of your key terms. This will give you a long list of items, some of which are very useful and some of no use at all. But if you know that what you want to find out is 'What are the most striking genetic variations among Amazonian butterflies in Brazil?', you can make your way through a list much more efficiently. (See Chapter 8, 'Researching a topic'.)

A written assignment that is to be part of a *group project* involves:

— agreeing on a topic that the whole group will explore

— turning the topic into a research question

— deciding which specific aspects of the topic each person or subgroup will research, and

— clarifying how each person's work will contribute to the overall assignment and to the total project (see 'Collaborative learning groups', Chapter 12).

Once the group has agreed on a topic, the process outlined in steps 1 to 9 can be applied to it, so that the group can collectively prepare a written definition of the topic and a research question before beginning research.

Your initial working definition

Before you begin full-scale research for an essay, write down:

- the precise topic set, with all of its parts
- a brief statement of your aims and the outcomes stated in your unit materials and by your teacher, and
- your responses to your analysis of the topic under the headings:
  - the directive verbs in the topic
  - any assumptions that seem to underpin the topic
  - the key concepts
  - ways of limiting the scope of the assignment
  - a possible thesis or theme
  - possible main points
  - a list of useful search terms, and
  - an initial research question.

Unless the essay is short and straightforward it is unlikely that you will have a final research question, a definitive statement of your thesis or theme, or a complete list of likely main points from which you can choose. As yet you may not be able to determine a final structure. If you have trouble analysing a topic, write down any ideas you have on it and discuss them with other people. Expressing your thoughts accurately in writing or verbally to others will help you clarify them (see 'The process of writing', Chapter 13).

It can be useful to return to this initial definition of the topic as you go about your research. And when you have completed your research, repeat the process of defining your topic (see 'Your revised definition', Chapter 8).

These initial steps in analysing a topic largely determine the material you select for research and how you finally present your assignment. However, as you proceed with your research, the information you gather can reshape your original definition of the topic and the research process may even lead you to change to another topic. Analysing your topic, developing an initial research question and undertaking the actual research are interdependent processes, rather than separate activities.

. . . movement through the different facets of research is not linear, but frequently recursive.   JOHN WILLISON and KERRY O'REGAN

TEN TIPS

1 Think about what you want to learn by doing an assignment.
2 Clarify any explicit requirements and what is expected of you.
3 If you have a choice of topics, consider several possibilities rather than settling for the obvious one.
4 Think about how your personal opinions might influence what you write.
5 Make a realistic estimate of how much time you have for each stage of the assignment.
6 Analyse the exact wording of a topic, including any directive words.
7 Work out an initial thesis or theme which you can express in one sentence.
8 Identify probable main points.
9 Devise a list of useful search terms.
10 Turn the topic into a question to guide your research.

REFERENCE

Maddox, H. 1967. *How to Study.* 2nd ed. London: Pan Books.

Researching a topic

8

Research and the use of research or inquiry-based methods of teaching and learning are becoming increasingly important in a world that requires graduates to be lifelong learners.

MURDOCH UNIVERSITY

The basis for selecting potentially relevant sources is your initial definition of the topic (see 'Your initial working definition', Chapter 7). This includes:

— a precise statement of the topic (with its parts), either as provided or as you have defined it so far

— the outcomes stated for the assignment in unit materials

— a brief statement of your aims for the assignment

— any directive verbs in the topic

— any assumptions that seem to underpin the topic

— key concepts central to the topic

— how much breadth and depth is possible

— a possible thesis or theme

— your possible main points

— a list of useful search terms, and

— your initial research question.

This working definition may be reasonably clear at this stage if the assignment is short and straightforward. But it is more likely that you will not have a definitive statement of your thesis or theme, a definite list of likely supporting points, or a final structure. As you engage in research, guided by the list above, identify possible sources and evaluate these possibilities to decide which to use and which to exclude.

The next step is to think about where and how you might find material. You will be given information in lectures and tutorials, supplied with reference lists for units, and perhaps directed to sources such as the websites, the media or an organisation. At times you may have to search out and know how to use less obvious sources so that you don't overlook material that could make a significant difference to the quality of your work.

This plethora of material can be overwhelming, particularly as information on most subjects is increasing rapidly all the time. You may feel bewildered because you want or are apparently expected to absorb so much. When researching a topic it is easy to become sidetracked by fascinating but irrelevant information, locked into an Internet search, held up by little or no information, or bewitched by mystifying technical language. A list of appropriate search terms provides at least a useful starting point; and refining your original research question is integral to selecting the most useful resources as quickly as possible.

The initial stages

Do at least some preliminary research early on—you may have a wonderful idea for tackling a topic, but if material on the topic is limited, it is better to discover this as soon as possible. Starting early also means that you can be alert to useful ideas from unexpected sources. Your first place to look for material should be any of the required unit lectures, readings or websites, particularly since you are expected to know these sources well.

1 Practical considerations

Time available

How much time do you realistically have available for your research? Break the overall task of producing the assignment into stages: major research, writing a complete draft, editing, finding last-minute information, and producing a final draft. Working out how you can schedule in each of these stages—in real life, not in an ideal world—will give you some idea of how much time you have to do the bulk of your research.

Download, print, copy, borrow or buy?

Your choice of whether you download, print, copy, borrow or buy material depends on:

— your finances

— whether the materials are easily available through a library, online, from another student, or from a teacher

— how heavily you will use the material

— how much you rely on unit materials and references for stimulation, for instance, if you have little opportunity to discuss your work with others

— whether you remember more if you underline the books or articles you read, and

— whether or not the material will be useful in other units or your current occupation or in your future.

Some material you are likely to want to refer to again, such as a unit text or a reference book that you will need for a final exam or seminar paper. If you do need to consult material more than once, you may want to obtain your own copy—buy a book, download or photocopy an article. If you need to use borrowed material heavily, take full notes on the content and note source details such as page numbers. When deciding which books to buy, be wary of relying on printed unit booklists. Some lists are drawn up well before a unit starts and may change, or a different edition or translation of a book may be recommended. Check online for up-to-date unit lists.

Even if you use the Internet heavily, sometimes you will encounter problems with material you need because you can't borrow it through a library, perhaps because it is in high demand. Often you can avoid this problem by doing your research well in advance, seeking out electronic sources of similar items, finding out if an alternative reference is possible, making an early appointment to see an interviewee, or borrowing material from friends. You might need to reconsider your choice of a topic or question in the light of available resources.

2 Selecting likely material

There are several steps in selecting the most relevant material as quickly as possible.

● First, check carefully which resources you are expected to use.

● Next, identify any other likely useful resources.

● And finally, critically evaluate these resources to determine their usefulness.

As you go through these steps, keep in mind the outcomes expected of you as well as your aims for the assignment. Keep in mind why you want the material you are selecting. Is it for a major assignment, preliminary reading for a lecture or discussion paper, follow-up reading to a field trip, or study material for an exam? 'Your purposes' in Chapter 10 looks at why you might want to read a book. ('Previewing', Chapter 10, suggests questions that help to clarify how useful a book is for your purpose.)

Some material, such as a unit text, you use for more than one purpose. Sometimes different materials may complement each other, such as two books each with different information on a topic, or a lecture and an article that present the same information from different perspectives. Sometimes you have to choose between materials because they are repetitious, such as two video documentaries covering essentially the same ground.

a Devising a reference list

Pay close attention to any references suggested in the unit or by a teacher who will read your work. If you are not given a list of references from which to choose, check the available information sources and make up a list of material relevant to your topic (see 'Topics and questions', Chapter 7). Consult any unit guides, handouts and reference lists for suggestions. If in doubt, ask your teacher for guidance on which material is essential and which material to read first. Consider both primary and secondary sources on your question (see 'Primary and secondary sources', Chapter 9). The length of your list should depend on the time available for your research.

b Key terms

When analysing your topic you should have drawn up a list of the main points and key search terms. Keep these firmly in mind and use them in your research. Think also about alternative or related terms you might need. Online, look at terms highlighted as links within the text or listed below it. Search subject dictionaries or a thesaurus or a specialist wiki to look up your initial list and find related terms.

c Finding extra sources

Look for material on your topic that is not obvious or recommended. For example, one of your own books or a reader from a previous unit may contain suggestions for further reading, or an organisation you contact for information may refer you to another source.

Like any kind of exploratory activity, library research benefits from good planning and proficient technique (for example, subject searches, catalogues, indexes) . . . but it also profits from unplanned encounters with the unknown. Contrast the tunnel vision effect produced by a data base that only reports what you ask it. Try wandering down the stacks; let yourself get distracted by what's in the vicinity of the item you're hunting. Who knows what exciting or inspiring adventures in knowledge lurk there?   ZOE SOFOULIS

As well as using required reading as a springboard to other items, a certain amount of browsing for material can be highly enjoyable and productive—as long as you keep time constraints in mind. When browsing you may come across material that isn't precisely on your topic but deals with the general principles underlying it. An article on scientific methods, for example, can spark off ideas about an individual question in physics. Other material may provide valuable background. For example, a conversation with a person who lived through the Depression years in Australia may help you more fully understand a specific aspect of this era. Occasionally an idea can be illuminated by juxtaposing it with material from an unexpected source; for instance, astronomy with Alice in Wonderland, semiotics with Sufi philosophy, poetry with popular music.

d Recording and filing references

As you select possible material, record pertinent details in an easily accessible form. For example, photocopy the abstract of an article, download a valuable reference list, record parts of an interview, or take photographs. You will probably record most of your information in note form even if preparing an oral or audiovisual assignment. (See Chapters 10 and 11 for more on selecting information and making notes from reading and lectures.)

Read material and edit notes before you consider filing them. Can you identify a specific use for the material? A growing pile of items to read indicates that you need to be more realistic about the amount of information you can take in and use. An efficient system is of little use if all it yields is an impressive collection of electronic files whose contents you have mostly forgotten, a stack of folders full of photocopied articles you intend to read one day, or an elaborate database the construction of which has been of more interest to you than its contents.

Some information you won't need to record and keep because it is relatively accessible. However, some information which you may want again might be available to you only once (such as material in an interview or radio program) or could be difficult to find again (such as information from a person awkward to contact or a book that isn't readily available). In these instances, as you select the information you want, think how you can best record and store it.

Knowledge is of two kinds. We know a subject ourselves, or we know where we can find information upon it.   SAMUEL JOHNSON

The basic reasons for systematically filing information are so that you can easily find it again, can add to or subtract from it, and can rearrange it when necessary. Taking time to set up an effective filing system also means that you avoid a last minute hunt for a crucial reference. Compare the usefulness of various types of software designed for creating a database or a filing system for collating references. Alternatively, you might prefer stationery such as looseleaf paper and a ring binder, a box of file cards, a concertina file or several filing trays to make it easier to arrange and rearrange material. A filing system often needs to be portable so that you can work in different places. Because of this, even if you have a laptop you might use a folder or file cards for part of your notes. Be selective about what you print out in hard copy, and make sure you always back up your research material.

Methods for filing information depend on the specific purposes for which you need it. Often it is convenient to organise and file material according to its *content* or its *source*, as in the following examples.

● To follow the development of themes within a unit, keep your lecture notes in sequence in a looseleaf folder. You can then interleave notes from discussion groups, field work and research wherever their content is related to a theme.

● When preparing to write an essay in which you are expected to base your ideas on a careful examination of primary source material, keep your notes from the reading of primary sources separate from those taken from secondary sources.

You might choose instead to organise and file your material in chronological order (such as dates on lecture notes), alphabetical order (such as web addresses or authors of books read), and/or numerical order (with each item or each page of notes numbered). Record the source of your information *in detail*, including page numbers, in case you want to find it again or cite the reference. Set up a 'contents' page so that you have an overview of what is in your notes.

e The medium

Consider the practical steps for selecting information from the research material you will use. For example, you gain more from a book if you are aware of what is involved in the process of reading and how you might improve your reading skills, both in print and online. You learn more from a lecture or podcast if you have thought about how these media convey and structure information and what you need to do in order to listen more effectively. (See 'Using sources effectively', Chapter 9; the introduction to Chapter 10, 'Reading'; Chapter 11, 'Listening to lectures'.)

Perhaps you are more comfortable using some media than others. You might, for example, usually take in more from printed journal articles or online unit materials than from lectures because you can revisit difficult sections in the former. Any medium becomes familiar if you use it often enough, but if there is no time for this before selecting material, opt for media which usually yield you the most information (and learn how to use the others later).

f Searching the Internet

The Internet is an invaluable research tool, but before going to it for your research make sure you are familiar with what your required unit materials have to offer. Searching online is then useful in all sorts of ways, particularly if it is difficult to get access to a teacher for help. For example, you might need general background information on a subject, specific material on a person or place, or a definition of a word or concept. Always cross-check what you find across several sites, or you may end up with inaccurate information.

You might also encounter a situation in which a teacher refers you to a considerable number of websites either because they consider all of them important, or to give you plenty of choice. A busy teacher might have put together a hasty collection of web addresses, or simply told you to 'look for information on the Net' but provided little in the way of what they expect or how to conduct an effective search.

Developing skills in conducting an effective Internet search for academic purposes is a time-saving skill. To help acquire such skills, find out what your institution's library or the study skills advisers offer by way of face-to-face or online tutorials on using search engines, or refer to the search engine's own help pages.

- You might simply search using a couple of your key terms in a scatter gun approach to see what comes up. But choosing to use only the first few items from the first page of results is unlikely to yield the best material for your aims; and checking lots of vaguely related material is very time-consuming.

  You need a clear aim and a lucid research question and some criteria for what you'll choose. You could skim newspaper headlines, and perhaps the first paragraphs in articles, but doing only this can be seriously misleading if you need to discover what the articles are all about. Similarly, in an Internet search, don't choose items based only on the couple of lines of description given under an item heading (see 'The Internet', Chapter 9, for more on this).

- When using the Internet, think carefully before following a trail of web links. Browsing through material which is vaguely connected with your question can be highly enjoyable, and while it does not constitute seriously selecting material for full-scale research on the topic, it can lead to serendipitous insights. But following links can be haphazard, and accessing them can be slowed down by the visual clutter (including advertising) on many web pages. Keep in mind your time constraints, and if you have a heavy workload, beware of spending too much time browsing. Don't feel obliged to search the Internet exhaustively simply because it's there; and if you have done a reasonable amount of research, don't fall into the trap of doing yet another search just in case there's a crucial item you might have missed.

> Thanks to the staggering informational power of new media, time is more than ever our most precious resource. It is the one quantity of which all of the world's technology cannot conjure a particle more . . .
>
> TOM CHATFIELD

- Bookmark sites to which you will want to return; and create clearly named folders for organising your bookmarks. In this way you build up a database from your searches, and you can refer to this for later assignments. Avoid simply collecting lots of possible sites, since then you have to go back and re-check each one for its usefulness, which is very time consuming.

- Global search engines (such as Google) search and index their findings in different ways, so it's worth using your key words to search on the same topic using different engines to see how the results vary or overlap. Try specialist search engines as well as global ones. And when looking for background information such as a definition or a biography, check out wikis other than Wikipedia (such as those specialising in philosophy or science). Make use of subject directories, and sites maintained by professional associations (such as the American Psychological Association) or discipline-based ones (such as ERIC for education).

- Because there are multiple pathways from one site to another, and these pathways are part of webs rather than hierarchies, repetition is built in; so during a search you might find yourself coming across the same site more than once. Such recurrences can be frustrating, as can the experience of putting in a search command and receiving large numbers of references to unrelated sites.

- Even careful searches can yield a large number of items, so develop skills to make a search more precise and to exclude some items. To learn about the value of combining more search terms, experiment with doing a search using one of your key terms, then three of them, then five, and notice how many results each search elicits.

> You throw a query to the wind and who knows what will come back to you? You may get 234 468 supposed references to whatever you want to know. Perhaps one in a 1000 might help you. But it's easy to be sidetracked or frustrated as you try to go through those web pages one by one. Unfortunately they're not arranged in order of importance.
>
> DAVID ROTHENBURG

To direct your search more accurately, become familiar with how to use the **Boolean operators** AND, OR and NOT. In addition, find out:

— what happens when you use brackets or double inverted commas around certain word combinations, and

— why you might use a truncation symbol (*) or a wildcard (?) in a search.

Entering the words within the < > signs can produce different types of results, as in the following examples:

- If you enter <Australia AND marine AND mammals>, you receive a smaller range of results each of which contains all three words, whereas a search without using AND would list a many results each with possibly only one of the words.
- If you search for <"straw bales"> your search produces items containing that exact phrase, and excludes items which only concern either 'straw' or 'bales'.
- Searching for <wom?n > yields results containing 'woman' or 'women'.
- Searching for <heat*> will use all forms of the word, such as 'heats', 'heated' and 'heater'.
- If you enter <mammals NOT marine>, you will not be presented with any information on marine mammals.
- A search for <jargon OR slang> would expand your results because it would list pages including either or both the terms. This sort of search is handy when authors commonly use alternative terms for the same subject.
- And you can combine Boolean operators, as in <(macadamias NOT peanuts) AND (tropics OR agriculture OR farming)>, where the search will start with the item you list first.

When you have a list of key terms for an assignment, using these operators can save you time, help you find the most relevant items, and exclude irrelevant but not relevant ones. Search queries use the operators in the order ( ) then NOT then AND then OR.

g Developing your research question

As you find likely material, begin to refine your initial research question so that you are clearer about what you actually want to find out (and what you are not so interested in). You might find that what now seems like too broad a topic takes on a more specific direction; or particular aspects of a topic might start to grab your attention. For example, if your initial research question was 'Do human activities affect the crown of thorns starfish population on the Great Barrier Reef?' you might replace 'human activities' with the more specific 'agricultural runoff'. Then as you start to pursue this question, you might come up with the more precise 'Are there particular types of agricultural run-off that seem to have a greater effect on the crown of thorns starfish population in the Great Barrier Reef?'

Remember, as you refine your question, take time to check back with the topic you were set to make sure you are still responding to this and haven't gone off track.

3 Evaluating your selection

Once you have selected relevant material, critically evaluate it according to its reliability and usefulness and its complexity for you. You need thorough and well-respected knowledge—you wouldn't do the equivalent of asking the first couple of people you meet in the street for reliable information on nuclear physics or existential philosophy.

Keep your research question in mind. Be prepared to discover that some of the material you have selected may not be as useful as you hoped, and don't expect that set or suggested references will completely suit your definition of the question. If you feel such material is of limited use, abandon it as a source or try to incorporate a criticism of it into your assignment.

Previewing selected material

Previewing helps you choose between possible items so that you select those which appear most directly relevant to your topic and research question (see 'Previewing', Chapter 10). Now that you have a more precise list of references, you need to evaluate each for reliability, to decide which source accords with your aims. Although the questions in Table 8.1 apply to web pages, you can use some of them for a preliminary evaluation of other sources. Decide if material is worth working with in depth, or whether any further use of it will waste time that could be better spent on another source.

- Previewing material can help you discover the complexity of the text or material and hence the background knowledge you require to use it.

- The structure, format and writing style of material can make it easy or challenging for you to follow.

- The material might or might not be interesting or familiar to you, and may or may not accord with your beliefs and biases. If a topic or perspective is new to you, you might not fully understand the material, but its very newness can be exciting. Don't automatically reject apparently difficult material—even as a beginning it may provide you with one or two important ideas, and later you may find it easier to understand and very stimulating.

> You can only understand a textbook when you are at the point where you almost don't need to read it, where it helps you comprehend (if it is any good) some higher-order connections among things which you separately have already worked your way through or around.   DAVID HAWKINS

If material you are required to use seems too advanced or too basic for you, discuss this with your teacher and with other students. There may be other material you can use, or if you must use the material for an assignment, you might need to choose another topic.

Evaluating web pages

When using material from websites, it is critically important to check whether information is reputable. For example, look for 'peer reviewed' or 'refereed' journal articles since the journal editor will have had each article critiqued and evaluated by experts in the field. Your teachers are unlikely to be impressed by information that turns out to be from a strongly biased source, such as apparently scientific writing on evolution that comes from a fundamentalist Bible college. And images in sites can also be easily manipulated electronically. Unless you know your subject well or have guidance from someone who does, acquire some basic familiarity with the area through recommended sources such as key texts and knowledgeable academics.

On the Internet, there is no quality control as there would be in any school library. If a bibliography on the real, historical Aztecs surfaces amid the gleanings it may very well be out of date and unattributed. It might be the work of an amateur Aztec enthusiast in Peoria who never read basic materials in the field. If there is an essay on the Aztecs it may have been written by a fellow in Moose Jaw who has rather unusual theories about pre-Columbian peoples and space aliens. The Internet is a free-for-all, as enjoyable as any conversation one might strike up in a saloon or coffee house. But it is hardly governed by the critical safeguards and intellectual structures that have been developed across the centuries to discriminate between honest thought and rampant eccentricity.

THEODORE ROSZAK

Table 8.1 'Evaluating web pages' lists some questions to answer on a site or page itself. When first encountering a site which you plan to draw on heavily, make it a practice to do a quick check of boxes such as 'About Us', 'Contact Us', 'FAQs', 'Sponsors', 'Our Philosophy' and 'Biography' to see what these tell you about a site. To answer other questions in the table may mean checking other sites for further information, such as an author biography or information on an organisation.

You won't be able to find answers to all of the questions for each web page, but as you use the questions repeatedly, you'll discover that some of them are more useful than others. Running through the questions will become automatic, and using even a few questions from each category will increase the likelihood that information you rely on is reputable.

TABLE 8.1	**Evaluating web pages**

Audience and objectivity   Why?

- Why do you think the site was created, for example, to provide useful information to the public, to advertise a product, to contribute to serious discussion, or to promote the ideas of a particular political or social group?
- Is the material aimed at a particular audience, for example, the general public, academics, a special interest group, business, or professionals?
- Does the material set out to inform or explain or persuade?
- What does the writing style or vocabulary tell you about the purpose of the item?
- Is the item scholarly or popular?
- Does the author present clear or indirect opinions?
- Does the material make claims without strong evidence?
- Is the information free of advertising? Does a page appear to be a lead-in to advertising?
- If there is advertising, is it clearly differentiated from the information content?   *continued*

TABLE
8.1   **continued**

Authority   Who?

- Who wrote this information?
- How can you find out more about the author?
- Is an author biography included? Could you contact them?
- Does the author have the qualifications and experience in the field?
- Are they a known expert in the field? Do they work for a reputable institution?
- Is the author widely published on this subject?
- Is the author quoted by other sources?
- Does the author cite other sources?
- Is the item on the author's personal website or on a professional one?
- Who owns or publishes this site?
- Who published the document?
- Are there contact details which allow you to check if the publisher is legitimate?
- Does the publisher produce other titles in the field?
- Does an institution or parent organisation support or endorse the information?
- What is the purpose of the organisation behind the site?
- Is it a local or national or international institution?
- Do other reputable sites link to or review the page?
- Is the publisher separate from the webmaster or developer or administrator?

Currency   When?

- When was it produced?
- When was it last updated?
- Is there outdated information on the page?
- Are the links current or updated regularly? Or dead?

Accuracy   What?

- Is the information factual, detailed, correct and comprehensive?
- Can the information be verified by research, statistics or studies?
- Can you find a couple of other sources to confirm the information?
- Why does it appear to be either credible or unreliable?
- Is a reference list or bibliography included?
- Are there mistakes in content, spelling or grammar?

Coverage   How much?

- Does the page seem to be complete or still under construction?
- How much of the page is text and how much is images? Is this appropriate for the subject?
- Is the information abridged? If so, does it refer to valuable further information?
- Is there enough depth to the information presented?
- Does the information support or update information you've already found?
- Does the reference list or bibliography indicate that the material is comprehensive?

Accessibility   How?

- Is the site easy to navigate?
- Is there an option for text only, or frames, or a suggested browser for better viewing?
- If a page requires particular software to view it, how much are you missing if you don't have the software?
- If there is a print equivalent to the web page, is there a clear indication of whether the entire work or only parts of it are available?
- Is any free information complete or only a sample of a longer item?

Working with selected material

By now you have evaluated possible sources and narrowed your list of references to those that you are most likely to rely on and refer to in your assignment.

Questioning and critiquing

> Where there is much desire to learn, there of necessity will be much arguing, much writing, many opinions; for opinion in good men [*sic*] is but knowledge in the making.   JOHN MILTON

As you work more closely with your chosen items—a book, a lecture, a website or a video—question the information they offer. You have already evaluated items for reliability and accuracy. Continue to do this as you go into more depth, but turn your focus to examining the purpose, argument, content, structure and presentation of the material for its general quality and for its specific relevance to your aims and the topic. (See Chapters 10 and 11 for details on how to examine information from readings and lectures.)

As part of critiquing resources for your research, hopefully you will learn to interpret primary sources confidently. In some assignments you are expected to use both your interpretation of primary source material and your opinion from secondary sources. For example, when you conduct an experiment, you may be expected to interpret the data yourself and to refer to other people's interpretations of data from a similar experiment. In an essay you may be expected to criticise a well-known author's works (a primary source) and also use other critics' evaluations of them (a secondary source). You might feel uncertain about presenting your own argument and ideas, and think that you should play it safe and rely mostly on secondary sources; or you might come from an intellectual culture where what you write is expected to rely heavily on presenting ideas from authorities. To develop your confidence in presenting your own ideas on primary sources, practise the following:

- Get to know the primary source material thoroughly, and see what ideas and interests this sparks off in you.
- Refer to secondary sources to help clarify points you don't understand in the primary source material.
- Read selectively among secondary sources and critically examine other people's interpretations of the primary ideas or data you are studying.
- Use secondary sources for occasional new insights and for any unexpected connections they may make.

As you become a more experienced researcher, you will be better able to trust your common sense in questioning and evaluating research material.

In a private debate the scholar Salih Awami said to Sufi Rahimi:

'What you have just said lacks references and proofs through quotations from ancient authority.' 'Not at all,' said Rahimi, 'for I have them all here, chapter and verse.' The scholar went away, saying, 'That was what I wanted to know.' The next day he made his famous speech on Rahimi which began: 'The lecture which you are about to hear from Sheikh Rahimi lacks conviction. Why, he is so unsure of himself that he actually adducted written proofs and authorities to what he says.'   IDRIES SHAH

Integrating your ideas with information

When preparing for an assignment, as you research and think about your topic or question you need to organise and integrate your ideas with the information you find—for example, so that it supports your thesis in a persuasive essay or your theme in an expository essay (see 'Genres', Chapter 7). The following method is one way of doing this for an essay:

- In an argumentative essay, write out a tentative statement of your thesis. Capture the essence of your argument in a sentence. For an expository essay, clarify the theme. Keep this in front of you as you work.
- Write each of the possible main points as a heading on separate electronic files or sheets of paper. You might use the outlining function on appropriate software

to help order these points. At this stage, if doing your research in a library, a laptop or a portable system such as looseleaf paper can be more convenient.

- As you find relevant information and ideas (and references to any graphic or audiovisual material) enter these under the appropriate heading.

- As you build your research notes, add a new heading if you decide on another main point to support your thesis. Alternatively, you may decide to delete a point that comes to appear less significant. If you have much more information for one heading than for others, and if that main point is central to the question and clearly supports your thesis, consider whether you should base your whole assignment on this point or perhaps rethink your thesis. In this case, develop new main points under that heading. If necessary, reorganise and delete material.

- Check the number of main points you want to make against the possible assignment length and the time available. It is better to err on the side of making a few points clearly, with plenty of evidence, examples and explanation, rather than trying to cover a large number of possible major points superficially.

- Check that each main point clearly supports your thesis or focus and is clearly relevant to your topic or question (see 'Analysing a topic and developing a research question', Chapter 7).

Organising your information and ideas in this way helps you to see the main points more clearly. You begin to understand how they could effectively be part of your argument and connect to one another, and the order in which to develop them. Your researching, thinking and organising should extend and clarify your original analysis of the topic. As you continue your research, you will probably revise your original working definition of the topic and begin to structure the content.

Communicating your ideas

'Don't grunt,' said Alice, 'that's not at all a proper way of expressing yourself.'

LEWIS CARROLL

Talking with others about the ideas and the information from your research helps you begin to sort out your thoughts and become accustomed to putting them into words. For example, in an online unit you may have the chance through a discussion list to work collaboratively with other students in researching and drafting an essay.

As you carry out your research, it is often valuable to write individual paragraphs or sentences so that you capture an idea you may use later. Put these ideas down when you think of them in case they vanish; and if you have a half-formed idea in your head, try expressing it without editing and see how it takes shape. If you can use a word processor for this, it is easier at a later stage to refine what you want to say. Trying to express your current thoughts accurately can lead you to other useful ideas (see 'Free writing', Chapters 13 and 14).

Towards the end of your research

When your research is almost complete and you are ready to begin to make use of the material, try to allow yourself time to sort out your ideas, for your thoughts to sift and settle. Do this rather than read another article or conduct another interview, especially if you are finding it difficult to work out what you want to say. Look at your notes as a whole. This will refresh your mind about your ideas on the topic and allow you to review the information you have selected from your material.

Talk again about your ideas and information with others, perhaps in a discussion or writing group, so that you begin to express your thoughts orally or in writing. New ideas and relationships will emerge, and any difficulties you might have in deciding and articulating what you want to say often resolve themselves. To clarify your thesis or theme, look at the connections between your main points, and ask yourself again what strikes you as most important and interesting about the question.

Your revised definition

Before you began your research you came up with an initial definition (see 'Your initial definition', at the beginning of this chapter). After your research, review your written statement about the assignment learning outcomes, and produce a revised definition.

- Look again at the question, paying special attention to any directive verbs and key concepts.
- Using the questions in 'Analysing a topic and developing a research question', Chapter 7, make notes again outlining your thesis or theme, the main points you have chosen, and the way in which you will structure them.
- Compare the initial and revised definitions. Have you omitted anything important? Does your revised definition still reflect your aims for the essay?
- Make sure, especially in the case of specific topics, that you are addressing all parts of the topic.
- With topics of your own choice, re-read any guidelines to ensure that you have incorporated all the requirements when developing your definition. Remember that focusing your written work around a thesis is a fundamental expectation for argumentative essays.

Now that your research is more or less complete, your thesis or theme and the main points that you will cover should be reasonably definite. If you find that you have omitted any important content, you may need to do some further research. The way in which you structure your assignment—how you will show the relationship between the main points and organise them so that they support your thesis or focus—may be quite clear now or may still be tentative. In either case, leave some flexibility so that if necessary you can revise your definition further when expressing your thoughts and information in writing your assignment (see 'Before you begin writing', Chapter 14).

An assignment is designed for a specific, limited purpose, rather than to find out all you are ever likely to know on a topic. Analysing a question and researching a topic should enable you to select from your current knowledge of that topic, even if your knowledge continues to grow and expand in areas far beyond the focus of your assignment.

TEN TIPS

1   Identifying how much time you actually have for each stage of your assignment—research, writing, editing—provides a realistic framework for your research.

2   Drawing up a thoughtful list of key terms and your likely main points saves time because it enables you to focus your research.

3   The first place to look for relevant material is your unit materials, especially if these are required sources.

4   Even if you regularly search the Internet in your daily life, developing the range of skills needed for effective academic research can save you a lot of time.

5   As you select and bookmark relevant sites, organising them into folders is useful for a particular assignment and also for future research.

6   Learn how Boolean operators can help you make your searches more precise and accurate.

7   Acquire the habit of evaluating websites for objectivity, authority, currency, accuracy, coverage and accessibility.

8   Look for less obvious sources which can enrich your thinking and make your assignment more original.

9   Taking time to construct an effective filing system for your notes will pay off when you need to quickly find references again.

10   Find opportunities to discuss your research with others as a way of clarifying your ideas.

Using information sources

9

. . . in the space of just over a decade, innovations in processing ever huger data sets have shifted our sense of what authority means further than during any comparable period in history—at the same time challenging some of our most central notions of cultural and intellectual value.

TOM CHATFIELD

We live in the midst of information networks. In the face-to-face and virtual worlds, you are a point in many networks, sometimes giving information and sometimes seeking it. No one can possibly learn all there is to know about a subject, so you can be both a learner and a teacher in subjects that interest you. Even as an interested beginner, you probably know enough about an area to teach someone else a little about it. If you can't answer someone's queries on a subject, you can probably direct them to another part of a network where they are likely to find what they want to know. Which network you plug into when seeking information depends on what you want to know, why you want to know it and whether you know which information sources are available, as well as how to use them effectively.

Where would you go first if you wanted to find out about emus? Or about the writer Isaac Asimov? Or about double-entry bookkeeping?

We tend to have preferences for finding information, depending on how we learnt in the past, and our preferred learning style. For example, to find out about emus you might want to see a live emu, or you might prefer to talk with a park ranger or a farmer, or to search online, or to find a book with pictures.

Starting points

Not even the largest 'multiversity' can offer all the resources needed by students today.   UNIVERSITY WITHOUT WALLS

An initial step in choosing information sources on a topic is to become aware of the range of possible sources. As a student in an educational institution, you have some obvious sources such as:

— classes, including lectures, laboratory sessions and discussion groups

— people, including teachers and other students, and

— printed and multimedia material, such as unit guides, laboratory manuals, handouts, recommended books and library materials.

Being able to use a range of information sources requires:

— defining your aims and analysing a question as clearly as you can

— locating a range of potential information sources

— choosing and evaluating sources that suit your subject, and

— examining sources to find out how to use them most effectively.

Unit materials

If you use the Internet often in everyday life, it may well be your first choice for finding information at university. However, recognise that unit coordinators carefully choose specific materials, reference lists and audio or video items as particularly valuable for certain subjects. In addition, assignments are set with the expectation that you will draw thoughtfully on specified materials, so it would be wise to make these your starting point. Materials provided by a unit coordinator can include:

— general sources such as lecture notes, or a bulletin board with updated information and a FAQs section

— online lectures or podcasts which provide specific information on a particular topic and which you can listen to as often as you need, or

— a blog used to discuss specific subjects, with ongoing contributions by the coordinator and which may or may not allow comments (see 'Blogs', Chapter 13).

Students can also contribute to unit materials if, for example, you are asked:

— to write your own blog

— to contribute to a wiki, that is, an open-access collaboratively created web page for writing projects, or

— to take part in a forum which is teacher-moderated or primarily for peer discussions.

In some units the information comes from field work, experiments, studio sessions and workshops. In other units, you might be directed to develop thoughtful questionnaires for interviews with individuals or groups. Learning with and from other people face-to-face presents unique challenges and satisfactions, especially at a time when vast amounts of disembodied information can be accessed on the Internet. And while the Internet has become the first place that many students go for information, university libraries are a rich resource specifically designed to meet student and staff research needs, so it makes sense to explore and get to know them.

Libraries

There are various types of libraries which have many different functions. They include:

— large state libraries, with special sections such as archives and history collections

— university libraries, often with individual subject libraries, branch libraries and departmental libraries attached

— government departmental libraries

— specialist collections, such as a historical society library, a photographic collection, or a substantial private collection

— public libraries serving a local community

— corporation libraries, and

— school and college libraries.

If you have access to more than one library, explore each one to find out what it offers you. Look at each as a possible place to work. Consider the facilities and services, material in your areas of interest, and staff expertise and helpfulness. It takes time to become familiar with the contents and organisation of a large library, and it takes practice to learn how to access library facilities and support services. To update, extend and diversify your knowledge of the information that any library has to offer, explore its online resources when new topics stimulate your curiosity.

> A researcher in San Francisco might, without leaving the desk, reach into the database of the British Library to grab a copy of the Lindisfarne Gospels, while another researcher in London rummages through the collections of the Library of Congress trying to find various Federalist papers. Instead of fortresses of knowledge, there will be oceans of information.
>
> J. BROWNING

Using a university library once meant hunting through physical collections. But it is now more appropriate to think in terms of accessing library services and library networks where virtual and physical spaces and services are integrated. Many materials from the core collections of academic libraries are online, and this provides 24-hour access to the full text of materials that can usually be downloaded and read online, or printed. As a tertiary education student you need the skills to discover online information, and most university libraries provide courses and support to help you develop these.

Information and learning spaces

While libraries are a node in information networks, they are also buildings within which there are different types of learning spaces, each with a different function. For example, large university libraries often contain a 'learning commons' with individual workstations, places for group work, and software which enables you to collaboratively record the results of your research. Staff expertise is usually available nearby for both content requests and for information technology support. Learning support services may also be available, for example, assistance with essay writing.

As well as interactive spaces, libraries still provide quiet corners where you can concentrate on study, whether or not you are using library materials. This is especially useful if there are distractions at home, or if because of home or work commitments you have to treat study as a daytime activity which you mostly leave behind when you go off campus.

Become familiar with the layout of a campus library—find out where different types of materials are located, and where facilities such as computers, printers, photocopiers and audiovisual equipment can be found. Most libraries have maps and publications describing their layout and operation, but it is easy to fall into the habit of using only one section of a library and being unaware of what other areas have to offer.

Types of collections

- **Unit materials** identified by lecturers as important are often placed in a reserve collection or an online equivalent e-Reserve collection. Links to an e-Reserve Collection are also often available through the unit web pages.

- **Electronic research databases** include indexes to articles and may include the full text of publications from newspapers, journals, statistical publications, encyclopedias and legal materials. These can include multimedia materials and visuals (such as photographs and drawings), sound (such as music and foreign language phrases) or both (such as videos and film clips). The databases can be searched for information on specific subjects, using key words or concepts relevant to your research topic. In most cases, the references you find can then be downloaded or printed.

- An important group of books in any library is **the reference collection**, for example, standard references such as *The Encyclopaedia Britannica* and *The Oxford Dictionary*. Reference collections can also contain works such as:

  — specialist encyclopedias or dictionaries, such as *The Encyclopedia of Philosophy*, and the *Dictionary of Film Makers*

  — atlases, gazetteers and guidebooks, such as the *Archaeological Atlas of the World*, and the *Bartholomew Gazetteer of Britain*

  — yearbooks and almanacs which give relatively up-to-date statistical information and which are often government publications, such as *The West Australian Yearbook*

  — handbooks, which contain useful and detailed information for people in specific fields, such as teaching, writing, surveying or skin diving

  — bibliographies which list books and other types of material by a particular subject, author, printer or country, for example, the *Current Bibliographies on African Affairs*, *The International Bibliography of Economics* and *A Bibliography of Sex Rites and Customs*, and

  — resource directories, which are catalogues of useful material, people and places, such as a directory for a particular city or small interest group.

  While some of these items may only be available in print in the library's reference collection, many are available online and can be found by conducting a subject search in the library's search system.

- **Books** are familiar sources of information, and may be available as e-books or as printed books (see Chapter 10, 'Reading', for suggestions on reading printed material effectively), but a wide range of other material may be available, such as journals or periodicals, newspapers, bulletins and other serial publications and government publications, such as reports, yearbooks and manuals.

  Twenty-two acknowledged concubines, and a library of sixty-two thousand volumes, attested the variety of his inclination . . .   EDWARD GIBBON

- In addition, there is **other material** and the following list may include materials unfamiliar to you or which you have not considered for academic research:

— graphic material, such as maps, prints, illustrations, paintings and models

— audiovisual material, such as video and films

— microform collections of research material, such as back issues of rare newspapers, and

— collections of ephemeral material, such as newsletters, posters, advertisements and lapel buttons.

Discovering useful resources

Most of us turn to Google and other search engines and tools when we want to find information in everyday life. However, if the work you produce as a student is to meet your teachers' expectations you also need to make in-depth use of academic libraries.

Guides and support

● Do not feel that you are alone in requiring help to carry out your library research. Knowing where to begin can be daunting, whether you are a new student entering the library for the first time or more advanced and about to begin research in a totally new area. When you need help in using the library, its resources or services, don't hesitate to ask the *library staff* for assistance. They are usually very helpful with anything from the most basic to the most esoteric of queries, and there are staff with specialist knowledge.

● Large libraries have extensive *websites* which act as gateways to all the resources and services. Become familiar with all parts of your library's website so that you can quickly and efficiently locate information and online resources. Attend a library tutorial to find out about using your library and searching for information, or ask the librarians for help.

● Explore the various *guides* the library has to enable you to locate material. These cover a wide range of topics, from finding key resources in specific subject areas, to citing your sources correctly, and organising your citations so that you can retrieve and re-use them effectively.

Searching for and retrieving information

Learning how to use the library's search systems effectively is the most important thing you can do to help you discover and retrieve relevant information. Most large libraries provide multiple ways of searching for resources. Make sure that you understand which content you're searching for when you use the library's search systems, and use a list of search terms central to a topic (see 'Analysing a topic and developing a research question', Chapter 7, and 'Selecting likely material', Chapter 8). Online instructions and guides will usually be available to assist you.

● A library website usually offers a Google-like search box where you can enter search terms to discover all the items available to you: books, journal articles, newspapers, theses, videos, archival collections, unit materials and others. Searching in this manner often results in retrieval of many items. You can refine your search results in various ways, for example:

— by year of publication

— by type of publication (such as books or articles)

— by subject

— by library location, and

— by full text availability (useful if you need it quickly).

Instructions on how to search effectively are normally available on the website.

- Some libraries also let you search the library catalogue as a subset of the broader search system—this provides information about everything the library has acquired and made available online, or on the shelves. You might find that searching for a known book is easier to accomplish by using the library catalogue than by using the larger search system. Your search for a book will, for example:

— retrieve those books which the library holds in its collection as well as e-books

— provide full details about the publication including title, authors, publication and edition

— provide information about where to locate the book on the shelf, or link to it online

— indicate whether it is out on loan and when it will be next available, and

— allow you to recall it from loan.

The system will help you to manage the books you have on loan by checking return dates, and possibly listing titles you've already borrowed and returned.

- You can also search within individual databases to find articles or other materials on a topic.

- If you fail to find anything of interest, consider whether you've used the correct search terms. If you have searched for a known item which you expected the library to hold—a reference from a unit guide, for example—check that you have the precise details such as author name or title of a book or article. While search systems can be quite forgiving and provide a range of alternatives, having the correct citation to start with is important.

- Once you've discovered an interesting item, you need to retrieve it for use. Online resources normally require you to have logged into the system to gain access, especially if you're using your own device on campus, or are searching from off campus. Normally your campus network login will work for library resources, but check that you have the correct information about remote access to online, licensed resources. The library or IT services will help you with this if needed. Printed items will be available within the library, shelved according to the library-specific system for organising collections. Make sure that you are aware of how to locate printed items in the library—library staff will help you if you're having trouble; they understand that it takes time to become acquainted with a system.

Off-campus access

With access to the Internet, you gain 24-hour access to the library, can conduct subject searches and can obtain high-quality copies of articles as well as links to e-books and other e-resources. This library service means you do not have to go on campus and enables you to study at a time and place that suits you. For students who are isolated in the long term (due to physical constraints, for example) or in the short term (due to illness or one-off commitments), online access to library services is invaluable. If you have an ongoing disability, find out what assistive technology is available in the library.

If you are not able to visit the campus library easily, perhaps because you have physical limitations or are a part-time or external student, be particularly well-informed about the services offered and the facilities you need to use most often, such as special loan arrangements. If you do manage to visit the library, be very clear about the sort of information you are seeking.

If accessing the library from home presents problems (such as unreliable Internet access or a slow download speed), check if there are other ways of gaining Internet access locally, via a local public library or via an employer or a government agency if in remote areas or small towns. Identify any books you are required to use extensively, and be prepared to buy these (see 'Download, print, copy, borrow or buy?', Chapter 8). The cost of mailing books or making special trips to a library can soon add up to the price of several books, and libraries don't regard provision of textbooks in large numbers as one of their functions.

The Internet

For centuries, it has been the case that no one can individually possess, consume or meaningfully search even a fraction of the world's knowledge. So we have always turned to others to advise and to select materials for us—and to determine what gains entry to those fields of permanent record in the first place.

Today, the process of selection is no longer one that happens before something is sent into the world . . . Almost anything and everything is now in front of the world's gaze, sifted not by gatekeepers but by public taste.   TOM CHATFIELD

Search engines

Many of us are familiar with at least one of the global search engines which create huge databases as a result of trawling the Internet. For your research, at times you might find it more appropriate to identify smaller more specialised search engines, or to conduct a thorough search within a particular site. A search aggregator gathers results from multiple search engines simultaneously, and can allow you to select specific search engines to be combed for information in response to a particular research question.

More academically focused search engines (such as Google Scholar) can be a convenient way to do a broad search for scholarly materials in a field, such as books, journal articles, conference papers and other literature. These search tools may:

— indicate where free online copies of items can be found
— help identify significant experts in a field
— suggest key search terms, and
— provide a starting point for finding other relevant literature.

Examples of different types of sites useful for study include:

— archive sites, which preserve valuable content which may otherwise disappear
— community sites, which serve as a forum for people with shared interests via chat and message boards
— organisation sites, belonging to corporations, businesses or other bodies
— information sites, belonging to bodies such as government or educational institutions
— media sharing and gallery sites, where users can upload and access images and music
— microblogging sites, where posts are limited in length
— news or political sites, with information and commentary on current events
— portals, which provide a gateway to an intranet or to other Internet resources
— 'question and answer' sites
— review sites, and
— wikis, where information is openly constructed in a collaborative way.

When you search online, go past the most obvious sites or those most easily found. Any individual site can change rapidly, but there are categories of sites which can be especially valuable to students. For example, sites which offer high-quality talks for a wide audience are useful because what is said needs to be clear and not assume extensive prior knowledge. Once you begin to find generally reliable sites which offer thoughtful and well-researched views and information, compile a list to which you can return. Swap lists with other students, and ask academics for sites that they find repeatedly stimulating or which are regarded as the most valued sites for a particular discipline.

Net neutrality?

Within the anonymous pixels of identical screens across the world, I encounter their service as if it were something found and not made.   TOM CHATFIELD

It is unrealistic to assume that knowledge on the Internet is neutral. This is obvious in some sites, but sometimes the abstract technological nature of the way in which we are presented with information can give the impression that such information is balanced and does not embody particular world views.

And while 'crowdsourcing' of knowledge may over time lead to more balanced and reliable information on a subject, the opinions of many rather than a few are not a guarantee of neutrality. For example, despite the open and collaborative construction of knowledge in Wikipedia, with systems in place for editing and for handling disputes over content, its current input is mostly from contributors who are male and from developed countries. (You can see how information on a subject is being constructed by looking at the 'History' and 'Disputes' tabs.) And while some specialist wikis are moderated by experts in the field, in more generalist wikis the views of experts in a subject are given no more weight than those of novices.

It is also important to give at least passing thought to the politics and economics of the Internet. The digitisation of a large quantity of books and of the contents of some libraries can make this material much more accessible to a much wider number of people; but if there is a charge for access, the material has become valuable as a commodity rather than for its own sake. It is also worth considering why particular material is selected for digitisation and who makes the choice.

'. . . those of us who are spending hours a day on Facebook are really living and interacting with people inside a marketing platform,' cautions Douglas Rushkoff. 'Those of us who are going on the world wide web are in a business space, as much as it is a social space.'   ANTONY FUNNELL

If you usually rely on the top few results from a search, are you aware how certain results manage to be ranked above others? Have you given thought to the possibly circular nature of some rankings, where an item with most previous hits receives a high ranking, which can result in more people accessing it, so it continues to receive a high ranking regardless of its relative merit? (Think about the repeated airplay received by big-name groups as compared to a new band trying to get noticed.)

So if this circular effect does apply to what you look for—for example, if a company notes what you previously looked at and so next time presents you with related items—how might you manage to access a wider range of sites? Going past the first page of results is one tactic, as is learning how to evaluate websites for your purposes (see 'Evaluating web pages', Chapter 8).

Then there is the question of who decides what we search for and how. While there is an enormous diversity of material on the Internet, are you aware of how many (or how few) very big 'for profit' companies control much of it? Or who makes money from this medium, for example, by collecting data on you? Consider how the profit motive might shape what you are presented with, and the ways in which it might be lucrative to manipulate the choices you make. If you have a habit of flicking from one web page to another, think about why commercial companies might prefer that you skip quickly from one source to another instead of staying to read in a leisurely way.

Information is coming at us from everywhere, and while this can be exciting and valuable, as a student it becomes vital to work out how to exclude information that you don't need or want. It is easy to feel overloaded with information possibilities, but you do have a choice about how much information to consume, so think about why you make certain choices. For example, consuming lots of information within a narrow band which mostly confirms what we already know or think can leave us just as ignorant as being under-informed.

> . . . there is no evidence that quantity becomes quality in matters of human expression or achievement. What matters instead, I believe, is a sense of focus, a mind in effective concentration, and an adventurous individual imagination that is distinct from the crowd.
>
> JARON LANIER

Information literacy

Being 'literate' in how to use the Internet for academic study involves more than knowing how to do a few quick searches on a topic. And knowing how to use online media in personal life doesn't mean that you automatically know how it might, or might not, be effective for study purposes.

University-level Internet

> People who think education equals information have no idea what either education or information is . . . A good working definition of information might be: it is an answer to a question that purports to be a fact. At least a definition like that reminds us that the quality of the question is more important than the quantity of data that appears as an answer.
>
> THEODORE ROSZAK

- Glancing through heaps of material on a topic, and perhaps downloading it, does not equate to knowing more about the topic; quantity isn't the same as quality, and amassing data isn't the same as developing an in-depth understanding of a subject.

- To build knowledge on a subject, take time to think critically, analytically and reflectively about what you find (see 'Critical thinking', Chapter 3), and to look at how different sources complement or contradict each other.

- Going after information because you continually want new stimuli is not the same as genuine curiosity which seeks to understand a subject.

- Knowing how is not the same as knowing why (see 'What questions might you ask?', Chapter 6).

- You wouldn't assume you were more knowledgeable simply because you walked into a library which had lots of books. Similarly, because we live in a time when there is a lot of material on the Internet, we cannot assume that we are somehow smarter or better informed. Information exists only on the Internet until you first, access it, and second, engage with it thoughtfully and with some purpose in mind.

- Learning how to evaluate web pages is an essential university skill (see Table 8.1, 'Evaluating web pages').

Skills needed

If you are a savvy everyday user of electronic media some aspects of it are very familiar to you, but you need to discover which parts of this experience could be useful in academic research. For example:

- Which skills do you need to competently use a library search system?
- When you are dealing with a long online article, which practical skills might be most useful, such as reducing the download size by disabling images?
- Could you benefit from assistive or adaptive technologies such as alternatives to using a mouse, or universal access features such as captioned audio, screen magnification, voice over, or flashing alerts?

With social media, think about the characteristics of each type, and then consider whether or not you could effectively use some of these features in academic work. For example, instant messaging doesn't allow for in-depth dialogue but could be an efficient way to exchange small bits of data quickly, or to conduct multiple simultaneous conversations.

While for many of us the Internet is now like the water we drink, as a student it is worth taking time to reflect on your existing Internet habits, or the quality of the water you're drinking. For example:

- How do you use the Internet to communicate?
- When seeking answers which sorts of questions do you most often use? Are the questions to find out about 'who' or 'how' or 'what' or 'when', or perhaps about 'why'? (See Chapter 6, 'Asking your own questions'.)
- When you use the Internet to seek information, what steps do you take? What skills do these steps require? Are the skills possibly transferable to your academic research?
- Do you generally use a systematic or a scatter gun approach to finding information?
- How often do you use electronic tools to actively seek out views different from your own, or to look for information which significantly enlarges your knowledge in an area?
- Or do you mostly look for ideas and 'facts' which agree with what you already believe or think you know (the 'echo chamber' effect)?

- If you look mostly for input from people who share your world view and ideas, does this mean that you feel more assertive about what you believe?

- Do you feel that you are more cosmopolitan and global simply because there is an abundance of diverse ideas 'out there' which you could access if you wanted to?

The 'wisdom of crowds' effect should be thought of as a tool. The value of a tool is its usefulness in accomplishing a task. The point should never be the glorification of the tool.

JARON LANIER

Using sources effectively

As a student, one of your primary tasks is to develop the capacity to ascertain which sources are regarded as academically reputable. However, you might sometimes overlook potential information if you stick only to academic sources. So as well as automatically consulting your lecture notes or accessing the Internet for information, ask yourself:

○○○○ *How would I find what I want to know if I wasn't a student with access to these sources?*

For example, you can learn much in your formal education from groups and individuals who are not formally considered experts or teachers. If you are studying local history, you can gain a wealth of information from an historical society made up of people who have lived in your community for a long time. If you are studying insect behaviour, the person next door who has kept bees for many years can be extremely helpful.

Communities offer a wide variety of organisations which can be helpful. The following are just a few possibilities:

— public agencies and institutions, such as museums, government departments, art galleries, courts, and scientific research organisations

— commercial businesses, such as mining companies, factories, insurance companies, shopping centres, and

— community groups, such as church organisations, business associations, environmental groups, women's healthcare houses, or ethnic broadcasting groups.

Some organisations offer library and public information facilities. You also have access to services and organisations designed to provide information, such as consumer advice groups and local government information offices. Often a person or group can refer you to further sources. Organisations and community groups receive many requests for information, so before you approach them it is courteous to have done some preliminary research on your topic and on the organisation, to find out who is likely to be the most appropriate person to help you, and to be as specific as possible about what you want to find out. This process of finding material is a valuable learning exercise in itself. Remember though that most organisations have a particular purpose; their approach to information is only part of the picture and may be biased (see 'Evaluating web pages', Chapter 8).

To make the most of a source:

- Think about its nature—what characteristics distinguish it from other sources? What might be its strengths and its limitations?
- Learn about different types of sources recognised in academic research (such as primary and secondary material) and the skills needed to use them effectively.

The mass media

Even if you receive much of your information on current events from social media and electronic journalism, the mass media are still a pervasive presence in our society. If you read a daily paper or watch the TV news, you see your community, your society and your world as they are selected, reflected and shaped by journalists. These 'gatekeepers' are in turn responding to the demands of a voracious 24-hour news cycle and are competing with other sources to be first with 'the news'. The extent to which the media influence you is particularly strong if you are not usually a critical reader or viewer of complex material.

> The newspaper format . . . offers short, discrete articles that give important facts first and then taper off to incidental details, which may be, and often are, eliminated by the make-up man. The fact that reporters cannot control the length of their articles means that, in writing them, emphasis can't be placed on structure, at least in the traditional linear sense, with climax or conclusion at the end.   EDMUND CARPENTER

But receiving news 'as it happens' makes it difficult to stand back from the information conveyed. For example, it is difficult to evaluate and use a 10-minute TV special on a 'hot' topic in the same way as you could a documentary or a book. And because much of the media deal almost entirely with topical issues and events, they frequently select information that makes 'a good story' or has visual appeal, rather than presenting a balanced view of a subject. In cases where the ownership of large sections of the media is concentrated in the hands of a few people, the information with which you are presented is likely to be limited in its scope. Use the mass media, but keep their limitations in mind.

If you want to use media information in academic research, seek out quality investigative journalism online. For example, you are more likely to find reliable and well-researched current material from public broadcasters and their websites. This material might include regular programs in areas such as science, gender issues, current affairs, wildlife and music; and special programs on major historical events and on complex issues such as nuclear power and racial discrimination.

Primary and secondary sources

When undertaking research, sometimes you can go directly to your subject for first-hand information. For example, if your subject is the ideas of Mao Tse-Tung you may be able to obtain and read translations of his writings, or if you are studying goldfish behaviour you might have access to facilities where you can conduct experiments. At other times, you will have to rely on other people's reports about your subject. For example, you may read a journal article about Mao Tse-Tung if you can't obtain his books, or you might ask an aquarium owner about the behaviour of goldfish. Often you will use both first-hand (or primary) and second-hand (or secondary) information.

If you are studying a local community group and you gather your information on them by attending several meetings, your source is also your subject and is described as a primary source. If you read a newspaper article on the group to obtain your information, the article is a secondary source, that is, the information doesn't come directly from your subject.

Similarly, if your subject is a scientific research organisation, a filmed interview with the head of the organisation is a primary source, whereas someone else's written report about the interview is a secondary source. If you are studying an historical event, the testimonies of participants and witnesses are primary sources, while a source of secondary information would be a biography written by an historian using these testimonies.

Quantitative and qualitative sources

You will often see the words 'qualitative' and 'quantitative' used to describe approaches to research. Put simplistically, the latter is about numbers and observations about 'facts', while the former is about narratives, words and phrases, images and documents that are assembled for analysis and interpretation. Most sources you use, whether primary or secondary, will contain two types of information: quantitative and qualitative. News bulletins, for example, use numbers to explain some aspects of a topic while other aspects are described in detail using words only.

Research may be conducted using quantitative methods, qualitative methods or some combination of both. For example, you may find data being reported where a table of numbers representing opinions is given, but alongside this table will be quotations that support the analysis. You need to understand what the numbers mean while gaining an insight into the situation from the narrative that goes with it.

Quantitative data, such as a chart of the unemployment rate over time, may be created from information that is being kept by an agency for people who are looking for work. Information may be obtained from each person, such as their age, marital status or place of birth, and then the data combined for the hundreds of people seen by the agency. This combination of single cases (people) then allows some sort of mathematical calculation. This generates quantitative information that can be used in research. Quantitative data can be analysed so as to generalise to the wider population to which the data applies.

Qualitative data, on the other hand, involves words, often combined with or explained through pictures or diagrams. The data may be obtained through methods such as interviews, observation or analysis of text (such as letters, books, reports, newscasts), and will produce a rich source of information. It is not possible to generalise from the data to a wider context but can still inform understandings, policy making and other decisions.

Research: a complex process

Think about how we gather information in everyday life. For example, when we are curious about a subject we can learn much by attentive observation. If we think about what is involved in observing, we will realise that it can be much more than 'just looking'. We can listen and look closely, and use our senses of taste, smell and touch if appropriate. If we observe a subject consistently and intently over a period of days or weeks, we come to see it with new eyes. We can observe the natural physical environment—phenomena such as a sunset, a bird, trees, rain and mountains. We can observe our manufactured and technological environment, with its aeroplanes and advertisements, its technology and toys. We can observe the people in our world such as parents, friends, work colleagues or strangers.

Observing people and seeking information from them are activities in which we engage for many of our waking hours, and we consciously or unconsciously learn much of what we need to know from interacting with others. Most of us think that we can understand other people simply by observation, partly because we are also people. And, we can learn much and arrive at some interesting descriptions by observing people. But to deliberately obtain reliable information from and about people requires forethought, and ongoing practice in skills such as observing and listening.

A similarly painstaking, systematic and analytical approach is required in academic research. For example:

- To obtain information through a questionnaire, you need to do more than throw together a long list of questions. A poorly constructed questionnaire is likely to result in spurious information; and skilled researchers recognise the need for a clear research question and are very cautious about drawing conclusions from their data.
- Research needs to be conducted according to ethical standards—be aware that universities take research ethics seriously. You may be familiar with debates around ethical research using animals, but you also need to consider any ethical questions which might be involved in research involving people. For example,

will your research be conducted with and for your interviewees, or is it purely for your own ends? How will you protect any highly personal information?

● Research techniques can be more of a hindrance than a help if used without sensitivity to the complexity of people and environments, or if used in the belief that they provide 'objective' answers.

Each discipline has evolved methodologies for carrying out different types of research, and there are ongoing controversies about various research tools. The skills developed by a botanist won't equip them to study human society, likewise the skills learned by a sociologist won't help them study a tree fungus (it will help them study botanists though). So when you go to an academic source (especially if it is refereed), the information you find should be the result of careful and deliberate research which draws on discipline-appropriate methods. Social science research draws on methods developed for studying people; and without such methods we can't properly generalise about a group or population.

Anyone interested in human beings and why we act as we do won't want to limit their inquiry to reading books or listening to lectures. The raw material of all our understanding of human behaviour is observations of people—ourselves and others. These observations describe how people act in certain situations and what they say about how they feel and why they do things. From these observations it is common for researchers to infer people's motives, values, attitudes, and opinions. Social science has developed a whole array of tools to assist in these analyses. These tools include questionnaires, interviews, field studies, participant observation, laboratory studies, and unobtrusive measures.

Each of these techniques is an entire skill area in itself and consists of a whole series of sub-techniques. For example, an interview may be open-ended or closed, structured or unstructured, in-depth or limited. The proper construction of a reliable and valid questionnaire is a skill requiring months or years of training and experience. Unobtrusive measures for observing people can range from activities such as measuring carpet wear patterns in an art gallery to find out which paintings are most popular, to gathering statistics from pharmaceutical companies about sales of oral contraceptives to Catholic and non-Catholic communities.

Each technique has its own characteristic strengths and weaknesses. The nature of the question being asked, the population being studied, the resources available, and the preferences of the questioner, all influence the choice of appropriate techniques. This area of 'research methodology' is one of the most complex and difficult in the social sciences and scholars spend entire lifetimes studying small aspects of it.

The interpretation of the data is equally complex and requires a sophisticated level of skill if it is to be properly done. The path which leads from initial formulation of a question in the mind through gathering data from observations of people to drawing valid conclusions from those observations is a long and thorny path which is pitted with traps for the unwary. Expert guidance is essential.   JOHN RASER

Humans don't follow neat patterns of behaviour, don't act in totally predictable ways, and are distinctly prone to present a researcher with a mass of complex material to analyse. As you acquire information, hopefully your clear definition of what you want to know will remain the same in substance, but it will inevitably change in shape as you come to grips with the uniqueness of another human being. To acquire skill in using research techniques, practise them and learn from your successes and failures how each technique can best be applied.

Even when you have considerable skill with such tools you will continue to learn more about their use because of the unpredictable nature of your 'subjects'. This very unpredictability shows the limited use of even sophisticated research tools, unless you seriously consider the nature of the relationship between yourself as a researcher and the people from whom you are seeking information. For example, if you treat interviewees only as information sources who should confine themselves to passively answering your questions, you ignore the input that these individuals can make to the substance and validity of your research. Or if you assume that you are a neutral observer or interviewer, you overlook how the way in which you are perceived might influence the responses you are given.

Another aspect of this research relationship concerns your cultural background, since this affects how you interpret the responses you receive from someone whose background differs from your own. Imagine, for example, how the responses of an older female factory worker might be interpreted differently by an affluent young male student, by a senior professional woman and by an older unemployed man whose mother worked in a factory. When you do not share the cultural background of the person you are interviewing, it is advisable to seek guidance when planning and interpreting your research.

> . . . the active voice of the subject should be heard in the account. Our interpretations should avoid transforming the acting and thinking human being solely into an object of study, while recognising that some objectification is inherent in the process of interpretation or reconstruction. Moreover . . . the theoretical reconstruction must be able to account for the investigator as well as for those who are investigated.
>
> JOAN ACKER et al.

TEN TIPS

1   Think about where and from whom you usually acquire information about current events and controversial issues.

2   Brainstorm to create a list of as many sources of information as you can.

3   For each unit you are taking, identify the essential sources with which you need to become familiar.

4   Check if you understand the difference between primary and secondary sources.

5   Take a tour of your university library (online or in person) to discover the sorts of collections it holds and how to access them as quickly as possible.

6   Learn how the library's web pages can save you time when you need to do things such as reserve a book or ask a librarian a specific question.

7   Ask library staff for help, especially in your first year or when you are taking a unit whose subject is unfamiliar.

8   Learn about the different types of Internet search engines and web pages.

9   Do an Internet search on a couple of topics and look at each entry on the first 2–3 pages to compare them to the three top-ranked results.

10 Choose a currently controversial topic and locate three different viewpoints on it.

Reading

10

I would sooner read a time-table or a catalogue than nothing at all.

SOMERSET MAUGHAM

As you silently read this paragraph, your eyes are moving from left to right in a series of quick jumps along the line of print. Each time your eyes stop, they focus on individual words or a cluster of words. The number of words you take in depends on your eye span and your word recognition skills.

You instantly perceive and recognise familiar words by their shape without needing to think consciously about their spelling, pronunciation or origin. However, sometimes you need a context to give a familiar word meaning. For example, how do you understand 'read' in 'I have read six books' or in 'You need to read between the lines'? At other times you need knowledge or experience to identify the intended meaning of a word. For example, the meaning of 'the table is too short' will vary according to the context in which this statement occurs.

When you come to a word you have never seen before, such as 'transmogrify' or 'simulacrum', your eyes focus on it for longer. You might re-read the sentence or paragraph to understand the meaning of the word from its context, or you might refer to a dictionary. Perhaps you recognise parts of the word ('trans-' in 'transmogrify'), or you attempt to divide the word into syllables (trans-mog-ri-fy, sim-u-la-crum) and pronounce it to see if you have ever heard the word spoken. Sometimes the word reminds you of another familiar word ('simulacrum' may remind you of 'similar', 'simulate', 'simultaneous' or 'fulcrum'). You might skip the word and move on.

There is much more to understanding what you read than the physical movement of your eyes and your ability to recognise words. When reading the paragraphs above, you gained an overall impression of what was written without needing to identify every word or literally reconstruct the printed message. You filtered the message through who you are as a reader and this was influenced by your cultural background, experiences and world view. These in turn have influenced your knowledge of and interest in the subject, your reading purpose, your reading abilities, your feelings about reading and your understanding and interpretation of what you read.

This reading process applies to reading longer passages of text whether printed or on screen. Different processes apply when reading on the web (see 'Information literacy', Chapter 9).

Recent theory . . . argues that experience is not personal but cultural. That is, although you, as an individual, may have an experience—such as falling off a bike, loving someone or winning a prize—you can only think about those experiences in particular ways that are available to you. So, it is argued that texts are read and gaps filled by readers, not with ideas that they personally 'make up', but with meanings that are already available in their culture.   BRONWYN MELLOR, ANNETTE PATTERSON and MARNIE O'NEILL

Stop for a few minutes to think about and answer the following questions about you as a reader:

Do you like to read? Why?

If you don't enjoy reading, why not?

What genres do you like to read? Historical novels? Scientific journal articles? Biographies? Cookbooks? Newspapers?

When do you read? Before you go to sleep? Whenever you have a spare moment? While cleaning your teeth?

Where do you most enjoy reading? In the bath? On the bus or train?

Do you read online? Do you own a digital device such as a tablet? If so, what do you read on it — newspapers, novels, journal articles, magazines, websites?

Do you enjoy reading on a digital device such as a tablet or computer, or do you prefer to print out the information and read it in hard copy? If so, why?

Do you have several books 'on the go' at the same time?

Do you talk to others about what and how you read?

Have you ever read a book that changed the way you think or act?

As a reader, you differ from other people in what you read, when and where you read, and how much you enjoy reading. You have your own reading 'personality' which is influenced by your cultural background and began developing when you first made contact with words and books as a small child. This reading personality influences the type of reading material or genres you prefer, and your attitudes and approaches to reading as a student. If you like to read novels, you can sit absorbed in them for hours. If you prefer magazines, you may be accustomed to reading in short bursts. If you usually read a newspaper, you probably read some articles closely and glance through others. If you read online to locate information, you probably flit from site to site and scan text to find what you need.

When confronted with reading material for your university study, only some of your everyday reading habits are appropriate. The way in which academic materials are presented can differ from discipline to discipline, and the way in which you are expected to read them also varies. You shouldn't read medical texts as you would science fiction, and novels in a literature unit require a different approach from magazines. However, if you enjoy reading and read a lot, you can build on this enjoyment and transfer any appropriate reading skills to your sustained academic reading.

Most of the academic print material you read in journals and books is organised in a linear form with the information beginning in the first sentence, paragraph or chapter and concluding in the final sentence, paragraph or chapter (see Table 11.1, 'Notemaking methods'). This linear text is based on the idea that the reader begins at the beginning and follows a coherently and consistently organised argument or exposition to the end. The writer uses guides to lead the reader through the material (for example, see Table 10.1, 'The anatomy of a book'). Within this structure the reader has the freedom to move backwards and forwards or to dip into the text.

> To communicate . . . experience through print means that it must first be broken down into parts and then mediated, eye dropper fashion, one thing at a time, in an abstract, linear, fragmented, sequential way. This is the essential structure of print. JOHN M. CULKIN

Many of the documents you read on a screen and some online websites are presented in this linear fashion, and similar strategies and ideas apply as when reading hard copy. If you are required to read large chunks of text on screen, you may find it preferable to print out the material and read it in hard copy, applying the techniques outlined in this chapter for printed material. However, much online material is presented through links whereby segments of information are connected conceptually by association or relationship. Hyperlinks open multiple pathways to other material, and you can click on a link embedded in a highlighted word or graphic, which opens up new information, which then provides further choices, and so on. The information can be accessed at multiple points, enabling you to follow the links that are most suitable for your reading purposes. Links on the web connect you with a variety of other media, which makes visual literacy important in 'reading' material. Many websites include visual material which can be directly relevant to the text (such as a diagram) or distracting (such as advertising).

- When you first open a web page that includes visual material, what do you first attend to—the text itself or the related graphics or advertising?
- If you need to follow long passages of online text, what strategies do you use to focus on the text and not on the non-essential graphics (see 'Focusing', Chapter 4)?

> . . . how does instant access to any piece of data, connected to any other piece of data by the slenderest of threads, how does this translate into knowledge, let alone understanding? And how will knowledge be imparted and how will children's brains be trained if the joys of hypertext make the concept of the linear argument redundant? We'll end up with soundbite education, just as we've got soundbite politics and soundbite journalism. JOHN NIEUWENHUIZEN

Whether you are reading offline (either print or on screen) or online, learn to read actively as opposed to passively. A passive reader looks at and recognises the words on a page or screen but doesn't actively engage with the material. Have you ever 'read' a passage or several pages and realised that you haven't taken any of it in? If when you read you sit looking at the text and your mind is elsewhere, and if you cannot recall or explain or ask questions about what you have read, then you are reading passively.

Reading actively means constructing your own meaning from the ideas expressed and how they are organised. It means discerning the author's argument and evaluating how effectively a thesis is supported by reasons. If the material doesn't contain an argument, active reading means finding the main theme and the information used to expand on it. Such reading involves criticising the material to uncover how the argument or theme has been affected by the author's background, purpose or theoretical framework. You also need to pay attention to visual images and materials such as figures, graphs, charts, tables and diagrams, instead of skimming over them. And active reading involves determining how what you are reading relates to other material in the field and to your own learning and purpose for reading. An active reader is aware of the author's writing style and method of presentation.

> . . . she continued with the process of taking a fragment here and a sentence there, and built them into her mind, which was now the most extraordinary structure of disconnected bits of poetry, prose, fact and fantasy.   DORIS LESSING

Preparing to read

Your purposes

Why you are reading influences any preparation you do before you read, your reading rate and whether you underline or make notes. Before you read, clearly articulate your reading purpose which could be for your teacher's objectives and/or your own aims. Ask yourself:

How thoroughly do I want or need to understand this material?

Do I need to read for an in-depth understanding?

How much do I want to remember?

Do I need to critique the material?

Do I need to relate the text to material in the lectures or discussions on the topic?

Imagine that you are reading to prepare for a discussion on an unfamiliar topic. A few days before the discussion you look through a couple of online references or check in your textbook to identify some of the main issues of the topic, using guides to help, such as the introduction, index, chapter titles or layout. Or imagine that you have to write a detailed critique of an article. First, you read for an overview and then you read slowly, underlining or making notes on the theoretical framework and the argument, and re-reading if necessary. To critique the article you might read other texts on the topic that present different or conflicting perspectives.

Sometimes you read the same material for several purposes. For example, you may be required to read the same text for background information for a unit as well as to understand it in-depth to answer an assignment question. You approach the material differently to meet each of these requirements.

Examining your material

When browsing in a bookshop or library, why does one book appeal to you more than another? When leafing through an academic journal, why do you pause over some articles and not others? When surfing the Internet, why do you pay more attention to one website than to another? Perhaps a book's appearance or title attracts you, or the author is someone whose writing you usually enjoy. Perhaps an article seems relevant to one of your interests or useful for a particular purpose. Perhaps the visuals on a website complement the written text rather than detract from it. The layout, writing style, or author's approach to the subject may lead you to buy a book, borrow a journal or bookmark a website. Each book, journal article or website is different, and your response to each will depend on who you are as a reader.

Previewing

a Why preview?

Systematic previewing fosters active reading and is a preliminary step to becoming thoroughly familiar with material. This preparation helps you understand why the material was written, its theoretical framework, the author's argument or focus and how the information is organised and presented. Previewing can indicate which parts of the text could be most useful for your purpose and how thoroughly you want or need to read different sections. Below are some further reasons why previewing is beneficial:

- If material on a topic is limited, previewing can help you get the most out of what is available because it helps you read in more depth.
- Reading complex material can be made easier if you have an overall idea of what you are about to read and can break it into manageable chunks.
- Previewing can help make a piece of unappealing required reading more interesting.
- Once previewing becomes a habit, it saves time because you have made some intelligent guesses about what you expect to find in an item.
- When selecting material to read in depth, previewing saves time because it can help you choose the most useful items.

b Previewing a book chapter or a journal article

There are different levels of previewing, depending on your purpose for reading (see 'Approaches to reading', later in the chapter). For example, if you want to select a few items from a long reading list, it makes sense to undertake a quick preview of each one. As a minimum, if you are choosing from a list of book chapters or journal articles, check:

— the title of the chapter or article

— the title of the book or journal from which the item is taken

— any information about the author

— an abstract, if there is one

— any subheadings, and

— the first and last paragraphs.

To develop your skills, use Table 10.1 to preview a couple of books in depth. It would be useful to choose one book that is an edited collection of articles and another book that is the work of a single author. When familiar with the range of questions in Table 10.1, use those that are most valuable for your purpose in reading.

There are various systematic steps you can take when previewing a book, but their order depends on your preference. You might start by reading the first chapter to become immediately involved with the content and the author's style, or you may prefer to check through the information that surrounds the text, such as the publication details and the index. As you preview, write down any ideas, questions or statements that seem relevant to your purpose and might help you understand and critique the book. Try to determine the author's position on the topic. This kind of previewing helps you read actively because you have a framework into which the information fits; as you read you consciously look for answers to your questions, and for information that supports or disagrees with your original ideas on the book.

Apply the questions in Table 10.1 for a fuller sense of what **a book** is about. For example, a quick thumb through the index can indicate the major areas covered by the book; and a glance at the publication details gives information about the book in its field, such as how recent it is, whether it has sold enough copies to be reprinted, whether it has been published in more than one country.

If you have **a set text** that you need to use extensively, it is very helpful to start with an in-depth previewing (by checking which of the questions in Table 10.1 apply to the text). In contrast, to simply get the feel of a book you might glance through it, read the back cover blurb, look at the pictures or diagrams, think about the meaning of the title and perhaps check through the table of contents and read the introduction.

Previewing **an edited collection** written by a range of authors is different from reading a book written by one author. Many unit textbooks are collections and you need to preview them by adapting the questions in Table 10.1. Identify any articles that are familiar, those that look interesting and those that you think will be particularly difficult or easy.

Most of the steps described for previewing a book also apply to previewing parts of books or articles, so first read Table 10.1 and adapt the questions to the chapter or article. Second, as you preview, read the introduction and conclusion and any section headings.

c Previewing online text

When previewing linear text online, first scroll through to determine the length of the material and to locate any headings and subheadings. Work out whether all the headings are at the same level or at different levels. In a long document note these headings so you can quickly search for them again. Second, make use of any navigational guides and site maps as you explore the material. Apply the appropriate questions from Table 10.1 to the material and read the introduction and conclusion. Make sure you note the source of the material, when it was written or updated, and the credentials of the author.

TABLE 10.1   The anatomy of a book

Title/subtitle

What is the author trying to convey in the title (and any subtitle)?

Cover/dustjacket

What information does the cover of the book give about the contents, the author and the book within its field?

How reliable is any information on the cover of the book?

Author/editor/translator

Is there any information inside the book about the author's (or editor's or translator's) background, other publications, or experience relevant to the subject?

Do you know anything else about the author or any other of his/her writings?

Publication details

When was the book written?

What is the publication date of your copy of the book?

Has the book been revised?

Which edition is the book? Has the book been reprinted?

If the book is a translation, what is the date of this?

Who is the publisher?

In which countries has the book been published?

Table of contents

Is the table of contents sufficiently detailed to be helpful?

Which sections appear to be interesting, familiar or difficult to you?

How do the contents relate to your purpose and to other material you are studying?

Preface/foreword/introduction

If the book includes a preface, foreword or introduction, have they been written by the author or editor, or by someone else?

What information do these sections give you about why the book was written, its place in its field, and how to read it?

Has the book been written to argue a case, or is it an exposition describing or outlining a subject?

Is the author's position on the subject explained? Does the position fit within a theoretical paradigm?

Text of the book

What do the introduction and conclusion tell you about the book?

Are there guides to your reading of the book, such as summaries of chapters, and subheadings?

Does the author spell out the argument of the book in the introduction or conclusion? If the whole argument is not made explicit, can you identify the thesis?

How does the structure of the book—for example, chapters or sections—develop the argument?

Layout

How are headings and subheadings used?

How is emphasis indicated within the text? For example, are italics used?

Graphics and visuals

Does the book contain much graphic or visual material?

Is any graphic material (such as diagrams, photographs, figures, graphs and charts, tables, maps) easy to follow?

How does any visual material (images or representations) seem to relate to the written text?

Glossary

If the book has a glossary, are many words unfamiliar to you?

Bibliography and references

How comprehensive are any footnotes, endnotes or a bibliography?

Does the author use recently published items in references and the bibliography?

Is the list of works at the end of the text a bibliography (i.e., all sources consulted) or a list of references (i.e., those sources cited in the text)?

continued

TABLE
10.1   **continued**

Is the bibliography divided into subject areas?

Is it a comprehensive or selected bibliography?

Do the references include sources other than written materials?

Index

What does an examination of the index add to your understanding of the contents of the book? Which subject areas are given prominence?

Does the index list mostly ideas and concepts, or more factual entries such as names of places and people?

Has the index sufficient detail to enable you to locate your areas of interest easily?

d Complexity of material

> People who read well . . . learn by plunging into books that are 'too hard' for them, enjoying what they can understand, wondering and guessing about what they do not, and not worrying when they cannot find an answer.   JOHN HOLT

How complex you find material depends on your knowledge of the subject, your interest in it, and whether or not the material accords with familiar perspectives or your world view. Even if you are familiar with a topic, material can be complex because it expresses new ideas in unfamiliar language, because of its style and format, or because it is poorly written, organised or presented. ('Evaluating your selection' in Chapter 8 looks at determining the complexity of material when deciding whether to use it in research.) If material seems too simple for your purpose, you may need to check that you really do understand it thoroughly—even basic material sometimes has points to offer that you may be able to use to support your ideas in a discussion or essay.

When you need to read material that seems difficult, the first step in doing this is to try to articulate why this is so.

- If the material is difficult because the subject doesn't interest you, read a little of it and use the techniques described later in this chapter to make your reading more effective. On closer acquaintance the material may become more interesting, particularly if you can relate the subject to one that interests you.

- If the material conflicts with your 'common sense' understandings or with your beliefs and biases, discuss these conflicts with someone who doesn't share your attitudes but is open-minded. It can help you to see your beliefs and biases in a new light if you play devil's advocate to them. Understanding different or conflicting perspectives is essential to thinking critically (see 'Critical thinking', Chapter 3).

- If the theoretical perspectives or key concepts on which the material is based are unfamiliar, you may need to read other, perhaps simpler, material that deals with the same perspectives or concepts, and it may take you time to understand the material fully.

- If the material deals with an unfamiliar area or if you have a mental block about the subject, preview the material first, then read the easiest sections before you attempt more advanced ones. If you can't get past the basics, ask for help.

- If the material appears complex, first preview it, then read it slowly and look for the argument or theme—sometimes material that seems complex at first becomes clear after a careful reading. Making notes or drawing a diagram or pattern of the material as you read can help your understanding. You may later find it both easier to understand and very stimulating.

- If you have a tendency to skip difficult segments of texts, determine why you find these difficult (for example, unfamiliar concepts or vocabulary, or complex sentences). Then break the text into manageable chunks and read each one carefully, perhaps aloud, and ascertain the meanings of difficult concepts or terms (see 'Developing your vocabulary' below).

e *The discipline area*

> She took the book to her refuge, the tree, and read it through; and wondered why it was that she could read the most obscure and complicated poetry with ease, while she could not read the simplest sort of book on what she called 'facts' without the greatest effort of concentration.   DORIS LESSING

How you read is also influenced by the discipline area of the material. The methodologies and conventions for communicating in writing vary from discipline to discipline; and within disciplines writers have different styles and ways of presenting information. For example, in maths understanding what you read can depend on mastering information one step at a time. In geography, you may refer frequently to maps and other visual material as you read. In literature, reading a literary work to savour the language differs from reading literary criticism to select the central points. How much you are expected to read varies from discipline to discipline, and this in turn also influences how you read. For example, first year students are usually required to spend more time reading in the social sciences and humanities disciplines than in the physical sciences.

As a newcomer to a discipline you may find its specialised language difficult to understand and even familiar, everyday words may have new and distinct meanings. For example, the word 'program' has different meanings in psychology, computing and education, and the meaning of 'character' is different in literature, mathematics and biology. Some words embody concepts that have changed over time; and words such as 'culture', 'power', 'subject' or 'class' have evolved specific meanings in different disciplines. You need a specialist dictionary to understand the meanings of some words and to be clear how the words are used in the context of your reading. You might also need to become visually literate (to read images and other representations) or numerate (for example, to learn how to read different kinds of figures and tables).

In the materials you read there will be varying amounts of quantitative information. This information may be obviously mathematical in forms such as graphs or charts, tables, formulae or symbols, or it may be embedded in prose so that the mathematical meaning lies within words such as 'rate', 'decreasing inflation', 'exponential growth' and 'inversely proportional'. The degree to which you deal with this quantitative information depends to a large extent on your purpose in reading, the nature of the material itself and your attitude towards those mathematical representations.

People usually read non-fiction materials to gain information. In doing so, it is essential to consider the inferences and conclusions based on evidence of both qualitative and quantitative kinds (see 'Data presentation', Chapter 15 and 'Quantitative and qualitative sources', Chapter 9). Although it is common for people to skim over figures, tables, formulae and symbols, it is only by paying close attention to them that you can decide whether to accept the inferences and conclusions of the author that are based on the data. This does not necessarily mean that every single number of a table, for example, needs to be considered in detail. However, an ability to make inferences, consider comparisons, see the 'big picture' and pick up inconsistencies is a valuable skill. In some cases, it is helpful to make transformations between the kinds of representations; for example, from a graph to a table, from formulae to words, or from words to a graph. In general, it is advisable to change your reading speed and consider these quantitative aspects more slowly than the rest of the text.

When you have to learn a new 'language', such as in a new discipline, the following tips are useful:

- Talk about difficulties with a teacher or with other students, listen carefully to relevant lectures, ask for a glossary of terms or consult a specialised dictionary on the subject.

- Search the Internet and/or read some basic books on the subject.

- Make a real attempt to understand the new language; and if you still have difficulties or think too much is expected of you, let your teachers know. The language may be second nature to them and they can easily forget that it may be incomprehensible jargon to you.

- Compile your own list of new or unfamiliar terms. Write out their meanings.

'Twas brillig, and the slithy toves
Did gyre and gimble in the wabe:
All mimsy were the borogroves,
And the momeraths outgrabe.   LEWIS CARROLL

Developing your vocabulary

If you read widely you can improve your vocabulary—that is, your understanding of the words you read and hear, and the words you use in writing and speaking. You can actively work at improving your vocabulary by consulting a general dictionary, technical glossary or specialist dictionary, and by developing a system for recording and using your new words. Try a notebook or card system or keep a computer document in which you write the unfamiliar term, the context in which it appeared, its dictionary definition and your own sentence using it. If you have a learning log or blog, set aside part of it for this purpose. Practise using these words in your writing and speaking. Try them out on other students and your friends. Ask for feedback from a teacher on your use of the words. Learn a new term each day or several a week.

When you begin studying in a new discipline or embark on a new unit, pay particular attention to the vocabulary. If you find there are many terms or concepts that you don't understand, start with those that are central to the area or those that keep recurring. When you understand these terms, start on the others.

Before you read, use your preview to look for frequently used or unfamiliar words and concepts and look these up before you read. Use the index or leaf through the text to find these terms. This will help you read more quickly and you will not be slowed down by continually consulting a dictionary. However, if you are reading and you do come across terms that you don't understand, don't skip over ones which are used frequently. Take the time to stop and look them up.

> The student's success is not simply a function of the number of words he or she has read and remembered. Rather, it is the degree to which the student—through that reading—has gone inside of the literature, has become used to the shape of relevant academic conversations, and has grappled with the unfamiliar language until it becomes his or her own language.   RONALD BARNETT

As you read

How you read material depends largely on why and what you are reading. You probably read a detective story straight through to find out 'What happens next?' With many academic books you affirm or reject what you read on the basis of your world view, theoretical perspective, knowledge, experience and interests. Maybe you read with pencil in hand, jotting down notes or with a document open on your computer for recording thoughts and ideas. Perhaps you underline anything that strikes you as useful, significant, puzzling or appealing, or ask yourself questions about what you are reading. Are you conscious of varying your reading rate according to your material?

> It is possible to question readings of stories which may seem 'natural' and normal by paying attention to the ways a story conforms to or differs from familiar patterns.
>
> BRONWYN MELLOR, ANNETTE PATTERSON and MARNIE O'NEILL

Do you talk about what you are reading with your friends and urge them to read it too? How you read is also influenced by whether or not you share your reading, perhaps discussing what you have read afterwards. Reading with others, either silently or aloud, gives you the opportunity to share immediate reactions to material. Some material, such as poetry, plays or novels, lends itself readily to being spoken and listened to with another person or a group; and listening to material read aloud can also give you new insight into the use of language and the pace and style of the text. You may also like to share with your teachers and other students, either face-to-face or online, the challenges and pleasures you have with material. Because peoples' perceptions of what they read differs, opinions vary, and so hearing different viewpoints can help you understand material more fully. (To set up a group to read each other's writing, see 'Share your writing', Chapter 13.)

Approaches to reading

> Some books are to be tasted, others to be swallowed, and some few to be chewed and digested; that is, some books are to be read only in parts; others to be read but not curiously; and some few to be read wholly, and with diligence and attention.
>
> FRANCIS BACON

Different reading techniques are sometimes given names, such as 'skimming' or 'scanning', and actual reading rates of words per minute are suggested for each. Such terms can be confusing and, while generalised reading rates may apply, in practice how you read varies. It depends on your purpose, the material and your concentration when you read. This section describes six different reading approaches that arise from your reading purpose and the material, but it doesn't assign reading rates to each approach. It looks first at the breadth and depth of the understanding you are seeking from your material, and then at reading rates.

Imagine you are planning a visit to a city that you have never visited before. Why are you going there? Six possible purposes are:

— to stroll around the central shopping area for pleasure

— to experience the city atmosphere

— to visit a famous art gallery or a zoo

— to familiarise yourself with the key features of the city

— to explore thoroughly as much of the city as possible, or

— to evaluate whether or not you could live in the city.

Your purpose in visiting the city influences how you prepare for your visit, what you do when you arrive and how long you stay.

Now imagine that you are planning to read a book you have not read before. Are you going to read this book:

— for entertainment?

— to gain an overall impression of it?

— to locate a specific idea or section?

— to familiarise yourself with the argument or theme?

— to understand and get to know the whole book in depth? or

— to critique or review the book?

Similarly to your purpose for visiting a new city, your purpose for reading a book influences how you prepare for the experience. The above six purposes and how they influence your approach to reading are explained below.

1 Entertainment reading

What do you read for relaxation? A favourite magazine? A detective story? A friend's blog? A collection of poems? An abstract philosophical work?

Entertainment reading (that is, reading without any specific intention of criticising or remembering what you read) can be more than reading for relaxation on free evenings or holidays. When studying, relevant light material can be a pleasurable way of getting yourself into the right frame of mind for in-depth study on a topic, and can provide you with general background on the subject.

When you read for entertainment, you probably read fairly quickly or browse through the material. You might pause to ponder over a particular passage, image or item of information, but you probably do not make a conscious effort to remember what you read. You might use entertainment reading as part of formal study when you intend:

— to read the quotes in a chapter of this book as stimulus for reading the chapter in detail

— to enjoy an historical novel before beginning an intensive study of the era in which the novel is set

— to peruse several different websites on a topic, or

— to read a biography of a scientist whose discoveries you are studying.

2 Overview reading

Reading for an overview of material entails reading quite rapidly, reading the introductory and concluding paragraphs, noting the argument or theme, noting how any graphic or visual items fit into the material, and forming an overall impression of what you read. You are not concerned with specific details or a complete understanding of the material. Read for an overview when, for example, you want:

— to find out how this *Guide* might be useful to you

— to decide whether to read a book in more depth

— to add to your store of information on a familiar subject area or topic, or

— to decide if a website is appropriate for your purpose.

3 Reading for specific information

> I have always been able to forget what I have read, retaining, however, a sort of geographical memory that would send me quickly to the right page in the right book to find something I had half forgotten but wished to remember.   ARTHUR RANSOME

To locate (or relocate) a specific item or section in material, read through most of the material quite rapidly, using such features as the table of contents, the index, chapter headings and subheadings to guide you to the item or section you want. Then read the section thoroughly, possibly making notes or underlining. If you are reading online you might choose to print out the relevant section (see Chapter 8, 'Researching a topic'). Read for specific information if, for example, your purpose is:

— to look for a specific section in this *Guide*

— to locate biographical details on a literary figure

— to locate up-to-date data from the web, or

— to find evidence for or against a case you will debate.

4 Reading for the argument or theme

To familiarise yourself with the argument or theme in material (see 'Genres', Chapter 7), first take an overview of it. Examine the structure of the material and find the thesis and supporting premises (see Table 10.2).

Read for the argument or theme when, for example, you want:

— to familiarise yourself with the main approaches to study presented in this book

— to read an article as background for a research paper

— to describe an item you plan to include in an annotated bibliography

— to prepare for a discussion on the material, or

— to understand the central conclusions in an experimental report.

TABLE
10.2 **Asking questions as you read**

As you read a section of a book or article, look for information to help you answer the following questions:

Author's purpose

Why has the author written the material? Are these purposes explicitly stated? Are there other implicit purposes?

For whom is the material intended?

Author's approach

What theoretical perspective has the author taken? How does this perspective relate to other material in the field?

Has a contemporary issue or a particular paradigm or philosophy influenced the author's purpose?

What are the author's underlying assumptions? Are these stated explicitly?

Is there any evidence of covert or overt bias, such as interpretation of material or choice of sources or of information? (See the Appendix for examples of discrimination in language and attitudes.)

Content

What is the argument or, if no argument, the theme in the material?

What evidence, examples or explanations are used to support the thesis or theme?

How does the author develop the thesis from one reason to another?

Do the supporting evidence, examples and explanations seem well researched and accurate?

Is the factual information correct as far as you know?

Which aspects of the topic has the author chosen to concentrate on and which to omit?

Does the material presented have breadth and/or depth? Is the material dealt with fully and accurately or is the subject treated superficially?

Is any irrelevant material included?

Does any graphic or quantitative material illustrate or restate the written content?

How are any visual images linked with the written text?

Which of your questions about the subject does the author answer? Which are not answered?

How do the contents relate to what you know about the topic?

Do any items puzzle or intrigue you?

continued

10

TABLE
10.2   **continued**

Structure

What framework is used to organise the material? Is the framework clearly explained and logical?

How is the argument or, if no argument, the theme reflected in the structure?

How is the supporting material organised and developed within the framework?

How does the author introduce the argument?

Does the author recapitulate at appropriate points what has been said?

How does the conclusion relate to the introduction and to the rest of the material?

Style and format

In what style is the material written? For example, is it formal or informal, simple or complex, descriptive or critical, didactic or persuasive, narrative, analytical?

How does the style and format influence your reaction to the material?

5 Reading for an in-depth understanding

When reading to understand an entire book or article as thoroughly as possible, first preview the material. Determine the structure of the material, then read to identify the thesis and supporting reasons or, if there is no argument, the theme and associated points. Then take the material section by section, reading the supporting evidence and identifying more fully the relationship between the thesis and its support (see Table 10.2). Seek out material that shows objections to the argument. Ferret out its theoretical perspective and any underlying assumptions.

Reading in this depth doesn't mean laboriously reading every page, or screen, word by word. It does involve making sure that you read actively, understanding each section so that with the material set aside, you can clearly construct your own understanding of what you have read and can see how each section fits into the whole argument or exposition. Seeing clearly how material is organised or structured can help you to understand its content. (Refer to Table 14.2, 'Transitional words and phrases', to alert yourself to the words and phrases that are signposts to the structure.) Make notes or underline important information to help reinforce your understanding.

Read for an in-depth understanding if, for example, your purpose is:

— to identify the assumptions underlying this *Guide*

— to summarise or paraphrase material

— to follow a complex argument

— to understand each stage of an experiment in order to repeat it yourself, and

— to understand material thoroughly so that you can build on it in further learning, or critique it as outlined below.

6 Reading to question and critique

To question and critique what you read, you need to read for an in-depth under-standing of the material as outlined in 5 above and also apply the suggestions below.

Before reading you should have evaluated the material to find out whether it is useful for your purpose and how complex it is for you, and to check whether its subject matter is relevant and interesting (see 'Evaluating your selection', Chapter 8). You begin to evaluate material critically during your preview and as you read, but you also need to think about it critically when you have finished reading and can see the text as a whole.

To critique material as you read it, take the text section by section. A section may be a group of chapters, a chapter, or just a paragraph, depending on the length of the text, how much visual or graphic material is involved, your purpose and how complex or familiar the material is. Before you begin a large section, preview it. As you read, ask yourself the questions in Table 10.2. These questions should help you identify the author's theoretical perspective, objectives and assumptions; understand the argument or theme and its structure; and evaluate the style and format of the material. At the end of the section, recapitulate what you have read. Check whether you understand the contents of the section as thoroughly as you need to, and try to understand the relationship of the section to the whole. When you finish reading each section, put the material aside and evaluate its usefulness for your purpose. Decide what information you want to underline or include in your notes.

If you have difficulty answering the questions in Table 10.2, discuss the material with other people. First, try to reach agreement on the argument—the thesis and supporting material—or, if there is no argument, the theme. Then discuss any differing opinions on the argument or focus for the material as a whole and for individual sections of the material. (Note that the questions asked in Table 10.2 are similar to those you should ask when evaluating your essays, as in 'Working with your rough draft', Chapter 14.)

Specific instances of when you might need to do this include:

— to write a critical review of this *Guide*

— to include a critical summary of the material in an assignment

— to prepare for an in-depth debate on the material, or

— to critique the theoretical perspective taken by an author.

Reading rates

> Speed, which becomes a virtue when it is found in a horse, by itself has no advantages.
>
> IDRIES SHAH

When feeling overwhelmed by long reading lists or the time it takes to get through a book or the plethora of websites, you might wish you could increase your reading rate or speed. Although learning to read more rapidly can save you study time, fast reading rates are useful only if you can understand and recall what you read as fully as you need to. They do not in themselves ensure better comprehension. Reading effectively involves varying your reading rate according to your purpose and to the difficulty of the material for you (see Table 10.3).

You can improve your reading rate while still constructing an understanding of what you read.

TABLE
10.3 **Varying your reading rate**

This table suggests how you might read Chapter 11 'Listening to lectures' in this book.

Your purpose	The material	Your rate
• To warm up	Boxed quotes	Fast
• To read for an overview of the chapter	Whole chapter, especially the introduction and conclusion	Quite fast
• To locate specific information to help you make more useful lecture notes	Section on 'Making notes'	Fast until you locate the section you want, then slowly within the section
• To familiarise yourself with the theme	Whole chapter	Slowly, making use of the introduction and the headings
• To gain an in-depth familiarity with the chapter	Whole chapter	Slowly and thoroughly, underlining or making notes
• To critique the assumptions and theme of the chapter for a discussion	Whole chapter	Slowly and thoroughly, section by section

- Check how fast you can read while still understanding what you read. Time the number of words you read per minute for:
  — a light novel you are reading for background
  — a journal article you are reading to familiarise yourself with the central ideas, and
  — a chapter in a unit text that you have to understand in depth.

  Read at least ten paragraphs of each one. In each case, when you finish reading, set aside the material and try to recall it in as much detail as you need. If you have trouble remembering the material, your reading rate probably needs to be slower and you may need to try the techniques in the following points.

- Preview all material before you read it, perhaps jotting down the major headings. Although this may appear to take extra time in the beginning, if you have a framework in which to place what you read, as you read it you can vary your rate according to the importance of the information and ideas. This framework will also help you remember the material later.

- Push yourself to read as fast as you can for 10–15 minutes each day for a week, then check your rate and comprehension. Remember your reading rate will regress if you seldom read and if you don't practise reading faster.

- Make a habit of reading material that is as complex as your study material. Becoming accustomed to reading material that is more demanding than light fiction or the sports pages can make it easier to read your study material.

- If you find that it slows you down to consult a specialist dictionary or technical glossary as you read, make a list of unfamiliar terms as you read and look them up as you need them. (See a method for doing this in 'Developing your vocabulary', earlier in this chapter.)

- Pay attention to any quantitative material such as tables and statistics; ask for help if you have difficulty interpreting them.

- Use visual material and layout clues, such as headings, to help you quickly understand written text.

The aim of improving your reading rates is to save you time, but you only save this time if you understand and remember what you read as thoroughly as you need. Without understanding, you have to go over the material repeatedly until you do understand it, and your initial time-saving is lost.

Notemaking and/or underlining

Books that you may carry to the fire, and hold readily in your hand, are the most useful after all.
SAMUEL JOHNSON

You might underline your own books because you want to make your responses to what you read part of the material itself. You might make notes either with pen and paper or on the screen because you don't want to mark your books, because referring to the book later is difficult, because a précis of the information is more useful for your purpose, or because notemaking helps you recall the information later (see 'Download, print, copy, borrow or buy?', Chapter 8).

On rare occasions you come across a piece of writing which encapsulates ideas that are especially significant for you so that you want to download, photocopy or buy the material. However, usually it is better to close the book or document and try to express what you have read in your own words, as this helps you to remember it. Be selective and avoid downloading or photocopying material you will never read. When under pressure and short of time, you may tend to download or photocopy everything rather than read any one item carefully (see 'Recording and filing references', Chapter 8).

Why make notes or underline?

You might do this:

— to help you see the structure in what you read

— because what you read strikes you as useful, puzzling, interesting or brilliant

— to remember what you read

— to be able to refer to it later, for instance, for an assignment or an exam in a few months time, or

— to help you concentrate on and understand what you read.

What to note or underline

Depending on your purposes for reading, there is a range of items you may need to note or underline. These include:

— the author's objectives, theoretical framework and assumptions (explicit and implicit)

— key elements, such as the argument, major characters or crucial information

— single phrases or sentences that encapsulate key elements or the author's objectives and assumptions

— a juicy quote

— details or facts that appeal to you, such as a useful statistic or a vivid image, or

— items to follow up, such as a question, an idea that offers further possibilities, a puzzling comment, an unfamiliar word, an explanation you don't understand or an opinion you question.

How much to note or underline

The amount of underlining you do or the quantity of notes you make depends on why you read, what you read and whether you have easy access to the material again.

If you have limited time and access to material, it is easy to opt for the apparent safety of making notes of everything you read 'just in case' you need the information later. However, if you are researching an essay topic and you analyse your question before reading, you need fewer notes and underline less. Having a clear idea of your reading purpose prevents you finishing up with masses of notes and no idea of how to organise or use them (see 'Integrating your ideas with information', Chapter 8).

Check that you understand what you have underlined, typed or written down (see 'Questioning and critiquing', Chapter 8). Underlining a lot or making detailed notes can be necessary, but it may indicate your inability to discriminate what is important from what is not, and can give you a false sense of achievement because you have a large quantity of work to show, regardless of its quality. When material is new or complex for you, you might fall into the trap of underlining or highlighting much of an article because it all seems important. If you find that you are doing this, try only underlining in pencil as you read, and then at the end review the whole text and highlight only what you can now see as the main points or erase much of the underlining.

If you often record lengthy quotes or paraphrases to use in assignments because the material 'says it much better than I can', try instead to select a limited number of quotes and paraphrases to support your own argument (see 'Paraphrasing and summarising', Chapter 16). Although, in Western higher education, your teachers usually expect you to display familiarity with the arguments and ideas in key literature in a field, relying mostly on authorities shows a lack of confidence in your opinions and a belief that there is a right answer for a question (see 'Questioning and critiquing', Chapter 8).

You probably don't need to underline or make many notes if you are reading mostly for entertainment, if you are familiar with the subject or if you have an excellent visual or conceptual memory. But if you need the material later, take down at least a bare outline of its contents and notes on where to find it again. Two weeks and ten websites later you will find it surprisingly difficult to recall what you have read unless you have some record of it.

'The horror of that moment,' the King went on, 'I shall never, never forget!' 'You will, though,' the Queen said, 'if you don't make a memorandum of it.'   LEWIS CARROLL

How to make notes or underline

Develop your own method of notemaking or underlining that differentiates between the thesis or focus and supporting material (see 'Genres', Chapter 7). Work out a way of indicating the author's position and assumptions or attitudes, the details that appeal to you and items to follow up. If you have a strong visual memory, you might decide to develop a mind map or patterned notes (see Table 11.1, 'Notemaking methods', for ways to do this). If you use patterned notes creatively, when planning an essay for example, the open-ended nature of the pattern can enable your brain to make new connections far more easily. Note that you can create a pattern as part of your assignment preparation to help you to link the concepts in your assignment.

When beginning to make notes:

— write down full details of the author, title and publication

— on each page of notes, write the author or title and list the page numbers of the book or article in the margin of your notes. This habit is essential for quoting exactly, referencing assignments and checking the content of an idea you want to paraphrase

— use quotation marks to clearly indicate the beginning and end of material you have copied exactly

— clearly identify the beginning and end of material you have paraphrased (see 'Paraphrasing and summarising', Chapter 16), and

— note any numerical information accurately.

(To integrate your own ideas with those from your reading, try the system suggested in 'Integrating your ideas with information', Chapter 8. See Table 11.1, 'Notemaking methods', for more ideas on how to make notes.)

After you read

> Some . . . sell their textbooks when they're through with them, but I intend to keep mine. Then after I've graduated I shall have my whole education in a row in the bookcase, and when I need to use a detail, I can turn to it without the slightest hesitation. So much easier and more accurate than trying to keep it in your head.   JEAN WEBSTER

When you have finished reading, do you close your book or article with a sigh of satisfaction or relief and not think about it again unless you have to use it? To remember and use what you have read, review the material as a whole and use it as soon, as often and as widely as possible (see 'Transferring and using what you learn', Chapter 5).

● Look at the material in relation to your reading purpose. If you are researching an assignment, ask yourself the following questions:
Does the material lead you to revise how you have analysed your question? Is the book central or peripheral to your understanding of a topic? Does the material provide the necessary level of information for your research? What parts of the material apply particularly to the thesis or focus of your essay?

● Find out whether your initial impressions and any questions raised during your preview have been confirmed or answered. To help revise what you learned from the text, look again at those parts of the material you examined during your preview. For instance, check through the index to help recall what you read and to give you a fuller understanding of the scope of a book.

● Look at the material as a whole and ask yourself the same questions about the objectives, approach, content, structure, style and format as you asked about each section while reading.

- Review your notes or underlining to ensure that you remember what you have read and to see how the various sections fit together. Draw up patterned notes of the whole chapter or article, or write a summary of it.

- Compile a list of questions the material has raised that you want to follow up. Edit your notes, or summarise them further if necessary, and file them (see 'Recording and filing references', Chapter 8).

- Think about the material and how your construction of its meaning is shaped by your world view, theoretical perspective, knowledge, experience and interests. Do any of the ideas affect your beliefs or actions?

- Reflect on how the material's style and format compares with your own writing. Perhaps the material is in a genre that can provide an example on which you can model your own writing, especially in relation to how you might structure what you write or how to use the language of a discipline. The material might also provide an example of what not to do.

Whether or not you think about what you have read when you finish reading depends largely on the impact it had on you and whether you are required to use it. You might remember an argument that changes your thinking or recall particular ideas or information. You may read further works by the same author or on the same subject, and in time re-read the original work. If an article or web page pleased or irritated you, stimulated or satisfied your curiosity, you are likely to reflect on it and discuss it with other people. Articulating your ideas and responses to material helps to clarify them, and you may also be required to convey your ideas about a book or article in a written review (see Table 10.4, overleaf).

Reviewing the chapter

1   Look through this chapter, taking each heading in turn and recalling what you can about it. Which section can you recall in most detail? Why?

2   Choose one section that is useful to re-read. As you re-read it, think about how you are reading and why.

3   Could you explain the structure and contents of the whole chapter to someone else?

4   Summarise this chapter using patterned notes (see 'Making notes', Chapter 11).

TABLE 10.4   Writing a review

'. . . What is the use of a book,' thought Alice, 'without pictures or conversations?'

LEWIS CARROLL

The overall purpose of a review is to interest and inform potential readers and to give your considered opinion of a book or article. As well as summarising or succinctly describing the contents of the material, the review should evaluate the overall strengths and weaknesses of the material from your perspective. The review should give enough of the content of the material for the reader to be able to understand your critique of it without having to read the original. Depending on your specific purpose for the review and any word limit, you should include some or all of the following information:

Context of the material

— full details of the author, title and publication
— when the material was originally written and/or revised, and
— the author's qualifications and experience.

Summary of the material

— brief outline of the book's contents
— summary of the book's argument or theme, and
— the author's purpose in writing the book.

A critique of the material

This would include an evaluation of:

— the theoretical perspective taken in relation to other perspectives on the topic
— the material in relation to other material in the field, including whether the book introduces any new concepts or data and/or reviews, and whether it contradicts or supports previous material
— the depth and thoroughness of the treatment of the subject matter in relation to the length of the material
— any data presented
— whether the conclusions are based on reasons or evidence, contain suggestions or recommendations, or are theoretical or practical
— how the book relates to your knowledge, your experience, your interests and your beliefs
— the author's style, and
— comments by other reviewers about the book.

Presentation of material

— the standard of the index, bibliography, graphic or visual material, and
— the overall quality of the presentation, such as layout, quality of paper and binding.

The review should follow the conventions for writing an essay with an introduction, body and conclusion. The body of the review should contain a summary of the book and the critique of it. Your review should be an argument with a thesis that expresses your judgement of the material. Support any statements you make, including your opinions, with evidence, explanations and examples. A few well-chosen quotations can convey the flavour of the author's style as well as illustrating a point. (Give the page reference for a quote immediately afterwards.)

Your own honest and well thought-out opinion of the material is of more value to your learning and to your readers than your version of someone else's opinion. A review can be technically excellent but dull to read unless you convey to your reader the impact the material has on you.

TEN TIPS

1   Think about how your everyday reading habits—of print material or on a screen—might help or hinder the reading you need to do at university.

2   Clarify what it means to read actively rather than passively.

3   Learning how to effectively preview material is one of the most time-saving skills you can acquire.

4   Become aware of what you first focus on when reading on a screen where there are images as well as text, and how this shapes your understanding of the text.

5   Identify strategies which help you keep going when you come to a section of text that you find difficult to understand.

6   Making a determined effort to become familiar with new vocabulary will soon help you read more easily.

7   Before you read new material, think about your purpose for reading so that you can choose how best to approach the task.

8   Learn what is involved in reading to identify how a writer develops a complex argument.

9   Be selective in your underlining, rather than finishing up with pages covered in highlighted text.

10   'Speed reading' practice can help—if your reading rate enables you to understand what you read.

Listening to lectures

11

The uptake of web-based lecture technologies for recording and delivering live lectures has increased markedly in recent years. Students have responded positively, and for many their use has transformed learning—freeing them up from rigid timetables by providing choice in lecture attendance and supporting learning by extending the lecture experience and enabling them to revisit key concepts and ideas in their own time.

MAREE GOSPER

Why lectures?

Preparing for a lecture

As you listen
    Making notes
    Overcoming concentration difficulties

After a lecture

Depending on who you are—your prior knowledge and skills, your world view, your experience and how you are feeling—you react to and select from what you hear. Each person responds differently to the pitch and intensity of sounds. One person's music is someone else's noise. If you live in the country the noise of traffic can be deafening when you visit the city; for an enthusiastic motorbike rider the roar of a 750 cc engine is music to the ears; and the crackle of a favourite breakfast cereal can be irritatingly loud to someone with a hangover.

Do you consider yourself a good listener?

Do you listen closely to your friends when they talk about their troubles?

Have you ever felt your eyes glaze over as you listened to a teacher's monologue?

Have you ever found your mind far away in the final stages of a lecture?

Do learning aids such as lecture outlines or slides increase your ability to focus on a lecture?

Do you concentrate and take in more if you attend a live lecture or if you listen to it online?

There is a difference between hearing sounds passively, and actively listening. Concentrating on what you hear is one of the basic requirements for listening to lectures. But even when you are keenly interested in a subject, it can be difficult to concentrate for a long time while sitting passively without the opportunity to respond.

Lectures are usually a one-way communication process. The lecturer lectures and you listen, whether the lecture lasts for five minutes or two hours, whether the lecture is delivered to twenty students in a classroom or to several hundred people in a large lecture hall, or whether you listen to it live or online. A lecturer may follow the customary university lecture format and talk for almost the entire time with little or no student interaction. Alternatively, part of the lecture may be set aside for students to respond to and discuss what is said. Most lectures are available online so you can choose whether to listen online or attend.

Why lectures?

... a lecture should have a certain kind of electricity and spontaneity, and a good lecture does. A good lecture is never just information conveyed and often actually being in the room makes a difference. The students know it if they come across lectures that are alive ...   ROBERT MANNE

For a long time lectures have been the most common form of tertiary teaching, so it is worth thinking about their objectives. These can include:

— imparting information to large numbers of people
— providing a common ground for formal discussion
— serving as a starting point for private study
— drawing together the main ideas in a new research area

— providing a preliminary map of difficult reading material

— reviewing research or literature that is difficult to locate, and

— adapting a topic for a particular audience in a way that a standard unit textbook can't.

> I cannot see that lectures can do so much good as reading the books from which the lectures are taken.　　　　　　　　　　　　　　　　SAMUEL JOHNSON

Educators debate the effectiveness of lectures in achieving many teaching objectives. For example, it is often stated that lectures don't encourage students to think for themselves and that students should discuss the lecture content rather than simply listen to it in lectures. It is also argued that lectures are widely used not because of their effectiveness, but because they are the cheapest way of teaching large numbers of students. In online units any lectures that have been transferred to the online medium without adapting them to that specific audience may be difficult to follow, especially without support materials.

You probably will have your own opinions on how valuable lectures are in achieving your learning aims, and it will be up to you to discover whether your learning style means that you take in information more effectively from listening to lectures, from discussing them or from reading.

The prevalence of online lectures means that universities are re-thinking the role of the traditional one-hour lecture delivered in a large lecture theatre to all students in a unit. Increasingly, online lectures are delivered in shorter, more targeted chunks, and lecture theatres are being re-designed. However, for the time being and especially in first year and in large units, the lecture is likely to remain central to your learning.

> 'Should a lecturer cover the ground laid down in his [sic] syllabus, even when some students don't understand, or go at a slower pace and get behind?' . . . If lecturers considered their courses in terms of the learning being achieved by students rather than as a succession of performances by lecturers, this question would seldom be asked.　　　　DONALD A. BLIGH

Lecturers who think seriously about how much can be learned and retained from particular lectures adapt their lecturing methods to their objectives and are willing to depart from the traditional lecture format. So not all of the lectures you attend will be a monologue from a teacher.

● The lecturer may present either an argumentative or expository lecture—be aware of these different frameworks (see 'Genres', Chapter 7).

● If the subject matter is difficult and involves a sequence of reasoning or events, the lecturer might present the material in chunks, perhaps using a series of short lectures, each followed by a few minutes for students to discuss or work on a related question.

● Interactive lectures, which involve an exchange of questions and comments with students, require both lecture time for student participation and a lecturer who knows the subject well and can present it logically, restructuring it on the spot in response to discussion.

- Lectures designed to encourage maximum participation from a large class might involve a concise lecture followed by a preliminary class discussion, individual student work, a small group discussion and a brief summary by the whole class. Another option might be a discussion based on comments posted beforehand on an online forum; or having students listen to an online lecture or podcast and using the lecture time for discussion.

Because lecturing styles and abilities differ, you inevitably learn more from some lecturers than others. Not all lecturers are talented communicators, but skilled lecturers vary their method of presentation, pace of delivery, voice and position in relation to the audience. They may be storytellers, actors or humorists or someone whose pleasure in the subject is contagious. Some lecturers read their lectures, while others use brief notes or speak extemporaneously. Others rely heavily on slides or other electronic aids to guide their presentation. A lecturer who is sensitive to an audience and responsive to shifts in mood and attention is always more enjoyable. You may or may not share a lecturer's enthusiasm for a topic, but a talented lecturer is a pleasure to listen to and can hold your attention almost regardless of the topic.

> If you go to a great performance of music, being in the concert hall is different from hearing the CD . . . I know that students feel that in the same way.   ROBERT MANNE

For some students attending or listening to lectures is something they do because it is in their timetable and for fear of missing something important. Many internal students rush to lectures from home, work, another class or from chatting with friends, and once the lecture is finished, they close their notes and only look at them again for exams or assignments. Online students may find a spare hour here and there to listen to lectures, perhaps when travelling to university by bus or car or when exercising, which can be a very effective use of time. Whenever or however you listen to lectures, learning from them requires at least some effort on your part. If you consistently prepare for lectures, actively concentrate on what is said and think back over it afterwards, you will get more out of lectures, even those that are not so well presented.

Preparing for a lecture

> . . . students are quite strategic about the choices they make, basing decisions on lecture attendance around three types of factors: educational value; convenience and flexibility; and social opportunities to meet other students, exchange ideas and make new friendships.   MAREE GOSPER

Usually, you will hear a face-to-face lecture only once, so preparing beforehand will help you understand it more fully. Although you probably won't use all of the suggestions listed below, try them out to see which ones work best for you.

- Most lectures are available online, so if you are an internal student first decide if you will attend or listen online.

- If the lecture is only presented live, occasionally you may want to record it if, for example, the topic is challenging, or if you want to listen the first time round without making notes. If you know you will miss an important lecture, you may need to ask another student to record it for you.

- If available, download any slides, material, or visual aids that accompany an online or live lecture and refer to these before and while you listen.

- Think about how useful a lecture could be in achieving your learning aims. For instance, if you are attending or listening to a lecture as well as discussing or reading a book on the topic, which is more effective for your learning? You might listen to the lecture to find information that is difficult and time-consuming to locate elsewhere, or to hear a gifted lecturer present a familiar topic in a new way. Your main incentive could be to absorb information for exams and assignments; or you might attend out of habit or because attendance is compulsory.

- Prepare for a lecture by thinking about where the topic fits within the broader framework of a unit—check the lecture schedule and review previous lecture topics. Read any materials you have downloaded for the lecture, and if you have time, preview some of the suggested reading on the topic. You may find material (such as a summary of main points, a map, a timeline or a list of biographical dates) that you can take to the lecture to help you follow it. As part of your preparation, list any questions or ideas that come to mind. You can use these as reference points when listening to the lecture, so that you are less likely to be overwhelmed by a mass of unfamiliar information.

- Consider your alternatives for making notes from the lecture. Will you use a laptop, or pen and paper? You may want to arrange to compare your notes with someone else's after the lecture (see 'Making notes', below). If you can only listen to the lecture live, you might decide to share attending lectures in turn with another student, and agree that you will each take clear and thoughtful notes when it is your turn.

- Immediately before a live lecture or before you listen online, think about how you feel. If you feel physically or emotionally low, do what you can to improve things for the next hour (see 'Emotions', Chapter 1). If you need to miss a live lecture ask someone to record it or to share their notes with you.

- If you need to listen to an online lecture or a podcast, choose a time without frequent interruptions.

- Arrive early at a live lecture or settle yourself before listening online. Pay close attention to the very beginning as this often:

  — provides an outline to help you follow what is to come

— relates the topic to reference material, to a theoretical framework, or to the rest of the unit

— states a problem the lecture will address

— tells a joke or story to lead into the topic, or

— gives significant information on how the lecture relates to assignments.

If you are an internal student, be aware that before a live lecture starts there may be announcements about vital information such as details of assignment due dates.

As you listen

'I think I should understand that better,' Alice said very politely, 'if I had it written down: but I can't quite follow it as you say it.'

'That's nothing to what I could say if I chose,' the Duchess replied, in a pleased tone.

LEWIS CARROLL

Thoughts can move faster than speech, so your attention can easily wander during lectures unless you actively concentrate on what is being said (see 'Overcoming concentration difficulties', later in this chapter). With online lectures or podcasts you can replay bits when your concentration lapses, but try to focus fully so that you only spend time on replaying material you find difficult. To sustain your concentration so that you understand more fully what you hear, try to question what is being said, anticipate what will be said, and frequently review what has been said.

Ask yourself questions about the objectives, approach, content, structure, style and format of the lecture. Most of the questions suggested in Table 10.2, 'Asking questions as you read', also apply to lectures. The questions you ask as you listen can form the basis for any notes you make. You may have other questions specifically related to the lecturing style, such as 'What is the lecturer conveying by his or her stance, distance from the audience and voice tones?'

Making notes

'Write that down,' the King said to the jury; and the jury wrote down all three dates on their slates, and then added them up, and reduced the answer to shillings and pence.

LEWIS CARROLL

You make notes from your lectures, your reading and discussions. The term 'note-making' is used here to indicate that you need to take an active role in creating notes and that your notes are more than a passive record of a lecture or reading. As a learner you should be making your own notes, processing and selecting information so that you make notes that are useful for your own aims. These notes should show at a glance the relative importance of information; that is, you should use methods of notemaking that clearly separate the main from the minor points. Most people find the easiest way to make notes from lectures and reading is to use linear notes. However, you may find linear notes more appropriate for lectures and patterned notes useful for reading or as a visual summary of your linear notes. Refer to Table 11.1 for more information on notemaking, and to the example of a patterned summary later in this chapter.

TABLE
11.1   **Notemaking methods**

Linear notes

To use linear notemaking effectively, try these suggestions:
— use headings and subheadings to break up your text
— note key words
— use numbering, and
— use coloured pens to differentiate the relative importance of information.

Another idea is to divide your page into two columns: use the left-hand column for headings and the key words in the main points. Use the rest of the page for minor points or important details. This method ensures that, before you write anything, you have to decide on the relative importance of the information.

As you become adept at the method add a third column, a narrow right-hand column, in which you record your responses to the information— references to check, points of particular interest, questions to ask about material you don't understand, aspects you know about, or exclamations.

Patterned notes

These notes are also called 'explosion charts' (see later in the chapter). The method involves starting in the centre of the page and branching to the edges. The argument or theme of the information is in the centre of the page, and the main and subpoints radiate from it. Minor points or details radiate from the subpoints. You can also show 'cross-connections' between, for example, main points. The pattern can be drawn to represent the structure of the material as presented, or the structure that most closely suits your intended use of the material. Patterns of notes are a visual aid to learning the material that complements the usual oral/textual format in which we store information.

The advantages of this system over the linear form of notemaking are outlined by Buzan (2006, 19):
- The centre or main idea is more clearly defined.
- The relative importance of each idea is clearly indicated.
- The links between key concepts are immediately recognisable because of the proximity and connection.
- As a result of the above, recall and review is both more effective and rapid.
- The nature of the structure allows for the easy addition of new information without messy scratching out or squeezing in.
- Each pattern looks and is different from the other patterns. This aids recall.

Source: Marshall 1991.

It is impossible to reproduce most of the content of a lecture exactly, and if you try to do so you will miss the overall pattern of the lecture and the main points. In addition, you very rarely want this much detail. Instead, your notes should be your consciously selected version of the material offered, so that you *make* notes rather than take them. The previous chapter on reading suggests why you might make notes and what your notes could include (see 'Notemaking and/or underlining', Chapter 10) and the same points apply to lectures. But how you make notes when listening to a once-only live lecture differs from making notes from a lecture you can listen to again or from printed material you can re-read. (Table 11.1 offers some suggestions on notemaking that you can apply to both your lectures and reading.)

Find a balance for each lecture between making useful notes and listening carefully—making notes constantly or making none at all are both of dubious value. In lectures that are meant to stimulate your imagination, spend most of your time sitting back and listening. In lectures that are densely packed with information and ideas you take more notes, but select from and condense what is said so that you can listen closely enough to understand. For instance, if you are given a lot of data or examples, you can often summarise what they mean rather than frantically trying to copy them all. Sometimes a sketch version of a graph can be useful to trigger your memory. If you have printed out slides or handouts, annotate these as you listen to the lecture.

Be alert for phrases such as 'The following three factors are . . .' or 'It's important to note that . . .' as these are designed to help you identify the structure of the lecture and indicate which points to note (see Table 14.2, 'Transitional words and phrases').

If you prepare for a lecture and quickly go over your notes very soon afterwards, you can usually strike a happy balance between making satisfactory notes and listening attentively to what is said. Try the following methods to experiment with how detailed your notes need to be and how much time to spend listening:

- Make as many notes as you think you will need. Go over them immediately after the lecture, asking yourself if you understand all you have written, and try to reproduce the way in which the lecture developed. If you can't, you have possibly spent too much time writing during the lecture—or the lecture itself was very confusing.

- Listen intently to an online lecture and make notes on the structure of what is said. Immediately after, see if you can write a satisfactory précis of what you have just heard, perhaps in a patterned format. Then quickly review your notes.

- When listening to an online lecture or podcast, take advantage of being able to stop and replay it at any point—something you can't do with a live lecture.

The above are suggestions and you should develop your own method of distinguishing the structure of what is said, separating main points from subpoints and supporting details. Lecture notes in which you can see the structure are easier to remember. Leave space for your own comments, questions, references to follow up and items to think about further. On each page include the lecture title, date and the lecturer's name. This is vital in case you need to use the material as a source in an assignment.

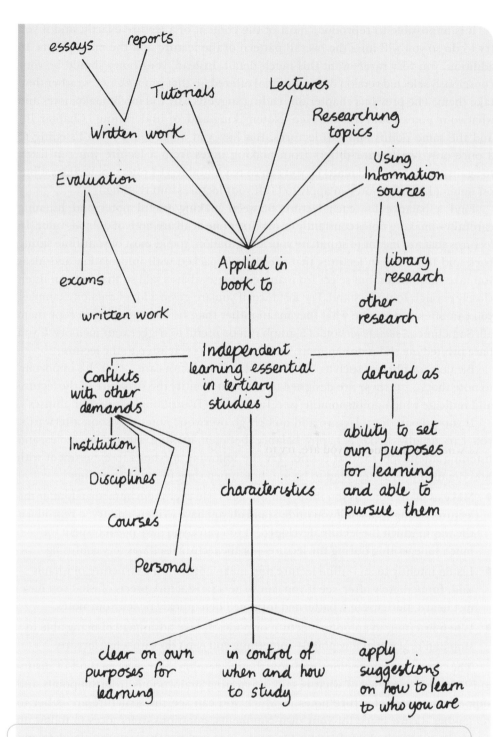

essays   reports

Tutorials   Lectures

Written work   Researching topics

Evaluation   Using Information Sources

exams   Applied in book to   library research

written work   other research

Conflicts with other demands   Independent learning essential in tertiary studies   defined as

Institution   ability to set own purposes for learning and able to pursue them

Disciplines   characteristics

Courses

Personal

clear on own purposes for learning   in control of when and how to study   apply suggestions on how to learn to who you are

A student's patterned summary of key points found in this book.

Overcoming concentration difficulties

Now I lay me back to sleep,
The speaker's dull, the subject's deep.
If he should stop before I wake,
Give me a nudge for goodness' sake.   ANON.

Try to overcome difficulties that prevent you concentrating on and understanding a lecture (see 'Concentrating', Chapter 4). Your concentration is usually better at the beginning of a lecture—if you are able to put aside the thoughts or distractions that were occupying you before the lecture began, and if you give yourself a few minutes to settle before the lecture. You also concentrate better when you know that the lecture is nearly over—unless you are impatient to finish. During a lecture your maximum concentration span is probably 20–25 minutes. In a long lecture, revive your concentration by changing your sitting position, by quickly reviewing your notes, or by formulating a question about a point you don't understand.

- Try to minimise distractions in your physical surroundings—a hard chair, a wobbly desk, a cold room or loud hammering nearby are not conducive to full concentration.

- If you find it difficult to listen to an online lecture because you can't see the lecturer's expressions or gestures, listen intently and replay parts if necessary. If you still have trouble, make full use of any slides, notes or handouts.

- If a lecture seems to offer little that is new to you, ask yourself 'Am I really listening to what is being said?' If you are, try to anticipate what will come next, relate what is being said to what you already know about the topic, and review any notes you have made as you listen. Make a game of trying to find new information.

- If a lecture contains too much unfamiliar material, make a list of questions on points you don't understand, and try to clarify these points afterwards.

- If the content of the lecture seems irrelevant or uninteresting, jot down at least an outline in case the topic becomes relevant or interesting at a later date. You might prefer to leave the lecture quietly and do some other work rather than feeling that you are wasting time.

- A lecturer may make it difficult for you to follow the lecture because they don't organise the material clearly, don't provide a written or oral lecture outline, or don't adequately prepare slides and other aids. When you can't follow a lecture easily, leave plenty of space to add to and edit your notes afterwards.

- If a lecturer's style is difficult or dull for you, think about why this is so. You can probably do little to change the idiosyncrasies of lecturers' styles, but let a lecturer know if you can't hear what is said. Don't dismiss lecturers you find difficult to follow as useless after only a couple of lectures. They may know their subject well and, as you become more familiar with their individual styles, it is often easier to concentrate on and understand what they are saying. And you never know, they may just be a world expert on the topic.

● If you turn up for a live lecture but spend much of the time socialising on your phone or laptop, you will miss much of what is said and are unlikely to follow the development of the lecture material or be able to distinguish main points from details. You also unfairly distract people nearby who are trying to concentrate. You need to decide if in future you will skip lectures (and miss important information) or give lectures your full attention.

After a lecture

Before I came here I was confused about this subject. Having listened to your lecture I am still confused. But on a higher level.   ENRICO FERMI

As you hear most lectures only once, *reviewing your notes* as soon as possible—preferably immediately after a lecture or the same day—helps you remember what you have heard. Ask yourself:

● Do I understand everything I have written?

● Can I identify the argument of the lecture—the thesis and reasons? If the lecture has no argument, can I distinguish the theme, main points and subpoints, and how the lecture developed from one point to another? It may help to underline or highlight the main points as you review your notes.

● Is there a clearly identifiable theoretical framework for the lecture?

● Do I need to edit my notes so that they reflect the lecture more accurately and read more easily?

● Do I need to expand my notes so that I can still understand them in a month's time?

● Can I integrate any slides or handouts with my notes?

● Do I have a relevant article or other material to file with my notes? Could I usefully include references to a couple of multimedia items?

● Would it be useful to express all or part of my notes in another form, for example, as a flow chart, a diagram or in a pattern? (See Table 11.1, 'Notemaking methods'.)

If you have *persistent problems* identifying the structure of lectures and under-standing your notes:

— listen to the lecture online if possible

— make sure that you are preparing thoroughly for lectures

— compare your notes with someone else's and discuss the differences to help clarify ways to improve your notemaking

— read some more on the topic so that the lecture isn't your only source of information, or

— ask a lecturer or study skills adviser for help with the problem (see 'Approaching teachers', Chapter 3).

Your problems with lectures may be due to the lecturer. If you have difficulty understanding an important lecture, you might go and see the lecturer soon afterwards to ask about the topic. Sometimes a person who's awkward in front of an audience is helpful when discussing information on a one-to-one basis. (Think how you feel when delivering a seminar paper and when discussing the same topic with one other person.) Giving an inspired lecture is a talent that few people possess naturally, so constructive comments can help lecturers improve their skill. Such comments can be made tactfully by asking questions on points you don't understand. Provide feedback on the lecturer when you have the chance to comment in unit surveys.

Since most lectures are a one-way communication, *using and discussing the lecture material* is essential if you are to understand the information and ideas fully.

- Do you have items you want to follow up—for example, an idea that interested you, a reference you noted, a point you didn't fully understand, or a quote you want to check out?

- Did the lecturer suggest any follow-up to the lecture, such as a reference to read, a problem to solve, an exercise to do, or a couple of questions to think about?

- File your notes for easy future reference (see 'Recording and filing references', Chapter 8).

Some lectures contain ideas or information that are especially significant to you. These lectures are easy to remember and use. Otherwise, you are most likely to use what you have heard and written down if you need the material for an assignment or an exam, for a seminar or online discussion, or when talking to friends or a teacher. Informal discussions over coffee straight after a lecture can be very helpful. For example, they can provide the opportunity:

— to compare notes

— to clarify points you didn't understand

— to exchange ideas that excited you, and

— to decide on questions or suggestions with which to approach the lecturer if necessary.

If you find some lectures boring and pointless, is it because you are sitting back and expecting to be entertained? If you are, think about why you are attending a lecture and prepare to take an active part as a listener. Inevitably some lectures seem a waste of time, and few people deliver an ideal lecture. But university lecturers are specialists in their subject, and can present you with insights into research on a topic. To make the most of the range of knowledge and lecturing styles you are offered, take the time to learn how to get the most out of lectures and, if necessary, pluck up the courage to try to change them.

TEN TIPS

1   If you have a choice between attending a live lecture and listening to it online, think about which works best for you.

2   Before each lecture, work out how the lecture fits within the unit by reviewing the unit guide and how you might use the information in any of your assignments.

3   Don't miss the introduction to a lecture.

4   Develop a method of making notes which can be adapted to different lecturing styles and content, and which enables you to capture the structure of a lecture.

5   Rather than writing everything down or taking only a few notes, practise finding a balance between listening so that you understand what's being said while also making notes of the more important material.

6   If listening to an online lecture, try to save time by listening attentively so that you only replay sections or parts you don't understand.

7   When you realise that your concentration has wandered, change positions, take a deep breath, and quickly look over your notes so far.

8   After a lecture, as soon as possible quickly review your notes and add to them or highlight parts so that they are clear for when you need to use them in the future.

9   To help you easily find your lecture notes again, note details such as the lecture title, the lecture date and the lecturer's name plus any key words.

10   Occasionally compare your lecture notemaking style with a couple of other students to see if you can learn new techniques from each other.

REFERENCES

Buzan, Tony. 2006. *Mind Mapping*. Harlow: BBC Active.

Marshall, Lorraine. 1991. *Learning Skills Tutors' Guide*. Perth, WA: Murdoch University.

Participating in discussions

12

'The time has come,' the Walrus said,
'To talk of many things:
Of shoes—and ships—and sealing wax –
Of cabbages—and kings –
Of why the sea is boiling hot –
And whether pigs have wings.'

LEWIS CARROLL

○○○ *Do you think of yourself as a 'talker' or a 'listener'?*

Which people or situations encourage you to talk? Face-to-face discussions? Online?

Who do you talk to in your daily life—about the weather, about personal matters or about current issues?

Do you find that many of your conversations (or online chats) are about other people, yourself, sex, ideas, events, leisure activities, technology, religion or politics?

Who do you particularly enjoy listening to?

Do you think that you learn more from talking face-to-face with people, participating in online groups, from listening, reading, writing or watching TV?

In online groups are you a 'contributor' or a 'listener'?

Do you chat with others by writing letters or emails?

Your discussions with other people, whether face-to-face or online, may be intense debates, rambling conversations, casual chats, exchanges of brilliant repartee or rituals of polite remarks about the weather. These discussions may be very brief, go on for several hours, or continue intermittently for weeks or even months. Perhaps you use discussion to sort out your ideas, share experiences, play with words, or learn something new.

As a tertiary student, you probably learn a great deal from informal ad hoc discussions over endless coffees or from chat groups. In universities, discussions are one of the contexts for debate and argument (see 'University culture', Chapter 2 and 'Critical thinking', Chapter 3). All members of the various disciplines, whether teachers or students, are participants in ongoing debates on a range of topics, questions and problems.

Why discussion groups?

Sharing your learning in discussion groups can allow you to collaboratively explore knowledge and ideas, which offsets the competitive pressures on you as a student. Discussion groups also provide an alternative to the solitary activities of private study and listening to presentations such as lectures.

Any discussion group can offer an opportunity:

— to integrate what you learn from your reading, writing and lectures

— to clarify your knowledge and ideas on a subject

— to stimulate you to study and think

— to sort out misunderstandings and problems in your work

— to practise communicating ideas to others

— to solve problems collaboratively, and

— to develop critical thinking skills and attitudes in a group context.

More specifically, student-organised study groups that meet regularly, whether face-to-face or online, can be an invaluable support and a source of feedback on work before you submit it. Within a unit, working collaboratively can stimulate you to think in new ways (see 'Collaborative learning', Chapter 3). Formal face-to-face or online tutorials and seminars can provide closer contact with a teacher, and feedback on your progress. Unfortunately, funding cutbacks to universities mean that some units no longer offer tutorials every week, or that students may work in large groups to complete set tasks with little whole-group discussion. In these circumstances, informal student-organised groups and online interactions become increasingly important.

Online discussion groups may be formal or informal, and can provide a much needed source of support and contact, particularly for distance, online and isolated students. Informal online discussions may focus on academic matters and/or provide social interaction. The academic discussions might take the form of regular formal tutorials or seminars, the collaborative production of an assignment, or shared informal problem solving.

Online groups can offer advantages to all students. Since the contributions are text-based, an active discussion list can construct a shared knowledge base, and a record of the group discussions builds up which can be stored and edited and easily revisited. Similarly, a group can build a wiki when working on a group assignment.

> . . . learning networks are groups of people who use CMC [computer mediated communications] networks to learn together, at a time, place and pace that best suits them and is appropriate to the task . . . The use of computer networks . . . introduces new options to transform teaching and learning relationships and outcomes . . .
>
> LINDA HARASIM

Types of discussion groups

Variety is the spice of discussion groups, whatever their origin, purpose and focus. Within a group, people of different ages, experiences, and backgrounds with different world views have much to offer each other when exchanging ideas; and a varied format and content for group meetings can be stimulating.

> I dogmatise and am contradicted, and in this conflict of opinions and sentiments I find delight.   SAMUEL JOHNSON

Most structured discussion groups in undergraduate education can be characterised according to who establishes them, their focus, and how much collaborative learning is involved.

- Groups may be set up by teachers for all or part of a unit, or by students who establish study groups that meet regularly.
- Discussions might focus on a particular segment of the content, on an assignment or other coursework, on study skills and/or provide student support.

- The extent of collaboration depends on such factors as the purpose of the group and a teacher's role.

Traditionally, in higher education formal small-group discussion is mostly conducted in face-to-face tutorials and seminars. These groups meet specifically for discussion as part of a unit and usually consist of a teacher as leader and a group of students. Such formal groups vary widely in structure and content. For example, they may be:

— a mini-lecture where the teacher imparts information

— a group in which the teacher remains relatively unobtrusive and the rest of the group manages itself

— a seminar series where each member takes a turn as chairperson

— a group that uses interactive exercises such as role-playing to learn about values and attitudes, or

— a session that emphasises the less subjective, rational aspects of learning.

Both tutorials and study groups may focus on:

— formal debates on issues, solving specific problems, or working on particular research

— discussions structured around a paper given by a group member or based on set reading, or

— sharing experiences and feelings as well as discussing intellectual issues.

Collaborative learning groups

> . . . these shared spaces can become the locus of rich and satisfying experiences in collaborative learning, an interactive group knowledge-building process in which the learner actively constructs knowledge by formulating ideas into words that are shared with and built upon through the reactions and responses of others.
>
> LINDA HARASIM

Collaborative learning groups can be informal and out-of-class, or be part of your formal learning. Collaborative learning in class can be a five-minute buzz group where you share information with other students, or a formal group with a life cycle of perhaps a few days or a few months. Weekly tutorials can be collaborative learning groups led by a tutor. To work more effectively in a collaborative group it is important to understand how groups work and the stages through which they pass (which are outlined in Table 12.1).

As well as pursuing your academic goals in discussions, work to develop skills for participating in the groups. This work involves actively reflecting on your interactions with the group, and taking initiatives both within the group and with your teacher to alleviate any difficulties (see 'Playing your part during discussions', later in this chapter).

TABLE
12.1

Group stages

If a group is to function well, face-to-face or online, apply the following four stages each time the group meets and over the life of the group. These stages involve both an analytical and a reflective component.

1   Find common ground with other group members. Allow some time for socialising to get to know each other and to discover what you have in common. Aim to understand each person's expectations of the group, identify conflicts and work at resolving them. Socialising—as long as it does not dominate—is not a waste of time and can lead to a more successful outcome. Online, a few comments about yourself before you get down to the business at hand can work wonders to situate you for the person or people 'listening' to you elsewhere on the Internet.

2   Clarify any different roles and goals for each person in the group. Do this early on and at the same time establish ground rules (see 'Ground rules', below).

3   Work to achieve the agreed outcomes of the group.

4   Reflect on the group's achievements, both the group's 'product' and the group process. Evaluating the group process should involve both individual and group evaluation.

Source: Based on Schmuck and Schmuck 1992.

Setting up discussion groups

Your teachers may have addressed the issues discussed in this section when establishing formal tutorials for face-to-face or online units. You should also address these issues if you are in a collaborative group with other students, within a unit or across related units, or if you are setting up a group. (If your group aims to concentrate specifically on writing, see 'Writing groups', Chapter 13.)

First things

Group size

Traditionally, 7–12 people is recognised as an effective number for tutorial groups, but this varies with the purpose of the discussion. Many people feel hesitant about speaking in front of a group, and ideally the group should be large enough to provide a variety of ideas and small enough to enable everyone to say something within the time available. If a group is too small, combine with another group if possible. If the group is too large, break into smaller groups for a part of each session or permanently.

For informal study groups three or four people can be ideal. This is also an optimum size for an online work group that needs to make decisions quickly.

When and where to meet

Agree on the length and frequency of meetings according to the size and purpose of the group. With an online group, your meetings can be time-independent (asynchronous) and place-independent. Decide whether or not to include any real-time (synchronous) meetings online or face-to-face.

Consider where to meet so that you can spend some uninterrupted and relaxing time together. Meeting outside formal settings, perhaps outdoors or off campus, can have a positive impact on formal discussions. Discussions are influenced by their physical setting, so if possible in formal settings seek out a comfortable room or adapt an unfriendly meeting place to a group's needs. A cold box-like room occupied by standard institutional chairs and tables and a blackboard is more conducive to monastic silence than heated debate. If the room is inappropriate, rearrange seating or desks so that everyone is more comfortable and, most importantly, can see everyone else. A leader need not be isolated in front of the group; a large open space in the middle of a group can be closed up; and if the room is carpeted people may be more relaxed sitting on the floor.

The first few meetings

Getting to know each other

Instead of plunging straight into talking about a topic or assignment and assessment, devote some time to becoming acquainted, perhaps over coffee. Names and faces become more familiar if each person, including the teacher, introduces themselves briefly and talks about their interests and hopes for the unit. Try icebreakers such as naming games or round robins. Breaking briefly into pairs to discuss a specific question gives people another opportunity to become acquainted. These strategies also provide a sense of the resources, strengths and expertise of group members. Such focused socialising actively contributes to the group process, and should occur in the first few meetings and be built into subsequent meetings (see Table 12.1, 'Group stages').

The group's role and focus

In the early stages, establish some shared initial expectations for the group. Some members may see the group's main role as enabling students to exchange ideas; others may see meetings as an occasion for the teacher to tell them about a subject; while some may see meetings as forums for discussing lectures or their special interests.

- If the group is part of a unit, make it a priority to discuss the group's role in the unit as a whole and how it should operate. Collectively decide (or find out from the teacher) if group participation will be assessed formally or informally and, if so, how.

- If the group is to work collaboratively on a project or assignment, the group needs to arrive at an initial understanding of how much work will be done together and the responsibilities of each person. It can be valuable to identify or develop a couple of smaller tasks as soon as possible so you practise working together.

- An online group need not be limited in its role and focus because of the medium. Consider setting up a virtual cafe (bring your own coffee), a debating team or a learning circle.

Ongoing meetings

Attending meetings

Regular attendance and contributions are important as this helps members feel comfortable with each other and confident enough to suggest ideas, ask questions, admit ignorance and respond honestly to other people's ideas. Developing a sense of give and take lessens the pressure to always have to say something and to impress others.

In online groups, participants need to agree on the frequency of new contributions, on the time frame for comments and on how often group members should log on.

Ground rules

> It is crucial to establish ground rules in a group because you've always got issues of power, and if you don't have ground rules it's basically a free-for-all.   JULIA HOBSON

Establishing ground rules (a code of behaviour) and abiding by them helps to ensure a harmonious working relationship that in turn helps the group achieve its aims. For example, if the aim of a group is to foster critical thinking skills and attitudes, the ground rules need to reflect this. Similarly, the ground rules for a writing group should reflect the specific outcomes sought by the group (see 'Writing groups', Chapter 13).

Ground rules for face-to-face or online groups should be developed collaboratively at the first meeting. If everyone contributes and agrees on the rules, people are more likely to abide by them. If a group does not seem to be working well, the ground rules may need to be renegotiated.

Possible ground rules might be:

— everyone will prepare for meetings

— when someone speaks everyone listens

— everyone will be on time, and

— discriminatory comments will not be allowed.

Ground rules to foster critical thinking and attitudes may be substantially the same as those for any effective group, but might also include:

— avoid being dogmatic

— don't silence others

— explain assumptions, and

— respect cultural differences and other people's opinions.

For online groups, you also need to abide by general Netiquette principles (generally accepted rules of conduct on the Net) and any online protocols specific to the group.

Preparing for a discussion

Once a group is established, consider how to make the most effective use of the time you spend together. If everyone in a group prepares, the discussion at least has the basis for success. If you prepare, you have a clearer idea of what you want to discuss and will remember the discussion more clearly. You can also challenge others who do not prepare and who rely on talking without much thought or preparation.

At times you may not be able to prepare as fully as you would like. However, if most people aren't preparing, discuss why not, and ensure that being prepared is a ground rule with which everyone agrees.

- Know as precisely as possible the topic planned for discussion, what preparation is required, and why.
- Do any required preparation such as reading or exercises.
- Formulate in writing at least one brief item to contribute to the discussion—a thought, a definition, a question, a piece of information, or a comment on your reading or lecture on the topic (see Chapter 6, 'Asking your own questions').
- Revise relevant lecture notes.
- Check reference books and follow up with more specific reading or websites if necessary.
- Read any notes you made during or after the last group meeting.

If you find the preparation required is too much or too difficult, if you have trouble obtaining necessary materials, or if you have other major demands on your time, ask the group leader as soon as possible for suggestions or information.

Immediately before the group meets, be aware of how you feel and try to put distractions behind you (see 'Your emotions', Chapter 1). You might read thoroughly a section from a relevant book or website to focus your mind on the discussion topic.

TABLE
12.2 **Preparing a discussion paper**

Prepare thoroughly if you are to give a paper. Your efforts will be assessed according to the content, how you structure the material, and your presentation.

- Research, plan and prepare the content of your paper. In a short paper, limit yourself to one or two main points. You need a clear introduction, and a summing-up that could be a statement or question for the group to debate. This is especially important if you do not make copies of your paper, as your listeners will have the material presented to them only once. (See Chapter 8 for information on researching, and Chapter 14 for ideas on how to plan and structure the content of a discussion paper.)
- Prepare visual aids, slides or notes, perhaps as handouts to help your audience follow you, especially if you plan to use data, maps or other information that may be difficult to absorb quickly.
- Decide whether to speak from notes or slides or to read a paper. Rehearse aloud, so that you know how long your presentation takes. Most listeners become restless after 15–20 minutes, so take this into account.
- Practise varying your presentation to hold the group's attention. You are more likely to engage your listeners if you invite questions or ask questions of the group at appropriate points in your talk.

Playing your part during discussions

Most university groups spend time talking about academic or practical matters, such as the next topic for discussion, the set reading or who will deliver a seminar paper, but they often neglect to explicitly consider group processes and interpersonal interactions within a group—the *hidden agenda*. Even group interactions of which every member is aware, such as frequent silences or an over-talkative person, aren't usually discussed by the whole group. The following are a few examples of this hidden agenda.

- The particular combination of people in a group plays a large part in shaping the discussions. For example, groups made up of school leavers approach a subject differently from groups of mature age students from a variety of backgrounds. People who are in a minority, such as women in a predominantly male discipline or a refugee in a group of Australians, often feel less free to speak.
- If people always sit in the same place or two or three people always sit together, this can set up habits of who talks to whom and where discussions centre.

12

- The person who decides the direction of a discussion may not be the teacher or a person with a lot to say, but someone who asks pertinent questions or who brings an aimless discussion back on track.

- How people contribute to a group is influenced by whether each person's participation is assessed and, if so, whether it is assessed by a teacher or by the whole group.

- When people contribute to a group discussion, they may be trying not to appear naive/over-clever/aggressive while at the same time seeming to be witty/intelligent/confident/sexually attractive.

> [in] working together across differences . . . the 'outsider' should sincerely attempt to carry out her attempted criticism of the insider's perceptions in such a way that it does not amount to, or even seem to amount to, an attempt to denigrate or dismiss the validity of the insider's point of view.   UMA NARAYAN

If you have little experience of taking responsibility for formal discussions and are anxious not to appear foolish in front of the other students or a teacher, you are unlikely to initiate discussions on how a group is working. If a teacher is unskilled in dealing with group dynamics, he or she is unlikely to instigate discussion with students about what is happening in a group. But the personal interactions within a group can't be separated from its intellectual discussions, and a group needs to spend time talking about both if it is to realise its full potential (see 'Collaborative learning groups', earlier in this chapter). If you feel that a hidden agenda item is being ignored at the cost of group effectiveness and your own learning, try to work up the courage—perhaps with someone else in the group—to bring the problem constructively into the open, using some of the suggestions below.

Each member of a group, even if remaining silent, influences how that group operates. The success of a discussion group depends largely on whether everyone plays a part in establishing ground rules, takes responsibility for how the group operates, and feels free to contribute fully.

Talking and listening skills

> . . . I find discussion as a whole . . . difficult, because I've never had to discuss anything before and haven't put my feelings into words . . . It takes me an awful long time to think about what I want to say and, sometimes, by the time I've thought about it, it's gone.   A STUDENT

Participating fully in a group discussion requires practice in the skills of:

— listening carefully

— asking useful questions, and

— talking as clearly and concisely as possible, even when trying to articulate new ideas.

These skills take time to develop, particularly with a group of people who initially are strangers; and for each combination of people you need to find your own balance between talking and listening. If you don't see asking questions as an essential part of conversations, practise the skills of genuinely listening and then asking questions.

Participating in a group is not the same as talking a great deal. Some of your alternatives include:

— listening closely for most of the time, occasionally contributing a well thought-out question or piece of information

— attempting to paraphrase what someone else said, to make sure you understood them

— asking questions that begin 'Do you mean that . . .?' 'What do you think about . . .?' or simply 'Why?'

— responding to someone else's contribution, as long as you really are responding and not just waiting to have your say, and

— affirming someone else's idea.

If you have prepared for the discussion you will have your own thoughts and questions to contribute. If a group is to help you sort out your ideas and become aware of your beliefs and biases, don't hold back because you feel you have to utter perfectly complete thoughts or that you can't play with ideas. But if outside university you often use social media to post completely spontaneous thoughts, be aware that in academic discussion you are trying to explore ideas in some depth; so take at least a little time to think before you speak.

You may come from a cultural background or educational system in which you do not speak up unless addressed directly by the teacher, or where your main contribution is to respond to factual questions asked of the class. In universities, you are expected to contribute knowledge as well as ideas, and to comment thoughtfully on what other members say.

● If you lack confidence in a group, remember that it takes time to gain experience in the skills of formal discussion and to settle into a new group of people. Even if you like the group members at the first meeting, you may still be cautious about venturing opinions until you know them a little better. You can gain confidence by:

— preparing for the discussion

— getting to know some members of the group outside the formal meeting time, and

— talking to the group leader or a helpful staff member about how you feel.

Others who at first seem to know more than you often don't; and even if they do, you still have your contribution to make (see 'Your cultural self', Chapter 1).

> Very few people know how to listen. Their haste pulls them out of the conversation, or they try internally to improve the situation, or they're preparing what their next speech will be when you shut up and it's their turn to take the stage.   PETER HØEG

- If you are aware that you talk too much, you may notice that others actually stop listening to you or find it difficult to follow what you say. For several meetings, try to ask other people questions whenever you feel tempted to talk—you will probably be surprised at how much they have to contribute. Ask yourself the following questions:

How much time do I usually spend talking and how much time asking questions and listening to what others say?

How much response do I usually give to other people's ideas?

Online, do I contribute frequently but only skim-read messages?

Your answers to these questions will probably vary for each group to which you belong. Reflect on why you put more effort into some groups than others.

Online discussions

Online discussions have some distinctive features when it comes to 'talking' and 'listening'. As they are independent of time and place you can decide when and where you want to contribute, which gives you the opportunity to reflect on an unfolding discussion before contributing, and to edit your initial response before posting it. This can be particularly useful if you prefer time to think before you write, if you have physical difficulties with writing or if English is not your first language. Also, you don't have to compete to contribute, and can be heard uninterrupted. If you are shy, you don't have to wait for a group leader to pick up visual signals indicating you want to say something. Even if you are initially hesitant, contribute as soon as you can rather than just reading other posts.

As well as learning some of the skills for contributing online, become familiar with the online communication tool being used. Online group discussion can be egalitarian because it is physically anonymous and so, for example, you are not judged by your appearance. However, because of the absence of visual cues, online discussions are likely to be less rich and nuanced than face-to-face interactions. You also have to learn the skills of 'talking' in chunks rather than being part of a conversation with its interruptions and interweaving of half-completed sentences, although many of these features are common when you interact on social media sites. In addition, sometimes you may feel that you are talking into space or feel vulnerable when you express ideas openly.

> The interface design must provide ease of navigation, a sense of human interaction, and helpfulness and responsiveness to the needs of learners studying in an information rich, self directed medium. Learners need to feel confident that they know where they

are at any one point in the course and that they can easily make contact with others as
the need arises.   ALLISON BROWN

Taking responsibility

Each person in a group influences the nature of the discussion, and the absence
of even one person can change the group atmosphere. Everyone needs to prepare
for and participate in discussions rather than seeing the group solely as the leader's
responsibility. If only one or two people contribute, even a skilful leader can do little
to make the group function satisfactorily. The amount of time each person talks
depends on factors such as their enthusiasm for a topic, their amount of preparation,
and their wellbeing at the time.

Some people prefer to contribute to a discussion only occasionally, but those who
rarely speak need encouragement. Most people indicate by facial expressions or body
movements when they're ready to speak, and everyone's sensitivity to these signs can
give a shy person an opportunity to speak. Someone who is quiet may gain confidence
if the group divides into smaller groups for part of the discussion. Reticent members
can be encouraged to speak, and garrulous individuals restrained, if each person
prepares a specific contribution for each session or takes a turn to comment briefly
on a topic. If you feel hesitant about participating in an online group, spend time
preparing the occasional thoughtful contribution.

However, the whole group needs to discourage a person who talks too much, and
usually this can be done politely but firmly by remarks such as 'That's interesting—
I'm curious to hear what other people have to say now'. If what the talker says is
irrelevant, the whole group will be grateful to someone who brings the discussion
back on track. But if the offender fails to take the hint, deal with the problem after
the meeting.

Leading and monitoring a group

The official group leader may not always be a teacher—he or she may be a student who
is giving a paper or is responsible for chairing the discussion. Most groups also have
unofficial leaders, even if 'leaderless'. Some groups rotate the leader or moderator so
that everyone has the opportunity to develop leadership skills.

If you are the group leader, even for one session, consider the following ideas:

- Devise a list of discussion questions (and possible answers to them) in case no
  one asks any questions (see Chapter 6, 'Asking your own questions').
- Think about different ways to organise the session—perhaps break the group
  into smaller brief buzz groups, or allow members time to reflect and/or write
  before they speak.
- Perhaps assign different roles to members, such as observers, monitors, reporters
  or questioners. Observers of the group process can check whether the ground

rules are being followed. Monitoring is particularly important for online groups, especially for members who are new to online discussions.

- Unless online discussions are password protected, others can log in.

Presentations

If you are responsible for a presentation, remember that your listeners are unlikely to be expecting a perfect presentation, and the content and structure of your talk is all-important. A confident presentation that rambles or says little will not be highly regarded. (See Chapter 14, 'Writing essays', for pointers on structuring introductions, conclusions and main points.)

With group presentations, the success depends on research and planning. Decide well beforehand who will be responsible for different aspects (and see 'Collaborative learning groups', above, for ideas on working as smoothly as possible with others). A group presentation means that you have moral support if you are nervous, and the range of individual skills can result in a high quality presentation.

> TABLE
> **12.3**   **Confident presentations**

> 'Begin at the beginning,' the King said, very gravely, 'and go on till you come to the end: then stop.'
>
> LEWIS CARROLL

Oral presentations are usually assessed on content, structure and delivery style, but it is often the latter that creates the most anxiety.

- Rehearse your talk thoroughly so that you are familiar with the material. Practise articulating and clarifying what you really want to say, and check that your talk is the right length.
- Tell a couple of people beforehand if you feel nervous and ask them to nod encouragingly during your talk. If you are expected to stimulate discussion at the end of your talk, give one or two people a couple of prepared questions to get the discussion going.
- To create a confident impression from the outset, prepare a succinct and clear introduction and learn the first few sentences by heart. Make eye contact with a few people in the room, and smile as you introduce yourself and your topic. Remember to breathe deeply before you start talking.
- Have water at hand to sip if your mouth becomes dry, and use this pause to gather your thoughts or to signal a move from one main point to another.
- Clearly indicate when you move from one part of your talk to the next. This helps you stay on track. Giving people a handout showing your main points also helps both you and them.

- Prepare your written material in a form that gives you most confidence when presenting. If you read from a written-out talk, build in pauses to make eye contact with your audience. If you are comfortable giving presentations, use slides, cards, a summary handout or overheads.

- Keep any visual aids simple and don't use too many. Limit the amount of information on each one, so that people have time to absorb it. Only use aids if you are going to make full use of the material in them.

- Nervousness can come from focusing on yourself rather than on the needs of your audience. Imagine yourself in the position of one of your listeners, and consider what you would want from a presenter.

- Your presentation is more likely to be interesting and confident if you are genuinely intrigued by your topic and want to share it. Whatever the topic, try to find an angle on it that fascinates you.

- Experienced presenters often feel nervous before a talk, but they have learnt to view these nerves as adrenalin which stimulates them to give a better talk.

- Tell everyone if you are happy to take questions or comments during your presentation, or if you would rather these were withheld until you finish. If you are responsible for the discussion afterwards, encourage others to take part. As well as improving the discussion, this can reduce your anxiety about being the centre of attention.

The teacher's authority in a group

The authority of those who teach is very often a hindrance to those who wish to learn.   CICERO

Where a teacher is responsible for a group, their authority usually overrides that of a student, even when the teacher tries to prevent this.

A teacher may have authority in a group because she or he is:

— an assessor of group members' work

— a specialist in a particular field of knowledge

— a skilled group leader

— a person older than most students in the group, or

— a dominant personality.

Leadership styles

He was leader by default—by de fault of de rest of de group.   ANON.

Some teachers consciously try to step back from a position of authority in a group, to encourage students to articulate their ideas and learn from each other. Such teachers face the challenge of being a *resource person* rather than an expert or an appointed leader. They try to use their personal skills with people or groups to foster the development of individuals and the whole group, instead of attempting to direct this process. If you are accustomed to having your learning firmly directed, you may find this approach disconcerting.

There are teachers who consciously prefer to be the *definite leader* in a group. This choice is consistent with a model that defines formal education as students receiving information from experts. Teachers who base their teaching on this model are likely to expect to be the focus of the group's comments and questions and to use group meetings to give mini-lectures. This approach can work when both teacher and students feel under pressure to cover a prescribed amount of material, but it discourages discussion between students and discounts the potential of small-group work.

Some teachers remain the *automatic leader* because they haven't given much thought to the bases of authority in a group—and even teachers who want to encourage student participation occasionally fall into accepting this authority. An inexperienced teacher may be glad of the security that the role of leader offers, and some teachers expect younger students to defer to them. Other teachers, because of their personality and experience, are accustomed to leading most groups in which they find themselves.

> The role of the teacher in an online environment is radically different to more traditional teacher–learner relationships. Once teachers have completed the syllabus and instructional design of the online course their role is then to observe, monitor, facilitate and provide information as appropriate, not to deliver a course in a fixed and rigid one-way format.
>
> ALLISON BROWN

Coping with a teacher's authority

If your teacher takes the authority, you may find it helps to work out why. For example:

- Some teachers don't recognise that their familiarity with the concepts and language of a subject automatically gives them authority. It can be difficult for such teachers to understand how complex the subject and language can be for beginners (see 'Developing your vocabulary', Chapter 10).
- Other teachers are anxious to cover a syllabus or eager to convey what they see as the important or exciting issues in a topic. Such teachers usually plan tutorials or seminars in depth and may ignore contributions that don't fit this plan, or which question the answers they have in mind. They may attempt to start a discussion at a level that is too advanced or at a pace that is too fast for most of the group, so that discussion is only possible if there are one or two students who are self-confident and familiar with the subject.

- Teachers who don't know how to encourage participation may not realise the need for a clearly defined starting point for discussion. Or they may hover over a group, rushing to break up silences instead of allowing people to collect their thoughts, or asking obvious questions and answering student questions so conclusively that further discussion is pointless.

All the tutors say, you know, do ask a question if you don't understand me, but if you really have no idea of what on earth they're going on about you can't very well say 'Well, would you start again at the beginning?'. You can't ask a question because you just don't know what to ask it about.   A STUDENT

How can a group cope with a teacher's authority? Start with the assumption that it is the responsibility of the whole group, not only the teacher, to make a group effective and ask yourself if you have contributed as fully as possible. A teacher who takes a dominant role may appear to determine a group's character, but she or he can only dominate if the rest of the group allows this to happen—if, for example, you seldom address comments or questions directly to each other. As a group, work out clearly what you expect and want from the discussions and develop ground rules to facilitate harmonious interactions. If you aren't prepared to take action, don't expect the situation to change.

What aims would you each like the group to have?

What do members have to offer in discussions, and what knowledge and skills does the teacher have?

What activities can the group undertake to help each person participate fully?

If you think assessment of contributions to the group is restricting full discussion, can you suggest alternatives?

If you don't understand an aspect of the discussion, are you each willing to ask about it?

If the discussion seems aimless, are you each willing to say so and suggest a definite direction for discussion?

Are you each prepared to renew the discussion after a silence?

You may want to talk about these and other questions during or outside group meetings. If possible, talk directly with the teacher about any problems rather than suffering in silence or grumbling and doing nothing. Teachers who are concerned about their students and their teaching know that they can often learn from students and welcome thoughtful suggestions. Such a direct discussion may require considerable courage if a teacher is authoritarian, and more than a little tact if a teacher is well-meaning but unskilled (see 'Approaching teachers', Chapter 3). It is usually easier to talk with a teacher if you have met on a one-to-one basis, because you see each other more as individuals with particular interests rather than as 'Teacher' and 'Student'. Whatever tack you take, include your comments on the quality of teaching in student satisfaction surveys.

After a group

After a group meeting, review the discussion by thinking about how it relates to you, your learning and the relevant unit. To remember what was discussed, make a brief summary as soon as possible and follow up anything you haven't understood. If you gave a talk, think back over your presentation and the ensuing discussion. If required, see the group leader to evaluate your paper. Make sure you know what the next topic for discussion will be and precisely what you are expected to prepare.

Another way to learn more from a formal discussion is to get together afterwards—possibly online—with one or two other students to talk informally about the topic. You can sort out points you didn't understand, make some of those comments that were lost in the larger group, and consolidate and build on what you did understand. The moral support that such discussions can give is invaluable, particularly for less confident students.

> . . . all my confidence diminished as I was to hear someone talk of *The Plague* all the time referring to the Germans in France during the War. What in heaven's name was she talking about? I had also read *The Plague* and found it a most interesting story of a town infested by bubonic plague, but it never entered my head that these things were all symbols. From that moment I was frightened to open my mouth. At coffee break, however, I was to learn a couple of others felt the same reaction to this piece of news.
>
> GWEN WESSON

If you have persistent problems in a group and feel dissatisfied, but have contributed as fully as you can, you might discuss your feelings one-to-one with the teacher. Perhaps approach other members of the group to see whether they share your feelings and if so, arrange to devote some of the formal discussion time to dealing with the problem. Maybe the group needs to revisit the ground rules and amend them. If your attempts don't succeed, you may be able to transfer into another group. Such a change often only involves asking the teacher concerned and is preferable to wasting your time.

Do you usually enjoy discussion groups? Most students feel confident and interested in some groups, and uncertain or bored in others. Remember that groups, even effective ones, have their off days. The success of a group as a whole depends on every member assuming responsibility for it; and the success of a group for you as an individual depends on your willingness to participate in critical debate and to speak and listen.

> Students should be enabled to develop the capacity to keep an eye on themselves, and to engage in critical dialogue with themselves in all they think and do . . . the student interrogates her/his thoughts or actions.
>
> RONALD BARNETT

TEN TIPS

1   If you regularly attend tutorials or participate in online discussions, you'll find it easier to contribute and ask questions as conversation threads develop.

2   For effective collaboration, pay attention to the four stages of groups if you are setting up or are part of a group.

3   Establishing ground rules and Netiquette in the early stages of a group helps make discussions more productive.

4   Listening carefully to what others say and asking thoughtful questions is just as important as having something to say.

5   Encourage quiet group members to participate, perhaps by watching for body language which suggests they are ready to contribute.

6   Everyone is responsible for a group, not just the teacher.

7   To help you feel confident when giving a talk, prepare a clear introduction and practise exactly what you want to say.

8   Rehearsing a presentation out loud several times helps you to be more articulate and to give a talk which is the right length.

9   Limit the number of visual aids (such as slides, overheads or handouts) you use for a talk, and limit the amount of information on each.

10   When giving a paper, tell the group if you will take questions as you go or if you prefer to have these at the end of your presentation.

REFERENCES

Schmuck, R. A. and P. A. Schmuck. 1992. *Group Processes in the Classroom*. 6th ed. Dubuque, IA: Wm C. Brown.

12

Developing your writing

13

From time to time I feel a need, sharp as thirst in summer, to note and to describe. And then I take up my pen again and attempt the perilous and elusive task of seizing and pinning down, under its flexible double-pointed nib, the many-hued, fugitive, thrilling adjective . . . The attack does not last long; it is but the itching of an old scar.

COLETTE

If writing is one way you often communicate and express yourself, you probably enjoy it and feel at ease with the process. Your formal academic writing will be enriched by your experience with the craft. In tertiary institutions, written expression is emphasised and learning is assessed primarily through writing essays, reports and examinations. You may have opportunities to take an oral exam, to deliver a paper orally, or to present an assignment in one of the following formats: a film, a website, a poster, a collection of photographs or drawings, a script, a blog or a poem. Don't overlook these. However, the reality is that to pass units in tertiary institutions you must be able to write prose. Even if you find that essay writing comes easily, it may take you time to learn to write reports in the style expected. When you are grappling with new concepts and trying to present them in an unfamiliar genre, your writing may not be as clear as when you write about material you understand in depth. In addition, you are expected to become familiar with the languages and methodologies of your disciplines and you may find it easier to write in one discipline than another (see 'Disciplines', Chapter 7).

Does writing usually come easily to you?

Do you prefer to write using pen and paper or on a computer or tablet?

Do you enjoy putting ideas, thoughts, feelings on paper or tapping away on a keyboard?

How does word processing influence the way you write?

Do you enjoy playing with different writing styles?

If you enjoy writing and write frequently, then you already have an enormous advantage when it comes to writing for academic purposes. You have probably worked out an effective range of approaches to your writing—sometimes waiting until the ideas settle in your mind before beginning, perhaps writing to a detailed plan, or maybe just sitting down and beginning to write. Be aware that the many genres of informal writing differ significantly from those of academic writing, but that if you like to write you have the major advantages of a positive attitude, a fluency with written language and practice with the craft of writing.

Do you lack confidence in your writing because your ability to write was undermined by severe criticism?

Do you have difficulty with writing because you think that what you write falls short of the standards expected by a teacher?

Do you think your vocabulary is limited?

Does your writing seem to deteriorate when you are writing about unfamiliar material or concepts that you find complex?

The 'academic style' that is appropriate for university writing is largely dependent on disciplinary conventions, and does not necessarily include long technical terms and convoluted sentences. Sometimes you do need to make use of particular terminology to convey a precise meaning, but such terminology can easily degenerate into jargon if used carelessly or to impress. When in doubt, opt for simplicity. The main aim of academic writing is to communicate what you want to say to your reader, and the basic need to be lucid and direct applies as much to scholarly writing as to any other kind.

There is no one perfect academic style of writing. Each student will assimilate and present ideas in an individual way. The forms and conventions must be followed but they are there to be used for your own writing aims. You are not expected to be an expert or a renowned author in your field, and it is preferable when writing essays or reports primarily to express your own honest, carefully considered response rather than paraphrasing or plagiarising other people's words and opinions, or indulging your prejudices (see Appendix, 'Discrimination').

You have your own way of using words when you speak and, while you may not be Shakespeare, you probably have your own style of writing. Use it in your academic writing. If your style includes irony, metaphor or an occasional flash of wit, use these elements to enhance your writing, unless they meet with strong disapproval from the people who assess your work.

The process of writing

> Communicating is surely an important objective of writing but not the only one, nor the first . . . the first use of writing is to think with—to articulate ideas—and by shaping these thoughts on paper, to communicate them.   V. A. HOWARD

Unless you are writing to articulate your thoughts purely to yourself, writing is communicating. This involves thinking about the genre in which you write and about your audience, the person or people who will read your writing. You are trying not only to express your thoughts fluently and accurately, but to do so in a certain style and in a way that your reader will understand. To do this you must be clear about what you want to say and why, and you will draw on any language, experiences and beliefs that you and your readers share.

> Find a subject you care about and which you in your heart feel others should care about. It is this genuine caring, and not your games with language, which will be the most compelling and seductive element in your style.   KURT VONNEGUT

Writing is a process that involves both a creative dimension and a critical dimension, and it is important to work on both of these in developing your writing. The creative phase is the process of generating words on the page or screen, of turning the thoughts, ideas, inspirations or dreams in your head into written words; and the critical phase is when you reflect on, constructively criticise and edit these outpourings. Your instruments for both phases can be pen and paper or keyboard and screen—which of these instruments you use and how you use them will depend on your personal preference.

Creating

The creative (generative) phase of writing involves thinking, reflecting and imagining as much as putting words on paper or tapping out sentences on a keyboard. This writing phase may at times involve writing to a plan or using a required genre. But the writing process can also be a way of actively constructing knowledge. The process can stimulate new thoughts and directions to which you respond in writing as you write. As you write you can uncover areas of seemingly forgotten knowledge, clarify unanswered questions about the content of your work, or identify the need for further research. So the process of writing can in itself be a learning process. Sometimes the creative phase of writing flows easily, while at other times the words just will not come. At these difficult times it can be a good idea to put your work aside and come back to it later, or to write about whatever else you have on your mind. Sometimes, especially when there are deadlines to meet, you need to struggle on in the hope that the flow will come.

> Thinking to oneself can be silent, or talking aloud to oneself, or writing. While all three are equally thinking, the most . . . accessible form is that which leaves a record on tape, disk or paper.   V. A. HOWARD

Editing

The editing (critical) phase of the writing process is different from the creative. In fact, the two phases are incompatible and it is difficult, if not impossible, to create and edit simultaneously. It is claimed that the creative facility resides in one hemisphere of our brain and the critical in the other, and that our brains are not capable of creating and criticising simultaneously. If this is so, it makes sense to separate these two processes in your writing.

Do you procrastinate when it's time to write because you don't know where to start on a topic? Do you feel that every sentence you write must be perfect? Perhaps you sit for a long time over one sentence or paragraph. This might be a sign that you are trying to combine the creative and the critical phases of your writing, and that trying to be critical is blocking your ability to generate ideas and to create. When you are generating thoughts, try not to edit. Think about having two hats: a creative one and an editing one, which you change as required. When you wear your creative hat, you might generate most of an assignment, or you may write for only a short time and cover only a section or even a paragraph of a total piece of work. Most importantly, don't stop the thinking and creating process by editing or criticising as you go. Write, let it flow (see 'Free writing', below) and, when you cannot generate any more thoughts, when you are written dry, only then go back and reflect and edit.

Once you have finished with the creative process of writing, do you put your work aside and not look at it again? Do you hand in the 'final' draft of your assignments to your teacher with only superficial changes from first to last draft? If so, you are not fully developing your writing, as an essential part of the writer's craft is reflecting on what you have written and learning to edit your work. This chapter and the two that follow provide help with editing. It may be useful to recognise that experienced writers often sit for hours over a page of work or produce several extensively revised drafts, introducing different ideas, changing the content and editing ruthlessly before producing the final draft. Even so, rarely is an expert writer entirely happy with the final version.

Developing your writing, including your formal academic writing, is a continuing process. You need to learn to vary elements of your style according to the discipline and genre in which you are writing, as well as the topic, your audience and your purpose for writing. One way to do this is to experiment with different ways of writing.

Write often and reflectively

> Learning to write again is . . . not a tightening up process. It is not a matter of learning lots of techniques. It is learning to relax one's muscles and one's brain.   GWEN WESSON

One of the most effective ways to improve your writing is to write, write, write— and then write some more. Make writing an integral part of your life, and write regularly and for extended periods. Play with words and write in as many genres as you can. Write informally about yourself and your life and write about your academic work: your lectures, readings, discussions and ideas. From time to time re-read your informal writing because, as with your formal writing, it is important to cast a critical eye over your creative endeavours. Assess your strengths so that you can build on them, and work on your weaknesses. To improve your writing, reflect on how you write and evaluate it in relation to what others say about the process.

Experiment with different methods

Free writing

> . . . freewriting is the best way to learn—in practice, not just in theory—to separate the producing process from the revising process. Freewriting exercises are push-ups in withholding judgement as you produce so that afterwards you can judge better.
>
> PETER ELBOW

When you free write, you write without attending to a plan and without editing as you write. The process of writing is the stimulus that helps you discover the focus and approach for what you want to say and how you want to say it. Free writing can help you generate meaning and coherence from ideas and words that are lying dormant or jumbled in your head. This method is particularly valuable if you freeze up when you have to write, or if you have a mental block when writing an assignment (see also 'Free writing', Chapter 14).

Sit quietly for 10–15 minutes while you write down or type the thoughts that flow through your mind. Don't stop to select, organise or edit what you are writing, and don't worry about details such as spelling and punctuation. If your mind suddenly flashes elsewhere, explore that sidetrack. *Don't stop writing.* If you can't think of anything to say, write 'I don't have anything to say' over and over until a thought hits you. It can help to imagine that you are writing to someone else, explaining your thoughts, as long as you don't stop to reflect on or edit what you are writing.

Practice in this way can develop your writing—try free writing about your dreams or problems, or about people or events. Incorporate this method into the initial stages of an essay or seminar paper. And use it when blogging. To help break the habit of always editing as you write, try free writing directly on a computer, or by speaking your thoughts into a voice recorder and then transcribing them. Once you have the words on the screen or page, you can look at them critically and begin the editing process.

Structured writing

It was his habit to prepare an extremely detailed synopsis, complete with chapter titles, so that he knew exactly what was to happen in each chapter. He then began writing whatever chapter took his fancy or seemed easiest, leaving the most difficult to last . . . Reading the smooth flowing narrative, building up to a climax, it is difficult to believe the book was written in this extraordinary way, but so it was.   ARTHUR RANSOME

Sometimes you need to write according to a plan because you are required to write in a specific genre or format. Using a plan is the writing method frequently taught and expected in formal education, and you are likely to use it when writing an essay, a report, an article or a business letter. However, even if you are working closely to an overall plan, as you express your ideas and information in words, try not to edit as you write. Once your ideas are sorted out on screen or paper, you can always go back and find the precise phrase you want.

Write in different genres

. . . creativity has much more to do with mastering a genre and then adjusting it to meet one's own purposes than with writing stories ninety percent of the time one puts pen to paper.   JIM MARTIN

While developing your writing is largely a matter of writing and receiving feedback on it, trying different genres is a way to explore different ways of structuring your work. Just as reading published diaries will give you ideas for the format and content of any journal writing, analysing well-written models of other people's work can give you insights into a genre. Similarly, reading other people's blogs can provide ideas on what to include and how to organise your own blog. Well-written student essays or reports can inform your own academic work, so when you are required to write an essay or a report on a topic, ask your teacher if it is possible to read copies of previous students' work on another topic. With your own work, ask for comments on why and how you have demonstrated that you have achieved the unit learning outcomes or the teacher's expectations. Take these points into consideration when you are editing and rewriting your own assignments.

Letters, articles, poems and other forms

> I am not urging you to write a novel . . . although I would not be sorry if you wrote one, provided you genuinely cared about something. A petition to the mayor about a pothole in front of your house or a love letter to the girl next door will do.   KURT VONNEGUT

Do you keep in touch with family, friends and colleagues by email? Write personal letters? Turn out business letters and reports as part of your job? Keep a blog or journal? Write an occasional poem or short story? Or send 'letters to the editor'? Many people who write in these forms don't see themselves as able to write because they are not producing a book, or because writing is not a major part of their job. But regular practice in a variety of writing genres can help you develop your writing.

If you haven't thought of letters, articles or poems as part of your writing, try experimenting with:

— writing emails or letters instead of phoning or texting your friends (and keep copies of your correspondence)

— capturing an experience or playing with words in poems, lyrics, short stories or dialogue

— writing a letter to the editor of your local paper if you feel strongly about an issue, or

— writing an article for the newsletter of a community group in which you are active.

If you are accustomed to writing letters, poems, plays or articles you could occasionally use these familiar forms in your assignments, but first check if this is permitted as your teacher may wish you to concentrate on learning how to write in a certain genre.

For example:

— an essay comparing Freud with Jung could take the form of an exchange of letters setting out the basis of the disagreement between the two men

— an assignment on evolution could be written as a dialogue between Bishop Samuel Wilberforce and Thomas Huxley, or

— a preface or introduction to an essay may be written as a poem or a personal letter.

Email or social media communication, and contributions to chat groups, are usually informal free-flowing writing, perhaps more akin to speaking than most other writing forms. Some social media messages are very brief and to the point and are often only one sentence or phrase. This informal writing can be a regular part of your overall writing output and can provide a space to write for an audience. It can provide practice in expressing yourself clearly and concisely, particularly if you write thoughtfully rather than trying to impress or blurting out the first thing that comes into your head.

Personal journals or diaries

> I never travel without my diary. One should always have something sensational to read in the train.
> OSCAR WILDE

If you have ever kept a journal or diary, what did you record in it? As a teenager, did you record those major events in a small notebook that you kept hidden, or did your entries read something like, 'Got up early this morning. School was OK except I got into trouble on the way home. Watched some videos.'? When travelling, have you ever kept a journal or diary as a record of places and events? During periods of emotional upset, have you written pages and pages that you destroyed afterwards? For some people, the thought of keeping a journal or diary conjures up images of monotonously recording facts and details, or pouring out secret feelings on paper. Some people are uncomfortable with putting personal reflections down on paper. A journal can consist of these, but it can also be much more.

What is a journal?

A journal is your reflective space—it is a place where you reflect in writing on whatever interests or concerns you. In a personal journal you write for yourself, it is a place where you can be honest with yourself, where your thoughts and ideas won't be judged by others, and where you are free to write in whatever style you like. You may use a journal to make an occasional entry, or write intensively for a couple of months and then let it lapse. You might write in a journal daily to describe the events, experiences, feelings, people and ideas from each day.

Journals can focus in on a specific area in as much or as little detail as you like, and can be about many things. For example, a journal might be about yourself:

— your dreams, daydreams and fantasies, descriptions of the circumstances in your life that connect with them, and discussion of them

— your emotions

— how your body feels

— your reflections, thoughts and reminiscences on your past, or

— your ideas, theories or inspirations.

A journal might be about your world:

— descriptions of a particular situation or event

13

— observations about people, or

— comments on public happenings or issues.

A journal could include items such as:

— poems, short stories, song lyrics that you write or collect

— important blogs

— clippings from newspapers or magazines and your comments on them, or

— notes on books, lectures, movies or videos.

If you write about your private life and thoughts in your journal, do you worry that other people might read it? You don't have to write about personal matters but if you do, be careful not to leave your journal where it might be found. You can use symbols instead of names and places, or write as if describing a fantasy or a dream that makes sense only to you.

A format

First, date each entry in your journal. You can keep your journal entries chronologically or organise them into sections. A looseleaf format enables you to organise or reshuffle your writing into sections, remove pages you want to share and elaborate on entries started long ago. You can also carry a couple of pages in your pocket or bag, in the glove box of your car or attached to your clipboard, and write when the impulse moves you. If you make your entries on computer, you can also set up files to reflect these sections. Some entries you might print out in hard copy to intersperse with handwritten material, or you might leave your journal as a computer folder. If you make your entries electronically, a laptop or tablet can provide flexibility.

> Never have I seen as clearly as tonight that my diary-writing is a vice . . . I glided into my bedroom, closed the curtains, threw a log into the fire, lit a cigarette, pulled the diary out of its last hiding place under my dressing table, threw it on the ivory silk quilt, and prepared for bed. I had the feeling that this is the way an opium smoker prepares for his opium pipe. For this is the moment when I relive my life in terms of a dream, a myth, an endless story.
>
> ANAÏS NIN

If you are already an avid journal writer, you will understand how Anaïs Nin felt about writing in her diary. If you haven't already done so, read the diaries of some well-known diarists such as Anaïs Nin or Charles Darwin to enrich your own journal writing. If keeping a journal is not part of your life and you think you would find it valuable, set aside a regular time so that you can enjoy writing it.

Learning journals or logs

A learning journal or log is a space where you keep track of your learning.

● It is a place where you reflect in writing on the ideas from your reading, discussions and other study tasks.

- It is where you document what you learn from a particular unit or from your learning overall.
- Keeping a personal learning journal as part of your studies can help you become aware of the experiences, passions, beliefs and biases you bring to your learning, and to understand who you are as a learner (see 'A learning portfolio', Chapter 17).
- Since a journal also provides an opportunity to experiment with and explore different writing styles without being judged, it can have a positive impact on your formal writing.
- If you are using the log to write about yourself as a learner, you could use it to respond to the questions you are asked throughout this book, such as those in Chapter 1, 'You'.
- If you haven't kept a log before, you can also use it to reflect on and explore your writing processes or the experience of keeping a log itself.

Writing is a way of constructing your knowledge, so the process of writing regularly in a log can be a learning process in itself. Even students who are initially reluctant about keeping a log usually come to find it a rewarding and valuable process.

The format for keeping a learning journal or log is similar to that for a personal journal.

- You can keep your log in looseleaf format or on a computer.
- Develop a system for dividing your log into sections that reflect the different areas about which you will write. For example, you might create sections for each of the units you are taking. Alternatively, you could use your log for work in only one unit and set up sections that separate notes on your reading and assignments from your reflections on the overall unit content.

In some units you may be required to keep a working journal, perhaps in the form of a reading log. If so, the content, format and style should be specified. For example, field journals in marine science units can have strict rules on what to include and how to structure both the original field notes and the journal entries that follow. If keeping a log is a formal requirement of a unit, a good idea is to use a looseleaf format so that you can easily remove entries you don't want anyone else to read. Of course, if the unit has provided format guidelines, make sure you stick to them.

Blogs

> And it occurred to me that there is no such thing as blogging. There is no such thing as a blogger. Blogging is just writing—writing using a particularly efficient type of publishing technology.
>
> SIMON DUMENCO

For many people the blog has replaced the traditional journal or diary and has become for some the repository for their other writing forms. In fact, a blog can be a space for presenting all of the writing genres mentioned above—letters, articles, creative writing, personal journals or logs and learning journals, and these can be public, or fully or partly private. However, blogs are also a writing genre in their own right. If you want to build an audience, blogs are all about developing discussion, interaction and conversation. Unlike the largely one-way nature of many traditional writing forms such as keeping a diary or writing an article for a newspaper, a blog invites and provides space for two-way communication.

If you like the idea of keeping a journal to practise your writing, but want to avoid the introspection that comes with keeping a private journal, a blog might be a happy medium. Many of the most successful bloggers started by writing about their own lives—the trials, tribulations and joys of their day-to-day existence.

Many blogs begin as a hobby, as a way of sharing thoughts on a particular topic or of contributing another voice to a debate. The subjects can be diverse, from good places to go for breakfast, to observational posts about travelling on the train to work each morning, to posts about one's garden, travels, pets, family or opinions. Some common types of blogs include:

— travel blogs that document a particular trip
— local blogs about events and places in your local area, such as cafes, live music, community events
— blogs that review books, movies, theatre, music
— expert blogs that provide an insight into your own field of expertise, for example, personal training, trading on the share market, making good coffee
— family and personal blogs that share the ups and downs of work, family or leisure
— commentary blogs, with thoughts on current affairs generally, or on a specific issue such as the representation of women in the media, and

— temporary blogs that are kept for a fixed time frame covering a project or experience that you are undertaking, for example, a travel blog, or perhaps a blog about your experience as a first year student or about a particular unit you are studying.

Blog posts don't have to be long—in fact, short posts are often more engaging for the reader and allow you to blog more often. Unlike articles, blog posts don't have to have definitive statements—you can blog in order to start a discussion, investigate a question, or consider what you already know about a subject, with 'space' left for your readers to contribute what they know. Collaborative blogs can facilitate an ongoing exchange of ideas (see 'Setting up a writing group', later in this chapter).

Successful blogs, those that build a large audience and promote discussion through the comments section and on social media, tend to find a niche and are written in an engaging, conversational manner. For examples of some well-written and/or popular blogs, visit the many major blogging platforms which offer a list of the best blogs hosted on their platform as a way of encouraging both readers and new bloggers.

You can also use search engines and social media to track down blogs relevant to your area of interest—but remember, the Internet is not curated so be careful which blogs you use as a model for your own writing. And be aware that anyone can read your blog unless you make it private, so you need to be extremely careful if you choose to write about other people. Also, give some thought to whether you are ready to handle aggressive (and possibly anonymous) responses to what you write.

Share your writing

The essential human act at the heart of writing is the act of giving . . . This central act of giving is curiously neglected in most writing instruction. . . . For most people, however, the experience of just sharing what they have written is rare.   PETER ELBOW

Do you ever write solely for yourself, or for one or two close friends?

If you write letters, short stories or poems, do you share them with friends?

Do you belong to an online discussion group in which you share your writing?

Writing alone is a traditional method of producing assignments, sitting for hours at your desk or computer with the aid of innumerable cups of black coffee the night before the assignment is due, and never discussing your thoughts and ideas with anyone. Since usually only your teacher reads your formal assignments, you receive only one person's perception and assessment of what and how you write.

Many students do not share with anyone else their written work or their ideas about how they will approach a written assignment. However, sharing and discussing your work can be valuable. Before you start any sustained writing, it can help you clarify what you want to put on paper if you explain your ideas to someone else. This is useful when you are beginning to formulate ideas on a topic or when thinking about how you intend to present your work. It is not necessary to talk to someone who is familiar with your area, although the feedback will be more valuable if you can find another student from your unit or discipline. If you cannot find such a student, it can help to explain your ideas verbally or in writing to a friend or member of your family who will listen carefully—or even to express them aloud to the family pet. But the ideal is to find someone taking similar units with whom you can share a mutual exchange of ideas and comments on written work. A working relationship such as this is invaluable, and from it you can both learn and improve your written work.

13

Computer-mediated communication, such as through email or social networks, has made it easy to share your ideas on an assignment with other students before you begin writing and as you write. It is also possible to share rough drafts and a final version of an assignment. Contrary to what many students believe, discussing your work with other students and clarifying your ideas is not cheating (see 'Peer evaluation', Chapter 17). Cheating is when you take other people's ideas and use them as your own without acknowledgement, or if another student writes parts of your work for you (see 'Academic integrity', Chapter 16).

Comments from others on your writing can be extremely useful. Have one or two friends read your writing and respond to it, or tell your teachers that you want to improve your writing and ask for specific feedback on your work. Perhaps you would like to share what you write with a wider audience but feel unsure of the criticism you might receive. If you work on your writing with a friend or a group of people who feel as you do, sharing your work and actually writing in their company is likely to give you confidence in developing your writing style.

Publicly accessible blogs that others can read are a good way to build your writing skills but only if you take more care about what and how you write because you have an audience. You can even ask your readers to take part in your journey to develop your writing skills. If you thrive on interaction and debate, perhaps you spend more time writing social media posts than keeping a diary. For you, a blog may provide a space to write in a focused manner while still engaging with other people.

Writing groups

Writing groups can be established with other students either face-to-face or online. They can be used to discuss informal writing or writing for assessment. Sometimes writing groups are set up by your teacher, and they can be important in collaborative group projects. If there are no formal mechanisms for establishing a writing group, you might decide to set one up yourself.

Why join a writing group?

1   If other people read (or listen to) what you have written and comment on it immediately or shortly after you submit it, you receive a variety of feedback which you can question and discuss. If this feedback is positive and accompanied by useful suggestions, you won't be devastated by criticism and you will have some ideas on how to change your writing.

2   Each member of the group will have their own way of expressing themselves. So reading or listening to other people's work gives you access to a variety of styles, approaches to topics and pieces of writing in a genre.

3 After some time, giving feedback on other people's work and receiving comments on your own writing can help you evolve your own standards for evaluating your own and others' writing.

4 Actually writing in the same place as other people who share a common writing purpose can provide a new stimulus for what to write about and how to write. Although in some cases you may be physically separated, it is possible for a group to meet in cyberspace in real time to compose electronically.

The written word is uniquely suited to the construction, group revision and sharing of knowledge. Practically all education is built around textbooks and written assignments, and computer-mediated communication (CMC) networks introduce an interactive text to enable information sharing and group knowledge building. Most CMC networks are asynchronous, a feature that with the text-based nature of communication, allows each participant to work at his or her individual learning pace and take as long as needed to read, reflect, write, and revise before sharing questions, insights, or information with others.

LINDA HARASIM

Setting up a writing group

The steps outlined below can be applied to face-to-face or online groups. They can also be used to set up a collaborative blog, or for a group to share and receive feedback on individual blog entries.

1 Find people with whom you share a purpose in writing, such as producing essays for a unit, making journal entries, a student magazine, or to improve your writing.

2 The group should be small enough for each person to contribute, yet have sufficient people to provide variety and depth in feedback.

3 Attend or contribute regularly, as people who get to know each other feel more comfortable about sharing their writing. After the first few meetings or contributions, don't admit new members. In an online group clarify whether all, some or none of your writing will be read by a teacher.

4 Agree on the length and frequency of meetings according to the size and purpose of the group. With an online group, decide if you will meet synchronously (that is, everyone meets at the same time) using video or audio communication software, or asynchronously (where people respond when they wish). If asynchronous, agree on how frequently new pieces of writing should be submitted, on the time frame for comments, and on how often members of the group will log on to receive messages.

5 Between meetings, do any necessary rewriting or preparation for the next meeting.

6 If a group member contributes a piece of writing to be discussed, provide copies for everyone to facilitate discussion. If online, make sure that the material is available in a format that everyone can access.

7 For the first meeting, consider writing about yourselves as a way of getting to know each other.

8 The group might decide to write on one of the following:

— free write on a set topic (as described earlier in this chapter)

— practise a particular style (such as narrative or expository) or form (such as dialogue or scientific report), or

— focus on a specific subject, such as the theory of evolution or a piece of music.

9 For a face-to-face group or a synchronous online group, participants might choose to write for part of the time they are together.

10 There should be no compulsion for people to share their writing as some people need more time to feel confident about this, but allow all members the opportunity to present their work. In some sessions the group might discuss everyone's work, while in others it may concentrate on the writing of one or two people.

11 Work out how much you expect to read and critique each other's work. For example, at every meeting you might read some of each other's writing, or after an initial exchange of everyone's work, you might focus on only one person's writing. Perhaps each person might present a key issue, dilemma or brilliant idea they want to try out. Another option is to decide what to do for the first meeting and then decide at each subsequent meeting the focus for next time.

12 Allow sufficient time for each piece of work to be read with care. In a face-to-face or online synchronous group, perhaps read the piece both silently and aloud. In an asynchronous online group, allow enough time for comments to be returned and read.

13 Agree on a standard and protocols for responses which should include the following:

- Feedback should be constructive, emphasising strengths rather than weaknesses. Initially, negative criticism that points out weaknesses should be avoided because it can undermine a beginning writer's confidence which the group is aiming to build. Destructive criticism is always taboo. When negative criticism is given, suggest how to make changes. Give feedback by responding to the piece spontaneously, or according to agreed-on criteria.

- Agree on ground rules and a code of conduct that do not permit discriminatory language and comments (see Appendix, 'Discrimination'). For online writing groups, agree on communication protocols and Netiquette principles (see 'Ground rules', Chapter 12).

14 Choose a member of the group to monitor the process. This is particularly important for online groups where problems can arise while protocols are still evolving.

Whether you write on your own or with other people depends on your aims and subject. You could make journal entries with a group of other students in a unit, write a report with one other person, or write poetry by yourself. Trying alternatives to find out which ones you enjoy is one way of discovering and exploring your writing voice.

> Put down everything that comes into your head and then you're a writer. But an author is one who can judge his [*sic*] own stuff's worth, without pity, and destroy most of it.
> COLETTE

Authors do not just sit down and instantly write a great book. They spend time practising the craft of writing and put in many hours on an individual book. Writing has become part of their daily lives as well as a talent that delights readers. You may not be a world-famous author, but writing frequently and experimenting with different genres can help you develop your writing and give you pleasure as a writer. And just as great writers refine their skills and thrive on the response of both their fellow writers and their readers, so you too can polish and enjoy your writing if you share it with others.

TEN TIPS

1   Perhaps you are already a 'writer'—think about the different types of non-study writing that you do.

2   Writing is a process that involves both creative and critical aspects, and developing your writing means working on both of these.

3   Writing short pieces frequently just for yourself or friends can be fun and help build your skills and confidence in getting words down on paper or on a screen.

4   Play with free writing if you have a mental block when it comes to expressing what you want to say.

5   Since writing can be useful in clarifying thoughts, consider jotting down your ideas or concerns or questions as a way of reflecting on them.

6   Keeping a personal learning journal can help you become aware of the experiences, enthusiasms, beliefs and biases you bring to your learning.

7   Writing a blog can give you practice in expressing yourself in a variety of forms and perhaps give you a chance to receive feedback on what you write.

8   If there are particular aspects of your writing you want to improve, consider setting up a writing group with others who have similar aims.

9   Establish clear ground rules for any writing group.

10   Learn about Netiquette if you share your writing online.

13

Writing essays

14

... *I always try to write on the principle of the iceberg. There is seven-eighths of it under water for every part that shows.*

ERNEST HEMINGWAY

Writing an essay is more than putting words on paper—defining your aims, analysing your topic, developing an appropriate research question and carrying out research are integral to what and how you write. Each activity requires careful thought as you integrate your aims with what is expected of you, and as you bring together your ideas and the information you find. Each activity can also have its own pleasures— discovering new information, turning ideas on a topic over in your mind, talking about them with other people or trying them out in different combinations and sequences. When you have more or less analysed a topic and located information on your research question, you can begin to focus on the task of writing the essay as a whole.

The framework offered here is useful only if you write frequently and receive feedback from others. Each essay is not an isolated end in itself—what you learn from writing one can help you with the next, even if the content and format of each differ and each is in a different discipline. Improving your writing takes time and practice, and your writing may seem worse before you notice any improvement—it takes time to change old habits and develop and refine new methods. Saying exactly what you want and in the style you need is easier if you have confidence in your writing abilities (see Chapter 13, 'Developing your writing'). But remember that even if you are a prolific and fluent writer in social media, academic writing requires a more disciplined and structured approach, and stream of consciousness writing, which assumes that the writer's personal opinions are always insightful, doesn't apply in essays.

Before you begin writing

An essay develops from your analysis of the set topic and a research question which you developed to guide your search for information and ideas (see 'Your revised definition', Chapter 8). As a result of your thinking and research, perhaps you have written sentences or paragraphs that capture thoughts you want to use. You will also have notes from your research.

Your definition of the topic

Your written definition should reflect the argument and structure of your essay. Developing a clear and comprehensive definition is crucial if you are writing an assignment collaboratively (see 'Collaborative learning groups', Chapter 12) and particularly if you are doing this online. Your definition should do the following.

- Make clear your **aims** for the essay. Ask yourself:

    Why am I writing an essay in the first place?

    Why was this piece of work set?

    What is my aim for writing this particular essay, and for choosing this topic?

    What outcomes am I expected to demonstrate in this piece of work?

14

- Check every word in **the set topic** and/or in the guidelines for the assignment.

  Am I clear about what any directive verbs are asking me to do?

  Have I identified any assumptions that seem to underpin the topic?

  Have I developed working definitions for the key concepts in the topic?

- Have you decided how you will limit **the scope** of the assignment?

- Clarify your **thesis or theme** (see 'Genres', Chapter 7).

  For an argumentative essay, ask yourself:

  What thesis will I advance for the topic?

  Does my thesis or theme directly reflect the question I used to guide my research?

  What reasons will I use to support my thesis?

  If your essay is expository, ask yourself:

  What evidence, explanations and examples will I use to support my theme?

- Consider how your **personal opinions** are reflected in your plan for the assignment, for example, in the choice of main points or in the scope chosen for your essay. Ask yourself:

  In my research, have I attempted to move beyond any biases or preconceptions I hold on the topic?

- Propose a **possible structure** that indicates how you will present the main points of the essay and how they are connected. Ask yourself:

  Exactly what is the topic?

  How many parts are there to the topic?

  What are my main points for the topic?

  How might I order the main points so that they support my thesis or theme?

  How do the directive verbs in the topic (see Table 7.1, 'Directive verbs') influence the structure of my essay?

- Make sure you are **addressing the topic**. Ask yourself:

  If I write the essay in this way, will I be responding to the exact topic in full?

Your readers

> I wish thee as much pleasure in the reading, as I had in the writing. FRANCIS QUARLES

Before you start writing the whole essay, think about your readers. Is your teacher the only one who will read your essay? Are you writing a paper to be read by a group of students, perhaps in an online unit? Is there a possibility your paper will be published in a collection of student work or elsewhere? What position do you think your readers might take on the topic? If you are uncertain of the level at which to pitch your writing, a good rule of thumb is to write for another student who is taking the unit but does not have an in-depth understanding of your topic. Don't slip into the conversational style you might use in social media. To communicate effectively:

— have clear in your mind the argument or theme you are presenting

— keep in mind your aim in presenting it

— be aware that you are communicating with someone

— take care to say exactly what you want to, and

— say it simply and succinctly.

Writing your rough draft

We would be given an assignment. I would take one look at it and think, 'That's the end of that. I won't be there next week so I won't have to worry about it.' After two harrowing days, when I kept thinking, 'Will I, won't I?' I'd sit down to look at it.   GWEN WESSON

For each essay you write, start with a rough draft. You may produce several drafts if your definition of the topic changes as you write or if you have the time. Reaching your final draft then involves editing your last rough draft.

When you write the rough draft of an essay, your main concerns should be the structure of the essay and the clear expression of your ideas. Concentrate on saying what you want, in the order you want, and as accurately as you can. When you are in the creative or generative phase of expressing your ideas, don't worry about a detailed structure or niceties of style or finding the precise word. And don't become bogged down with concerns about perfect spelling or correct and detailed conventions such as footnoting. Be as precise as you need to be to express your ideas clearly and fully, and leave perfecting the formalities to your final draft.

Most skilled writers produce several drafts of a work before arriving at a final version. Many students, however, sit down and expect to start writing the first sentence and to write straight through to the end, producing a more or less complete essay in one draft. This is not an effective way to produce a satisfactory essay—any method of writing relies on thoughtful research and time to mull over a topic before writing, and any method should lead you to a rough draft that has three clear sections: an introduction, a body and a conclusion. How these sections should be organised and written is outlined in 'The parts of your essay', later in this chapter. Once you have produced your draft, use the checklist of questions in 'Working with your rough draft', also later in this chapter. As a precaution against computer problems, print out a hard copy of your rough draft.

Writing methods

Working from your revised definition of the topic, you can produce your rough draft by free writing, working from a detailed plan, or a combination of these two methods. Any of these approaches can be effective.

14

Writing to a plan

An essay plan needs to be written down, whether it is an outline or developed in detail. Your plan might be linear (see Table 14.1, 'A sample essay plan') or an explosion chart or pattern (see Table 11.1, 'Notemaking methods'). When writing an essay more or less to a written plan, the plan structures and limits what you write and prevents you going off on a tangent. A plan includes a statement of:

— your thesis or theme

— an introduction and conclusion, and

— the structure, that is, how the main points are ordered, balanced and linked.

Don't be surprised if you don't follow your plan exactly. As you write, the process of expressing your ideas can stimulate new thoughts and directions and lead you to see familiar ideas in new ways (see 'The process of writing', Chapter 13). Actually expressing your ideas with clarity involves searching for and choosing words, phrases and sentences, so part of the structuring can only be done as you write. Integrating new ideas into your plan and making choices as you write can further clarify what you want to say and can lead you to revise your plan. Hopefully, such revisions will be only minor at this stage of your work.

Free writing

In free writing you use the act of writing to clarify your thoughts, without editing them as you write. Free writing can help get you started on your writing and can help you come up with a statement of your thesis or theme. Having completed your research, you may be surprised how the structure and main points emerge (see 'Free writing', Chapter 13).

If you have a mental block when writing essays, particularly when starting to write, it may be because you don't feel confident about your writing or your knowledge of a topic or how to organise your information, or because you are anxious about your study or have other pressures in your life (see 'Emotions', Chapter 1). Perhaps you are having difficulty defining or deciding on a thesis or theme. If you do experience a block, but you have to or want to write, sit down at your computer, or at your desk with lots of paper and a pen. Don't worry about notes or plans or references. Start typing or writing *anything* on your topic that comes to mind; and write *continuously* for about 10 minutes. If you can't think of what to write, write about why you can't think of what to write, or about the thoughts that are coming between you and the topic. When the time is up, look over what you have written. Some of it may be useful later or it may stimulate new thoughts. This free writing activity is often enough to shift a mental block and stop you procrastinating (see 'Procrastination', Chapter 4), but if it doesn't you may need to leave your work for a few hours or days, if possible. And remember that even for skilled writers sometimes writing refuses to flow smoothly.

The writer wandered to the water cooler, washed his hands, looked up the weather report, made some unnecessary phone calls, looked at his tongue in the mirror for symptoms of fatal disease and, when he had at last exhausted methods of killing time, went to his typewriter.   RUSSELL BAKER

Other writing methods

You can combine planning and free writing in various ways.

- Use a plan and write from this, with your notes and references in front of you. Use free writing whenever you are stuck. You could:
  — write the body of the essay first, and then the introduction and conclusion, or
  — begin with the introduction and write in the order you planned, right through to the conclusion, or
  — begin writing the section where your ideas are clearest, and proceed section by section until you have written the one that is least clear to you.

- Make a detailed plan and then free write each section of your rough draft putting aside your notes and references. If you don't understand a section well enough to write about it or if you need a quote or item of information, turn to your notes and references to refresh your memory—and then close them before you start writing again. When you finish writing your draft, check your work against your notes for completeness and for references you could cite.

It took me two hours to write this. I bit my finger-nails, cut my toenails, had a snack, crunched an apple and generally procrastinated. But I did it!   GWEN WESSON

The parts of your essay

An essay is constructed like a freight train. The argument is the engine, supplying power and direction and pulling the rest behind it. The cars are the paragraphs, each carrying a topic sentence and a load of specific sentences; the couplings are transitions holding the cars together, and the caboose is the conclusion, letting the reader know that the essay has come to an end. It is important to realise that the train exists to carry the freight: the essay is the vehicle for getting the meaningful specifics of your topic to the reader in an orderly condition, so they can unload and use them.   Adapted from text by FRED MORGAN

No matter which method you use to produce an essay, your rough draft should finish up with the following parts.

The introduction

The introduction outlines *what you are going to say*. It should make clear your definition of the topic and make your reader want to read on. You should:

— outline your thesis or theme

— indicate your main points

— state how your essay is structured

— outline your reasons for focusing on specific aspects of a general topic

— indicate the question you used to focus your research, and

— indicate the scope and limits of your essay.

To orient your reader to the topic you might:

— outline your theoretical position on the topic

— explain the significance of the topic, and/or

— provide a context for the essay.

You need to provide a definition of any concepts or terms that are central to the topic. This can usefully be done as part of your introduction; or you can define each concept when you are about to refer to it extensively. Such definitions provide you and your reader with a shared understanding for the rest of your essay.

To engage the reader and add interest or variety, you might:

— briefly review literature

— give selected data to establish an issue as worth writing about

— explain the significance of your research question in relation to the topic, or

— use a quote that conveys the key ideas you will discuss.

The body of your essay

Here you say *what you want to say*. You should order your main points effectively and provide links that make this order clear to your reader; present each main point as fully and accurately as necessary; write coherent paragraphs; and keep a balance between your main points.

a Ordering the main points

After the introduction, your argument or theme should be developed clearly and logically throughout the essay and restated in the conclusion. The following suggestions may help you decide on the order in which to develop the material you have selected.

● Refer back to your aims and definition of the topic.

● Keep your thesis or theme firmly in mind and, as you write, show how your main points link back to this.

● By now you should have decided on your main points. Ask yourself why you chose these and how they are connected to each other. In the moon topic, in Table 14.1, you might have chosen your points because they reflect significantly different aspects of the topic. In the moon topic, does an understanding of one point depend on explaining another point first?

TABLE 14.1   A sample essay plan

Your topic is 'Critically evaluate the theory that the moon is made of green cheese'. After reflection and research you decide to argue that the moon is made of green cheese. You think that the most important and interesting aspects of the topic are the beliefs for and against the theory, scientific research relevant to the theory, and astronauts' discoveries about the green-cheesiness or otherwise of the moon. You define the topic accordingly. The following basic model is one you could use to structure your essay.

Topic: *Critically evaluate the theory that the moon is made of green cheese.*

Introduction

Thesis:	That the moon is made of green cheese
Supporting reasons	(a) Historical beliefs for and against the theory
	(b) Scientific research
	(c) Astronauts' discoveries

Main point (a)	**Main point (b)**	**Main point (c)**
Historical beliefs for and against theory	Scientific research	Astronauts' discoveries
1. In Greek times	1. Geology of the Mice Age	1. Mice on the moon
2. In 19th-century industrial Europe	2. Properties of green cheese	2. Feline interest in the moon
3. In mid-20th century	3. Causes of craters on the moon	3. The Lunar Costa Verde
4. The Green Cheese Revivalist Movement		
Brief summary of these beliefs	Brief evaluation of key points in the research	

Conclusion

That the moon is made of green cheese

(a) Historical beliefs for and against the theory

(b) Scientific research

(c) Astronauts' discoveries

Personal conclusions and implications for future research.

14

- If, however, you still have several supporting points from which you will choose as you write, write each point out as a separate section of your essay. See what links emerge from what you have written, and then rewrite your final points as necessary to clarify the links between them and develop an ordered whole.

- If you prefer to write in longhand, use a separate page for each paragraph. When you come to order the whole essay, you can add or delete paragraphs and arrange them in the order that seems most logical.

b Linking information

As well as coherently developing each main point in turn, your argument or theme depends on indicating the links between each point and the reason for their order. In addition, within each main point you should make clear how your choice of explanations, examples and evidence works to support the point. If you assume that this connecting information is not essential, your reader is left to second-guess what you intend.

To convey these linking relationships, use transitional words or phrases (see Table 14.2) and use pointers such as 'Having discussed idea X, I now want to examine . . .' or 'However, Y contradicts idea X which I have just discussed . . .' or 'First, I discuss X then, second, I discuss Y . . .'. Use subheadings (if allowed) and if expected, include a plan or a detailed table of contents. Remember, to make clear the order of the main points in your essay and to indicate the links between them, they need to be clear in your mind.

> 'Then you should say what you mean,' the March Hare went on. 'I do,' Alice hastily replied; 'at least—at least I mean what I say—that's the same thing, you know.'   LEWIS CARROLL

c Presenting each main point fully and accurately

Saying what you want to say also entails presenting each of your main points fully and accurately. In academic writing you are expected to explain any general statements you make and back up any claims. To support a main point you might explain a point further, cite statistics or facts, refer to reputable research or use quotations. You can also present information that counters each of your points and explain why you do not think such information carries weight.

Don't expect your reader to be a mind reader. Remember, you have been researching and thinking about the topic recently, so a sentence you write which conveys a whole collection of ideas to you may not do so to your reader. Don't skim over points that need explanation. Don't assume that your reader automatically knows who or what Alcibiades was, or precisely what you mean when you use terms such as 'instinct', 'natural', 'good' or 'Western society'. Beware of unthinking generalisations. For example, if you write 'University students are very intelligent', do you mean all, most or some students? Have you located any research to support this claim? And what do you mean by 'intelligent'? When you make general statements, support them

TABLE 14.2 Transitional words and phrases

These are words and phrases that show relationships between two ideas or facts.

They indicate:

Addition

in addition, again, also, and, besides, finally, first, further, last, moreover, second, too, next

Cause and effect

accordingly, as a result, consequently, hence, otherwise, therefore, thus

Comparison

similarly, likewise

Contrast

in contrast, although, and yet, but, however, nevertheless, on the other hand, on the contrary

Examples or special features

for example, for instance, in other words, in illustration, in this case, in particular, specifically

Summary

in brief, in conclusion, in short, on the whole, to conclude, to summarise, to sum up

Connections in time

after a short time, afterwards, as long as, as soon as, at last, at length, at that time, at the same time, before, earlier, of late, immediately, in the meantime, lately, later, meanwhile, presently, shortly, since, soon, temporarily, thereafter, until, when, while

with *explanations, examples or evidence*. Consider whether it is appropriate to include quantitative material—in disciplines such as psychology, for example, tables might be included as an appendix.

Even if your teacher is the only person to read your finished work, check whether you are expected to write without assuming his or her knowledge of the topic so that you demonstrate your own knowledge fully. If you are in doubt about the level of writing required, imagine that you are writing for a reasonably intelligent student just about to begin the unit and with an interest in your topic. This helps to avoid pitfalls such as writing on the implications of Hegel's ideas without actually describing the ideas because you assume that your teacher knows what they are.

d Paragraphing

Each main point should consist of one or more paragraphs. Each paragraph should contain one key idea or cover one aspect relevant to a main point. This idea or aspect is frequently set out in a key sentence, which may come anywhere in a paragraph or may be implied by the total content of the paragraph rather than stated explicitly. If you are still mastering the craft of essay writing, it can be very helpful for both you and your reader if the first sentence of each paragraph states the central point of the paragraph. Then each of the other sentences in the paragraph should explain or illustrate or support the point the paragraph is making.

○○○ *Stop for a moment and think about what you have just read. Now look at the next paragraph. What is its key point? Is there an explicit key sentence? How does each of the sentences in the paragraph relate to the key point of the paragraph?*

A paragraph should be coherent, so that your reader is led smoothly from one sentence to the next and understands the connection between them. For example, if the paragraph uses a central metaphor, each sentence may echo and expand that metaphor. Words and phrases such as 'similarly', 'because', 'besides', 'in contrast', 'meanwhile', 'therefore' or 'for instance' help to indicate the links between sentences (see Table 14.2, 'Transitional words and phrases'). If a paragraph is not coherent, your reader will be faced with bewildering jumps of thought, events out of sequence or facts illogically arranged.

> Just as the sentence contains one idea in all its fullness, so the paragraph should embrace a distinct episode; and as sentences should follow one another in harmonious sequence, so paragraphs must fit into one another like the automatic couplings of railway carriages.   WINSTON CHURCHILL

A paragraph may vary in length from a couple of sentences to many (and such variety makes more interesting reading). As a *very* approximate rule of thumb for assignments, each paragraph averages about 100 words. Therefore in a 2000-word assignment, you would have approximately 20 paragraphs, which you might divide up into two for an introduction and conclusion, and an average of four or five paragraphs for each of three or four main points. Thinking of your assignment in this way can help you understand how many main points you can make fully and clearly.

e Balancing main points

Decide whether all your main points should have equal weighting within the essay. In the moon topic (Table 14.1, 'A sample essay plan'), you might decide to look more closely at the scientific research, or you might devote more space to the astronauts' discoveries because they are more recent.

Even with the most careful planning, as you actually write you may find that you need to devote more of the total essay to one point to explain it fully, to give less emphasis to another point, or to delete a point that no longer seems essential to your thesis. Some essays have a strict word length requirement. What do you do if you discover part-way through your essay that it will be too long if you present all the points you have planned to cover? You may need to reduce the number of points or to eliminate repetitive sections. Conversely, does your essay look as though it will fall short of the length required? If so, check that your plan hasn't been too skimpy on the number of points you cover and make sure you have supported each of your main points thoroughly. It is rare for students to do justice to a topic in less than the required length. When in doubt about whether or not to include or omit material, refer back to your aims for the essay, the outcomes and your argument or theme, and ask yourself if the material fits with these. Learning to discard material is an essential but often difficult part of writing—you may have to force yourself to do it.

> Have the guts to cut . . . If a sentence, no matter how excellent, does not illuminate your subject in some new and useful way, scratch it out.   KURT VONNEGUT

The conclusion

This draws together *what you have said* in the body of your essay. It should:

— sum up your argument

— restate your thesis or theme

— draw together your main points, and

— refer back to your introduction.

You should not introduce a new major point or a statement that needs detailed explanation. And as well as drawing together what you have said, the conclusion serves to round off your essay—don't make it so abrupt that your reader is surprised the essay is finished.

You might also:

— suggest a question that needs to be explored further, or

— raise one or two implications for further research.

> There are two things I am confident I can do very well; one is an introduction to any literary work, stating what it is to contain, and how it should be executed in the most perfect manner; the other is a conclusion, shewing from various causes why the execution has not been equal to what the author promised to himself and to the public.   SAMUEL JOHNSON

Working with your rough draft

Working with your rough draft is essentially a checking and rewriting stage, since by now you should have a clear idea of the aims, argument or exposition, content, structure, approach and basic writing style of your essay (see Table 14.3, 'Checking your rough draft'). Part of your work with the rough draft will probably be remedying oversights. For example, you may need to find full details for bibliography entries, or check on the precise wording of a quote or exact data for part of a graph. What else do you check for at this stage?

TABLE 14.3   **Checking your rough draft**

Aims

- Does the essay reflect your aims in:
  - — undertaking an essay in the first place
  - — doing this particular essay
  - — choosing this particular topic, and
  - — selecting your argument or theme within the topic?
- Does the essay reflect the objectives for which the essay was set?
- Does your writing demonstrate the learning outcomes expected?
- Have you checked that you have met all requirements for the essay?

Argument or exposition

- Does the essay have a thesis or theme?
- Have you clearly stated this in your introduction?
- Do the main points support your thesis or theme?
- Are you clear about the theoretical framework in which your argument or exposition is situated?

Content

- Is your topic clearly defined?
- Does the essay address the exact topic?
- Have central terms or concepts been clearly defined?
- Is all your material relevant to your definition of the topic?
- What are the main points of your essay?
- Are the main points presented as clearly and fully as necessary?
- Are the quotations and examples you have used integral to your essay?
- Do you have too much or too little material for the length of your essay?
- Is there any unnecessary repetition of minor points?
- Have you avoided discriminatory attitudes and language?

Structure

- Does your introduction:
  - — accurately outline your definition of the topic
  - — state your thesis or theme
  - — indicate the scope of your essay
  - — state your main points in the order in which you will present, and
  - — intrigue your reader?
- In the body of your essay:
  - — What is the structure of your essay?
  - — Does your structure logically and effectively develop your thesis or theme?
  - — Is there a balance between your main points?
  - — Are the main points clearly linked?
  - — Does each paragraph contain only one key idea, and is this idea clearly relevant to the thesis it is supporting?
  - — Have you clearly connected your paragraphs using transitional words, phrases or sentences?
- Does your conclusion:
  - — reinforce the thesis or theme of the essay
  - — relate to your introduction
  - — finish the essay smoothly, and
  - — suggest any further areas or questions to be followed up, without introducing any major new ideas?

Approach

- In your research, have you tried to deal with any personal biases on the topic?
- In an argumentative essay, have you incorporated your own ideas to develop the thesis, and have you supported these ideas?
- Have you followed any guidelines about the use of 'I' or 'we' and of active or passive voice?

Style

- Have you expressed your ideas clearly and simply?
- Is the writing style your own?
- Have you incorporated formal requirements regarding style and conventions into your writing?

14

> Reheating a piece of writing after it has cooled, tempering it, and sharpening it is enjoyable—if you know how. Otherwise it may turn out worse, brittle and misshapen.
>
> KEN MACRORIE

If you have researched, planned and written your essay thoughtfully you are less likely to have to make major revisions to your rough draft. However, sometimes when you re-read your draft you are struck with a new idea about the structure or content, or you suddenly see a major flaw in what you have written. If you have sufficient time, you may want to rework an initial rough draft substantially. Be prepared for this, but realise that at some stage you have to stop working on your essay and let it stand as it is, warts and all. If you are writing your essay at the last minute, you are unlikely to have the time for detailed rewriting. In this case, the amount of work depends on how clearly you really knew what you wanted to say before you started writing.

When you have finished writing and working on your rough draft, you have done most of the work on your essay. Wherever possible, write a rough draft, work on it and put it aside for at least a few days before you write the final one. You might discuss it with others, or have someone else read it and comment. If you are writing an assignment collaboratively, swap your pieces with other members of the group. You may want to change a phrase, add a word, rewrite a sentence or a paragraph. In any case, give yourself time to stand back from what you have written and time to reflect on your whole essay before you finally sit down and edit it.

Editing your final draft

In the final draft, you edit what you have written in order to polish your writing style and complete details of formalities such as punctuation, endnotes or references. Producing your final draft in a new form can help you proofread your work—for example, use a different font or use double spacing if your drafts have been single-spaced. If you have been writing on screen, it can be helpful to edit on a hard copy of your work—and this copy provides a backup if your computer crashes.

- Often a good essay is difficult to read because of inadequate proofreading. (Chapter 16, 'Using conventions', is designed to help you check details such as presentation, writing conventions and spelling.) Using a spelling or grammar checker on your computer is no substitute for thorough proofreading.

- The craft of improving your writing style involves imagination as well as hard work (see Chapter 13, 'Developing your writing'). When polishing your writing in an essay, check carefully for unnecessary repetition, inaccurate use of words of whose meanings you are uncertain, and ambiguous use of 'it', 'this', 'they', 'them'. Reading your essay aloud (particularly to someone else) is an effective way of checking for these problems. If possible, ask someone else to comment on your writing style in the essay.

Evaluating your essay

Ask yourself:

What were my aims for the essay?

How well have I achieved these?

How would I change what I researched, planned and wrote if I repeated the essay? Why?

Has working on my essay led me to any ideas or questions I might follow up?

You should be the first person to evaluate the strengths and weaknesses of what you write (see 'Your own evaluation', Chapter 17). If you include a written self-assessment (as well as your plan or detailed table of contents) with your essay, your readers then have a basis for constructive criticism, but first check with your teacher if this is acceptable to them.

> It's not healthy for the tightrope walker to be misunderstood by the person who's holding the rope.   PETER HØEG

The next stage is up to your readers. If your essays are usually read only by your teacher and the teacher provides helpful feedback, this feedback can provide encouragement for your next writing assignment even if you have difficulties to overcome. If your teacher provides only curt or cursory comments on your writing, find one or more other people who will spend time and care commenting on your work. If such help is not possible, you can discover a new perspective in your writing by reading your work aloud and recording and listening to it. Even if you have comments from other people, learning to evaluate your own work is part of the craft of writing.

If your way of writing essays or reports is criticised explicitly because it does not conform to the accepted conventions of your discipline at tertiary level, you may need to learn how to use the appropriate genre and to adapt to what is expected. Find out from your teacher why your written work does not meet the requirements, and read the relevant sections in this book.

The more useful the feedback you receive on an essay, the more you can evolve your own style and craft as a writer. Think carefully about any comments you are given and discuss them with your reader to learn more about your strengths and weaknesses as a writer. Remember that, for your writing, yours is the final evaluation. (See Chapter 17 for more on evaluating your own work.)

Hopefully, writing an essay is not a postscript to research, or a duty that you scribble through at the last minute. If you think of essay writing as a craft to be practised and as part of all the writing you do, you will understand that it can reward you for the time, care and imagination you put into it in ways that are more satisfying than achieving a good grade.

TEN TIPS

1   Before you start writing your rough draft, carefully re-read the set topic and revisit any requirements for the essay.

2   Check your definition of the topic using the list of questions at the start of this chapter.

3   If you are uncertain of the level at which to pitch your writing, a good rule of thumb is to write for another student who is taking the unit but does not have an in-depth understanding of your topic.

4   When you first sit down to produce a rough draft, focus on structuring your main points and getting your thoughts down as accurately as possible—leave editing what you've written until later.

5   Experiment with writing from a plan similar to that in Table 14.1 'A sample essay plan', and also with writing from a plan which is much more detailed, to find out which works best for you.

6   When you are unclear about what you want to say in a particular part of an essay, try free writing to help clarify your ideas.

7   Pay particular attention to crafting a clear and informative introduction—it is the first thing your reader will encounter.

8   Choose to develop a smaller selected number of main points in detail, rather than presenting many more points superficially.

9   Support the points you want to make rather than assuming that something that seems 'common sense' to you is something that everyone would agree with.

10 Each paragraph should have one central point, not simply be a collection of information about a topic.

Writing scientific reports

15

Some of the worst (articles in scientific journals) are produced by the kind of author who consciously pretends to a 'scientific scholarly' style. He [sic] takes what should be lively, inspiring and beautiful, and in an attempt to make it seem dignified, chokes it to death with stately abstract nouns; next, in the name of scientific impartiality, he [sic] fits it with a complete set of passive constructions to drain away any remaining life's blood or excitement; then he [sic] embalms the remains in molasses of polysyllable, wraps the corpse in an impenetrable veil of vogue words, and buries the stiff old mummy with such pomp and circumstance in the most distinguished journal that will take it. Considered either as a piece of scholarly work or as a vehicle of communication, the product is appalling. The question is, does it matter?

F. PETER WOODFORD

How you write a report does matter—whether your report is published in a scientific journal or is a unit requirement. Communicating your findings and observations in a report is an integral part of science, and communicating clearly is interwoven with thinking clearly. Unless your reports are clearly thought out and written, your practical work—no matter how good—is of limited value.

What do you bring to an experiment or field trip that affects the quality of your written report? Your knowledge of a subject—of underlying theory and specific detail—is obviously important and can be improved with preliminary reading. Your care in observation, your practical skills, and your expertise in experimental design and using research techniques also affect the standard of your scientific work and writing.

How you use this chapter depends on the detail in your laboratory manuals, the number of practical sessions you have each week and the extent to which you design your own research. Some examples follow:

— if your laboratory manual describes in great detail the experiments you are to carry out, focus on planning the experiments and use each section of this chapter as you write your reports

— if you have to write up three laboratory sessions each week, you could use this chapter to help you write any difficult sections, or

— if your research is substantially your own, the sections on writing styles and conventions may be particularly valuable.

Another facet that is basic to good research, experimental design and report writing is an awareness of the objectives set down for the research. Some of these objectives translate into specific learning outcomes, such as to test a particular hypothesis, or to observe a certain phenomenon. However, you also need to think about why you are doing the research in the first place. And as one of your aims is to communicate your findings, think about who will read the report. You might either:

— write a report on a routine laboratory experiment for your teacher, where both carrying out the practical work and writing about it are exercises in using a meticulous scientific method, or

— write a public report for a government department or the popular press, or a report for your work in an interdisciplinary course. Readers of such reports need emphasis on key ideas without too much scientific detail or too many bland descriptions.

Each individual research project and its report has a different purpose. Keeping your aims, the learning outcomes and your readers in mind when researching gives you a basic framework for clear report writing.

Beginning a report

Is 'writing up' something you see as a task to be done after the 'real work' of an experiment or field work is over? In practice, the process of writing can help you to clarify your thoughts and stimulate new ideas, so write at all stages of your laboratory and field work rather than leaving this activity to the end.

Writing as you plan

> If I had eight hours to chop down a tree, I'd spend six sharpening the axe.
>
> ABRAHAM LINCOLN

If you are expected to design all or part of an experiment, write as you do so. Your written design can then be built on as you carry out the experiment, providing a detailed and organised basis for your final report. Clearly state the purposes of the report, the problem you want to solve and your hypothesis or predictions. Write down the nature, frequency and duration of the necessary measurements and observations. For example:

— how you will choose samples

— the range and degree of precision required in measurements

— any controls needed to test for one or more variables

— how you will ensure reliability by avoiding systematic errors and assessing the size of any random errors

— methods for checking the accuracy of measurements and observations

— how you will record each measurement and the scales you will use, and

— if you will be presenting numerical data, samples of the likely format for tables and figures.

> It is possible to measure something other than what you expect to measure. For example, people frequently talk in everyday language about measuring intelligence. Yet it is not clear what is being measured: it may be ability in a specific subject, adaptability, expression, or something quite different. Alternatively you might be trying to measure a physical property like the fire retardant ability of a chemical. How can you be sure that your measurement is a valid measure of the retardant effect, and that it will give similar results to other measurements of fire retardant, or will be a good predictor of measurements of the fire retardant for other materials?   LORRAINE MARSHALL

Your laboratory or field notebook

Begin writing for a report during your practical work as you record methods and results, and immediately afterwards while the work is still fresh in your mind. Writing in this way helps you think critically about what you are doing, and can lead you to repeat an experiment while it is still set up or to fill in gaps in your field observations. Your notes should be a complete and chronological record of what you did and when, including calculations and diagrams of apparatus.

15

> . . . a lab notebook. Everything gets written down, formally, so that you know at all times where you are, where you have been, where you are going and where you want to get. In scientific work and electronics technology this is necessary because otherwise the problems get so complex you get lost in them and confused and forget what you know and what you don't know and have to give up . . . Sometimes just the act of writing down the problems straightens out your head as to what they really are.
>
> ROBERT M. PIRSIG

Write the name of each section of your report on separate pages of your notebook and record your ideas, observations and results under the appropriate heading. Don't worry at this stage about your writing style or the order of material within a section—concentrate on putting ideas and information down as clearly and concisely as possible.

Measurements, observations and calculations

Check that you understand and can follow all the steps required to make observations and take measurements. As you carry out and record research, your results are usually in the form of numbers. For example, if you are interested in how long it takes a one-celled animal to divide, you would measure the time from one division to the next with a number of these animals and then derive the average time. The results would be a set of numbers called *data*. In the early stages of analysing data, ordering them in tables or figures can help you see patterns emerging in your results. After collecting, recording and analysing initial data, check your data to determine whether you need to make further measurements. In your notebook, include a brief discussion of your main results or observations and record any unexpected developments in your experiment. Also make sure that you:

— label each measurement—including the units used—so that you can identify it later

— decide when measurements can be estimated, and when they need to be precise, and how precise they need to be

— take enough measurements and observations to be as accurate as necessary in the time available, but don't spend time on additional measurements which don't significantly improve accuracy, and

— if making calculations, decide how you will double-check for mistakes.

If you are not confident with basic aspects of numeracy that are essential to how you work with and present data (such as the difference between an average and a mean, or how to use percentages and fractions), attend a workshop on these or take an online tutorial.

Planning your writing

● Before you start writing your whole report, plan *what* you are going to say and how you are going to say it—this is where separate sheets of paper or pages in a computer document for the various sections are useful. Discussing your work with others—teachers, students and friends—gives you practice in explaining your ideas and results and helps to clarify what you want to say and how.

- Consider *how* you might write your report. You could tackle it in stages, editing each section as it is completed. You might start by writing up Materials and Methods and the Results, drafting your Discussion and the Conclusions, and leaving the Introduction until last. Another method is to write the rough draft of the whole report from start to finish, concentrating on conveying your ideas and information accurately, and then editing what you have written.

- *When* you write your report probably depends on when it is due and your overall workload. But the earlier you begin writing the more time you will have to set your completed report aside and think about it (see 'Writing to a plan', Chapter 14).

Check if your report has to be presented using specific software. And become familiar with a range of software and online tools recommended for report writing for functions such as data analysis, and for specific uses such as models and simulations.

As you write your report

A scientific or technical report usually follows a highly structured format, and is expected to follow certain conventions of data presentation and writing style.

Report sections

Think about your report as a whole, rather than as an assortment of sections. However, each section should by itself convey intelligible information to your reader.

When considering the sections that make up a report, it is important to realise that there is *a range of report genres*. For example:

— biomedical reports often consist of an Introduction, Materials and Methods, Results, and Discussion

— reports in descriptive field sciences are likely to include an Introduction, Materials and Methods, Geographical Context, Analysis of Data, and Results, and

— more theoretical papers may consist of an Introduction, Theoretical Analysis, Applications, and Conclusions.

Report formats can vary from one discipline to another, so make sure you are clear about what is expected.

For a first year student scientific report, you are probably given a title, expected to write a one- or two-sentence Introduction and describe the Materials and Methods as in the laboratory manual. Most of your effort on the report is spent on the Results and Discussion sections. Occasionally, reports require a cover page, a table of contents, illustrations or a preface and may include recommendations, appendices and acknowledgements. It is not unusual for two sections to be combined when this makes sense—for example, the Results and Discussion, or the Conclusions and Recommendations.

It is the *purpose of each section* of a report that is important. Even if you are told which sections to use in your report, don't follow the instructions blindly. Take time to reflect on the function of each section in the whole report.

The following descriptions of report sections include some points that apply more to articles for publication than to conventional student reports. These points are mentioned because they relate to the purpose of a section and need to be thought about early in your report writing career.

1 The title, or 'What is the specific problem or question being asked?'

Your title should attract a potential reader and should be short and specific—for example, 'Resources and Environmental Management: Fundamental Concepts and Definitions', or 'Numerical Data Bases for Australian Science and Technology'. Use a subtitle if a fuller description is necessary and, for the sake of brevity, omit words such as 'a', 'the' and 'on' where possible.

The title should state the problem posed or the question asked and can indicate how this problem or question was approached; but a title is not a summary of your report. On the page headed 'Title' in your notebook, list key words and write the title before you write your full report. Check it for accuracy afterwards and ask yourself, 'Do the results and discussions actually answer the specific question or problem set out in the title?'

2 The abstract or synopsis, or 'What are my main findings?'

Your abstract or synopsis is a précis of the content of your report and is meant to be read in conjunction with the title. It is usually no more than a paragraph and includes information on the field, the hypothesis, the research design and the main results. An abstract should enable your reader to decide whether to read the whole report, so it should be intelligible by itself and should not be full of technical jargon. To help you clarify your ideas and plan your material, it may be useful to write the abstract before the rest of your report. After the whole report is written, revise the abstract to ensure that it presents the essential content of your report in a balanced manner.

An abstract differs from a summary, the latter being a review included at the end of a report to help your readers understand your conclusions or recommendations. Such a summary includes more detail than an abstract and may contain tables and figures. The term 'abstract' is commonly used in academia, while the term 'synopsis' is used in government reports.

3 The introduction, or 'What did I investigate, and why?'

> In Part One of formal scientific method, which is the statement of the problem, the main skill is in stating absolutely no more than you are positive you know. It is much better to enter a statement 'Solve Problem: Why doesn't cycle work?' which sounds dumb but is correct, than it is to enter a statement 'Solve Problem: What is wrong with the electrical system?' when you don't absolutely know the trouble is in the electrical system. What you should state is 'Solve Problem: What is wrong with cycle?' and then state as the first entry of Part Two: 'Hypothesis Number One: The trouble is in the electrical system.'
> ROBERT M. PIRSIG

The introduction should state the specific problem or question under consideration, perhaps as an enlargement of the title.

- State clearly the purpose and scope of your work. If you are testing an hypothesis, introduce the relevant theoretical background.

- Discuss selected research studies which, when taken together, show that your particular experiment or observation is logical and worthwhile within its field. For example, you may have focused on gaps or dilemmas in a field or have tested a new application of previous work.

- Don't cite a large number of studies in the introduction. Either refer to papers that review the research literature relevant to the research question and methodology or, if you want to critically review a large body of research literature, add a separate section after the introduction or write a separate review.

- Explain any unusual or complicated theoretical aspects of the subject which aren't covered by the literature, particularly if your readers include people without a strong background in the field.

- Address any research findings that run counter to your proposed approach to the topic.

- State the assumptions and limitations of your work, and define technical terms.

- Summarise your conclusions if necessary, but without attempting to provide a review of them or of your results.

4 The materials and methods, or 'How did I go about what I did?'

This section describes what you did, usually in the order in which you did it, *so that a reader with experience in the same field could repeat the experiment or observations*. Strike a balance between being concise and giving sufficient detail—for example, a diagram of the apparatus used can be preferable to a long, written description of it.

- Broadly outline your overall experimental design unless this is obvious from your introduction.

- Under 'Materials', describe any field-work locations and list the equipment used, including software and items such as questionnaires.

- Refer to any preliminary experiments and any changes of techniques you have made.
- State the conditions and procedures of the experiment and observations. Indicate how safety or ethical concerns have been handled.
- Describe the main features of your samples and any sampling and control devices used.
- Describe the measurement techniques used.
- Include your reasons for choosing a particular method if there were alternatives.

5 The results, or 'What did I observe or find?'

The purpose of this section is to present in logical order a statement of your findings and observations. These should be supplemented with tables or figures (graphs and charts) derived from an analysis of data recorded (see 'Data presentation', later in this chapter). In a practical report, present your results accurately but don't simply provide large amounts of raw data—you are expected to show that you have thought about the raw data and summarised them into an appropriate format. Your results should be presented with your hypothesis in mind, and provide the building material for the discussion where you interpret the results.

The Results section should be coherent on its own. You may be able to report the results fully in a few words or numbers or in a clear table or figure, accompanied by comments on the most significant patterns in the data. If your results led to further experiments that produced further results (and so on), you might want to combine your Results and Discussion sections.

- Display data in a reliable and systematic manner.
- Any raw data, or data to more decimal places than appropriate for the summaries in your results, should be placed in an appendix.
- State the number of results obtained and your reasons for omitting any of them from this section.
- Give results that support your conclusions (or lack thereof), but be careful that your selection doesn't distort the results in order to reach a particular conclusion.

6 The discussion, or 'How have I interpreted the results and what are my answers to the specific question asked?'

I am appalled by the frequent publication of papers that describe most minutely what experiments were done, and how, but with no hint of why, or what they mean. Cast thy data upon the waters, the authors seem to think, and they will come back interpreted.

F. PETER WOODFORD

In some student practical reports you are only required to discuss whether your hypothesis is tenable or whether you have answered the question asked. Nevertheless, the Discussion is the heart of your report and the section where you have the greatest opportunity for critical analysis. Your aims here are to interpret your results; to show their significance in relation to your introduction; to explain how the results add to what is already known; to say whether or not your hypothesis is sustainable; and to discuss your work in relation to the theory underlying similar studies.

- Discuss the precision of your results. Refer to or take them as read, rather than summarising them.

- Explain any irregularities, shortcomings or unexpected results. Note that these discrepancies, rather than being a problem, can often alert you to significant findings.

- Avoid obviously subjective judgements, such as 'excellent results' or 'highly useful data'.

- Indicate the limits of your research.

- Compare your results with the findings of studies that you mentioned in your introduction. To do this satisfactorily (if you have time), check the original studies to find out exactly what other researchers did, how they did it and the conclusions they drew, then report these findings accurately.

- Consider any positions which apparently contradict your own.

- Give theoretical explanations for the data discussed.

- If appropriate, briefly suggest one or two possible directions for future research in the area.

The points in your discussion should be logically argued and developed, but the section should not be too discursive. Use subheadings to help your reader follow the stages of your argument unless your discussion is brief. The reader should be able to judge the validity of your conclusions from the information in the discussion.

7 The conclusions, or 'What can justifiably be concluded?'

> The TV scientist who mutters sadly, 'The experiment is a failure; we have failed to achieve what we had hoped for,' is suffering mainly from a bad scriptwriter. The experiment is never a failure solely because it fails to achieve predicted results. An experiment is a failure only when it also fails adequately to test the hypothesis in question, when the data it produces don't prove anything one way or another.   ROBERT M. PIRSIG

State succinctly the conclusions which can justifiably be drawn from your work, and indicate their significance for your original research question. If your results are inconclusive (for example, after a short student practical session), say so, give reasons for this and suggest improvements or further work to be done. Don't present another summary of your results.

8 The references, or 'Which studies did I cite?'

Your list of references should be in alphabetical order and should consist only of reports or studies cited in your report, not literature consulted. When citing from references that report on other people's experiments, each reference should, if possible, be checked to ensure that any errors in citing the original experiment are not repeated (see 'Conventions' and 'Questions and mistakes', later in this chapter).

Teachers' objectives for asking you to write reports include teaching you about a scientific method and a subject area, as well as providing an exercise in writing. In this case, you may be faced with the apparently conflicting aims of showing your teacher how much you know about a subject, while including only necessary detail as expected in a professional report. When confronted with this dilemma, don't rehash textbook material on basic theory, and don't bury your Discussion and Conclusions under a mass of detail.

If possible talk about the problem with your teacher for suggestions on how the different aims can be reconciled or which one should have priority. When deciding what to include and what to omit, remember that in professional reports the readers usually know less about the subject than the author, while the reverse is presumably true of the readers and writers of student reports. However, don't assume that because your teacher knows a subject you should not explain it fully and clearly. Your teacher needs to know that you understand the basic principles of a subject.

Data presentation

Your data sets must be ordered, presented in a clear format and interpreted, or your readers won't be able to make sense of them. How you order and present your data depends on a host of factors, but the guiding principle is always clarity. To achieve clarity, data are usually presented in tables and figures, accompanied by explanatory text.

Why use tables or figures?

Use tables or figures if they enable your reader to understand the data more clearly. Use them if, for example, they present data more concisely than words could; or use figures such as graphs and charts at the beginning and end of your results analysis to show the overall relationships between variables. Don't use tables or figures simply for the sake of having them in the report.

How will you present data?

This depends on the information you have to convey. For example, don't use graphs if you don't have the data for a sufficient number of points. Use bar or line graphs, pie charts or flow charts if you want to clearly demonstrate trends in results. Use tables where you want to present your data with accurate values. Consider which form of presentation might be appropriate for your data when it is simple and when it is complex, when it is new and when it is repetitive.

Ordering data in tables

There is more than one way of ordering data in a table. If your reader has sufficient knowledge of the type of data you are presenting, you can arrange your information so that the patterns and exceptions are easily seen. If you can't assume your reader has this knowledge, supply a sentence or two clearly interpreting the information presented. To achieve this clarity, think carefully about the ordering of your data, rather than putting it down in the first format that comes to mind. For example, when presenting tables there are several points to consider.

- Decide to what degree of accuracy you will present your data. Depending on the purpose of your tables and the precision of your experiment, you may be able to round off the numbers without losing any vital information. Your reader may do this anyway in order to understand the table.

- Consider whether to present your data primarily in columns so that your reader's eye is led down the page, or in rows across the page. Which form makes it easier to see the patterns and exceptions in the data presented? In which form will the table fit most easily on the page?

- Decide whether to include aids, such as averages, totals, maxima/minima or percentages, to help your reader interpret your data.

- Think about how to set out and space your material, for example, where and how to separate columns of numbers.

Amount of information

There is a limit to the amount of information you can convey in one table or figure. Often it is better to opt for several small tables or figures rather than a large complex one. This allows you to place each one close to the relevant text and helps your reader focus on one or two aspects of your data at a time. If you find that in a table you have frequent blank spaces or repeated data, you may need to create smaller tables.

Labelling

To label your tables or figures:

— number them in consecutive order

— give each one a title that is precise but concise, and a legend to explain the elements it contains

— consider whether to present the data in several smaller formats if you find yourself developing a complex system of legends and footnotes for a large table or figure

— in tables specify the units used in the headings of the columns and rows, so that each entry in the column or row need be a number only

— ensure that your reader can easily see if a heading refers to a column or a row, and

— indicate units and magnitudes clearly on the axes of a graph or chart.

TABLE 15.1 **A sample table**

Higher education students. By mode of study and full- or part-time load — 2010

In 2010, just under 1 million (81%) of higher education students were studying internally (on campus), 12% were external students and the remaining 7% were in multi-modal programs (partially delivered on campus and partially through distance and/or online delivery). Of the internal students, 77% were studying full-time and 23% were studying part-time (table 12.18). A similar distribution was found among students in multi-modal programs. In contrast, the ratios were reversed among students studying externally, with 79% studying part-time and 21% studying full-time.

12.18 HIGHER EDUCATION STUDENTS,
By mode of study and full- or part-time load—2010

	Full-time students		Part-time students		Total	
	'000	%	'000	%	'000	%
Internal	743.1	77.1	221.3	22.9	964.4	100.0
External	31.4	21.5	114.9	78.5	146.3	100.0
Multi-modal	63.8	77.9	18.1	22.1	81.9	100.0
All students	838.3	70.3	354.3	29.7	1 192.7	100.0

Source: Australia. DEEWR 2010. Reproduced in: ABS 2012. Copyright Commonwealth of Australia, reproduced with permission.

Note that the authors have:
• presented the data as raw data and as percentages
• given an explanatory title for the table, and
• provided an accompanying précis of the data.

Presenting data in tables and figures is an integral part of communicating your findings from practical work. In student practical sessions you may have little latitude to opt for different forms of data presentation. But when you design experiments, ask someone who knows your subject to look at your initial data presentation to see what it conveys to them. Try different formats and ordering of your data to see which one conveys most precisely what you want to say. Data presentation is a complex skill, and this section touches on only a few of the basic points. To learn how to convey information as concisely and unambiguously as possible, find people who are skilled in the use of data presentation techniques and work with them on the results of your own experiments.

Writing styles and conventions

. . . execrable writing . . . is the product of shoddy thinking, or careless condescension, or of pretentiousness.   F. PETER WOODFORD

Your writing style in scientific and technical reports is likely to be shaped by conventions about what 'scientific' thinking is. For example, you are usually expected to avoid using 'I' or 'we' when describing what you did or found because scientists are supposed to be impartial observers. Become familiar with the range of techniques available and practise these often so that they become part of your writing repertoire. Whatever conventions and style you choose, use them to help you report your findings more clearly, rather than to impress your reader or to hide ignorance. The principles that underlie all successful communication also apply to scientific writing. Be lucid and unambiguous, and ask yourself:

Exactly what do I want to say?

Why do I want to say it?

How can I say it most effectively?

To whom am I saying it?

Style

Reports should describe concisely and accurately what happened in an experiment or in field work—they should not be written in a narrative or storytelling style. Events are usually presented in chronological order or in order of significance, and the description should develop logically, step-by-step. Write most of your report in prose and avoid the overuse of formulae and other abbreviations when the information they convey could easily be expressed in words.

The **language** you use should be neither too technical nor too elementary. Your level of writing should be aimed at whoever will read your report.

- Define any new words or mathematical symbols when you first use them.
- Use subject specific language.
- Use technical terms accurately (for example, 'constant' and 'efficient') and avoid the careless use of words that can have a technical meaning (such as 'parameter' or 'factor').
- Use chemical and pharmacological names rather than unfamiliar trade names.
- Write scientific names, proper names, numerical data, equations and formulae correctly.
- Opt for familiar, short or concrete words rather than unfamiliar, long or abstract ones.

I am a Bear of Very Little Brain, and long words Bother me.   A.A. MILNE

If poor **grammar, spelling and punctuation** prevent you communicating clearly, work on these with the help of a good reference text on the subject (see 'Grammar, spelling and punctuation', Chapter 16). Find a patient friend who is proficient in these skills and willing to proofread your work. Consult a study skills adviser.

Keep your **sentences** short and simple if in doubt about their length. Construct your **paragraphs** so that each one contains one idea (see 'The body of your essay', Chapter 14). If you have trouble writing coherent sentences and paragraphs, work with someone who will help you improve these skills. Read and analyse plenty of well-written articles to get the feel of effective writing—*Science* and *Nature* are good sources.

Conventions

Check with your teacher which conventions you are expected to follow in a report. Some examples follow.

- Are you expected to use passive voice rather than active? For example, are you expected to write 'pH4 was needed by the enzyme' (passive) instead of 'the enzyme needed pH4' (active)? Using the passive voice does not in itself make your writing more scholarly, and the active voice generally makes your writing more direct.

- Are you required to use past tense when describing your methods and reporting your results? Are you expected to use the present tense when stating facts that are generally agreed on?

- Are some numbers to be written in words and some in figures? How are times and dates to be recorded?

- Will you number your report sections and subsections using the decimal system, as in '2.1.1', '2.1.2', '2.1.3'?

To cite *references*, it is customary in scientific reports to use the author's name and the year of publication in the body of the text, rather than using footnotes. For example:

According to Brown (1959) . . .
Recent studies (Black 1975; White 1976) show that . . .
After a thorough training, 'The student can no longer write; he pontificates' (Woodford 1967).

For references you cite but have not seen in the original:

The mouse ran up the clock (Green cited by Blue 1971) . . .

If you refer frequently to other research literature, the text may become so cluttered with bracketed references that it is difficult to read. In this case, number each item and list all references at the end of the text in order of appearance. You can use a computer automated system such as EndNote® to do this. To cite one of these references, quote the number of that reference in your text. For example:

The mouse ran up the clock[31]

or

The mouse ran up the clock (31).

See Chapter 16, 'Using conventions', for detailed information on correct referencing, including citing online references.

Editing the report

When your report is finished, set it aside if you have the time, so that you can come back to it with something of the approach of a person reading it for the first time. While it is set aside, think about what you have written and make occasional corrections—but allow yourself some distance from it before you prepare your final version.

Check through the **contents** of your report. If some of it seems irrelevant or too detailed, prune ruthlessly. See if you have covered all the points in 'As you write your report', above. For example, have you:

— recorded all experimental information such as strength of solutions, ambient temperatures, specifications of instruments

— put units against all your measurements and results

— defined all symbols

— checked your calculations

— compared your results with expected or established results, and

— dated your work?

Look at your **writing style**. Be prepared to replace an inappropriate word and to rewrite a clumsy sentence or paragraph. Proofread your report for mistakes or omissions in details such as spelling, grammar and punctuation, or ask someone else to read your work to point out incorrect details and suggest ways in which you can polish your writing style.

When you have edited the content and style of your report, produce a clean, legible copy (see 'Presentation', Chapter 16).

Writing a scientific report involves putting words on paper, but it also involves thinking about and planning what you want to say as you take notes during an experiment or field work, as you begin to draft the whole report, and when working on your final draft. As you try to express exactly what you want to say, the process of writing itself can spark new ideas and make you look again at old ones. And remember, writing a report is you communicating about your work to your reader, so think about who will read your report and what you need to tell them.

15

Questions and mistakes

Many students see experiments and practical work as exercises to be gone through to find the Right Answers. Yet any real learning for you as an individual follows from the questions you ask for information, because you want to know. Following procedures laid down by someone else to answer a question asked by someone else inevitably leads to someone else's answers. You can learn from someone else's answers—but only if their answers have a connection with your questions (see Chapter 6, 'Asking your own questions').

You interpret the results of an experiment according to the hypothesis being tested and what you expected to find. The way a question is asked, a problem stated or an hypothesis worded influences the results you are likely to come up with. Even researchers who start with the same hypothesis and arrive at similar results can and do interpret those results to reach considerably different conclusions. Their results and conclusions are then interpreted by other researchers in the light of their own hypotheses, findings and opinions. To discover how scientific research has developed in an area and just how shaky 'facts' can be, take a paper on a specific topic and read through the originals of any studies cited in that paper. Read these original studies carefully and compare their actual findings with the way in which these findings have been cited in the later paper. It is not uncommon to find noticeable discrepancies between the two.

> School books even more rarely tell us how thinkers of the past have gone about trying to answer their own questions, and still more rarely, what mistakes they made along the way. A graduate student in Psychology suggested one day to a noted professor in that field that there should be a publication in which psychologists would write about their mistakes, the hunches that had not worked out, the experiments that had not proved what they meant to prove; or didn't prove anything. The professor agreed that such a publication would teach students a great deal about the doing of psychology. But, he said, there was no use even thinking about such a publication, because no-one with a reputation to defend would ever put anything in it. So we find it hard to find most of our mistakes because we are so rarely told how the do-ers of the past came to make and later find theirs.
>
> JOHN HOLT

If, at the end of an experiment or field work, you have not found the answers you expected, if your results are inconclusive or point to other answers, don't automatically think you have failed. Think about what you did and try to discover why your results were inconclusive or unexpected. If you made a mistake, acknowledge it. If your work could be improved, suggest how this might be done. If you discover related questions, or areas to be explored for a more complete answer, suggest these as part of your report. Don't try to hide your unexpected or inconclusive results, or distort them to produce the right answers. You can learn much by analysing your mistakes.

You can learn as much from writing a report of observations made in the laboratory or field as you can from doing the practical work about which you write. The challenge of trying to describe your work accurately, logically and lucidly for someone else to read and understand should make you think about what you actually did. It will also help you critically evaluate other people's reports. In serious research, describing your work helps you to think about how to design and conduct experiments or a set of observations, about the disciplines in which you are working and writing, and about the strengths and limits of scientific knowledge. What do you think science is all about? Or technology? Your answers to these questions will shape and be shaped by the reports you write about your scientific and technical work.

TEN TIPS

1   Identify the learning outcomes set for report.
2   Think about who will read your report.
3   Start your writing as you carry out your research, rather than leaving it until the end.
4   Check which software can make your report writing and data analysis easier.
5   Ensure that you understand each of the stages required for your experiment or research.
6   Clarify the function of each section of a report and which sections you are expected to include in a particular report.
7   Think about which format for presenting your data will make it easiest to follow.
8   Be familiar with the conventions you are expected to follow in presenting your report.
9   Report all results, even if they do not support your hypothesis.
10 When the results are not what you expected, take time to reflect on what you can learn from this.

REFERENCES

Australia. Department of Education, Employment and Workplace Relations. 2010. *DEEWR Higher Education Statistics, All Students, 2010*, Table 12.18. Canberra: DEEWR. Reproduced in: Australian Bureau of Statistics. 2012. 'Education and Training'. In *Higher Education Yearbook Australia, 2012 (cat. no. 1301.0)*. http://www.abs.gov.au/ausstats/abs@.nsf/Lookup/by%20Subject/1301.0~2012~Main%20Features~Higher%20education~107.html.

15

Using conventions

16

'. . . that's not a regular rule; you invented it just now.' 'It's the oldest rule in the book,' said the King. 'Then it ought to be Number One,' said Alice.

LEWIS CARROLL

When using conventions in your assignment writing it is useful to understand why they exist rather than simply following rules. For example, the standard referencing conventions used in academic writing by most Western publishers serve as shorthand to succinctly convey information on sources used. Much of this shorthand has its origins in the reporting of research where the reader needs to be able to follow up references to understand the original citations and evaluate their use.

As a university student, when you use material written or produced by someone else you do so by either quoting from the original source, paraphrasing it or summarising it. Scholars are expected to acknowledge the source of any material they have not written or produced themselves, and you are also expected to understand and use the appropriate methods for citing all material which you take from other sources. The process of acknowledgement is called referencing, and is fundamental to communication in academic culture and an integral part of academic debate (see 'University culture', Chapter 2). Skilful choice and application of references shows an awareness of nuances in academic dialogues or controversy.

In your **first year** you need to learn when it is appropriate to quote, paraphrase and summarise, and how to do this. You will come to realise that references are used for a variety of purposes, such as demonstrating the breadth of your research on a topic (see 'Why include references?', later in this chapter). If you are new to academia, you may be mostly concerned to reference correctly, especially when you are inevitably confronted with different disciplines and teachers expecting different referencing formats. To avoid confusion, learn the basic elements for referencing and other conventions so that you can adapt them as required—and remember that your longer-term aim is to use sources to engage in academic debate.

When citing a reference, acknowledge your source and give full details of the reference. For example:

Savage, Jo. 2012. *The Film 'Fangs'*. Anchorage, AK: Wolf Publications.

In the text you would cite the source as (Savage 2012, 54) and give full details in the reference. It may seem unimportant and pedantic to have to follow academic conventions. However, if you omit any of this information (for example, if you refer only to 'Savage's book on the movie *Fangs*'), your reader will not know who the author is, the book's title, when and where the book was published, and on which page in the book to find the cited reference.

Individual academic disciplines, publications and teachers frequently adopt their own variations of the standard conventions. The essential elements are the same, but the formatting details may vary considerably. Whichever format you use, be *consistent* and *accurate*. Early on, check with your teachers or the unit materials so that you are clear about the conventions expected in your discipline, course, unit or assignment; and in each unit find out the personal preferences of the unit coordinator and your teacher in these matters. This is particularly important if your

16

teacher strongly prefers a particular referencing style and gives lower grades for any deviation from this style.

Either stick to tradition or see that your inventions be consistent.   HORACE

However, don't let the punctilious observance of correct conventions become the focus of your writing. Use them as necessary to help you communicate more clearly— and if in doubt about which convention to use, rely on your common sense to convey clearly and accurately to your reader what you want to say.

The Chicago style of referencing is used in this chapter and throughout this book. The list of References at the end of some chapters and the Quotation Sources at the end of this book are all in Chicago. However, for the quotations in the book the style has been varied, with the author's name in capitals following the quote, and the publication date and page number available in the Quotation Sources.

Most of the examples in this chapter are taken from material written about the sea, a place where human conventions are subservient to nature.

Academic integrity

On the Internet it is common to circulate other people's words, ideas and images, often without acknowledgement. This is not acceptable in academic culture.

Modern writers and researchers in the Western academic traditions expect to be fully acknowledged if their ideas or their work (including words, images and sounds) are referred to in any way. This differs from some cultures where it is accepted that you are showing respect for authorities by copying their words without detailed acknowledgement. In Western higher education, deliberately copying without acknowledgement (plagiarism) is seen as unethical and is treated seriously in universities.

University scholarship is based on honesty and trust, and within the university community these values are called 'academic integrity'. All scholars are expected to be ethical—to honestly report their research findings, and when they use work which is not their own, to attribute it to the other person. As a student you are also expected to be honest in acknowledging when you use material which is not your own, so that you build trust with your teachers and become part of the academic community.

When a person writes or produces something they then usually own this material; it becomes their intellectual property (IP). Using someone else's material without acknowledgement is regarded as stealing their property. Further, authors or producers (or publishers) own the copyright to this material, which means that legally it cannot be used without prior permission except in specified quantities and for specific purposes; and it must be acknowledged and in some cases purchased.

Plagiarism and collusion

Most students try to use other authors' material honestly. However, because of a limited understanding of referencing conventions, at times new students inadvertently do not acknowledge their use of phrases, sentences or paragraphs from another source. *Plagiarism* occurs when you take someone else's ideas, images or writings and present them as your own. There are varying degrees of plagiarism. Extreme forms occur when a student copies, with or without minor changes, large extracts from the web, sections of an article or chapter, or another student's essay.

Collusion, which is a form of cheating, occurs when a student has another person complete for them some assessable work such as an exam or assignment, and perhaps pays for this. Collusion differs from collaboration in that the intention in the former is to deceive the teacher who will assess the work, whereas in collaboration each person presents their own work (see 'Collaborative learning', Chapter 3, 'Playing your part during discussions', Chapter 12 and 'Peer evaluation', Chapter 17).

Plagiarism often results in an unsatisfactory piece of work because, for example, the student's own writing style differs awkwardly from that of the plagiarised piece, or the section that has been copied is not exactly relevant to the overall argument. Reading the work of a student who has plagiarised someone else's words and ideas is a disheartening experience for a teacher. In many instances, teachers can easily detect a case of plagiarism because they notice a shift in writing style and are familiar with the relevant source material. They may then ask another teacher to read a student's work, or may make a thorough search for the original source (perhaps using plagiarism detection software) or discuss the paper with the student.

Detecting plagiarism from the web is a relatively simple matter of putting a few phrases or sentences into a search engine using the appropriate software. Most universities have invested in plagiarism-detection software and students may be invited or required to submit their assignments to this system which generates a report that is submitted with the assignment. You can make use of this software to learn how to reference correctly, and to check your own writing for any unintentional errors you have made in citing references.

It is usually a university requirement that teachers report all confirmed cases of plagiarism to the correct university authorities. Each case is dealt with individually, and the course of action will depend on the student's experience of university study and on the degree of plagiarism. Although university policies vary, the student may be asked to resubmit the assignment, or the assignment could be failed. The student can be required to take a special course or module on plagiarism. In serious cases, especially for repeated offences, official disciplinary action is taken and a student may fail the unit or be expelled from the institution.

There is considerable debate across the university sector about plagiarism. The web has made it very easy for students to copy material directly into an assignment.

16

Stringent measures to discourage plagiarism are still used, and concerns about cheating have led some universities to an increased use of exams or other supervised assessment. However, some academics argue that universities need to rethink their approach to plagiarism and notions of intellectual property, and others argue for radical change to university assessment.

> A better solution is needed than endlessly informing students that plagiarising is wrong. It might help if some of the pressures to complete assignments on time were removed, if students were given assignments, tests and exams that called for deep study and individualised responses and if they were in an episteme that did not see knowledge as property to be made private and kept private.   JOHN TIFFIN and LALITA RAJASINGHAM

How to avoid plagiarising

- You may be tempted to plagiarise if you are not confident about your knowledge of a subject or your writing ability, or because you feel pressured by too much work. If so, talk about these difficulties with someone who can help you (and use any relevant sections of this book) rather than resorting to plagiarism and being confronted with the same problems later on.

- If you have so much work to complete and so little time available that plagiarism seems to be an option, check to see if other students in your unit or course are having workload problems. If so, collectively approach your teacher. If not, see your teacher individually to discuss how to manage your workload more effectively.

- When taking notes from material, read a section, put the reference aside and paraphrase or summarise the material in your own words (see 'Notemaking and/or underlining', Chapter 10). If you copy any words exactly, put them in quotation marks; or if you want to closely re-phrase another writer's words, clearly identify the beginning and end of paraphrasing. In both cases note the page reference and full details of the source.

- When writing, put shorter quotes in inverted commas or indent longer quotes. For quotes, paraphrases and summaries, use footnotes, endnotes or textual references to acknowledge the source. Indicate clearly where a paraphrase or summary begins by acknowledging the author immediately before in your text. If you take an opinion from someone else, don't disguise it by using the passive tense, such as 'It has been said that . . .'. If you use factual information—for example, statistics that are not common knowledge—acknowledge the source.

- If you are a student from a culture where quoting authorities is handled differently, make certain that you understand Western referencing conventions.

Quoting, paraphrasing and summarising

Although assignments are supposed to be almost entirely your own words, you are also expected to support your argument by using source material which you quote, paraphrase or summarise. You need to balance your own words with material from others, being careful not to overuse other people's writing even though you might think 'they can say it better than me'.

> I might repeat to myself, slowly and soothingly, a list of quotations beautiful from minds profound; if I can remember any of the damn things.   DOROTHY PARKER

Why use quotations?

Quotations are short pieces which must be identical to the original source. You use quotations to:

— express a thought or concept succinctly

— illustrate a point you want to make

— convey the flavour of a work, and

— analyse in depth the exact words of an author.

How to present quotations

> With just enough of learning to misquote.   LORD BYRON

Long quotations

Only use long quotations if you intend to discuss the content of the quote in some detail. Long quotations should be set apart from the main body of your writing so that they are easily identified. If a quote is longer than about 30 words or a few lines of text, it is usual to apply most of the following conventions:

— introduce the quotation with a colon

— miss a line above and below the quotation

— indent from the left (some authors indent both sides)

— use single spacing when the rest of the text is one and a half or double-spaced

— do not use inverted commas (quotation marks), and

— reference the information as required (using either the author–date or footnote systems described in this chapter).

For example:

> In his book *Sailing to the Reefs*, Bernard Moitessier (1971, 83) discusses the motivation behind single-handed sailing:
>
>> And it is, I believe, this need not simply for novelty, but for physical and spiritual cleanliness which drives the lone sailor towards other shores; there, his body and mind are freed from their terrestrial ties and bondage, and can regain their essence and integrity in the natural elements which the ancients deified.
>
> This description captures the spirituality of the experience . . .

16

A familiar children's poem (Lear 1943, 251) describes an unusual sea voyage:

> The Owl and the Pussy-Cat went to sea
> In a beautiful pea-green boat,
> They took some honey, and plenty of money,
> Wrapped up in a five-pound note.

Short quotations

These are usually integrated into the text as part of a grammatically complete sentence and are enclosed by either single or double inverted commas. For example:

> Truly immersed in the experience, 'one forgets oneself, one forgets everything, seeing only the play of the boat with the sea, the play of the sea around the boat' (Moitessier 1975, 52) as the present takes priority over all else.

At times you will quote only a phrase or individual words and you should treat these as you would a short quotation.

If quoting a couple of lines of poetry within your text, you need not set them apart and can indicate the division between the lines with an oblique. For example:

> The single-handed sailor knows the power of being 'Alone, alone, all, all, alone, / Alone on a wide, wide sea!' (Coleridge 1912, 196)

All quotations

- The words must be identical to the original.

- The punctuation and spelling must be *exactly* the same as in the original. This includes details such as capital letters and inverted commas. If you wish to highlight a word or phrase in the quotation by underlining, bolding or using italics when none was used in the original, this must be indicated to the reader by adding in square brackets the words 'my emphasis' or 'emphasis added'. For example:

> Yet the neatness of a copy does not devalue a diary, because, paradoxically, formality was part of the *genre* [emphasis added], and even diaries written at sea had aspirations beyond that of a briefly scribbled note.

- If you choose to abridge a quotation (that is, omit some words or phrases), the convention is to use three dots (an ellipsis) to show that something has been left out. Note that the meaning and intent of the original must not be altered. For example:

> To working people who were unable to work for wages while at sea the purchase of a notebook . . . represented a costly investment to preserve an account of the voyage.

When abridging a longer quote, you may have to change the punctuation or the grammar so that the quotation still makes sense. In this case, the convention is to indicate your additions within square brackets, as in the following example:

> All diaries aspired to the status of the printed book, and the notebooks . . . in which diaries were kept show a common ambition among diarists [at sea] to produce a lasting memento [of their voyage].

- If you want to draw the reader's attention to an error or inappropriate language in the writing of another author, use the word *sic* (Latin for 'thus') within square brackets to indicate that those were the exact words of the author and that the mistake is not yours. In the following example, sexist language has been signalled:

> They all know that man's [*sic*] destiny is linked to our planet, a living creature like ourselves (Moitessier 1975, 185).

Paraphrasing and summarising

When researching a topic you may come across passages of text which you want to borrow for your assignment. If you decide to use these in your writing, you may quote exactly, or you may choose to write either:

— *a summary* of a long segment of text, or

— *a paraphrase* of shorter discrete passages of text, that is, a restatement in your own words of the meaning and sense of the text.

The following conventions should always apply to paraphrases and summaries:

- In both cases you must acknowledge the source.
- You need to be certain that you fully understand what you have read and that you capture the information relevant to what you want to say.
- At times a paraphrase or summary may be written as a short paragraph which you integrate into your text.
- If you want to incorporate into your paraphrase or summary even a few words taken directly from the original, you must put this text in inverted commas to show that you are quoting.
- Changing only a few words in a quotation, and then presenting the quote without inverted commas (as if it were a paraphrase), is not paraphrasing but in fact is plagiarism, even if you acknowledge the source.
- When you re-express material in your own words, you will probably use synonyms or change the sentence structure.
- Clearly indicate where a paraphrase or summary begins by acknowledging the author immediately before in your text—for example, 'Humphries says . . .'.

16

- When you use a summary in your writing, you basically create your own synopsis or outline of the material. To summarise argumentative material note the thesis and supporting premises; and for expository material note the main idea and supporting points (see 'Genres', Chapter 7).

- Integrate the paraphrase or summary into your text so that the sentences follow smoothly, and use a reference to acknowledge the source. For example:

  > When out of sight of land for several days, life beyond the boat and the ocean pales into insignificance for the single handed sailer. It is evident that these adventurers focus only on the vessel and the ocean (Moitessier 1975). Such experiences are akin to other types of adventure whereby . . .

- If you are acknowledging an idea or theme that runs throughout the material you do not need to include the page reference (as shown in the example immediately above).

References

Why include references?

References may have any of the following functions:

— to give the source of a quotation, paraphrase or summary so that your readers can locate and refer to this item

— to give the source of authority for a 'fact' which a reader might question as true

— to make a cross-reference to another part of your text

— to lend authority or support to your ideas

— to demonstrate the breadth of your research on the topic, or

— to show that you have checked facts relating to the topic.

When to reference

You must reference when:

— quoting someone else's words

— paraphrasing or summarising what someone else has said, or

— using another person's intellectual property, such as their ideas, theories, images or information.

You need not reference what you have written if:

— the material is entirely your own, or

— you are using known and accepted facts (such as the population of Australia), rather than facts obtained from research findings and/or 'facts' that are open to dispute.

How to reference

The first practical steps need to happen when you start to take notes from a source. At this stage you may be uncertain how extensively you will rely on a particular source in your final assignment. So to be on the safe side, at the beginning of your notes *record every source detail* (such as page numbers) as if you will use the material. Then if you do use it, you won't have to undertake a time-consuming hunt for the details or to forgo using it because you can't track down the details required to reference it.

Start with the common sense approach of thinking about what your reader needs in order to understand the nature of your references, and to be able to quickly find the source of a quote, paraphrase or summary. Think about the following questions:

- In the text of your essay:

  Why is it useful to include the year for a reference as well as the author's name?

  Why do you need to include the page reference for a quote, paraphrase or summary at the appropriate point in your essay, rather than in the reference list at the end of your essay?

  If an item has more than one author, why is it inappropriate to name only the first author?

- In your reference list:

  Why do you need to put the items in alphabetical order of first authors' surnames?

  Why are publication details useful if your reader wants to find an item in a library?

  For Internet items, why include the date on which you accessed the item?

Unfortunately for new students, different referencing styles are used in different academic disciplines. However, there are variations of the author–date style (also known as 'included references' or 'adjacent referencing') which include the Chicago style and the numbered or notational style (or footnote/endnote style).

The *author–date system* uses author–date citations within the text; and the full details of all the references cited are listed alphabetically by surname in a reference list at the end of the assignment.

The *footnote/endnote system* uses consecutive numbers (either in superscript or bracketed) in the text for each reference, and the full referencing details are listed in numerical order either at the foot of the page or at the end of the essay.

Bibliographic software programs, such as EndNote® or RefWorks, are available to help you store and manage your references in a personal electronic library. You can also transfer the references in your database to create a reference list using whichever referencing style is required. Investigate which software your university library provides for students, and learn how to use it by attending a workshop or taking an online tutorial. Such software is invaluable for storing all reference material

16

in all units; to facilitate accurate referencing; and to help you avoid inadvertently plagiarising material. It is a good idea to start using this software in your first year because then you begin to build a personal reference library that you can use throughout your studies and beyond.

Author–date references

Author–date references within a text enable a reader to continue reading your text smoothly. For example:

> In his book *Sailing to the Reefs*, Bernard Moitessier (1971, 83) discusses the motivation behind single-handed sailing.

This system is the accepted form of referencing in most scientific disciplines and in many disciplines in the social sciences and humanities, and paraphrases and summaries are cited in the text in the same way as direct quotations. Author–date references give the author's surname and (in brackets) the year of publication, and should include a page number for a quote. At times the author's surname, the year of publication and the page number are all in the brackets. For example:

> Bernard Moitessier (1975, 4) describes sailboats as living creatures.

> or

> Sailboats are sometimes described as living creatures (Moitessier 1975, 4).

Note that there is a comma between the year and the page number. Many styles, including Chicago, use very limited punctuation (Moitessier 1975, 4). Some styles use 'p.' before the page number (or 'pp.' where several pages are involved).

The details involved in citations using the author–date system vary depending, for example, on whether the Chicago or American Psychological Association (APA) or Modern Language Association of America (MLA) style is employed. The following list (in Chicago style) is not meant to be exhaustive.

- Use only the author's surname in a textual reference, unless initials are needed to distinguish two authors with the same surname:

    > The theory was first propounded in 1970 (Larsen, A.E. 1971), but since then has been refuted; M.K. Larsen (1983) is among those most energetic in their opposition.

- If you refer to more than one publication in a year by the same author, distinguish them with a letter after the year:

    > 1978a and 1978b

- If you cite more than one author in the same sentence, present them in either of the following ways:

    > According to these two authors (Moitessier 1975; Letcher 1974), . . .

or

According to Moitessier (1975) and Letcher (1974) . . .

- If a work has two authors, use either of the following formats:

  As the authors (Pardey and Pardey 1979) argue in their book . . .

  or

  Pardey and Pardey (1979) argue that . . .

- If a work has more than two authors, some styles use the abbreviation et al. after the first author's name in the citation in the text. Chicago requires all authors' names to be given for up to and including three authors, for example: (Lester, Brown, and Withers 1987, 26). For four or more authors, only the surname of the first listed author is used, followed either by 'and others' or more commonly 'et al.', for example: (Forman et al. 1987, 62–63). In Chicago 'et al.' is not italicised.

  Adamson et al. (1988, 236) contend that leadership cannot be eliminated entirely but will become 'covert'.

- In the reference list at the end of the assignment, give names of all authors with initials or full names.

  Adamson, Nancy, Linda Briskin and Margaret McPhail. 1988. *Feminists Organizing for Change: The Contemporary Women's Movement in Canada.* Toronto: Oxford University Press.

- For works with no publication date, follow the author's name with (n.d.).

  Johnson (n.d.) has suggested . . .

- For works with no author, cite the title in the text and in the reference list.

  . . . as stated in Phillip's report (*The Voyage of Governor Phillip to Botany Bay,* 1790).

Footnotes

Footnotes allow for more information on the same page about your source than is possible in a textual reference. As well as being used to acknowledge a source in detail, a footnote may comment on or support what you have written in the main text.[1] Footnotes appear on the same page as the reference. A number follows the quotation or paraphrase you are referencing and is repeated at the foot of the page.[2] Footnotes

---

1   Lengthy footnotes suggest that your essay has not been planned with sufficient care, and they break the flow of the text for your reader. In such cases, ask yourself if the footnote information is really necessary. If it is, consider whether the information should be incorporated into the assignment or placed as an appendix to the text.

2   The quotation or paraphrase may be a word or phrase, a sentence or a paragraph.

may be numbered consecutively throughout the text or numbered separately for each page, section or chapter.

The first time you acknowledge a particular book in a footnote, give whichever of the following details are applicable so that your readers can locate the work if they want to. The order of these details may vary according to the referencing style adopted. In the examples below the Chicago style is used; but note that within this style, footnote referencing differs significantly from author–date referencing (discussed earlier in this chapter), and as a general rule the two referencing styles should not be mixed in an assignment. See below for details on footnote referencing:

— author/editor's name (surname last)

— title of the book (generally italicised, but may be underlined or capitalised)

— translator/illustrator/reviser's name

— publication details (edition, place, publisher, year), and

— page reference.

For example:

> Francis Chichester, *Gipsy Moth Circles the World* (London: Hodder & Stoughton, 1967), 67.

For immediately consecutive footnotes referring to the same source, in the second or subsequent footnotes use the author's surname, the book title and the new page numbers. For example:

> 1. David Lewis, *Children of Three Oceans* (London: Collins, 1969), 60.
> 2. Lewis, *Children of Three Oceans*, 66.

If there is more than one item by the same author, give the author's name in each case and follow it with the year, title and page numbers of the individual item.

If there is more than one author with the same surname, also give initials and (depending on the style) possibly first names.

Endnotes

These serve the same purposes as footnotes, and are used more often. If too much space would be taken up in your text with numerous, lengthy or complicated footnotes, use endnotes. They are simpler to lay out in the final draft of an assignment. However, as with footnotes, if you have too many endnotes in relation to the length of your assignment, consider whether the assignment is adequately planned.

When compiling endnotes, all reference notes that would have appeared as footnotes are collected at the end of your assignment. Number these references consecutively throughout your text and apply the same rules of abbreviation to them as to footnotes. Your word processing software can deal with footnotes or endnotes and change between them.

It is useful for your reader if endnotes can be placed on a separate page and detached from your text for easier reference, and if they are headed 'Endnotes' to distinguish them instantly from a bibliography or reference list.

Refer to Table 16.1 for abbreviations and contractions that you may need in your referencing.

Reference lists and bibliographies

> . . . the vastness of the subject and the limitations of the author, would make such a list, gathered under the prestigious title of 'Bibliography', seem both mysteriously erratic and hopelessly incomplete.   ALBERTO MANGUEL

Some of the sources that you rely on for an assignment you will actually refer to in your work, and some will remain as 'background' sources.

Reference lists

You must include a reference list for all assignments, whether written, oral or multimedia, to provide full details of the works to which you refer in your text. Only include in your list the sources to which you have actually referred; and give all the details that a reader would need to find such an item easily. In the author–date system, a reference list is arranged alphabetically according to the authors' surnames.

Bibliographies

If you are required to provide a *simple bibliography*, this enables you to provide a complete or selected list of the significant sources you consulted in preparation for writing the assignment but which you have not actually cited in your assignment. (Avoid any temptation to pad this list out—your teachers can easily identify when you do this.)

An *extensive bibliography* is a self-contained work that gives a complete list of items on a topic.

At times you may be asked to provide an *annotated bibliography* of all sources used, including those to which you have referred in your text. In this case you provide brief commentaries on your sources.

How to present a reference list and bibliography

The initial step in getting this right is to check in your unit materials and with the person who will assess your work, first, which referencing conventions you are expected to follow; and second, if there is any specific software you are expected to use to do this. The following points outline general principles in referencing, but they are only general guidelines and are presented in Chicago style.

TABLE
16.1   **Abbreviations and contractions**

app.	— appendix
bk, bks	— book(s)
©	— copyright
c. (*circa*)	— about a certain date [as in 'c. 1901']
ch., chs (or chap., chaps)	— chapter(s)
col., cols	— column(s)
diss.	— dissertation
ed., eds	— editor(s)
edn (or ed.)	— edition
et al. (*et alii*)	— 'and others' [used when a book has several authors as in 'P. March et al.']
et seq. (et sequentes)	— 'and following' [as in 'pp. 64 et seq.']
f., ff.	— 'and the following' [to refer to page numbers as in 'pp. 30 ff.']
facsim.	— facsimile [i.e. an exact copy of writing, printing, picture]
fol., fols	— folio(s)
front.	— frontispiece
ibid. (*ibidem*)	— 'in the same work' [as previously cited]
ill., ills	— illustrator(s)
loc. cit. (*loco citato*)	— 'in the same place (already) cited' [i.e. in the same passage referred to in a recent reference note]
ms., mss	— manuscript(s)
n., nn.	— note(s) [as 'p. 56, n. 3' or 'p. 56n.']
n.d.	— no date [of publication]
n.p.	— no place [of publication]
op. cit. (*opere citato*)	— in the work [recently] cited
p., pp.	— page(s)
passim	— 'throughout the work' [rather than on specific pages]
q.v., qq.v. (*quod vide*)	— 'which see' [used in cross-referencing]
rev.	— revised [by], reviser
[*sic*]	— 'thus' [to guarantee exact quotation when the reader might doubt this]
trans., tr.	— translator, -ion, -ed
v., vv.	— verse(s)
viz. (*videlicet*)	— 'namely', 'in other words' [usually after words or statements about to be elaborated]
vol., vols	— volume(s)

Book entry

The basic format for a book entry is:

— author or editor's name (surname first, followed by first name or initials)

— year of publication

— title (generally italicised, but may be underlined or capitalised)

— translator, illustrator or reviser's name, and

— publication details (place of publication and name of publisher).

For example:

Colgate, Stephen. 1978. *Fundamentals of Sailing, Cruising and Racing.* New York: W. W. Norton & Company.

Article, chapter or anthology item

The basic format for these entries is:

— author or editor's name (surname first, followed by first name or initials)

— year of publication

— title of article, chapter or item, possibly enclosed by inverted commas

— author or editor of the book in which the chapter or item is found

— title (underlined or italicised) of the periodical, book, anthology or newspaper from which the item was taken

— publication details of periodical or book (include publication details for overseas periodicals), and

— page numbers of article, chapter or item.

For example:

Burke, K. M. 1979. 'A Dream in Ice and Snow.' *Cruising World* 5(1): 60–63.

Additional points

● Publication details are as follows:

— periodical: volume number, issue number (if pages are numbered afresh for each issue), date.

— book: edition (if not the first edition), place, publisher, date.

● If there is more than one entry for an author, list in chronological order of publication.

● Bibliography entries may be classified into groups according to topic or the nature of the material. For example:

— 'Primary sources' and 'Secondary sources'

— 'Books' and 'Articles', and

— 'Items from newspapers' and 'Personal conversations'.

16

- The heading of a bibliography should indicate its scope; for example, 'Selected bibliography', 'Brief annotated bibliography' or 'A general bibliography'.

The finishing touches

You are expected to present your work clearly and to use correct grammar, spelling and punctuation in assignments and reports. If you are uncertain about the conventions you are expected to follow in these matters, check with a teacher and with referencing guides.

Grammar, spelling and punctuation

'He has got no good red blood in his body,' said Sir James.

'No. Somebody put a drop under a magnifying-glass, and it was all semi-colons and parentheses,' said Mrs. Cadwallader.   GEORGE ELIOT

A sound knowledge of grammar helps you write more fluently and is an important part of the writer's craft. Your ideas have less impact if your grammar, spelling and punctuation are poor, since your reader frequently has to re-read what you have written to clarify what you meant to say.

To improve these skills, consult books and ask for help from other people. You may have to learn by heart the correct forms and usages, but if you can discover underlying reasons for a particular rule you remember the correct version more easily. Read your work aloud to yourself (possibly into a voice recorder) and check the grammar and punctuation of any sections which don't flow smoothly. Use the spelling and grammar checking tools on your software; and develop your own electronic dictionary, especially if you have a learning disability which results in repeated spelling errors. If English is not your first language and you have trouble with grammar and punctuation, seek help from a language adviser.

I struggle through the alphabet as if it had been a bramble bush; getting considerably worried and scratched by every letter.   CHARLES DICKENS

Presentation

Whether you are submitting your assignments in hard copy or online, the purpose of presenting work clearly is to help your reader. Assignments are rarely handwritten as you are expected to use a computer to type them, and increasingly you are required to submit them electronically.

- Keep an electronic or hard copy as a backup for the rare occasion when your reader happens to lose your assignment.
- Do not overcrowd each page. Use more than single spacing. Leave margins on both sides and at the top and bottom. A wide left-hand margin (at least 2.5 cm) enables your reader to write full and detailed comments. Often a unit guide will specify requirements such as these.

- For easy identification, provide a cover sheet giving your name, the assignment title, unit, teacher's name, date on which the assignment is due and the date of submission. Some schools or departments have their own cover sheet template you are expected to use. The cover sheet may also include an abstract or synopsis (see 'Report sections', Chapter 15).

- Number the pages.

- To help your reader understand the structure of a long assignment you may decide to provide a contents page. This could be accompanied by a list of any diagrams, graphs or appendices. Check if headings are permissible, or perhaps required, within the assignment.

- If you submit your work in hard copy, write or type on only one side of the paper, particularly if you write in ink or on lightweight paper. However, as this is environmentally wasteful, if you want to save paper explain this to your teacher, but follow unit instructions. Secure all pages firmly together. Any appendices to which the reader will refer frequently should be detachable (for example, endnotes or tables of results).

- If handwriting your assignment, write clearly in ink, and take care with details such as dotting the 'i's accurately or forming the 'r's clearly as these make your writing surprisingly easier to read. Legible writing saves your reader from eye strain and irritation. If your handwriting is atrocious or if you have physical difficulties with writing, persuade a friend or a proficient typist to type your assignments for you, or learn to type yourself.

- Be judicious in your use of headers or footers. For example, while it is a good idea to include your name on each page don't repeat the essay topic or date page after page.

No publication, whatever its nature, should be expected to follow slavishly any set of rules—by whomsoever prescribed—if to do so would have an adverse effect on the text as a whole. What counts above all is consistency of approach and treatment; and for that reason, discretion, sensitivity and sheer common sense should always prevail in writing and editing.   AUSTRALIAN GOVERNMENT PUBLICATION SERVICE

Use conventions to help you say what you want to as lucidly as possible. Particularly in early drafts, don't worry about the correct form of academic conventions so much that they prevent you from expressing your ideas effectively. Become familiar with the basic conventions and their purposes, check which forms to follow for a particular piece of work, and then rely on your common sense to convey what you want to say to a reader. If you have trouble with using any convention, seek advice and work at overcoming your difficulties. At the start of your studies, putting in some solid groundwork so that you understand how to appropriately acknowledge sources will set you up well for the remainder of your academic pursuits.

On the one hand, learning to use academic conventions may seem tedious and pedantic. On the other hand, these conventions assist communication; and paying attention to them helps you understand more about the nuances of scholarship in the university culture, and how the conventions are used in academic dialogue or controversies.

TEN TIPS

1   Keeping in mind *why* referencing is used helps you to understand how to reference correctly.
2   Think about the details you need to provide so that your reader can quickly locate a quote, paraphrase, summary or reference in the original source.
3   Whichever format you use for quoting and referencing, be consistent and accurate.
4   Limit the number of long quotations you use, and only use them if you are going to draw on their content in your assignment.
5   As well as following any unit requirements for quoting and referencing, check with your tutor about their personal preferences since it is likely they will assess your work.
6   Check that you are clear on the difference between paraphrasing and plagiarism, and between collaboration and collusion.
7   Find out how software which detects plagiarism can help you reference correctly.
8   Check if a unit requires you to use particular software for referencing.
9   When you are new to academic referencing conventions, taking an online or face-to-face workshop on these can be very helpful.
10 If you are uncertain about punctuation, such as when to use a comma or full stop, read your work aloud and notice where you need to pause to make it easier for your reader to follow what you write.

REFERENCES

Coleridge. Ernest Hartley, ed. 1912. *The Poems of Samuel Taylor Coleridge*. London: Oxford University Press.

Lear, Edward. 1943. *Nonsense Omnibus*. London: Frederick Warne & Company.

Letcher, John S. Jr. 1974. *Self Steering for Sailing Craft*. Camden, ME: International Marine Publishing Company.

Moitessier, Bernard. 1971. *Sailing to the Reefs*. Translated by Rene Hague. London: Hollis & Carter.

Moitessier, Bernard. 1975. *The Long Way*. Translated by William Rodamor. London: Granada.

Pardey, Lin and Larry Pardey. 1979. *Seraffyn's European Adventure*. New York: W. W. Norton & Company.

Learning from evaluation

17

> . . . the process of evaluation [is like using] a small
> torch to glimpse what sort of animal might be in front
> of you in a huge, dark cave. In this metaphor, the
> cave is the process being investigated, and the torch is
> the evaluation. The cave is large and complex, and
> the torch beam is narrow and weak; each evaluative
> question is equivalent to pointing the torch in a
> particular direction, to see what is there and what
> walks into the light.
>
> STEPHEN C. EHRMANN

If you want to learn to speak Spanish, you learn more quickly if you live in a Spanish-speaking country. You can evaluate your pronunciation constantly by comparing it with what you hear, and you receive instant feedback when you practise your new language skills. In informal online forums, if you want to play a more effective role you need frequent practice in contributing appropriately and in carefully reading other people's posts. At the same time, you need to reflect on your strengths and weaknesses as a group member, and how to improve. You can then evaluate your participation and make better use of any feedback you receive from other people in the group.

In both these instances of informal self-directed learning, reflection, self-evaluation and feedback from others are fundamental to your learning. Your own evaluation inevitably involves checking your pronunciation against that of a native speaker, or comparing your online participation with that of a group member whose participation you admire. These comparisons can provide criteria against which you judge the standard of your development. On the basis of why and what you want to learn, you appraise your learning so that your strengths and weaknesses emerge more clearly, and perhaps you then re-adjust your aims accordingly. You may discover, for example, that you want to learn more colloquial Spanish so that you can take part in day-to-day conversations, or you may decide that in online discussions you need to respond in more depth to other people's posts. These discoveries provide you with more refined criteria for reflecting on and evaluating what you learn—and so the learning process continues.

When it comes to formal learning, consider for a moment how you would prefer your learning to be evaluated. For example, if you had a choice, how would you like your knowledge of an assignment topic to be formally assessed?

○○○ *Would I submit my written work, other people's comments on my work and/or my own evaluation?*

What type of evidence might adequately demonstrate what I have learned?

Would I prefer to discuss what I know with the people assessing me, or to take an exam?

What particular aspects of my learning would I want tested?

Who do I think could best evaluate my learning?

Answering these questions involves thinking about your reasons for learning. These reflections might lead you to ask whether you wanted or needed someone else to assess your knowledge at all, and to ask 'What are the purposes of evaluation?'

Why evaluation?

Your aims

One explicit purpose attributed to formal evaluation is to further your learning—to help you progress towards your overall goals and your learning aims (see 'Why remember?', Chapter 5). Being able to ask for and actively use evaluation requires you to reflect on your aims for undertaking a unit or an assignment. Think about why you want to learn, and ask yourself what, how and when you want to learn. These questions are often too complex to answer fully, but unless you are willing only to follow the objectives other people set for you, you need to consider the questions seriously. Your aims will inevitably evolve during your learning, so reformulate them as this happens. If your aims are clear, you can use them to develop your own criteria by which to evaluate whether, what and how well you are learning.

You are likely to modify your knowledge, skills or behaviour according to the evaluation you receive when you communicate and demonstrate what you have learned. These modifications may be slight, for instance when you learn how to pronounce a word more accurately; or they may be a new cornerstone in your learning, for instance if you gain a significant new insight into how people behave in online groups. The evaluation you have received then becomes an integral part of learning according to your aims. (This contrasts, for example, with a multiple choice exam at the end of a unit which judges your knowledge according to others' objectives and from which you gain no feedback.)

However, sometimes you don't have enough knowledge and experience to make use of the information in the response you receive, and at other times you reject feedback because it 'feels wrong' or doesn't fit with your world view or knowledge.

Other people's objectives

A schoolgirl answered the question 'In what countries are elephants found?'

'Elephants are very large and intelligent animals, and are seldom lost.'   JAMES AGATE

An explicit purpose of formal evaluation is demonstrating and proving your knowledge to satisfy other people's learning objectives (see Table 3.1, 'Learning outcomes and objectives'). These people are the teachers who directly assess your work, and unit coordinators who develop a curriculum, prepare the unit guide and set the assessment tasks. Like you, teachers often develop new objectives as a course or unit progresses, perhaps as implicit aims become obvious, or in response to the particular group of students taking the unit. As new objectives emerge the teacher should discuss these with you.

Formal assessment is often used to judge if you are ready to move on to more complex material. This occurs in subjects that teach a sequence of skills, where a thorough knowledge of the preliminary steps is necessary to cope with more demanding ones, or when understanding of basic concepts is essential before moving to more complex ones. For example, unless you can demonstrate an elementary grasp of a language you are usually not permitted to move to more advanced units. One purpose of continuous assessment is to judge your readiness for the next stage within a unit.

> . . . reading, unlike dancing, is not a muscular act, and it is a serious mistake to treat it like one. The dance master must stretch and strengthen the student's muscles so that the student may make the next movement, and without injury. But one cannot injure oneself with a difficult thought.   JOHN HOLT

Who evaluates your learning?

It is much more difficult to judge oneself than to judge others.   A. DE SAINT-EXUPÈRY

Teachers often say: 'Assessment drives learning. If you want students to learn something it has to be part of the assessment, and the weight or percentage of the assessment task will influence how much time and effort students will put into it.' In effect, teachers are saying that students are only motivated to learn what is assessed. This does not take into account a student's own long-term goals and short-term study aims (see 'Focusing on your goals and aims', Chapter 3).

○○○ *Do I mostly learn material that is connected to the continuous or final assessment?*

Do I have my own aims for each of the units and assignments I undertake?

What are my goals for the course of study in which I am enrolled?

You should be the first person to evaluate your work. Make this more than a passing thought or a casual comment to a friend. Take time to reflect. Check what you have learned against your aims and against the outcomes set for a course, unit or assignment. If when you hand in an assignment you also submit a brief written self-evaluation of the assignment, your teacher is better able to provide you with comments to help further your learning.

A peer group, such as a discussion or study group to which you belong, can give you feedback on work such as an essay plan or a seminar presentation (see 'Share your writing', Chapter 13). The group may formally assess some or all of your work. This alternative to teacher-only feedback and assessment requires thorough planning to work well, but students in groups that undertake this collective responsibility can gain from their involvement in each other's learning. When you feel ready to have your biases and assumptions challenged, you might actively seek comments from a group with a range of backgrounds and a diversity of abilities, knowledge and ideas.

An adviser whom you seek out as your sounding board can provide help ranging from correcting spelling errors to giving a detailed critique of a major assignment. This person might be a learning skills adviser, a language adviser, a member of an online study group, a student who has previously taken the unit, a friend or a sympathetic teacher. Ideally, the person who comments on your writing and work should be someone whose expertise you respect and/or you find stimulating as a thinker, and someone who is easily accessible. Perhaps they have particular expertise that you value, such as proofreading or advising on grammar and punctuation.

Your teachers are usually responsible for formally assessing your work, sometimes in collaboration with you or other teaching staff. The amount of informal feedback teachers provide varies according to their teaching styles—and to your willingness to ask for comments.

> I wrote my name at the top of the page. I wrote down the number of the question '1'. After much reflection, I put a bracket around it thus '(1)'. But thereafter I could not think of anything connected with it that was either relevant or true. . . . It was from these slender indications of scholarship that Mr Welldon drew the conclusion that I was worthy to pass into Harrow. It is very much to his credit.   WINSTON CHURCHILL

At times your class teacher may not be available, or they may give you little or no feedback on your work. In these situations make an appointment or send an email indicating politely the time frame in which a reply would be useful to you, and ask for comments on particular aspects of your work (see 'Approaching teachers', Chapter 3).

If your attempts don't change the situation, find another person (or group of people) with whom you can discuss your learning. As your teacher is the person who formally assesses your work, you need to be prepared to approach her or him if you want to discuss or question an assessment you receive.

How is your learning evaluated?

Your own evaluation

> Self-assessment is essential for progress as a learner: for understanding of selves as learners, for an increasingly complex understanding of tasks and learning goals, and for strategic knowledge of how to go about improving.   D. R. SADLER

Reflecting on your learning, and then preparing your own written evaluation of this, provides a perspective on what you have contributed to and what you have gained from a course, unit or assessment item. In a self-evaluation for a particular subject or piece of work, you may comment on your aims, your informal learning, the relationship between your formal and informal learning, your approach to studying, and the relevance of other work or units.

Self-evaluations can vary in length from a couple of paragraphs about a specific assignment, to several pages about a unit, or to three months of diary or blog entries reflecting on your tertiary study. The guidelines in Table 17.1 were used by students writing self-evaluations for a half-hour discussion with their teacher at the end of a unit. They may suggest some ideas for assessing your own learning.

TABLE 17.1   A self-evaluation

Imagine you are writing for someone you will meet in the future. This unknown person wants to know about you and your work during the unit.

- What were my goals and objectives when I started the unit?
- How effectively did I achieve them?
- What strengths did I feel I possessed?
- What were my weaknesses?
- How did I apply my strengths?
- How did I try to overcome my weaknesses?
- What work did I accomplish in quality and quantity (for example, in assignments or for tutorials)?
- How much recommended reading did I do for the unit and for tutorials?
- What reading did I do beyond recommended readings (author, title and any comments)?
- What ideas came from my 'outside' reading, and how did they relate to the unit?
- What do I feel I learned:
  — about tutorials
  — about university
  — about myself
  — about improving my ability to learn, and
  — about directions I want to pursue in future learning?

A self-evaluation should not be only a compilation of your real or imagined shortcomings, or a prosaic listing of the number of books read and lectures attended. Write about your strengths as well as your weaknesses. Evaluate your learning so that if you read the evaluation again in a couple of years' time it would tell you about this one aspect of yourself. Your evaluation is not a formal unit assignment to be judged, and will be next to worthless if you are not honest with and about yourself.

Peer evaluation

Peers have an important role to play in all our lives, be it in kindergarten, university, workplace or social club. Through interaction, we learn and develop . . . peer involvement in assessment during formal education has the potential to encourage learning and develop assessment skills that will last a lifetime.   NANCY FALCHIKOV

In your informal learning, whenever you ask a friend to comment on or give you feedback on such learning you are involved in peer evaluation. In fact, throughout our lives and in a wide range of contexts peers assess our work and learning; so peer assessment is viewed by some educators as essential for developing a skill transferable to everyday life.

In your formal education, peer assessment occurs when another student either provides feedback on or assesses your work. Peers can contribute to assessing a wide range of academic work including written assignments, oral presentations, and portfolios, and may do this in pairs or groups, possibly on a reciprocal basis. Informally evaluating another student's work can give you valuable insights into how to go about formal peer assessment.

If a friend asks for helpful comments on an essay, there are several ways you might respond. You could respond with the first thoughts that come into your head. You might provide detailed written feedback, confine yourself to a few pithy statements at the end of the essay, or discuss your comments with your friend. If you do discuss your comments, you will probably modify some of your feedback as you come to understand more clearly what your friend was trying to achieve. And if you don't already realise it, you will soon come to know that your feedback is subjective—it comes from your preferences and beliefs which arise from your knowledge and experiences of learning. For example, do you believe that you know what constitutes a 'good' essay? If you judge your friend's work according to criteria that are based on a particular model of an academic essay, you need to explain this model and the criteria so that your friend can accept or reject them. Your feedback, both your praise and criticisms, will be more useful if you make it clear that you are giving your personal reaction to the work.

Imagine what you would do in one of the following situations and discuss it with friends if you can:

- *You have spent two weeks carefully preparing and writing an assignment. When it is returned, you skim through the pages and find the only comment on the final page is 'Pass, Satisfactory work'. How might one of your peers provide comments on your work that help explain this grade?*

- *If asked to contribute to the formal assessment of another student's scientific report, on what might you base your assessment?*

Teachers' evaluations

> When the cook tastes the soup, that's formative; when the guests taste the soup, that's summative.   R. STAKE

Your teacher may give you feedback during a unit to help you improve (formative assessment), or give you an assessment that will contribute to your final grade (summative assessment). Feedback may be officially recorded, or informal and unrecorded.

Formative evaluation

Formative evaluation can be used to assess your progress, identify your learning needs, give you direction and shape your learning. The person giving you such feedback should give constructive comments on both the strengths and the weaknesses of your work in relation to the outcomes you are expected to demonstrate and against set criteria. In addition, if you want feedback on a particular aspect of your work, ask for it. While your teacher is usually the person who provides formative feedback, give some thought to who else might usefully do so, for example, a study skills adviser.

What form might feedback and comments take?

Ideally, this depends mostly on your needs. The comments might be written or oral; they might be given ad hoc, or structured according to a specific situation or specific criteria. They might be given when an assignment is returned to you, or be part of a required individual consultation with your teacher at the end of a unit. At times a teacher will give feedback to the whole class as part of a general discussion and not give it to you specifically. In online units you might receive feedback via email, perhaps when working on the draft of an assignment.

Formative feedback needs to be given in a way you understand. For example, if you ask for an idea to be clarified, you need an explanation which gives you more information but doesn't overwhelm you with detail; or if you have used a word inaccurately, you need to see it in different contexts so that you understand its correct meaning. However, if you repeatedly make the same error, don't expect the person marking your work to correct every error. They are likely to correct the first few, highlight the next few, and then leave it to you to identify further examples and any other similar errors you make.

Formative feedback is most useful if given immediately or when you want it. For example:

— if you have feedback from the first essay in a unit to refer to when writing the second essay

— if you receive the results of a diagnostic test that indicates your preparedness for the next phase of learning

— if a teacher gives you useful hints when you are attempting to remember the proof of a theorem, or

— if your peers comment on and discuss a seminar paper immediately after you deliver it.

Summative assessment

For most of the students, the competitive grade has come to be the essence. The naive teacher points to the beauty of the subject and the ingenuity of the research; the shrewd student asks if he is responsible for that on the final exam.   PAUL GOODMAN

Summative assessment may include formal structured comments, but more usually it consists of a letter/number grade, a percentage or a pass/fail mark. It may be based on continuous assessment and/or on a major final paper or exam. 'Continuous assessment' refers to frequent cumulative assessments of your learning by methods such as weekly laboratory reports, regular seminar papers, quizzes, monthly assignments, or a combination of these. It may be used on its own or in combination with a major final assessment.

Educators debate the value of both forms of assessment. For example, if your work is assessed only or mostly at the end of a unit, you may receive little feedback on your learning during a unit, so you have no formal indication of your progress until the end, and it is difficult to convey your total understanding of a subject in one final assessment. On the other hand, continuous assessment means that you are rarely free from assessment tasks which means that you can feel continually under pressure and have little time for serendipitous learning.

The effect of grades and percentages on students' learning is controversial. Grades and percentages enable student performances to be ranked, which can help future employers to quickly judge prospective employees. Good grades are certainly important when applying for a postgraduate place. However, grading creates pressures that can hinder your learning, and at least some aspects of student learning which are difficult to measure cannot be graded, for example, the development of attitudes such as being open to different opinions (see 'Developing skills and attitudes', Chapter 3).

Criteria and standards

For each course, unit or assignment, you need to know:

— the specific criteria on which you will be assessed, based on the outcomes you are expected to demonstrate, and

— the standard you are expected to reach to pass or achieve a particular grade or percentage.

Criteria

Your learning should be assessed according to explicit criteria which reflect the stated learning outcomes (see Table 3.1, 'Learning outcomes and objectives'). For example, if you are expected to demonstrate knowledge about a particular topic, the criteria should specify which knowledge and the depth and breadth needed. If the outcome is to demonstrate the ability to write an argumentative essay, this specific skill needs to be defined in detail and specify items such as outlining the thesis in the introduction, integrating research, and summarising the argument in the conclusion. When assessing your essay, the teacher can then judge the standard of your work according to these criteria, which are often included in unit materials as marking or assessment guides. Read these guides very carefully; clarify what they mean; and check that your work attempts to meet the standard required.

The criteria used for an assessment task may be explicitly set out, widely accepted and clearly defined in the unit materials and in an individual teacher's mind, but this doesn't make the use of these criteria objective. In practice, a teacher adopts some of the cultural and discipline-based guidelines used for assessing learning in a subject, and combines them with a personal preference for certain academic conventions. And when applying these criteria to your work, the final result is partly based on the teacher's subjective judgement. All students are familiar with the game of trying to uncover the subjective approaches that each teacher brings to assessment.

> After some years it began to happen that I would find myself in the middle of writing a comment and begin to wonder whether it could really be trusted, whether it was really useful . . . If I were in a different mood or the paper were in a different place in the stack, perhaps I wouldn't have made the comment I did.   PETER ELBOW

It is impossible for humans to be totally objective, yet when teachers make decisions about the methods, criteria and standards of assessment they may assume that they are being objective. In practice their decisions are based on an array of beliefs and assumptions about the nature of education, of university, of knowledge and of students.

The criteria by which your learning is assessed may appear to be objective, because it is part of a system of percentages, exams and 'weighted averages', 'full-time equivalent students' and confidential files. How else, it is argued by some, will a teacher, an employment agency or postgraduate selection panel know the 'excellent' students unless students have top marks or grades on an official record, or unless a student has produced a thesis on an acceptable topic? As a student you can appeal against an assessment if you believe it demonstrates that you have achieved the learning outcomes and if it meets the set criteria but this has not been recognised by the teacher. Find out what is required to lodge an appeal if you believe your work has not been accurately graded.

> Objectivity, in short, has the logical status of a myth: it builds up one sense of reality rather than others . . .   MICHAEL NOVAK

Some teachers acknowledge and attempt to spell out the assumptions, criteria, biases and beliefs by which they evaluate your learning. They don't assume that a practice which has 'always' been carried out, or which is used 'everywhere else' or is 'efficient' is necessarily the best system. These teachers will usually give you the opportunity to negotiate decisions about the assessment of your work if you have valid reasons, understand the set outcomes and criteria expected, and if you are clear about your learning aims.

Standards

Each university has descriptors which explain what each assessment grade means (such as a C grade or a Distinction), and these descriptors are applied to all assignments and across all areas of the university. It is important that you understand what each grade means, and how it is interpreted in your particular discipline and depending on the extent of your tertiary education. If you are unclear about this, check your unit materials and ask your teacher to explain. Note that it is common in first year units to receive a result such as a 'Credit' or 'Satisfactory' even if in secondary school you received high marks.

Your assignment may be graded according to criteria such as the selection of content, use of quotations and general writing style. If the result is recorded by a single letter grade (for example), the letter you are given does not tell you how well you have done on each criteria. Neither does it indicate how your teacher averaged or added up your performance for each criteria to arrive at a single grade. To learn from assessment it is vital that you know explicitly why your teacher chose that particular letter grade; what the grade means; and how the grade relates to the criteria on which you were assessed. If summative assessment is to be useful to you, it needs to be accompanied by detailed comments. Ideally, the recorded assessments you receive are formalities which follow on from the comments on your work.

In addition to applying specified standards to your work, when a teacher assesses your learning they can also be influenced by:

— your previous knowledge or work in an area

— the work of other students on a topic or subject area

— whether or not you have achieved the stated learning outcomes for the unit or assessment item

— specific standards determined by one or more of the teachers who developed a unit or set the assessment task

— the educational/cultural models and preferences of an individual teacher who directly assesses your work, and

— the requirements of professional organisations.

Decisions about the criteria and standards used to evaluate learning are made by unit coordinators, individual teachers, groups of teachers, administrators, other educational institutions or—at a fundamental level—society in general. There are, for example, academic and administrative committees within a university, professional bodies and prospective employers, all of which play a role in determining what should be taught and the standards of that assessment. An individual teacher will judge whether your work meets the criteria and the standard expected that may lead to you becoming a doctor; but that teacher is mostly making that decision on behalf of stakeholders, including a professional medical association that sets down standards for doctors, patients who expect certain skills in doctors, and government bodies that make decisions about the number of doctors needed.

Administrative requirements

As well as the academic standards by which your work is judged, the assessment of your work is shaped by administrative requirements. These may include university policies that demand a proportion of the assessment of all units be supervised (such as in an examination) or for assessment methods that require minimum staff time or results that can be recorded in a particular computer format. The methods may reflect a desire to conform to practices in other institutions, or the implicit expectations of employers and professional organisations.

When, or even before, you enrol in a unit you need to know:

— what work you are expected to complete for assessment, and when

— whether you must pass each assessment item in a unit (or each unit in a program) or whether you can fail one or two of the individual assignments/units and still gain an overall pass

— whether results are given as a Pass/Fail, a grade, a percentage and/or as comments

— whether the person who will assess your work is your tutor or lecturer or someone you don't know

— the degree of choice you have in the four previous points

— any academic requirements, such as those pertaining to correct referencing (see 'Academic integrity', Chapter 16) and assignment submission

— whether you are able or expected to contribute to the assessment of your work

— whether and how you can appeal against or record a dissent from an assessment in your official file, and

— protocols about the time frame for returning work to students.

When a formal assessment item is due your teacher should have set aside time to give feedback on and assess the work submitted by each member of the class; your responsibility is to hand the work in on time. Most units have requirements about the time frame for returning work to students. If your work hasn't been returned by this time, ask when you can expect it back. It is particularly important to receive comments in time if you need feedback to proceed with your next assignment.

A learning portfolio

During your formal education, you might choose to build a learning portfolio either in a traditional form or as an e-portfolio. What you collect into your portfolio can give you a sense of your learning development as an independent learner, and it can become a central repository from which to choose material when applying for a future job or trying to gain entry to further study.

What might you include in a learning portfolio?

● Items you have written about yourself as a learner—your overall goals and study aims, your questions, your enthusiasms (see 'Learning journals or logs', Chapter 13). Your self-evaluations (see Table 17.1) are an important part of this.

e-portfolios

An electronic portfolio is a web-based collection of evidence of your knowledge and skills, your learning achievements, and reflections on your learning. E-portfolios differ from traditional portfolios in that you can include written, audio, video and photographic material, and you can provide links which present more detailed information on particular parts. In your e-portfolio you can include:

— documents such as your CV

— written appraisals of your work

— examples of your best work

— links to websites, audio or video files, and

— a blog.

Ensure your e-portfolio is password protected so that you decide who can evaluate it, for how long and which sections they can view. In the structured environment of the classroom, when an e-portfolio forms part of the assessment, only your teacher or other students in your group might have access. When applying for a postgraduate place or a job, access can be provided for members of a selection panel. Some universities use specific e-portfolio software and you may be able to access this for a while beyond graduation.

- Selected pieces of work that demonstrate particular skills or knowledge, along with comments and evaluations by yourself or others.

- Material such as drawings you have completed in response to an idea, items of information you want to follow up, articles which have been particularly significant for you.

- Evaluations of an internship or of a paid job or voluntary work relevant to your learning.

- Your structured reflections on your learning,

His [*sic*] '*noteworthy contribution*' is an essential step demonstrating a student's readiness for a degree. This may be a work of art, a research finding, or a community service. It will be intended to show that the candidate for a degree is more than a consumer of what earlier scholars, creative artists, and social leaders have given to him [*sic*].   UNIVERSITY WITHOUT WALLS

17

TEN TIPS

1   Think creatively about who might best provide feedback on a particular aspect of your work.

2   Before you choose an elective unit, look at the assessment requirements and methods.

3   For each unit or assignment, be clear about the criteria against which you will be assessed and the standard required to achieve a particular grade or percentage.

4   Look carefully at how the formal assessment in a unit relates to the outcomes and objectives set down for the unit.

5   Take advantage of any opportunities for peer assessment and for feedback from other students.

6   Before you submit an assignment, take a few minutes to write your own self-evaluation of its strengths and weaknesses, and then learn from comparing your judgement with that of your teacher.

7   When you are given only a brief comment and a grade or mark for an assignment, it is helpful to follow up and find out how different aspects of your work contributed to the overall result.

8   When your teacher puts time and effort into giving thoughtful written comments on your work, they expect you to read these carefully and apply them in your next assignment.

9   At the end of a unit, take time to write an honest self-evaluation of what you have put into it and what you have learned from it.

10 Give serious consideration to building up a learning portfolio during your formal education.

Appendix

Discrimination: sexist language and attitudes

Discrimination legislation has often been concerned mostly with stereotypes based on sex, sexual preference, disability and race. Other stereotypes commonly perpetuated in our culture relate to a person's age, religion, politics, economic circumstances and occupation. Trying to counter such stereotypes may be dismissed as 'politically correct'. However, in any society some ways of speaking and writing are more powerful than others because they are taken for granted as 'normal'; and we need to reflect on what we consider to be 'common sense' to realise that such language can be hurtful or offensive to the people being labelled. The discourses mocked as 'politically correct', such as 'chairperson' or 'indigenous', by opponents, are part of the attempt by less powerful groups, such as women and Aborigines, to be treated more fairly and courteously.

Using language that depicts people according to stereotypes is undesirable for two reasons:

1   It shows a lack of awareness of our biases and prejudices. We can never be totally objective, and it is essential to our learning and communicating that we are as honest as possible about our particular forms of subjectivity.

2   It reveals insufficient thought and care about what we are communicating. Some manifestations of the shoddy use of language are unsupported generalisations, terms that are not defined clearly, and clichés.

- 'Australians are easy-going.' Does this apply to all, most, many or a few? Has this general statement been supported and explained?

- In 'a neurotic woman' or 'the average Italian', 'neurotic' and 'average' are both terms that have precise meanings in certain disciplines. Has their meaning in the particular context been defined?

- The phrase 'a career woman' is sometimes used to describe a woman seriously interested in her work, or 'a dole bludger' to describe someone who is unemployed. Why have these clichés been used?

In this appendix we look at sexist language and attitudes as an example of discrimination.

Avoiding sexist language

Sexist language is based on stereotypes which assume that being biologically male or female implies a whole range of associated characteristics. Occasionally, it is relevant to describe a woman as petite or a man as solid, or to describe a female person as someone's wife or mother; but all too often adjectives such as these form part of a description in which they are irrelevant.

'Janet Smith, a petite brunette, has just become the first woman truck driver for the company.'

'Henry Jones, a solid ex-footballer, today graduated as a male nurse.'

One useful test for sexist language is to substitute mention of a woman where a man is mentioned and vice versa. Would you write 'Fred Smith, a tall redhead who is married to a typist, was today awarded his second gold medal'? How do you react to reading 'The engineer should at all times protect her clients' interests'?

Pronouns—'he/him/his'?

'He' is commonly used to refer to both females and males; for example, 'The best time to teach a child maths is when he is about two years old'. This convention limits our view of reality. Studies have shown that children literally think of a male when they read or hear the word 'he', and many people who argue for the use of 'he' as a convenient shorthand to include both sexes object to the suggestion that 'she' might serve the same purpose. There are alternatives to using only 'he', 'him' and 'his'. Instead of using sexist language as in: 'This monograph is for a teacher concerned with improving his communication with his students . . . The intention of the authors is to share experiences with a teacher who may find some of them helpful in his own situations.

- Change from singular to plural:
  This monograph is for **teachers** concerned with improving **their** communication with **their** students . . . The intention of the authors is to share experiences with **teachers** who may find some of them helpful in **their** own situations.

- Reword to eliminate unnecessary gender pronouns:
  This monograph is for **a teacher** concerned with improving communication with **students** . . . The intention of the authors is to share experiences so that **a reader** may find some of them helpful in teaching situations.

- Replace the masculine pronoun with 'one' or 'you'. You can also replace the pronoun with 'he or she', 'him or her', 'her or his', or with 'he/she', or 's/he', but these constructions are clumsy and infrequently used.

  This monograph is useful if **you** are a teacher concerned with improving communication with **your** students. The intention of the authors is to share experiences so that **you** may find some of them helpful in **your** teaching situations.

'Man'?

The word 'man' has an ambiguous double usage—to refer to a male person and to describe humanity in general. As with the use of 'he', the word 'man' creates a male image. When we read the words 'man the hunter' we visualise a male adult and forget about the women (and children and elderly people) who are supposedly part of the total picture.

Instead of:	Consider:
• man or mankind	humanity, human beings, people, the human race, men and women
• manpower	human resources, human energy, workers, workforce
• the man in the street	a typical person, the average person, lay person
• man-made	synthetic, artificial, manufactured, constructed
• chairman	chairperson, the chair, leader, coordinator, convenor

Apples are apples and oranges are oranges; but apples and oranges are fruit.

WITHOUT BIAS

'A man's job'? 'Woman's work'?

Our language is based on assumptions, frequently outdated, about the occupations of women and men (for example, nurses are assumed to be female and surgeons male). Women are often categorised primarily as mothers and wives, despite the high proportion of women who are in the paid workforce. We read newspaper headlines such as 'Rebel mum of three suicides in cell' to describe the prison death of a prominent political activist and journalist; or 'Dr Samuel Keep, a leading physician, and his wife Margaret' is used to introduce two doctors who are married. Women should be treated as people in their own right, and women in traditionally masculine fields (or men in traditionally feminine fields) should not be singled out.

Instead of:	Consider:
• 'Anna Clarke, career girl' to describe a woman who takes her work seriously	describing the woman's occupation as 'Anna Clarke, teacher' or 'Anna Clarke, engineer'
• terms such as 'male secretary', 'female executive' or 'woman doctor'	the terms 'secretary', 'executive' or 'doctor' to apply to both men and women
• workmen	worker, labourer, employee or staff member
• author or authoress	author
• waiter or waitress	steward or attendant
• the lady of the house, housewife	the consumer, homemaker, housekeeper
• cleaning lady, cleaning woman	domestic help, cleaner

Names

Different attitudes of men and women are reflected in the inconsistent use of first names and surnames—for example, 'Peter Braithwaite and Miss Smith', 'Braithwaite and Janet Smith'. The use of titles also reveals attitudes—for example, 'Dr White and Alison Black' (instead of 'Dr Black'). One of the most common examples of discrimination by title is that the title 'Mr' refers to both married and single men while the terms 'Mrs' and 'Miss' are used for women, thus assuming that marital status should be an important part of a woman's identity, but not a man's.

Instead of:	Consider:
• Peter Braithwaite and Miss Smith	Mr Braithwaite and Ms Smith, or Peter Braithwaite and Janet Smith
• 'Dr Tom Jones and Ms Margot Thomas recently published a book on marine biology. Margot is now doing further research on this topic. Dr Jones is acting as her assistant.'	'Ms Margot Thomas and Dr Tom Jones recently published a book on marine biology. Ms Thomas is now doing further research on this topic. Dr Jones is acting as her assistant.'

Put-downs

Patronising descriptions of women are unnecessary and are often clichés.

Instead of:	Consider:
• the girls, the ladies, the fair sex, the weaker sex	the women
• the missus, the wife, the little lady, the better half	wife (or refer to the woman concerned by her name)
• chicks, birds, girls	girls (for younger women), women
• femocrats	feminists

- Issues that seriously concern women should not be considered trivial or funny—for example, sharing housework, discrimination in employment, or rape.

- Jokes that are based on stereotypes of both women and men are offensive to many people—for example, jokes about incompetent women drivers, frustrated spinsters, gossiping housewives, men-hating women's libbers, husbands, helpless house-husbands, or effeminate males.

- Referring to 'men and ladies' instead of 'men and women' or 'ladies and gentlemen' is discriminatory.

- Don't always refer to 'men and women' or 'he and she'; use 'women and men' or 'she and he' as well.

- Avoid talking about 'man and wife'; instead use 'partners', 'husband and wife', 'a man and a woman' or 'a couple'.

Identity
'Who's she?' they asked
and straight away
I answered back,
'She's Brian's wife'.
Why say it so?
Why not just say
'She's Josephine'?
A rose by any name
should smell as sweet.
But Josephine's a sweeter name
by far, than
'Brian's wife'
or 'Jenny's mum'
or 'Noelene's friend'. GWEN WESSON

Male and female characteristics

- Instead of assuming that only women can be gentle, compassionate or sensitive, and only men can be decisive, logical, assertive, strong or adventurous, think of these qualities as human rather than sex-based. Similarly, avoid the assumption that only women are passive, helpless or emotional, and only men are insensitive, angry or ruthless.

- Women who don't comply with the stereotype of a passive female and men who don't conform to the image of an aggressive male are often described in a negative way.

Instead of:	Consider:
• a pushy woman	a powerful woman
• a gossiping woman	a talkative woman
• an effeminate man	a gentle man
• an hysterical woman	a woman who is upset
• an aggressive woman	an assertive woman

Avoiding sexist attitudes

Sexist language is a subtly pervasive yet tangible way of perpetuating stereotypes. Sexist attitudes are equally pervasive and subtle. Following are some instances of sexist attitudes that you are likely to find in written material.

- The **'invisible woman'** attitude occurs when women as part of a group of people or society are ignored or rarely included in writings or media products about that group or society. For example:

  —in writings on human evolution, where only hunting societies and the activities of male *homo sapiens* are considered, with little or no reference to the female of the species

- —in gender-blind statistics which give figures for the amount of unpaid domestic work but fail to break these figures down according to gender
- —in medical research which studies conditions common to men and women but conducts research mostly on men, and
- —in movies or video games where women play only token roles.

● The '**token woman**' position is evident when individual women are described because they are unusual but the majority of women are still ignored. This occurs, for example, in history texts which include descriptions of the life of a woman who is prominent as a social reformer (such as Elizabeth Fry) or a pioneer in a traditionally male field (such as Elizabeth Blackwell), but which neglect the 'ordinary' female contemporaries of these women.

● The '**patronised woman**' approach occurs when a special section is allocated to women without a corresponding section for men—for example, a book index that has an entry for 'Women' but not for 'Men'.

● **Stereotypes** of women and men are common. Examples include:

- —anthropology texts which assume that women are wives and mothers and that men are breadwinners, and
- —career information brochures which assume that women are nurses and men are doctors or that females have few serious work interests.

Instances of these attitudes can also be found when discrimination is based on grounds other than sex. For example, the 'invisible' ethnic group; the invisibility of people in poverty; the 'token' black or working-class representative; the patronised handicapped person; stereotypes of homosexuals or elderly people or socialists.

In writing, reading and speaking, being aware of discriminatory attitudes or language in ourselves and in others requires that we question and evaluate what is communicated. The discriminatory thought patterns of many disciplines need to be redressed; but trying to develop new patterns should not just be academic exercises. Such developments involve being aware of the world views we bring to our learning, of how we see other human beings, and of how we might change as individuals. Changing thought patterns can only be achieved with consistent and conscious effort, because our discriminatory attitudes and language are part of our cultural understandings—of who we have learned to be.

Quotation sources

The page number on which the quote appears is provided before the reference in bold.

1 You

1 Eliot, T. S. 1963. 'Little Gidding.' In *Collected Poems 1909–1962*, 222. London: Faber & Faber. Excerpt from 'Little Gidding' from *Four Quartets* by T.S. Eliot. Copyright 1942 by Houghton Mifflin Harcourt Publishing Company; Copyright © renewed by T.S. Eliot. Reprinted by permission of Houghton Mifflin Harcourt Publishing Company. All rights reserved.

3 Luce, Gay Gaer. 1973. *Body Time: The Natural Rhythms of the Body*, 177. St Albans, UK: Paladin.

4 Waugh, Evelyn. 1928. *Decline and Fall*, 143. London: Chapman & Hall.

5 Woolf, Virginia. 1929. *A Room of One's Own*, 18. New York: Harcourt, Brace & World.

5 Olinekova, Gayle. 1982. *Go for It*, 142. New York: Simon & Schuster.

6 Morgan, Fred. 1972. *Here and Now II: An Approach to Writing through Perception*, 3. New York: Harcourt Brace Jovanovich.

7 World Health Organization. 1946. *Preamble to the Constitution of the World Health Organization: Official Records of the World Health Organization (and entered into force on 7 April 1948), no. 2,* 100. New York: WHO.

8 Carpenter, Liz. 1977. 'The All-American Complaint, "If I Only Had the Time . . ."' *Ms*, January: 48.

9 Bashkirtseff, Marie, quoted in Webster, Jean. (1912) 1988. *Daddy-long-legs*, 75. New York: Scholastic Inc.

10 Austen, Jane. (1813) 1999. *Pride and Prejudice*, 191. London: Penguin Books.

11 Foucault, Michel, quoted in Martin, Rux. 1988. 'Truth, Power, Self: An Interview with Michel Foucault, October 25, 1982.' In *Technologies of the Self: A Seminar with Michel Foucault*, edited by L. H. Martin, H. Gutman and P. H. Hutton, 14. Amherst, MA: University of Massachusetts Press.

13 Simon, Sidney B., L. W. Howe and H. Kirschenbaum. 1972. *Values Clarification: A Handbook of Practical Strategies for Teachers and Students*, 13–14. New York: Hart Publishing.

14 Csikszentmihayi, Mihaly. 1992. *Flow: The Psychology of Happiness*, 242. Sydney: Rider.

15 Eight-year-old girl, quoted in Edwards, Hazel, ed. 1975. *Women Returning to Study*, 43. Richmond, VIC: Primary Education.

16 Webster, Jean. (1912) 1988. *Daddy-long-legs*, 22. New York: Scholastic Inc.

17 Turkle, Sherry. 1995. *Identity in the Age of the Internet: Life on the Screen*, 9. New York: Simon & Schuster.

18 Shakespeare, William. 1963. *The Tragedy of Hamlet, Prince of Denmark*, Act I, Scene iii, Line 78. Edited by Edward Hubler. New York: Signet Classics.

2   Becoming a university student

19   Priest, Ann Marie. 2007. 'Expression of the Interesting.' *The Australian: Higher Education Supplement*, October 10. http://www.theaustralian.com.au/higher-education/appointments/expression-of-the-interesting/story-e6frgckf-1111114605535.html.

20   Tucker, Robert E. 1995. 'Argument, Ideology, and Databases: On the Corporatization of Academic Debate.' *Argumentation and Advocacy* 32(1): 30.

22   Webster, Jean. (1912) 1988. *Daddy-long-legs*, 79. New York: Scholastic Inc.

22   Boyer, Ernest L. 1990. *Scholarship Reconsidered: Priorities of the Professoriate*, 77. Princeton, NJ: Carnegie Foundation for the Advancement of Teaching.

23   McInnis, Craig, Richard James and Carmel McNaught. 1995. *First Year on Campus: Diversity in the Initial Experience of Australian Undergraduates*, 69. Canberra: AGPS.

23   Lowe, Ian. 1990. 'The Dying of the Light.' *Australian Universities Review* 33(1): 13–18.

23   Taylor, Harold. 1969. *Students Without Teachers*, xii. New York: McGraw-Hill.

24   Harasim, L., S. R. Hiltz, L. Teles and M. Turoff. 1996. *Learning Networks: A Field Guide to Teaching and Learning Online*, 3. Cambridge, MA: MIT Press. Reproduced with kind permission.

25   Franklin, Benjamin. 1706–1790. *The Quotations Page*. http://www.quotationspage.com/quote/41369.html.

25   Carroll, Lewis. 1970. *The Annotated Alice: Alice's Adventures in Wonderland and Through the Looking-glass*, 88. Revised ed. Harmondsworth, UK: Penguin.

26   Høeg, Peter. 1994. *Miss Smilla's Feeling for Snow*, 298. Translated by F. David. London: Flamingo.

27   Deakin, Michael. 1973. *The Children on the Hill: The Story of an Extraordinary Family*, 27. London: Quartet Books.

27   Yorke, Mantz and Bernard Longden. 2004. *Retention and Success in Higher Education*, 39. London: Society for Research into Higher Education and Open University Press.

28   Carroll, Lewis. 1970. *The Annotated Alice: Alice's Adventures in Wonderland and Through the Looking-glass*, 128. Revised ed. Harmondsworth, UK: Penguin.

31   Moodie, Gavin. 2005. 'How to Study the Course.' *The Australian*, June 8: 33.

31   Leavis, F. R., quoted in Wyatt, J. 1990. *Commitment to Higher Education: Seven West European Thinkers on the Essence of the University*, 82. Buckingham, UK: Society for Research into Higher Education and Open University Press.

32   Watling, Sue. 2009. 'Technology-enhanced Learning: A New Digital Divide.' In *The Future of Higher Education: Policy, Pedagogy and the Student Experience*, edited by Les Bell, Mike Neary and Howard Stevenson, 95. London: Continuum Books.

33   McInnis, Craig, Richard James and Carmel McNaught. 1995. *First Year on Campus: Diversity in the Initial Experience of Australian Undergraduates*, 121. Canberra: AGPS.

3   Engaging with university

37   Brookfield, Stephen D. 1989. *Developing Critical Thinkers: Challenging Adults to Explore Alternative Ways of Thinking and Acting*, 7. San Francisco: Jossey Bass.

38   McInnis, Craig, Richard James and Carmel McNaught. 1995. *First Year on Campus: Diversity in the Initial Experience of Australian Undergraduates*, 47. Canberra: AGPS.

39   Wesson, Gwen, ed. 1975. *Brian's Wife, Jenny's Mum*, 164–165. Blackburn, VIC: Dove Communications.

42   Axelson, Rick D. and Arend Flick. 2010. 'Defining Student Engagement.' *Change: The Magazine of Higher Learning* 43(1): 38–43.

42   Barrie, Simon and Michael Prosser. 2004. 'Generic Graduate Attributes: Citizens for an Uncertain Future.' *Higher Education Research and Development* 23(3): 1.

43   Brookfield, Stephen D. 1989. *Developing Critical Thinkers: Challenging Adults to Explore Alternative Ways of Thinking and Acting*, 14. San Francisco: Jossey Bass.

44   Jewell, Paul. 1992. 'Snake Oil, Sophistry and Sterile Syllogisms.' In *On the Same Premises: Proceedings of the Second National Conference on Reasoning*, edited by Paul Jewell, 3. Adelaide: Flinders University Press.

44   Ballard, Brigid and John Clanchy. 1988. 'Literacy in the University: An "Anthropological" Approach.' In *Literacy by Degrees*, edited by Gordon Taylor et al., 14. Milton Keynes, UK: Society for Research into Higher Education and the Open University Press.

45   Healey, M. 2003. 'What Disciplinary Communities Can Do to Develop Teaching and Research Links.' Paper presented at the American Association for Higher Education Conference, Washington DC, 14–17 March: 15. Cited in Willison, John and Kerry O'Regan. 2007. 'Commonly Known, Commonly Not Known, Totally Unknown: A Framework for Students Becoming Researchers.' *Higher Education Research and Development* 26(4): 393–409.

45   Organisation for Economic Cooperation and Development. 2002. *Frascati Manual: Proposed Standard Practice for Surveys on Research and Experimental Development* 30. Paris: OECD.

46   Lombardi, Vince. 2008. 'Individual Commitment to the Team.' *Quote of the Day*. http://www.theteliosgroup.com/quotes/individual-commitment-to-the-team-2.html.

47   Shakespeare, William. 1968. *Henry IV*, Act I, Scene iii, Line 42. Edited by John Dover Wilson. London: Cambridge University Press.

49   Yorke, Mantz and Bernard Longden. 2004. *Retention and Success in Higher Education*, 7–8. London: Society for Research into Higher Education and Open University Press.

49   Foucault, Michel, quoted in Martin, Rux. 1988. 'Truth, Power, Self: An Interview with Michel Foucault, October 25, 1982.' In *Technologies of the Self: A Seminar with Michel Foucault*, edited by L. H. Martin, H. Gutman and P. H. Hutton, 9. Amherst, MA: University of Massachusetts Press.

50   Webster, Jean. (1912) 1988. *Daddy-long-legs*, 103. New York: Scholastic Inc.

52 Høeg, Peter. 1994. *Miss Smilla's Feeling for Snow*, 95. Translated by F. David. London: Flamingo.

53 Thoreau, Henry James. 1960. *Walden*, 214. New York: Signet Classic.

54 Yorke, Mantz and Bernard Longden. 2004. *Retention and Success in Higher Education*, 8. London: Society for Research into Higher Education and Open University Press.

4 Planning your study

57 Gleick, James. 1999. *FSTR: The Acceleration of Just about Everything,* 62. London: Abacus.

59 Gleick, James. 1999. *FSTR: The Acceleration of Just about Everything,* 62. London: Abacus.

61 Schlenger, S. and R. Roesch. 1990. *How to Be Organized in Spite of Yourself.* Ringwood, VIC: Signet.

62 Jerome, Jerome K. 1947. *The Idle Thoughts of an Idle Fellow*, 51. Bristol, UK: J. W. Arrowsmith.

64 Anon.

64 Juster, Norton. 1962. *The Phantom Tollbooth*, 24. London: William Collins.

68 Western proverb.

69 Bliss, Edwin C. 1977. *Getting Things Done: The ABCs of Time Management*, 32–33. Melbourne: Macmillan.

70 Anon.

73 A student, quoted in Funnell, Antony. 2012. *The Future and Related Nonsense*, 59. Sydney: ABC Books.

74 Chatfield, Tom. 2012. *How to Thrive in the Digital Age*, 30. London: MacMillan.

76 Chatfield, Tom. 2012. *How to Thrive in the Digital Age*, 49. London: MacMillan.

76 Carroll, Lewis. 1970. *The Annotated Alice: Alice's Adventures in Wonderland and Through the Looking-glass*, 304. Revised ed. Harmondsworth, UK: Penguin.

77 Vivienne, quoted in Edwards, Hazel, ed. 1975. *Women Returning to Study*, 26. Richmond, VIC: Primary Education.

79 Carroll, Lewis. 1970. *The Annotated Alice: Alice's Adventures in Wonderland and Through the Looking-glass*, 322. Revised ed. Harmondsworth, UK: Penguin.

80 Sher, Barbara. 1979. *Wishcraft: How to Get What You Really Want*, 213. New York: Ballantine Books.

81 Norton, Margaret, quoted in Hall, Allan, ed. [1972]. *Worse Verse: From the Look! Pages of The Sunday Times*. London: Times Newspapers, London.

5 Learning and remembering

84 Nash, Ogden. 1972. 'Who Did Which? or Who Indeed?' In *I Wouldn't Have Missed It: Selected Poems of Ogden Nash*, 224. Boston: Little, Brown & Co.

85 Keen, Sam. 1970. *To a Dancing God*, 32. New York: Harper & Row.

86 Carroll, Lewis. 1970. *The Annotated Alice: Alice's Adventures in Wonderland and Through the Looking-glass*, 137–138. Revised ed. Harmondsworth, UK: Penguin.

86 Hobson, Julia. 1996. Interview for *Critical Thinking in Context.* Videorecording. Produced by Murdoch University, Western Australia.

87 Van Doren, Mark, quoted in Ellis, Dave, ed. 1994. *Becoming a Master Student*, 97. 7th ed. Boston: Houghton Mifflin.

89 Carroll, Lewis. 1970. *The Annotated Alice: Alice's Adventures in Wonderland and Through the Looking-glass*, 149. Revised ed. Harmondsworth, UK: Penguin.

89 Chatfield, Tom. 2012. *How to Thrive in the Digital Age*, 47. London: MacMillan.

90 O'Brian, Patrick. 1994. *Testimonies*. Harper Collins. Audiotape. Read by Patrick Tull. Bath, UK: Stirling Audio, 1996.

90 Hesse, Hermann. Source unknown.

91 Hallen, Patsy. 1996. Interview for *Critical Thinking in Context.* Videorecording. And quoted in the booklet *A Teacher's Guide to the Video*, 39. Produced by Murdoch University, Western Australia.

92 Barnett, Ronald. 1992. *Improving Higher Education: Total Quality Care*, 120. London: Society for Research into Higher Education and Open University Press.

92 Borges, Jorge Luis. 1972. 'Funes, the memorious.' In *A Personal Anthology*, 33. London: Picador.

93 Chaytor, Henry John. 1945. *From Script to Print: An Introduction to Medieval Vernacular Literature,* 116. Cambridge: Cambridge University Press.

93 Theobald, Robert. 1997. *The Future of Work*. Sunday Special. Radio program. Sydney: ABC Radio National, September 14.

94 Carroll, Lewis. 1970. *The Annotated Alice: Alice's Adventures in Wonderland and Through the Looking-glass*, 247–248. Revised ed. Harmondsworth, UK: Penguin.

95 Bridges, David. 1993. 'Transferable Skills: A Philosophical Perspective.' *Studies in Higher Education* 18(1): 50.

6 Asking your own questions

100 Lindsey, Crawford W. Jr. 1988. *Teaching Students to Teach Themselves*, 63–64 and 224. New York: Nichols Publishing.

101 Tiffin, John and Lalita Rajasingham. 2003. *The Global Virtual University*, 10. New York: RoutledgeFalmer.

102 Sutherland, Donald. 1951. *Gertrude Stein: A Biography of Her Work*, 203. New Haven, CT: Yale University Press.

102 Russell, Bertrand, quoted in Carstairs, G. M. 1944. 'Concepts of Insanity in Different Cultures.' In *The Listener* LXXII, July 30.

103 Berrill, N. J. 1958. *Man's Emerging Mind*, 158. London: Dennis Dobson.

103 Vonnegut, Kurt Jr. 1971. *Cat's Cradle*, 150. London: Victor Gollancz.

103   Feiffer, Jules. 1963. 'Crawling Arnold, Dramatists Play Service.' In *A Dictionary of Modern Quotations*, edited by J. M. & M. J. Cohen, 72. New York: Penguin.

104   Brookfield, Stephen D. 1989. *Developing Critical Thinkers: Challenging Adults to Explore Alternative Ways of Thinking and Acting*, 9. San Francisco: Jossey Bass.

104   Thomas, Dylan. 1954. *Quite Early One Morning*. New York: New Directions Publishing. Quoted in Kozlovsky, Daniel G. 1974. *An Ecological and Evolutionary Ethic*, 7. Englewood Cliffs, NJ: Prentice Hall.

105   Carroll, Lewis. 1970. *The Annotated Alice: Alice's Adventures in Wonderland and Through the Looking-glass*, 251. Revised ed. Harmondsworth, UK: Penguin.

106   Barnett, Ronald. 1992. *Improving Higher Education: Total Quality Care*, 120. London: Society for Research into Higher Education and Open University Press.

106   Holt, John. 1977. *Instead of Education: Ways to Help People Do Things Better*, 87–98. Harmondsworth, UK: Penguin Books.

107   Holt, John. 1977. *Instead of Education: Ways to Help People Do Things Better*, 20. Harmondsworth, UK: Penguin Books.

107   McInnis, Craig, Richard James and Carmel McNaught. 1995. *First Year on Campus: Diversity in the Initial Experience of Australian Undergraduates*, 124. Canberra: AGPS.

7   Choosing and analysing a topic

110   Willison, John and Kerry O'Regan. 2007. 'Commonly Known, Commonly Not Known, Totally Unknown: A Framework for Students Becoming Researchers.' *Higher Education Research and Development* 26(4): 393–409.

111   Carroll, Lewis. 1970. *The Annotated Alice: Alice's Adventures in Wonderland and Through the Looking-glass*, 137. Revised ed. Harmondsworth, UK: Penguin.

112   Juster, Norton. 1962. *The Phantom Tollbooth*, 17. London: William Collins.

113   Kress, Gunter. 1990. 'Two Kinds of Power.' *The English Magazine* 24(Autumn): 4.

116   Pirsig, Robert M. 1975. *Zen and the Art of Motorcycle Maintenance*, 166. New York: Bantam Books.

117   McLuhan, Marshall. 1969. 'Playboy Interview: Marshall McLuhan.' Interviewed by Eric Norden. *Playboy* March: 54.

121   Carroll, Lewis. 1970. *The Annotated Alice: Alice's Adventures in Wonderland and Through the Looking-glass*, 269. Revised ed. Harmondsworth, UK: Penguin.

123   Willison, John and Kerry O'Regan. 2007. 'Commonly Known, Commonly Not Known, Totally Unknown: A Framework for Students Becoming Researchers.' *Higher Education Research and Development* 26(4): 393–409.

8   Researching a topic

125   Murdoch University. Curriculum Commission. 2012. *Report from the Working Group on Embedding Research in Teaching*, 63. Green Paper, Appendix C. Murdoch, WA: Murdoch University.

129   Sofoulis, Zoe. 1992. 'Serendipitous Ventures.' In *STAR Guide: Study Techniques and Materials (A105) 1992*, 21. Murdoch, WA: Murdoch University.

129   Johnson, Samuel. 1979. In *The Oxford Dictionary of Quotations,* 276. 3rd ed. Oxford: Oxford University Press.

132   Chatfield, Tom. 2012. *How to Thrive in the Digital Age*, 34. London: MacMillan.

132   Rothenburg, David. 1997. 'Caught in the Web.' *The Australian*, August 27: 40.

134   Hawkins, David. 1973. 'What It Means to Teach.' *Teachers College Record* 75(1): 11.

135   Roszak, Theodore. 1969. *The Making of a Counter Culture: Reflections on the Technocratic Society and its Useful Opposition*, 12. Berkeley, CA: University of California Press.

137   Milton, John. 1979. In *The Oxford Dictionary of Quotations,* 352. 3rd ed. Oxford: Oxford University Press.

138   Shah ('Rahimi'), Idries. 1974. *Thinkers of the East*, 104. Harmondsworth, UK: Penguin Books.

139   Carroll, Lewis. 1970. *The Annotated Alice: Alice's Adventures in Wonderland and Through the Looking-glass*, 86. Revised ed. Harmondsworth, UK: Penguin.

9   Using information sources

142   Chatfield, Tom. 2012. *How to Thrive in the Digital Age*, 72. London: MacMillan.

143   University Without Walls. 1972. *The University Without Walls: A First Report.* 32. Yellow Spring, OH: Antioch College.

145   Browning, J. 1993. 'Libraries Without Walls for Books Without Pages.' *Wired*, Premier Issue: 62.

146   Gibbon, Edward. 1979. In *The Oxford Dictionary of Quotations,* 224. 3rd ed. Oxford: Oxford University Press.

149   Chatfield, Tom. 2012. *How to Thrive in the Digital Age*, 74. London: MacMillan.

150   Chatfield, Tom. 2012. *How to Thrive in the Digital Age*, 59. London: MacMillan.

151   Funnell, Antony. 2012. *The Future and Related Nonsense*, 27. Sydney: ABC Books.

152   Lanier, Jaron. 2011. *You are Not a Gadget: A Passionate Manifesto*, 50. Harmondsworth, UK: Penguin Books.

152   Roszak, Theodore. 1969. *The Making of a Counter Culture: Reflections on the Technocratic Society and its Useful Opposition*, 13. Berkeley, CA: University of California Press.

154   Lanier, Jaron. 2011. *You are Not a Gadget: A Passionate Manifesto*, 50. Harmondsworth, UK: Penguin Books.

155   Carpenter, Edmund. 1970. 'The New Languages.' In *Explorations in Communication: An Anthology,* edited by Edmund Carpenter and Marshall McLuhan, 163. London: Jonathan Cape.

158   Raser, John. 1980. Excerpt written for the first edition of this book.

159   Acker, Joan, Kate Barry and Joke Esseveld. 1983. 'Objectivity and Truth: Problems in Doing Feminist Research.' *Women's Studies International Forum* 6(4): 423–435.

10 Reading

161   Maugham, W. Somerset. 1967. *The Summing Up*, 92. London: William Heinemann.

162   Mellor, Bronwyn, Annette Patterson and Marnie O'Neill. 1991. *Reading Fiction*, 21. Scarborough, WA: Chalkface Press.

164   Culkin, John M. 'A Schoolman's Guide to Marshall McLuhan.' *Saturday Review*, March 18: 301.

164   Nieuwenhuizen, John. 1997. *Soundbite Education*. Ockhams Razor. Radio program. Sydney: ABC Radio National, June 15.

165   Lessing, Doris. 1970. *Martha Quest*, 200. New York: The New American Library.

170   Holt, John. 1977. *Instead of Education: Ways to Help People Do Things Better*, 74–75. Harmondsworth, UK: Penguin Books.

171   Lessing, Doris. 1970. *Martha Quest*, 28. New York: The New American Library.

172   Carroll, Lewis. 1970. *The Annotated Alice: Alice's Adventures in Wonderland and Through the Looking-glass*, 191. Revised ed. Harmondsworth, UK: Penguin.

173   Barnett, Ronald. 1992. *Improving Higher Education: Total Quality Care*, 39. London: Society for Research into Higher Education and Open University Press.

174   Mellor, Bronwyn, Annette Patterson and Marnie O'Neill. 1991. *Reading Fiction*, 44. Scarborough, WA: Chalkface Press.

174   Bacon, Francis. 1979. In *The Oxford Dictionary of Quotations,* 27. 3rd ed. Oxford: Oxford University Press.

176   Ransome, Arthur. 1976. *The Autobiography of Arthur Ransome*, 34. London: Jonathan Cape.

180   Shah, Idries. 1970. 'A Quality Must Have a Vehicle.' In *The Way of the Sufi*, 61. Harmondsworth, UK: Penguin Books.

181   Johnson, Samuel. 1979. In *The Oxford Dictionary of Quotations,* 280. 3rd ed. Oxford: Oxford University Press.

183   Carroll, Lewis. 1970. *The Annotated Alice: Alice's Adventures in Wonderland and Through the Looking-glass*, 189–190. Revised ed. Harmondsworth, UK: Penguin.

184   Webster, Jean. (1912) 1988. *Daddy-long-legs*, 36. New York: Scholastic Inc.

186   Carroll, Lewis. 1970. *The Annotated Alice: Alice's Adventures in Wonderland and Through the Looking-glass*, 25. Revised ed. Harmondsworth, UK: Penguin.

11 Listening to lectures

188   Gosper, Maree, Margot McNeill, Karen Woo, Rob Phillips, Greg Preston and David Green. 2010. 'Web-based Lecture Technologies and Learning and Teaching: A Study of Change in Four Australian Universities.' *Research in Learning Technology* 18(3): 251–263.

189 Manne, Robert, quoted in Preiss, Benjamin. 2013. 'A Teacher from the Old School to Call It a Day'. *The Age,* January 19: 16. http://m.theage.com.au/victoria/a-teacher-from-the-old-school-to-call-it-a-day-20130118-2czdi.html.

190 Johnson, Samuel. 1971. Quoted in Boswell, James. 1827. *The Life of Samuel Johnson, LL. D.: Comprehending an Account of His Studies, and Numerous Works, in Chronological Order; A Series of His Epistolary Correspondence, and Conversation with Many Eminent Persons; and Various Pieces of his Composition, Never Before Published,* 141. London: Jones & Co.

190 Bligh, Donald A. 1972. *What's the Use of Lectures?*, 61. Harmondsworth, UK: Penguin Books.

191 Manne, Robert, quoted in Preiss, Benjamin. 2013. 'A Teacher from the Old School to Call It a Day'. *The Age,* January 19: 16. http://m.theage.com.au/victoria/a-teacher-from-the-old-school-to-call-it-a-day-20130118-2czdi.html.

191 Gosper, Maree, Margot McNeill, Karen Woo, Rob Phillips, Greg Preston and David Green. 2010. 'Web-based Lecture Technologies and Learning and Teaching: A Study of Change in Four Australian Universities.' *Research in Learning Technology* 18(3): 251–263.

193 Carroll, Lewis. 1970. *The Annotated Alice: Alice's Adventures in Wonderland and Through the Looking-glass*, 122. Revised ed. Harmondsworth, UK: Penguin.

193 Carroll, Lewis. 1970. *The Annotated Alice: Alice's Adventures in Wonderland and Through the Looking-glass*, 146. Revised ed. Harmondsworth, UK: Penguin.

197 Anon. 2007. In *Oxford Dictionary of Modern Quotations,* 5. 3rd ed. Oxford: Oxford University Press.

198 Fermi, Enrico, quoted in Smith, Anthony. 1970. *The Body*, 16. Harmondsworth, UK: Penguin Books.

12 Participating in discussions

201 Carroll, Lewis. 1970. *The Annotated Alice: Alice's Adventures in Wonderland and Through the Looking-glass*, 235. Revised ed. Harmondsworth, UK: Penguin.

203 Harasim, L., S. R. Hiltz, L. Teles and M. Turoff. 1996. *Learning Networks: A Field Guide to Teaching and Learning Online*, 4–5. Cambridge, MA: MIT Press.

203 Johnson, Samuel. 1979. In *The Oxford Dictionary of Quotations,* 280. 3rd ed. Oxford: Oxford University Press.

204 Harasim, L., S. R. Hiltz, L. Teles and M. Turoff. 1996. *Learning Networks: A Field Guide to Teaching and Learning Online*, 4. Cambridge, MA: MIT Press.

207 Hobson, Julia. 1996. Interview for *Critical Thinking in Context.* Videorecording. Produced by Murdoch University, Western Australia.

210 Narayan, Uma. 1988. 'Working Together across Differences: Some Considerations on Emotions and Political Practice.' *Hypatia* (Summer): 38. Quoted in Warren, Karen J. 'Rewriting the Future: The Feminist Challenge to the Malestream Curriculum.' *Feminist Teacher* 4(2 & 3): 46–52.

210   A student, quoted in The Nuffield Foundation. 1976. *Small Group Teaching: Selected Papers*, 123. London: Group for Research and Innovation in Higher Education.

212   Høeg, Peter. 1994. *Miss Smilla's Feeling for Snow*, 37. Translated by F. David. London: Flamingo.

212   Brown, Allison. 1997. 'Teaching "Big Picture" Economics.' Unpublished paper, 6. Murdoch, WA: Murdoch University.

214   Carroll, Lewis. 1970. *The Annotated Alice: Alice's Adventures in Wonderland and Through the Looking-glass*, 158. Revised ed. Harmondsworth, UK: Penguin.

215   Cicero, Marcus Tullius. 2008. *The Nature of the Gods [De Natura Deorum]*, Book 1, Line 5. Translated by P. G. Walsh. Oxford: Oxford University Press.

215   Anon. Source unknown.

216   Brown, Allison. 1997. 'Teaching "Big Picture" Economics.' Unpublished paper, 8. Murdoch, WA: Murdoch University.

217   A student, quoted in The Nuffield Foundation. 1976. *Small Group Teaching: Selected Papers*, 122–123. London: Group for Research and Innovation in Higher Education.

218   Wesson, Gwen, ed. 1975. *Brian's Wife, Jenny's Mum*, 79–80. Blackburn, VIC: Dove Communications.

218   Barnett, Ronald. 1992. *Improving Higher Education: Total Quality Care*, 198. London: Society for Research into Higher Education and Open University Press.

13 Developing your writing

220   Colette. 1960. *The Vagabond*, 13. Translated by Enid McLeod. Harmondsworth, UK: Penguin Books.

222   Howard, V. A. 1990. 'Thinking on Paper: A Philosopher's Look at Writing.' In *Varieties of Thinking: Essays from Harvard's Philosophy of Education Research Center*, 84. New York: Routledge.

222   Vonnegut, Kurt. 1980. 'How to Write with Style.' Advertisement in *Psychology Today*, September: 58.

223   Howard, V. A. 1990. 'Thinking on Paper: A Philosopher's Look at Writing.' In *Varieties of Thinking: Essays from Harvard's Philosophy of Education Research Center*, 91. New York: Routledge.

224   Wesson, Gwen, ed. 1975. *Brian's Wife, Jenny's Mum*, 109. Blackburn, VIC: Dove Communications.

224   Elbow, Peter. 1981. *Writing with Power*, 14. Melbourne: Oxford University Press.

225   Ransome, Arthur. 1976. *The Autobiography of Arthur Ransome*, 9. London: Jonathan Cape.

225   Martin, Jim R. 1985. *Factual Writing: Exploring and Challenging Social Reality*, 15. Geelong: Deakin University Press.

226   Vonnegut, Kurt. 1980. 'How to Write with Style.' Advertisement in *Psychology Today*, September: 58.

227 Wilde, Oscar. 1977. 'The Importance of Being Earnest.' In *The Portable Oscar Wilde*, edited by Richard Aldington, 481. Harmondsworth, UK: Penguin Books.

228 Nin, Anaïs. 1966. *The Diary of Anaïs Nin 1931–1934,* 89. Edited by Gunther Stuhlmann. New York: A Harvest Book.

229 Dumenco, Simon, quoted in Scocco, Daniel. 2009. '50 Thoughful (*sic*), Funny and Polemic Blogging Quotes.' DailyBlogTips. http:///www.dailyblogtips.com/blogging-quotes/.

231 Elbow, Peter. 1981. *Writing with Power*, 20–21. Melbourne: Oxford University Press.

233 Harasim, L., S. R. Hiltz, L. Teles and M. Turoff. 1996. *Learning Networks: A Field Guide to Teaching and Learning Online*, 3–4. Cambridge, MA: MIT Press.

235 Colette. 1964. *Casual Chance.* Quoted in *Good Reads* http://www.goodreads.com/quotes/8018-put-down-everything-that-comes-into-your-head-and-then.

14 Writing essays

236 Hemingway, Ernest. 1965. *Writers at Work: The Paris Review Interviews*, 235. Interviewed by George Plimpton. New York: Viking.

238 Quarles, Francis. 1979. In *The Oxford Dictionary of Quotations,* 403. 3rd ed. Oxford: Oxford University Press.

239 Wesson, Gwen, ed. 1975. *Brian's Wife, Jenny's Mum*, 81. Blackburn, VIC: Dove Communications.

241 Baker, Russell. 1972. 'At Lunch.' In Frank, Joseph. *You*, 63. New York: Harcourt Brace Jovanovich.

241 Wesson, Gwen, ed. 1975. *Brian's Wife, Jenny's Mum*, 120. Blackburn, VIC: Dove Communications.

241 Morgan, Fred. 1968. *Here and Now: An Approach to Writing through Perception*, 153. New York: Harcourt, Brace & World.

244 Carroll, Lewis. 1970. *The Annotated Alice: Alice's Adventures in Wonderland and Through the Looking-glass*, 95. Revised ed. Harmondsworth, UK: Penguin.

246 Churchill, Winston. 1958. *My Early Life*, edited by Andrew Scotland, 143. School ed. London: Odhams Press.

247 Vonnegut, Kurt. 1980. 'How to Write with Style.' Advertisement in *Psychology Today,* September: 58.

247 Johnson, Samuel. 1979. In *The Oxford Dictionary of Quotations,* 274. 3rd ed. Oxford: Oxford University Press.

250 Macrorie, Ken. 1968. *Writing to Be Read*, 89. New York: Hayden Book Co.

251 Høeg, Peter. 1994. *Miss Smilla's Feeling for Snow*, 79. Translated by F. David. London: Flamingo.

15 Writing scientific reports

253 Woodford, F. Peter. 1967. 'Sounder Thinking through Clearer Writing.' *Science* 156(3776): 743. Reprinted with permission from AAAS.

255 Lincoln, Abraham. Source unknown.

255 Marshall, Lorraine. 1997. *A Learning Companion*, 310. 2nd ed. Murdoch, WA: Murdoch University.

256 Pirsig, Robert M. 1975. *Zen and the Art of Motorcycle Maintenance*, 100. New York: Bantam Books.

259 Pirsig, Robert M. 1975. *Zen and the Art of Motorcycle Maintenance*, 101. New York: Bantam Books.

260 Woodford, F. Peter. 1967. 'Sounder Thinking through Clearer Writing.' *Science* 156(3776): 744. Reprinted with permission from AAAS.

261 Pirsig, Robert M. 1975. *Zen and the Art of Motorcycle Maintenance*, 102. New York: Bantam Books.

265 Woodford, F. Peter. 1967. 'Sounder Thinking through Clearer Writing.' *Science* 156(3776): 744. Reprinted with permission from AAAS.

265 Milne, A. A. 1926. *Winnie the Pooh*, 48. London: Methuen & Co.

268 Holt, John. 1977. *Instead of Education: Ways to Help People Do Things Better*, 99–100. Harmondsworth, UK: Penguin Books.

16 Using conventions

270 Carroll, Lewis. 1970. *The Annotated Alice: Alice's Adventures in Wonderland and Through the Looking-glass*, 156. Revised ed. Harmondsworth, UK: Penguin.

272 Horace. 1936. 'The Art of Poetry.' Translated by Edward Henry Blakeney. In *The Complete Works*, edited by Casper J. Kraemer Jr, 401. New York: The Modern Library.

274 Tiffin, John and Lalita Rajasingham. 2003. *The Global Virtual University*, 82. New York: RoutledgeFalmer.

275 Parker, Dorothy. 1939. 'The Little Hours.' In *Here Lies: The Collected Stories of Dorothy Parker*, 209–210. London: Longmans, Green & Co.

275 Byron, Lord. 1945. 'English Bards and Scotch Reviewers', 1.66. In *The Poetical Works of Lord Byron*, 114. London: Oxford University Press.

283 Manguel, Alberto. 1996. *A History of Reading*, 323. London: Harper Collins.

286 Eliot, George. 1950. *Middlemarch*, 70. London: The Zodiac Press.

286 Dickens, Charles. n.d. *Great Expectations*, 50. London: Chapman & Hall.

287 Australian Government Publication Service. 1994. *Style Manual: For Authors, Editors and Printers of Australian Government Publications*, xi. 5th ed. Canberra: AGPS.

17 Learning from evaluation

289 Ehrmann, S. 1999b. *Flashlight Evaluation Handbook*. Flashlight Project. http://www. ctl.wsu.edu/CTLSilhouette/mode/author/flashlight/EvaluationHandbook. Quoted in Phillips, Rob, et al., eds. 2000. *Handbook for Learning-centred Evaluation of Computer-facilitated Learning Projects in Higher Education*. 1.3. Murdoch, WA: Murdoch University on behalf of a consortium of universities and the Australasian Society for Computers in Learning in Tertiary Education (ASCILITE).

291 Agate, James. 1979. In *The Oxford Dictionary of Quotations*, 2. 3rd ed. Oxford: Oxford University Press.

292 Holt, John. 1977. *Instead of Education: Ways to Help People Do Things Better*, 61. Harmondsworth, UK: Penguin Books.

292 de Saint-Exupèry, Antoine. 1943. *The Little Prince*, 39. New York: Harcourt, Brace & 293.

293 Churchill, Winston. 1958. *My Early Life*, edited by Andrew Scotland, 21–22. School ed. London: Odhams Press.

293 Sadler, D. R. 1983. Cited in S. M. Brookhart. 2001. 'Successful Students' Formative and Summative Uses of Assessment Information.' *Assessment in Education* 8(2): 153–169.

294 Falchikov, Nancy. 2007. 'The Place of Peers in Learning and Assessment.' In *Rethinking Assessment in Higher Education: Learning for the Longer Term*, edited by David Boud and Nancy Falchikov, 139–140. London: Routledge.

295 Stake, Robert. Quoted in Scriven, Michael. 1991. *Evaluation Thesaurus*, 169. 4th ed. Newbury Park, CA: Sage. Cited in Earl, L. 2004. *Assessment as Learning: Using Classroom Achievement to Maximize Student Learning. Experts in Assessment*. Thousand Oaks, CA: Corwin Press.

296 Goodman, Paul. 1971. *Compulsory Miseducation*, 106. Harmondsworth, UK: Penguin Books.

298 Elbow, Peter. 1981. *Writing with Power*, 118. Melbourne: Oxford University Press.

298 Novak, Michael. 1970. *The Experience of Nothingness*, 37. New York: Harper & Row.

301 University Without Walls. 1972. *The University Without Walls: A First Report*, 35. Yellow Spring, OH: Antioch College.

Appendix: Discrimination: sexist language and attitudes

305 International Association of Business Communicators. 1977. *Without Bias: A Guidebook for Nondiscriminatory Communication*, 22. San Francisco: IABC.

307 Wesson, Gwen, ed. 1975. *Brian's Wife, Jenny's Mum*, 26. Blackburn, VIC: Dove Communications.

Index

Note: **Bold** numbers indicate main entry; *italic* numbers indicate tables.